BLAKE'S NIGHT

BLAKE'S NIGHT

William Blake
and the Idea of Pastoral

DAVID WAGENKNECHT

The Belknap Press of
Harvard University Press
Cambridge, Massachusetts
1973

For Pat

Acknowledgments

Any critic trudging behind the likes of S. Foster Damon and Northrop Frye has reason to be grateful to his predecessors. Without the encouragement of their works, especially of Frye's, I could hardly have proceeded as I have. Every student of Blake must share my additional indebtedness to the historical and bibliographical work of David Erdman and Geoffrey Keynes. I also learned much from the book-length studies by John Middleton Murry, Milton Percival, Peter Fisher, Hazard Adams, Robert F. Gleckner, Thomas Altizer, Harold Bloom, and Morton Paley; and from the pictorial studies by Anthony Blunt and Jean Hagstrum. I am sure that my borrowings from these writers are more pervasive than annotation alone can demonstrate.

In addition, I have some more personal obligations, which are a pleasure to record. This study first saw light as a doctoral thesis at the University of Sussex, where Dr. Angus Ross helped keep the project, and its author, afloat by means of many indispensable kindnesses. The way would have been more difficult, and much less pleasant, without him, and I am enormously grateful. Professor Morton Paley, of the University of California at Berkeley, read the thesis as "outside examiner," pointed out some egregious errors, and made valuable suggestions for improvement. For his encouragement and tolerance in dealing with a work which sometimes comes to different conclusions from his own I am also very grateful. Needless to say, no one but myself is responsible for the errors and effects which remain.

All Blake's words are quoted from *The Poetry and Prose of William Blake*, edited by David Erdman and Harold Bloom, copyright © 1965 by David V. Erdman and Harold Bloom, and reprinted by permission of Doubleday & Company, Inc. The Clarendon Press of Oxford University Press has given its kind permission to quote from the following works: *Spenser's Faerie Queene*, ed. J. C. Smith (1909); *Spenser's Minor Poems*, ed. Ernest de Selincourt (1910); *The Poems & Letters of Andrew Marvell*, ed. H. M. Margoliouth (second edition, 1952); *The Poetical Works of John Milton*, ed. Helen Darbishire (1958); *The Landscape of the Mind*: *Pastoralism and Platonic Theory in Tasso's "Aminta" and Shakespeare's Early Comedies*, by Richard Cody (1969). Passages from Edgar Wind's *Pagan Mysteries in the Renaissance* (new and enlarged edition, 1967) are quoted by kind permission of Barnes & Noble (for American rights), and by Faber & Faber, Ltd. (for world rights). Passages from *Fearful Symmetry: A Study of William Blake*, by Northrop Frye (© 1947 by Princeton University Press: rev. paperback ed., 1969) are reprinted by permission of Princeton University Press.

August 1972   D.W.

Contents

Illustrations

BLAKE'S NIGHT

Preliminaries

My theme would suggest to most readers a very specialized, if not narrow, approach to the poems of Blake, and my first purpose, therefore, must be to explain how it is that the work is a comprehensive study—not comprehensive in that it comments on every last scrap Blake wrote, but in the sense that it interprets the whole of Blake's poetical career in terms of a single, unifying thematic concern or idea: the idea of pastoral. The simplest way to explain is to rehearse the study's development.

I began with the notion that Blake was an English epic poet, and must have felt bound therefore to consider himself in relationship to the English tradition of epic, that is, to Spenser and Milton. From there it was a short step to considering Blake in terms of the Virgilian idea of a poetic career: to learn one's craft writing pastorals (a naive notion which itself is part of the pastoral fiction) before moving on to higher song. That Blake was conscious of at least a general loyalty to the Virgilian program is manifest in the many pastorals of the very early *Poetical Sketches* (1783) and in the outline of his "canonical" career, the sequence of works he illustrated and etched with his own hands, beginning with *The Book of Thel* and *Songs of Innocence* (both dated 1789) and moving on to *Jerusalem*. In deciding to press the general loyalty for something critically more specific, I confess to having been motivated in part by a bias toward a "literary" Blake. We are often reminded that Blake regarded himself as a prophet without being reminded at the same time that the poet did not make the same kind of distinction between theological and secular meaning to which we are accustomed. It was a "plain fact" to Blake that "any man of mechanical talents may from the writings of Paracelsus or Jacob Behmen, produce ten thousand volumes of equal value with Swedenborg's. and from those of Dante or Shakespear, an infinite number" (*The Marriage of Heaven and Hell*). Beyond my bias, I was challenged into critical action by the fact that in *Songs of Innocence and of Experience* we have a collection of poems full of pastoral elements the meaning of which has never adequately been attempted (Harold Bloom, in a recent study, makes some interesting suggestions, but only to dismiss pastoralism as too simple a context for Blake's ironies).[1] It was apparent from the beginning that I was going to have to make a systematic comparison between the pastoralism of the *Songs* and that of some other collection. The obvious choice in terms of the tradition I was suggesting was Spenser's *Shepheardes Calender*.

While I worked on this comparison, my thoughts were equally devoted to another, as yet unrelated problem. I was working on the assumption that the fundamental thematic question of Blake's longer poems was the development of a conflict between the idea of the "Orc cycle" in the prophecies and the evolution of a character, Los-Urthona, designed to supersede that cycle. I was also of the opinion that something like a crisis in this conflict prevented Blake from bringing the *Vala/The Four Zoas* manuscript to a publishable conclusion. Both of these assumptions are staples of contemporary Blake criticism, and testify to the influence of Northrop Frye's magnificent study, *Fearful Symmetry* (Princeton, N.J.: Princeton University Press, 1947), especially its analysis of *Vala/The Four Zoas* (pp. 269–312). The "Orc cycle" was Frye's term for the mythological realization in Blake of a ceaseless conflict between Energy and Reason, a conflict which could be applied to the body politic in terms of Revolution and Repression, or to sexual relationships in terms of Impulse and the Female Will. Los, Blake's mythological figure who comes to represent the poetic imagination, includes in his make-up and his situation the struggles which constitute the Orc cycle, but he eventually transcends them by moving to an imaginatively higher ground. I decided that if pastoralism in Blake was going to be more important than scenery and motifs, it had better embody a mythological counterpart to the transcendence of the Orc cycle.

A primary myth for pastoralists has always been the story of

Venus and Adonis, the most influential treatment of which for the English Renaissance is to be found in Ovid's *Metamorphoses*, a book which Blake pronounced "fable," but one which contained "Vision in a Sublime degree" (*A Vision of the Last Judgment*). The relationship between this tale and the sexual aspect of the Orc cycle is obvious enough, but the relevance is not restricted to this aspect. As Ovid tells it, the tale of Venus and Adonis is matched against the awful cautionary tale of Myrrha, led by passion to seek her father's bed: the fate of Adonis is to repay Venus for visiting such passion on a mortal. There is a suggestive relationship between this pair of stories and Blake's cycle. So far as my comparison between Blake and Spenser was concerned, the latter was obviously open to the classical analogue: Adonis could easily be associated with "the daily cycle of the sun across the sky, the yearly cycle of the seasons, and the cycle of water, flowing from wells and fountains through rivers to the sea,"[2] which is substructure for so many of Spenser's poems.

It also seemed to me that Blake would inevitably associate "pastoral" with two primary texts: Spenser's *Epithalamion* and Milton's *Lycidas*. The two poems suggest a collision of *eros* and *thanatos* which it does not take great sophistication to trace to the Adonis myth. It is nevertheless comforting to be reminded that the collision is there, plain to see, in the earliest pastoral texts. Theocritus XV ("The Women at the Adonis-Festival") is a wedding song which looks forward to a dirge; Bion's "The Lament for Adonis" looks back to the wedding song.

All these ideas in fact proved useful, but they seemed to me at the time rather archetypally general for the kind of critical approach I wanted to make to Blake's poems. It was at this time that I received a critical illumination of great importance in the form of Richard Cody's exciting book, *The Landscape of the Mind* (Oxford: Oxford University Press, Clarendon Press, 1969; hereafter referred to as Cody). The critical problems of pastoralism all derive from a complex, three-cornered relationship shared by imagery, ideational content, and the idea of imitation. In brief, pastorals are puzzling because they present a fiction imitating an ideal difficult to credit in terms of the imagery which supports the fiction. The danger for the practicing critic is that he may approach the fiction on too literal a level. When Hallett Smith, for example, argues that "the simplicity of the shepherd's conditions makes for an invulnerability to appeals in the name of wealth or of chivalry,"[3] this is fine—but vulnerability to precisely these appeals is what pastorals like Spenser's most passionately express. Cody's book, which studies the relationship between pastoralism and "aesthetic platonism" in the Renaissance, is valuable not only because it contains the clearest statement I know of what pastorals are about but also because it discriminates so fluently in its critical judgments between imagery and fiction. Here, according to Cody, is the "idea of pastoral": "The message of pastoralism, communicated on the image level, as it has been called, is this: that this-worldliness and otherworldliness can be reconciled, and that a truly cultivated man, whatever his intimations of divinity, may find a natural human voice. The burden of the pastoral poet, however lightly felt, is thus an enactment of the Socratic compromise between artifice and naturalness, transcendence and immanence" (p. 12). The idea expressed here "on the image level" would seem to include nonchalance. But there is nothing nonchalant about the fictional, mythological figure the invocation of whom, Cody tells us, "in an appropriate context of love, landscape, and poetry can be said to signalize the Renaissance pastoral mode": Orpheus (p. 14). Orpheus because "both as lover and theologian, [he] is credited with finding a single voice for all the intimations of this world's beauty and the other world's that solicit a human mind" (p. 29). The essence of Orpheus is the authority and power of the poetic voice, and it seems that for the platonists of the Renaissance Orpheus used his powers to resolve the tensions beneath the bucolic mask of nonchalance. Ficino, whose commentary on the *Symposium* is an important document in the development of Orpheus as a syncretic and central mythological figure, is specific about the kinds of tension: "Orpheus, he explains, was possessed of all four divine madnesses distinguished by Socrates: that of poetry, or the Muses; that of ritual mystery, or Bacchus; that of prophecy, or Apollo; that of love, or Venus. The human soul, being full of discord, needs the music of poetry to temper it, the Bacchic sacrifice to unify its parts, the Apolline vision to reveal the transcendent unity behind and before it, and the passion for beauty to unite it with God" (Cody, pp. 28–29). It was clear by now that Orpheus transcended and absorbed the myth of Adonis, and I thought I had found my analogue to Blake's Los.

But at the same time, largely by means of comparison to *The Shepheardes Calender*, I made the discovery that Blake's *Songs* were more directly about the idea of pastoral than I had suspected; "The Lamb" and "The Tyger" were plainly enough addressed to the reconciliation of "this-worldliness and otherworldliness." More specifically, the confrontation between the two poems, in terms of the enigmatic terminology of "Innocence" and "Experience," testified to the difficulty Blake experienced in discovering a "natural human voice" for expressing reconciliation. In these poems a deceptive simplicity and lightly worn ambiguity of meaning are the bucolic mask over the passionate countenance of Orpheus. Innocence is a fiction imitating an ideal difficult to credit in terms of the imagery which supports the fiction. But Experience only makes it impossible to approach the fiction on the literal level, lest it function as a travesty of the real. Innocence is therefore dependent upon Experience in the sense that Experience protects Innocence by suffering, in a sense, for it. It was beginning to be apparent to me—and it proved a point of great relevance to Blake—why pastoralism was associated with the passion of Christ, as well as with that of Orpheus. The critical worth of the ideas revealed to me in the way I have described is, I hope, completely a question of the "readings" of the *Songs* I present below, and will accordingly depend on the reader's assessment of my interpretations. For in the final analysis—this I came to see clearly—the idea of pastoral was much more Blake's than it ever could be his critics'. A reading of the short poems is therefore an attempt to reveal as much of this idea as possible; the fundamental impotance of the idea could best be attested to by the coherence of the reading.

The same thing, of course, had to be true of the longer poems, the subject of the second half of the study. I had by now concluded that my constant critical problem was to be the identification of Blake's various "translations" of the idea of pastoral. It had by now appeared that the question of the Orc cycle and Los, of Adonis and Orpheus, was subordinate to this more fundamental question, and would probably be absorbed by it in the process of critical analysis. (This again appealed to my "literary" bias, because I had felt that analyses of the Orc-Los crisis had too often been made dependent on forces—Blake's supposed attitudes toward contemporary history or Christianity—elusive of critical description.) In terms of the *Songs* the idea of pastoral had emerged as the vehicle for conveying Blake's ambiguous and agonized approach to the problem of "Generation." In terms of imaginative language, the idea of pastoral was a reaction to the impossibility of articulating transcendence except in terms determined by the realm of immanence. What did this idea look like in the prophecies, and how could Milton—about whom I had yet said little—be implicated in its expression?

It appears that the whole aim of Blake's longer poems is the preparation of ground for apocalyptic statement. Here it is appropriate to invoke Northrop Frye's definition of apocalypse, which is largely derived from Blake in the first place. Apocalypse, Frye suggests in his *Anatomy of Criticism*, is "the imaginative conception of the whole of nature as the content of an infinite and eternal living body which, if not human, is closer to being human than to being inanimate."[4] Apocalyptic, therefore, can mean "metaphor as pure and potentially total identification, without regard to plausibility or ordinary experience" (Frye, *Anatomy*, p. 365). In reading the prophecies one recurrently meets a singular phenomenon, related to the question of Orc: the more "apocalyptic" the outlook, the greater is man's awareness of his fallen condition. The closer Blake comes to the achievement of imaginative transcendence, the more man comes to seem immersed in a satanic immanence. This in fact is what "the marriage of heaven and hell" means. I discovered two things about this phenomenon: one was that it expressed itself almost exclusively in terms of allusions to Milton, and the other was that the coincidence of apocalypse and Fall was only a very logical development, in Blake, of the idea of pastoral. The closer one came to achieving a total metaphorical form, the more heightened one's awareness of the tainted source of the imagery. After all, it is traditional to pastoralism to dream of the lion and the lamb lying down together; it seems quite beyond its powers to imagine a world where there are neither lions nor lambs.

Finally, it became clear that the central imaginative aim of Blake's poetic career was systematically related to the idea suggested. Blake's secular and religious concerns are one: to demonstrate that the ordinary world of extensive, fallen vision includes the imaginative wherewithal for that world's intensive, visionary transformation. This is an optimistic statement of the idea of pastoral. In *Milton* it functions epithalamically. In *Jerusalem* it suggests a universal form in which all individuals are identified, in which everything find itself *as* itself. Put this way, the resemblance between the universal form and that ideal, spiritual landscape where pastoral fictions are set ought—it is my feeling—to seem irresistible.

One more idea, which is not pursued or realized below. It is suggested by a remark of M. H. Abrams in *The Mirror and the*

Lamp (New York: Oxford University Press, 1953): "We also find in eighteenth-century criticism the beginnings of a more radical solution to the problem of poetic fictions, one which would sever supernatural poetry entirely from the principle of imitation, and from any responsibility to the empirical world. The key event in this development was the replacement of the metaphor of the poem as imitation, a 'mirror of nature,' by that of the poem as heterocosm, 'a second nature,' created by the poet in an act analogous to God's creation of the world" (p. 272). Most readers could be led easily enough from these remarks to Coleridge and Romantic critical theory, though it is interesting to reflect that in English criticism the idea of a second nature can be traced to Sidney. Blake is not exclusively a Romantic poet, nor is he an Elizabethan; he traffics, however, with both Romantic and Elizabethan ideas. I wonder, therefore, if the largest historical implication of the present study is not that pastoralism is the great unexplored link between Romantic and Renaissance ideas. To explore the suggestion, one would have to discard certain received critical doctrines. Mr. Abrams' distinction between "mirror of nature" and "second nature" would have to be reexamined. More seriously, the critical cliché still everywhere encountered, that pastoralism dies in the eighteenth century, apparently because the Romantics knew too much about sheep to be able to write poems about them, would have to be discarded too. A certain kind of pastoral poem does largely cease in the eighteenth century, for which one is grateful, but the idea of pastoral goes on. Blake's most explicit version of pastoral—though perhaps it is the least characteristic—illustrates what I mean.

In 1820–21 Blake undertook a commission from Dr. Robert J. Thornton (the same whose *The Lord's Prayer, Newly Translated* later moved him to nearly apoplectic marginalia) for some portraits and a series of illustrations in woodcut (an unusual medium for Blake) for an edition of Virgil's pastorals. Blake's receipt of the commission is instructive, for it includes his registration of the imaginative bankruptcy of the genre as practiced by too many eighteenth-century poets, but then goes on to transcend that bankruptcy. Where Ambrose Philips, whose insipidities Blake was hired to illustrate, had,

> First, then, shall lightsome birds forget to fly,
> The briny ocean turn to pastures dry,
> And every rapid river cease to flow,
> 'Ere I unmindful of *Menalcas* grow,

Blake as comment drew birds flying over a field, ships at sea, and a busy commercial river. (These drawings he did not even bother to cut into wood himself.) But elsewhere Blake's woodcuts are a searing and dramatic series of allusions to his own mythology and to the tensions of his career. We see the poet himself on the road to Felpham and the struggle with his patron, William Hayley; more poignantly we see an admonitory old man of Experience reduce a young companion to riven despair. Blake makes of Philips' inanities a dark allegory of the artist's subversion through patronage more suggestive of the self-conscious rusticities of Spenser than of eighteenth-century porcelains. Blake's vigor and originality, as usual, enable him to escape the limitations of his contemporaries, and free him to apply his own understandings where traditions were stale or misunderstood.

Finally, a note about my title, *Blake's Night*. This indicates the one image in Blake which most completely locates and circum-scribes my theme, and it serves to remind the reader that the key passages by means of which that theme is here developed are transformations of each other in Blake's remarkably consistent and persistent imagination. Blake's Night is the night of "Mad Song" and of "Night," of "Earth's Answer" and of "The Little Girl Lost & Found"; it is the night of Enitharmon's joy in *Europe*, and of her song in *Vala/The Four Zoas*, Night II. In *Paradise Lost* (as Blake read the poem) it is the night Satan pours dark dreams into the ear of Eve; likewise it is the scene of "To the Evening Star." In Blake's Night Luvah (in some sense) and Jesus and Milton's Satan and Milton himself and the Polypus descend into "eternal death." In Blake's Night, finally, while Ololon and Orc undergo different sorts of consummation, Los enters the portal of Experience and suffers a kind of passion as the darkness of the Covering Cherub is allowed to come between Albion and Jesus. Blake's Night, equally filled with eroticism and with death, is the ultimate *locus* of the idea of pastoral.

I refer throughout to one edition of Blake's poems: *The Poetry and Prose of William Blake*, edited by David V. Erdman (commentary by Harold Bloom), third printing with revisions, 1968 (New York: Doubleday & Co.). This is referred to throughout as "E," followed by a page number, for example, E34. I should, however, record that my study of *Vala/The Four Zoas* (thus referred to, however inelegantly, throughout the text because ultimately we have neither the one poem nor the other) was helped enormously by G. E. Bentley's edition for the Oxford

University Press (1963). Bentley's edition, though perhaps not so good a text,[5] seems to me on the whole preferable to Erdman's presentation because Bentley's editorial practice makes the poem more available. Erdman moves a whole Night out of serial order, and puts many of the textual variants in an appendix, where they are very difficult to apply to one's reading. For simplicity's sake, however, and because the Bentley edition is an expensive volume, I refer throughout to E.

Use of this text poses one stylistic issue: Blake punctuates eccentrically, and the critic who quotes extensively from an edition respecting this (E) has to decide whether or not to edit the text to the extent of adding end-punctuation to quotations within his own sentences. I sometimes compromise for the sake of clarity, but in general respect the poet's neglect of end-punctuation in quotations set off from the text which syntactically conclude statements of mine. This means that technically a number of my own sentences lack end-punctuation, but I think no one could be confused by this.

In discussing the illustrations to the *Songs*, I have referred often to the Rosenwald copy reproduced in facsimile by the Trianon Press for the Blake Trust, because a mass-produced version of this reproduction is now readily available in an Oxford University Press paperback edition, *Blake: Songs of Innocence and of Experience* (1970). The reader is reminded that Blake altered the colors, and very occasionally iconographic details, in his various copies of the *Songs*, and that my readings of these etchings are therefore subject to a comparative refinement which seemed inappropriate to my general purposes here. However, I have tried to ensure that such refinements as may be do not affect the tenor of any interpretation.

The abbreviations I use for Blake's poems are as follows: *Jerusalem*, J.; *Milton*, M.; *Vala/The Four Zoas*, F.Z.; and *Visions of the Daughters of Albion*, V.D.A. I refer often to *The Book of Thel* as *Thel*, and to *The Book of Urizen* as *Urizen*. In referring to Blake's poems, I always give E numbers, which refer to pages in the Erdman text (and of course unprefaced numbers refer to lines of particular poems under discussion), but I neglect to give fuller citations when I judge a reader with Erdman open before him can readily locate the relevant lines. For *Jerusalem* and *Milton* I give full citations: plate number first, line number(s) second, and finally the E number, for instance, J., 43.5–8; E189. For the *Vala/The Four Zoas* manuscript, and sometimes for *Tiriel*, I give the manuscript page number first (since these poems were never published on plates), followed by the line number(s) and the E number. For other works I give only the E number, except for some cases in *Urizen*; here it seems easier to use Blake's chapter and verse system of enumeration (roman and arabic numbers, respectively) rather than to allude to plate numbers.

References to Spenser are to the three-volume Clarendon Press edition (Oxford: Oxford University Press): *Spenser's Minor Poems*, edited by Ernest de Selincourt (1910), and *Spenser's Faerie Queene* (in two volumes), edited by J. C. Smith (1909). References to Milton are to *The Poetical Works of John Milton*, edited by Helen Darbishire (Oxford: Oxford University Press, 1958). The lines from a poem by Andrew Marvell were taken from *The Poems & Letters of Andrew Marvell* (in two volumes), edited by H. M. Margoliouth (Oxford: Oxford University Press, Clarendon Press, 1952). References to pages of these editions are given by page number, for instance, p. 34.

I refer to *Paradise Lost* by book and line numbers, roman and arabic enumeration respectively. For the *Faerie Queene* I use an arabic system of notation: 1.1.1.4–5 means book 1, canto 1, stanza 1, lines 4–5.

PART I
The Dream of the Lion

PASTORAL SONG

The initiation of a poetic career with a collection of pastorals is itself an indulgence in the sort of ambivalent fiction we associate with the kind: the face of ambition and interest, of *negotium*, wears the mask of humility and professes the virtues of *otium*. When *The Shepheardes Calender* appears to the world in 1579, it is not the rustic dialects and the assumption of rural innocence which tell the tale, but the "weeds" worn by the shepherd on this occasion; they include an introductory epistle and much learned argument in the annotations, elegant typefaces and carefully wrought wood-cuts—all of them forcing from the critic this declaration: "No English poet had ever been announced so pretentiously." It is plain enough to the initiated that Spenser "had decided to make of his career an *imitatio Vergilis*."[1]

In terms of career, William Blake was "brought on" much less certainly, and certainly less dramatically. His fledgling *Poetical Sketches* (1783) had to suffer the uncertain editorial practices and faint praises of his backers, but when he had come to see that the way forward was going to have to depend for its realization entirely on his own efforts, and he got down to his proper, canonical beginnings in poems written, etched, colored, bound, and published by his own hands, the resulting *Songs of Innocence* (1789), to be issued with their "contraries" in 1794 as *Songs of Innocence and of Experience*, are enough to recall the Spenserian precedent. As the most cursory survey of the relevant criticism will attest, there is in these poems an almost opaque simplicity masking passionate complexity of meaning. Just as certainly, as a glance at the illustrations will attest, the vocabulary of the *Songs* is pastoral. The exquisite presentation of the poems bespeaks (among other things) ambition.

The logic of these facts would seem to demand a situation where examination of Blake's lyrics against the background of pastoralism would be a cliché of criticism, but criticism has so far, with minor exceptions, resisted the cliché.[2] There are two general reasons for this. The first is that the poet's difficulty has until very recently kept him outside the purlieus of ordinary literary-critical examination; it has not been such a long time since Blake commentators could even coherently disagree with each other, and the supposed "specialness" of Blake's meaning has kept him insulated in a kind of perpetual foreground of eccentricity. The second reason, more germane, is that pastoralism reached Blake's immediate historical neighborhood in such an elegantly debased form that critics have perhaps been too willing to follow Dr. Johnson's lead and turn their backs on it. There is much willingness to regard the *Songs* as an *imitatio* of Anna Barbauld, or of Isaac Watts, or of Mary Wollstonecraft,[3] but little inclination to pierce the veil of gauzes and ecclesiastical bands and seek any of the minute particulars of the poems in a less specialized pastoral context.

Blake does, however, belong to a tradition of English literature, and his two obvious peers are Spenser and Milton, both of them epic poets whose reception of the Virgilian program (from pastoral to epic) was sufficiently enthusiastic to insure that pastoralism is an important element of their maturest work. They are also, after the Bible, the most important literary influences on Blake, and it would be odd, therefore, if pastoralism was not an important element of his work as well. It will be the burden of the following pages, therefore, to suggest that even in minute particulars there is nothing fanciful in the comparison between Blake's *Songs* and *The Shepheardes Calendar*, and that the most complete answers to the questions of context (where Blake distinguishes Innocence and Experience) and of point of view in the *Songs* are to be found in the pastoralism of the poets he admired and emulated. To see Blake thus, against the background of Spenser and Milton rather than of Barbauld and Wollstonecraft, is not only to clarify meaning but to imply evaluation as well. I am here willing to accept the implication, if only because to restore

Blake to the company he surely keeps is obliquely to reinforce my thesis. Otherwise Blake speaks everywhere implicitly on behalf of his own critical deserts more eloquently than I could hope to speak explicitly for them.

PASTORAL IGNORANCE

We have discovered aspiration, or ambition, wearing the pastoral disguise, or pretense, of artlessness. The assumption of simplicity is an important aspect of pastoralism, and I would like to propose for it the term "pastoral ignorance."

Pastoral ignorance is a complicated affair. It appears at first to be a rather light-hearted dramatic or rhetorical posture, but one of the first things we notice about the dramatic assumptions of pastoralism is that, while masks are worn nonchalantly or with as much grace as is consistent with rusticity, there is nothing frivolous about the act. Critics in the past have articulated this fact most often in terms of *decorum*, the ethics of a relationship between artificiality and nature, but the term "nature" begs many philosophical questions, and it ought to be remembered that in pastoralism an easy, commonsense distinction between "real" natural worlds and "ideal" dreamlike artificial ones would destroy much of the serious meaning of the genre. Theseus' grudging respect for Bottom's pastoral play in *A Midsummer Night's Dream* is not a function of decorum but depends on his discerning, however dimly, something like allegorical significance. To give another example, when in Spenser's "October" eclogue in *The Shepheardes Calender* Piers advises Cvddie,

> Abandon then the base and viler clowne,
> Lyft vp thy selfe out of the lowly dust:
> And sing of bloody Mars,
>
> (37–39)

critics have instinctively—and I think rightly—taken this passage from Venus to Mars quite seriously. There is no tendency to remember decorum or that the advice comes dramatically from a man named "Piers." Rather, the reader tends to inflate the passage to include spiritual advice of a high order.

Sometimes what seems like an issue of Social Substance or of Nature in a pastoral turns out to be an allegorical issue after all. No one has written more eloquently or intelligently about social cases of this kind than William Empson.[4] The paternity of many a pastoral heroine—is she peasant or the king's daughter?—is, as Empson makes clear, more of an allegorical question than a "natural" one. In fact, as Empson reads pastoral, nature is itself often a function of allegorical significance. The qualities which make the heroine a princess may perhaps seem to emanate from the soil, but are less a function of nature than of values which permeate the society even at the expense of distinctions otherwise assumed to be natural. This has its reflection in terms of pastoral ignorance also: the heroine is usually a foundling, and ignorant of her own paternity; there seems to be a link between her ignorance and the values which it makes available to the pastoral plot.

We have discovered, then, aspects of pastoral ignorance which are capable of relationship to the overriding concerns of the critics of Blake's *Songs*, specified by Northrop Frye to be point of view and context.[5] Point of view can be related to the rhetorical assumption of pastoral ignorance, and the latter can be seen as itself the vehicle of a largely inexplicit allegorical context. What with rhetorical pretense on one side and ineffable truths on the other, there would seem to be much about pastoral—where more is said than meets the ear—to discourage the critic. For the moment we must be content with establishing a connection between the two sorts of obscurity.

The connection will also help make the way clear before a comparison between so-called Arcadian pastoral and what Blake is doing in the *Songs*. The difficulty in the particular way of the *Calender* and the *Songs* is a reflection of the very different organizing principles of the two groups of poems. We approach the *Calender* instinctively as a dramatic structure, organized around the protagonist, Colin Clout. But merely the subtitle of Blake's 1794 collection ("Shewing the Two Contrary States of the Human Soul"; E7) leads us to expect a philosophical rather than a dramatic structure. In this case we expect the secret of the work to be an allegorical context. The connection between the two very different structural principles is the idea of pastoral ignorance.

PLATO'S *PHAEDRUS*

This connection has a *locus classicus* in Plato's *Phaedrus*. In examining it there, we can be assured that we are not straying from our subject, for if Theocritus is the ultimate source of

the pastoral manner, Plato is responsible for the fullest articulation of pastoralism's allegorical significance.[6] We can approach this significance initially in terms of a Socratic doctrine. (Quotations are from the translation by Benjamin Jowett; Oxford: Oxford University Press, 1892.)

Socrates has been discussing in pastoral surroundings the virtues of a kind of madness which "was a divine release of the soul from the yoke of custom and convention" (vol. I, p. 473). He explains:

> The divine madness was subdivided into four kinds, prophetic, initiatory, poetic, erotic, having four gods presiding over them; the first was the inspiration of Apollo, the second that of Dionysus, the third that of the Muses, the fourth that of Aphrodite and Eros. In the description of the last kind of madness, which was also said to be the best, we spoke of the affection of love in a figure ... which was also a hymn in honour of Love, who is your lord and also mine, Phaedrus, and the guardian of fair children, and to him we sung the hymn in measured and solemn strain.   (vol. I, pp. 473–474)

Marsilio Ficino was to make of Orpheus a syncretic figure possessed of all these forms of madness, the supreme poet, prophet, lover, and mystic, the "single voice for all the intimations of this world's beauty and the other world's that solicit a human mind" (Cody, p. 29). Hence, for Renaissance poets immersed in neoplatonism, and in the imagery of poets more mediate to this tradition also, Orpheus would come to seem the supreme pastoral figure, the synthesis of all the rest, expressing the final harmony of god, man, and nature. But Orpheus' ascent is erotic, and it is Eros of whom Socrates speaks. Since all pastoral conflict is erotic, we need to concentrate on this point.

Socrates gives his ideas about Eros their supreme development in the *Symposium*. There, Werner Jaeger writes in *Paideia*, "the concept of Eros becomes an epitome of all human striving to attain the good," and an illustration of a principle that might have interested Blake, "that man can never desire what he does not think to be good for him."[7] Even more interesting, for our purposes, is the "allegorical genealogy" which Socrates provides for Eros. Eros is the offspring of Plenty and Poverty: "He is a true philosopher, standing midway between wisdom and folly, and absorbed in constant striving and yearning." Eros, then, "is something between mortal and immortal. He is a great spirit: a daemon acting as intermediary between gods and men. This gives him a vitally important place in Platonic theology. He closes the gap between the earthly and celestial realms; he is the bond, the *syndesmos* that binds the whole universe together" (Jaeger, vol. II, p. 188). In short, if Eros were a character in Blake, he would inhabit Blake's pastoral realm, Beulah. In the case of Spenser we do not need to speculate: Cupid appears, in *propria persona*, in the "March" eclogue of *The Shepheardes Calender* (an imitation of Bion no. 4, "Love and the Fowler"), and although one critic has remarked sourly, "We resent this winged Cupid . . . in the English woods,"[8] Cupid's presence there is important. Before explaining this importance, however, we must turn back to the intricacies of the *Phaedrus*.

The *Phaedrus* seems to have two subjects: eroticism and rhetorical eloquence, and critics have professed some difficulty deciding which is the "real" subject. A. E. Taylor, after some hesitation, declares for rhetoric,[9] but the point of course is that Plato's two subjects are in fact one. Concerning the question whether the effective rhetorician need have any respect for the true, whether in fact too much respect for the complexities of truth might render him an inefficient persuader, Socrates solves the dilemma by arguing persuasively that only he who already knows the truth can successfully construct a persuasive (even if false) *simulacrum* for purposes of persuasion. This position is by no means distinct from the erotic subject matter of the dialogue. For the *Phaedrus*—and this is what is interesting to students of pastoralism—expresses an allegory of Eros rhetorically. The rhetorical aspect of the dialogue is the driving force of a drama shared by Phaedrus and Socrates (Lysias, Phaedrus' lover, is absent, but his invisible presence almost constitutes a third character). Moreover, Socrates' allegory of love is inseparable from this rhetorical drama.

In his image of charioteer drawn by two horses that represent respectively the higher and lower passions, Socrates represents a moral dilemma, and sketches the portrait of an erotic spirit who may become ensnared in sensuality but who can, through self-control and a harmonious philosophy, emancipate his soul. In the end, the successful spirit will be "light and winged for flight." "Nor," says Socrates, "can human discipline or divine inspiration confer any greater blessing on man than this" (vol. I, p. 463). In the course of articulating this idea, Socrates repeatedly refers to himself—sometimes seriously, sometimes in jest—as possessed by the Muses. At one point he must truncate an argument before possession by madness drives him too far (vol. I, p. 446). At the end of the dialogue, after a very long discussion of rhetorical organization, Socrates pauses before leaving the pastoral pleasance and addresses, ostensibly to Pan, a prayer which Werner Jaeger declares "is the only prayer in the whole of Plato, a pattern and an example of the philosopher's prayer" (Jaeger, vol. II, p. 196).

As suggested above, Plato's allegory exists in a rhetorical and dramatic context as interesting to students of pastoralism as the morality they express. At the end of Socrates' long and passionate discourse on the nature of Eros, Phaedrus remarks: "And I begin to be afraid that I shall lose conceit of Lysias, and that he will appear tame in comparison, even if he be willing to put another [speech] as fine and as long as yours into the field, which I doubt" (vol. I, p. 464). And indeed Socrates, though not in the sense at present understood by Phaedrus, is "seducing" the young man—though to a view of Eros rather than to his couch. We have already seen Socrates giving way to emotion— or pretending to give way. The rhetoric of the passages dealing with his emotions—which culminates in his moving prayer to Pan—is complex, but the idea central to its appeal is fundamental to the nature of pastoralism, and it is simple enough: it is the idea of interest (in the sexual sense) and, more generally, of ambition.

Sexual interestedness would of course hopelessly corrupt all of his fine words about Eros, yet Socrates himself, earlier in the dialogue, betrays an acute consciousness of it. His expression of this concerns us: "Consider this, fair youth, and know that in the friendship of the lover there is no real kindness; he has an appetite and wants to feed upon you: 'As wolves love lambs so lovers love their loves'" (vol. I, p. 446). This remark he later repudiates as a sin against Eros; his earlier rudeness, he suggests, was only called forth by the rhetorical necessities of his debate with Phaedrus. If we can take this disclaimer at its face value, Socrates seems to have successfully illustrated his own rhetorical principle: the rhetorical impact of his lies about Eros depended upon prior knowledge and deliberate falsification of the truth.

But I have suggested that success in Socrates' context of educative eroticism is precisely what is equivocal, lest the philosopher succeed only in luring Phaedrus from the bed of Lysias to his own. Plato's solution to this ambiguity is not the solution of the pastoral poet, for most poets would remain silent before it.

Indeed, we may argue that such silence itself is the source of pastoral ignorance, a pretense of knowing less than one knows. Socrates, however, is quite clear everywhere about the superiority of philosophy to poetry. In the *Phaedrus* he therefore lays down the rules for clear composition, and he speaks the plain truth about Eros. To do so is to illustrate a truth about rhetoric and to release it from the imputation that it is merely the art of maneuvering, but this release has to be accomplished at the expense of consciousness of the possible effect on Phaedrus. In a world composed, alas, of wolves and lambs, the truth must be told, even if to tell it entails pretending ignorance of the possible corrupting effect. To tell the truth in this way requires what I should call the highest form of pastoral ignorance. It requires what Blake thinks of as "organized innocence." It is at this point, then, in terms of what Blake calls "innocence," of what I have called "pastoral ignorance," that the link between rhetorical posture and allegorical significance becomes visible.

Before leaving the *Phaedrus*, some of the less important details of the rhetorical exchanges between Socrates and Phaedrus should be examined, for they also shed light on the habits of pastoralism. The erotic maneuvers of the dialogue are involved indeed, but capable of relationship to the general technique of pastorals, the disguising of ambition in pretense. For example, Phaedrus begins by reciting to Socrates the argument of his mentor and would-be lover that a young man ought to take as lover one who is not "in love" with him. The sort of eroticism at issue in the *Phaedrus* is an instrument of *paideia*, the ideals of culture expressed in terms of development and education. The ambition of which I have been speaking has its erotic manifestation in the attachment of a young man to an older, wiser mentor, and Plato expresses the meaning of this attachment in terms of the emancipation of the soul and the achievement of a harmonious, inward-looking life. The other possibility is, of course, pederasty. Spenser's "E.K." refers uncomfortably to "paederastice much to be praeferred before gynerastice" in the notes to "Ianuarie" (p. 17), but for Plato the issue was less hysterically an available choice between spiritual emancipation and physical enslavement. Indeed, this needs to be stressed, for the question of *dependency*, as we will see, is fundamental to both Spenser's and Blake's versions of pastoral. It is the issue to which the rhetoric of the *Phaedrus*, even more than the doctrine, most insistently points. Lysias' argument is that it is better for a young man to accept a lover who does not love him because the nonlover is more likely to be interested in the development, the manliness, the public exposure and welfare of his friend than the passionate lover. The latter will be possessive and will be interested in keeping the beloved passive, private, effeminate, and weak. In short, dependent.

Although the sexual conventions are very different, we can see a resemblance between the situation in the *Phaedrus* and the one depicted in *The Shepheardes Calender*. Colin Clout's pastoral ambitions are related to *paideia*; his eventual failure to realize those ambitions is related by Spenser to a declining state of culture, in which "Tom Piper makes vs better melodie" than the court poets ("October," 78). Further, Colin's situation is made poignant largely by means of the resemblance between his difficulties with his Proud Fair ("Shepheards deuise she hateth as the snake"; "Ianuarie," 65) and his difficulties with respect to preferment—that is, with the Queen, who seems, despite all the compliments lavished upon her, to represent the attitude of Proud Fair extended to include the circumference of Colin's world. We will see further on that this resemblance is realized even in Spenser's style, for the blazon to Eliza in the "Aprill" eclogue is very closely related in style and tone to the *Epithalamion*. Erotic success and careerism find a common vocabulary in pastoralism's concern with the problem of dependence.

Socrates has already demonstrated how the language of philosophy can cut through the equivocations of sexual interest and dependence, and speak clearly; his employment, in this context, of the word "ambition" is interesting: "If, on the other hand, they leave philosophy and lead the lower life of ambition, then probably, after wine or in some other careless hour, the two wanton animals take the two souls when off their guard and bring them together, and they accomplish that desire of their hearts which to the many is bliss; and this having once enjoyed they continue to enjoy, yet rarely because they have not the approval of the whole soul" (vol. I, p. 463). This is the language of morality, and we find nothing like its resolution in the poetic language of pastoralism. The pastoral language, self-consciously fictional, cannot choose. But if pastoral ignorance is a rhetorical sign that even in the pastoral world one cannot eliminate choices, one can create a context in which it is unnecessary to choose between them. We will see this repeatedly in Spenser; we will find Blake telling us specifically that his pastoral realm, Beulah, is one where "Contrarieties are equally True" (M., 30.1; E128).

And so perhaps the best that pastoralism which stops short of philosophy can do with Phaedrus' problem is expressed in

The CLOD & the PEBBLE

Love seeketh not Itself to please,
Nor for itself hath any care;
But for another gives its ease,
And builds a Heaven in Hells despair.

    So sang a little Clod of Clay,
    Trodden with the cattles feet:
    But a Pebble of the brook,
    Warbled out these metres meet.

Love seeketh only Self to please,
To bind another to its delight;
Joys in anothers loss of ease,
And builds a Hell in Heavens despite.

(E19)

THE SPRING OF THE YEAR

We should now be in a position to examine pastoral ignorance in two parallel but very different poems by Spenser and Blake, the former exploiting the rhetoric of ignorance and the latter developing Innocence as an allegorical context. Both poems are addressed to the seasonal beginning of the year, and the primary interest of the comparison is to see how such different poems are able to draw upon a common pastoral vocabulary to communicate themselves. The poems are Spenser's "March" eclogue and Blake's Song of Innocence "Spring."

If *The Shepheardes Calender* had been organized about the seasons instead of about the Christian calendar, "March" would have introduced the series. It is an imitation of Bion no. 4, "Love and the Fowler," the subject of which is the introduction of a boy to erotic experience. "Pastoral ignorance" takes the form of rusticity in this eclogue; the two boys of the dialogue, Thomalin and Willye, are rustics in fact, clearly not courtiers in disguise. We seem to be in a kind of Beatrix Potter world, for the only girl mentioned is named "Lettice," and one of the boys declares, "For als at home I have a syre, / A stepdame eke as whott as fyre" (40–41). The conversation he shares with his interlocutor reminds us of Tom Sawyer and Huckleberry Finn. Rusticity, moreover, is central to Spenser's purpose, which is to express with great poignance and humor the terrors of enslavement to eroticism. It is not that the discipline of love is being suppressed or criticized; Spenser merely suggests how ill-equipped poor innocent mankind is for its erotic task. Willye's emblem at the end (for each eclogue ends with an emblem) is: "To be wise and eke to loue, / Is graunted scarce to God aboue" (119–120). At the end of Thomalin's tale we see him pelting Cupid with "pumie stones." The weapons are harmless because they have passed through so much fire, and we shudder for Thomalin as much as laugh at him.

Thomalin's encounter with Cupid, a sort of allegory of adolescence, is moving precisely because of its narrator's ignorance. It is not a familiar story to him:

> But he, that earst seemd but to playe,
>   A shaft in earnest snatched,
> And hit me running in the heele:
> For then I little smart did feele:
>   But soone it sore encreased.
>
> (95–99)

The touch about the wound increasing is not in Spenser's original, and "E.K." picks up the point and reminds us of the heroic implications of a wound in the heel (p. 34). Spenser's tone, however, constantly underplays heroic implication and aims at pathos. Once, however, he achieves something more complex. Thomalin has been "tooting" for birds, and he fires at something in the undergrowth:

> But were it faerie, feend, or snake,
> My courage earnd it to awake,
>   And manfully therat shotte.
> With that sprong forth a naked swayne,
> With spotted winges like Peacocks trayne,
>   And laughing lope to a tree.
>
> (76–81)

Suddenly we seem to have found our way into the unsheltered world of fabliau; it is as if Cupid himself had been surprised as forked animal, exposed naked in the act he will inspire in poor Thomalin. The effect is to suggest, if only for a moment, that the world belongs to low, rude Thomalin rather than to his sophisticated tormentor. Pastoral ignorance has made the world rustic, even if it has not made it safe.

Spring

Sound the Flute!
Now it's mute.
Birds delight
Day and Night.
Nightingale
In the dale
Lark in Sky
Merrily
Merrily Merrily to welcome in the Year

Little Boy
Full of joy.
Little Girl
Sweet and small,
Cock does crow
So do you.
Merry voice
Infant noise
Merrily Merrily to welcome in the Year

Little Lamb
Here I am,
Come and lick
My white neck.
Let me pull
Your soft Wool.
Let me kiss
Your soft face.
Merrily Merrily we welcome in the Year

(E14–15)

This poem is pastoral in a way that goes beyond the pastoralism of "March" to the mythological roots of the genre, and it will be useful in the first place to verify this. The critical term most useful for interpreting the poem is "Orphic." It will be remembered that Orpheus became the supreme figure for Renaissance pastoralists of the neoplatonic persuasion because he included in his mythological person all four of the madnesses declared by Socrates to be divine, and his ability to tap these irrational sources of wisdom is what gives his music such power: it affects gods as well as men, and even the rocks respond to his song. It is the erotic power par excellence, and as we know from the tale of his head upon Lesbos, it transcends even death. Blake's "Spring" is a poem very much in the Orphic tradition, a poem about the season dancing to the flute of the god. The jangling rhymes are meant to jangle, and to seem childish, because they represent the very first, inexperienced responses to the magic flute of the first line, responses which bring the natural world out of the silence of line 2 into the light (and dark) of quotidian day. The simple, repetitive rhymes, like the magical "echo" of many a pastoral poem, represent the harmony between natural world and the powers of the piper. The process of creation is rendered for us in three stanzaic parts, and the successful conclusion of each aspect of the Orphic process is represented by an echoing and emphatic long concluding line. This suggests a voice having found itself. The poem celebrates the creation from the Orphic point of view, but it actually deals only with the first childish quarter of the creation: the voice and the nature which dances in response is still very young.

While language is pared almost to the point of abstraction, the three stages of the poem seem to move in the direction of dramatic specificity. Hazard Adams has remarked that the absence of definite article from "Lark in Sky" in the first stanza results not in "generalization but an immanence of larkness, rather than a particular, somewhat detached lark."[10] This is what we would expect of a creation out of an Orphic pipe, the evocation of all the various "nesses" which go to make a world. But the little boy and little girl of the second stanza seem *not* to represent boyness and girlness but more dramatically vivid presences before the speaker of the poem. The third stanza, in terms of situation, is more dramatic still. The speaking voice of the poem has moved from outside the creation (or fiction) to the inside, and we find it, in Blake's illustration, as child with lamb, first asking the lamb to respond ("Come and lick"), then wooing the lamb almost as a lover might ("Let me kiss"). We notice, then, that the Orphic speaker has succeeded in emotionally realizing the merriness which the refrain speaks of by moving himself dramatically ever closer to his creation: evocation yields to drama.

But to achieve this closeness, the voice of the poem comes perilously close to giving up its power *over* the creation which it has evoked. There is in terms of helplessness very little difference between the lamb and the infant of Blake's second illustration to the poem (see Fig. 1). This childish immanence, one can see, can be related to the "doctrines" of which Blake commentators are fond in two very different ways. One could talk on the one hand of the speaker's increasing immersion in the nature of his creation, and argue that this is bad. More commonly

1. "Spring," second plate

Blakeans argue that the immanence is a good thing, on the grounds that the similarity, the dramatic equality, of child and lamb suggest—by way of lines from "The Lamb"—Jesus: "He became a little child:/I a child & thou a lamb" (E9). Hazard Adams, for example, becomes quite enthusiastic in the service of this argument: "And who is the I—is he a lamb, a child, a man? It does not matter. Or to put it another way, he is all these things contained naturally in one thing, just as ultimately the one life is Jesus, who is man, child, and lamb. All is contained in a single spiritual body."[11] It is not my immediate business here to do more than note the contradiction between these views (one can get round it by evoking a Blakean version of the "fortunate Fall"—the merciful because clarifying naturalization of the fallen—but still understandably wonder whether Blake is applying Adams' doctrine to the adult sheep in his etching, which accordingly become God the Father and the Virgin Mary), but it is to the point to observe that argument in terms of the language of pastoral may be more helpful. That Spenser's "March" and "Spring" share a pastoral vocabulary now needs to be demonstrated.

Most of the elements of Spenser's eclogue can be discovered in Blake's twenty-seven-line poem. I suggested that when piper joins lamb on the greensward (according to the illustration) in Blake's third stanza, we could not be sure whether the god was in fact calling nature's tune any more. The similarity is not fortuitous between this question and the question of erotic decorum in Spenser's "March." In that poem the rustic's world of fabliau seemed for a moment to have overwhelmed Eros, and Cupid was forced to scamper away naked and awkward as any swain. In "Spring" Blake's lamb has the same sort of contextual effect on the piper that Thomalin's rusticity has on Cupid.

But any spring lambs in "March" were sure to be roasted, if not devoured, and for the comparison to be good we need to discover the theme of erotic dependency in "Spring." It is obvious enough, I think, that the progress of the poem describes, in its very innocent way, the passage to eroticism. The first stanza celebrates the delight of birds "day and night." (Their merriment occupies a cosmological spectrum similar to the "distant deeps or skies" evoked in "The Tyger": "Nightingale/In the dale/Lark in Sky.") We get a boy and a girl in the second stanza, and the metaphor "Cock does crow/So do you" subtly links the sexual merriment in the two stanzas to the ideas of betrayal and sacrifice.

As noted before, the infant in the third stanza woos his lamb.
All this is accomplished with a delicacy and lightness of touch
which critical analysis fails to imitate, and the reader might
correspondingly fail to see any relationship between Blake's infant's introduction to affection and Thomalin's, were it not for the
illustrations which accompany the poem. Blake is sparing with
words in "Spring" but prolix in illustration, for he etched this
very short poem on two plates. In the first, a young mother
holds her infant on her lap, while sitting under a tree—a posture
which everywhere in Blake represents dependence on nature. The
child is standing on his mother's lap and straining forward, arms
extended, toward the flock of sheep which is grazing right up
to the mother's feet. The import of the picture is clear, that the
mother is protecting the child just as mother, child, and sheep
are all protected by (or dependent upon) the tree which over-
arches them. The protecting tree is growing out of a slight knoll, on
the slopes of which the mother is resting, slightly above the level
of the sheep, and this difference in altitude plus the need for
protection implies at least two levels of nature in the picture. To
state a subtle and delicate suggestion crudely, the sheep represent
an experience for which the child is not ready, to which he must
descend. In the second illustration (Fig. 1), the protective tree has
disappeared, and so has the mother. We do get a stream, however—
surely with its traditional meaning of the flux of natural experience— flowing by the land on two sides of the picture. On the
dry land the child, who now seems somewhat older, is playing
with a young and amiable-looking lamb. The child has his hands
at the lamb's throat, but this is seemingly the better to guide the
creature's face so that he can lick the child's neck. Two sheep
recline complacently in the background, one of them apparently
asleep, and the inference is strong that these are the parents of
the lamb. The natural difference between child and lamb which
was emphasized in the first illustration has disappeared (the only
hint in the illustration that this might be a step down
rather than a step up is that the little angel closest to the
illustration—there are four such, cavorting in the midst of decor-
ative filigrees—is bowing his head in an attitude which suggests
mourning), and the need for protecting the child has apparently
disappeared also. But the presence of the lamb's parents, however
complacent (for sheep are not noted for their wisdom or prescience), together with the position of the child's hands, subtly
suggests dependency and a need for protection on the other side.

The point by now hardly needs stressing—and it is precisely the point we saw in Spenser's eclogue—the world of Spring is not safe.

Concerning "Spring" Hazard Adams remarks: "Blake shows that he can write well with vague words."[12] The vagueness and the lisping simplicity are related to what I have been calling pastoral ignorance. Blake uses the pretence of a childlike speaking voice as Spenser uses the ignorance of rustics, but Blake's is the more suggestive use of the device. "Spring" is a composite work of art; we need both words and pictures to deduce its meaning. But once we have, the Orphism of the text emerges poignantly as an idea of Innocence; the words are steadfastly innocent of their darker implications. This is a positive achievement of the imagination. Irony is much too crude a term for what Blake is doing; there would be irony if the speaker of the poem were only a child, only naive. But he is Orpheus as well, suffering the darker implications of the world his pipe calls forth. Without the vocabulary of pastoralism, this would be much more difficult to see.

EPITHALAMION AND ELEGY

If it can be taken for granted now that the language of Blake's *Songs* is pastoral, it becomes clear that an understanding of the vocabulary and grammar is a prerequisite to interpreting the poems. And since in Blake's English tradition pastoralism had expressed itself most eloquently in epithalamion and elegy, it might be useful to inquire what happens to these forms in Blake's hands. This question will take us to the end of the study; more immediately, to know something about pastoralism in Spenser's *Epithalamion* and in Milton's *Lycidas* will illuminate Blake's interest in it.

The history of the epithalamic and elegiac traditions is not what concerns us here, nor the role in that history of the individual talents of Spenser and Milton. The theme of the *Epithalamion* belonged to the pastoral tradition when Spenser picked it up, but probably not so irrevocably that he could not have depastoralized the poem if he had wanted to, and the fact that we think of the epithalamion today as an inevitably pastoral genre is partly a reflection of Spenser's genius and choice. That he chose as he did, however, testifies to something important in the pastoral tradition—Richard Cody remarks that "all pastoral aspires to the function of epithalamion, a Platonic dream of having life every way" (Cody, p. 73)—but there is no need here to seek that choice's specific rationale. Likewise, *Lycidas* has its history—which apparently returns all the way to the "Lament for Bion"—but as J. B. Leishman has pointed out, "*Lycidas* is a much more original . . . kind of poem than has been commonly supposed,"[13] and this originality includes the selection and arrangement of pastoral motifs from a great range of English and classical reading. But if pastoralism was idiosyncratic in the hands of Spenser and Milton—and that is greatly to overstate a case—the importance of the *Epithalamion* and of *Lycidas* would insure that their idiosyncracies would be seen by a poet of Blake's generation as central to a great tradition.

Not the least success of the *Epithalamion* is its translation of erotic wish-fulfillment into Orphic terms. The speaker of the poem is its erotic protagonist (an innovation of Spenser's),[14] and he evokes Orpheus in the very first stanza to account for this innovation ("So Orpheus did for his owne bride, / So I vnto my selfe alone will sing"; 16–17). Further, the crowning of his success is associated in the poem's famous refrain with Orphic responses from the world of nature: "The woods shall to me answer and my Eccho ring" (18). As this might suggest, if there is any difficulty to be found with the tone of the poem, it is that there is so much of the sweet smell of success about it. In the *Epithalamion*, *eros* triumphs, but Edmund Spenser, careerist, tends to overwhelm both the lover and the Christian. Reference has already been made to the blazon to Eliza in the "Aprill" eclogue of the *Calender*. This set-piece, a synthesis and pinnacle of the poet's technical virtuosity, is the first real resting place we get in the *Calender*. In it Spenser gather his powers, and applies them to the ambition of preferment. In places the tone becomes rather hectic and admonitory:

> Ye shepheards daughters, that dwell on the greene,
>   hye you there apace:
> Let none come there, but that Virgins bene,
>   to adorne her grace.
> And when you come, whereas shee is in place,
> See, that your rudenesse doe not you disgrace:
>   Binde your fillets faste,
>   And gird in your waste,
> For more finesse, with a tawdrie lace.
>
>   (127–135)

The same thing happens in the *Epithalamion,* where Spenser urges the "Nymphes of Mulla" to bind their locks and

> Behold your faces as the christall bright,
> That when you come whereas my loue doth lie,
> No blemish she may spie.
>
> (64–66)

It is clear that Spenser's preparation of a great occasion has as much to do with ambition as with devotion. Ambition works through time, and therefore A. Kent Hieatt's proposals concerning the temporal structure of the *Epithalamion* assume renewed interest.[15] Hieatt's idea is that Spenser carefully organized the poem in terms of the hours of light and darkness which prevailed the day of his wedding. But it seems odd that when we arrive at the hours of darkness, and the bedding of the bride, Spenser should dismiss the maids and the Orphic fiction in which they participated: "The woods no more shal answere, nor your echo ring" (314). Thomas M. Greene has observed that Spenser, as he approaches the consummation of the marriage, indulges in distinctly bourgeois delight in the richness of the lady's sheets and coverlets,[16] but it is the ambition of the poet taken in its widest sense which controls the peculiarities of the poem. Spenser's mind has run ahead to issue, and we are given to understand in the final stanzas that when the lady's womb conceives, there will be more answering and echoing.

The pathetic fallacy is one of the conceptual ribs of *The Shepheardes Calender,* and time is important here too. Whether we encounter it in elegy or epithalamion, pathetic fallacy represents the triumph of the imagination—erotic, poetic, or religious—over nature, and Spenser suggests that a failure of the imagination amounts to the triumph of time. Nature becomes antagonist rather than Orphic context. So in "Ianuarie" of *The Shepheardes Calender* he gives us what comes close to parody of pastoral—or antipastoral. Colin Clout in his sadness throws himself to the ground, in itself a pastoral gesture but accomplished here without pastoral nonchalance. Further, Colin breaks his pipes, stops his music, and insofar as the *Calender* has as its subject the ambitious Orphic imagination versus the nature of time the fundamental question becomes whether, through the course of the year's turning, Colin will regain imaginative control of the world. Hence his references to the season in "Ianuarie" constitute in a sense the antithesis of pathetic fallacy ("All so my lustfull leafe is drye and sere, / My timely buds with wayling all are wasted"; 37–38), for they represent the triumph of time rather than of the imagination:

> Thou barrein ground, whome winters wrath hath wasted,
> Art made a myrrhour, to behold my plight.
>
> (19–20)

The response of the mirror is not the aspiration of a would-be Orpheus, but the fate of Narcissus. Nature, time, the obdurate Lady, all have accumulated in the mirror which is the month. By "December" of the *Calender* the mirror triumphs. "October" suggests poetic ambition as means of access to a declining court, and as the instrument of its restoration; "November" provides us with an elegy offering the usual Christian solution to the problem of time. But neither oaten pipe nor Christ seems really relevant to Colin's problem, and in "December" he hangs his pipe upon a tree and bids farewell to love and lambs and court alike. The year has not brought even its natural harvest ("Nought reaped but a weedye crop of care"; 122), and so the *Calender* as a whole suggests the wasting hold of time on form.[17]

Milton employs the pathetic fallacy, too, in *Lycidas*, but there is no question of giving in to time, either in terms of the natural processes of the year or in terms of the unnatural and premature death of Edward King. Of course the eventual solution to the problem of time is Christian:

> So Lycidas sunk low, but mounted high,
> Through the dear might of him that walk'd the waves.
>
> (172–173)

But the poem, it ought not be necessary to say, is essentially, not circumstantially pastoral, and it is some support to Richard Cody's suggestion that the epithalamion is pastoralism's ultimate expression that the lines on the resurrection are followed by:

> Where other groves, and other streams along,
> With *Nectar* pure his oozy Locks he laves,
> And hears the unexpressive nuptiall Song,
> In the blest Kingdoms meek of joy and love.
>
> (174–177)

The tone of the poem is purely pastoral also. It ends not on a comic note, but on that note of nonchalance which in elegy dramatically embodies pastoral ignorance of tragedy:

At last he rose, and twitch'd his Mantle blew:
To morrow to fresh Woods, and Pastures new. (192–193)

Nor are the famous digressions unrelated to pastoral issues. It should not be surprising that one of them is devoted to the question of true fame. In the other, which has prompted even more critical agony, there is a suggestion of recidivism in the arts ("their lean and flashy songs / Grate on their scrannel Pipes of wretched straw"; 123–124), but Milton concentrates on moralizing at the expense of faithless clergy. Blake touches the same subject in "The Voice of the Ancient Bard" ("And wish to lead others when they should be led"; E32), as does Spenser in his "Maye" eclogue. Milton's imagery—except for that troubling "two-handed engine"—is perfectly indigenous to pastoralism. What has seemed to intrude is moralizing itself, but this too is a problem we have seen before, and defining the relationship between dramatic pretenses and dogmatic assurances has been an issue of pastoralism since the *Phaedrus*.

"TO THE EVENING STAR"

We are fortunate in having an early Blake poem, "To the Evening Star" (published 1783), a complete and polished poem in its own right, which he subsequently adapted to the purposes of the *Songs*, where it becomes "Night." I reproduce the earlier poem here with gaps in the typescript to underline its structure.

Thou fair-hair'd angel of the evening,
Now, while the sun rests on the mountains, light
Thy bright torch of love; thy radiant crown
Put on, and smile upon our evening bed!

Smile on our loves; and while thou drawest the
Blue curtains of the sky, scatter thy silver dew
On every flower that shuts its sweet eyes
In timely sleep.

Let thy west wind sleep on
The lake; speak si[l]ence with thy glimmering eyes,
And wash the dusk with silver.

> Soon, full soon,
> Dost thou withdraw; then the wolf rages wide,
> And the lion glares thro' the dun forest:
> The fleeces of our flocks are cover'd with
> Thy sacred dew: protect them with thine influence.
>
> (E402)

This exquisite sonnet variation within very small compass speaks a surprising range of the pastoral vocabulary. The poem begins in the epithalamic tradition; by the end, if not elegiac, it at any rate includes the strongly felt presence of death in a pastoral context. However, the closest analogy to its development we have so far seen is "Spring." The first quatrain of the poem is an invocation which seems to be personally interested ("smile upon our evening bed"), yet all the dramatic energy of the speaker's specific erotic situation has been drained off into the invocation. The speaker's address grows even less erotically specific as the poem progresses: "smile on our loves" in line 5 has either a general reference (as the plural implies) or no erotic reference at all. By the end of the poem the shepherd-speaker is clearly speaking for humanity in general, and the object of his address, considerably less clear a presence than in the first lines of the poem, is about to withdraw out of earshot. Nevertheless, at the end of the poem there are many specific, dramatized forces at work, and much more dramatic urgency than at the beginning.

The most efficient way to analyze the poem is to follow the fortunes of the central image. The image of the first quatrain is of the hymeneal torch of Venus, and of her "radiant crown." Light and heat—illumination, warmth, beneficence—are inextricably bound together. In the second stanza, the influence of the goddess has less specific epithalamic purpose (if any erotic purposes at all), and in terms of image it undergoes a corresponding division and cooling down. Warmth is rendered in the word "smile," repeated from the fourth line, but the light of the torch has gone into the "silver dew" of line 6. The silver dew is to be scattered "on every flower that shuts its sweet eyes / In timely sleep." That is, some sort of naturalization has taken place; the bed of love has been replaced by a bed of flowers (which should, at the very least, cause us to think of "The Sick Rose"). Further, a new tone has entered the poem. The reader will have noticed that erotic invocation has already given way to the need for protection, about which I have already said a good deal, and it is noteworthy that the tone of these lines, if not quite Miltonically moral, reminds us of the rather hectoring decorum exhibited by Spenser on important occasions. There is a certain nursery suggestion here that little flowers that will *not* shut their eyes in timely sleep must pay the consequences; we will see a lot more of this sinister maternalism in Blake. If we have sunk to nature, and love is now vegetating in a flower bed, it is interesting that this descent brings with it the suggestion that the flowers in the bed might have an independent power over their own destinies—if only, as in this case, one which gets them into trouble with the authorities. It is also interesting that the question of one's danger or safety depends on whether one is "timely." On this aspect of the poem the influence of Spenser has been great.

In the third section of the poem, the analysis of image is subtilized further. This is the stillest part of the night, and hence the safest. In terms of the poem's erotic fiction the moment of creation, achieved after the childish flowers have been put to bed, is being rendered. It is interesting to compare Blake's lines to the parallel passage in the *Epithalamion*:

Bvt let stil Silence trew night watches keepe,
That sacred peace may in assurance rayne,
And tymely sleep, when it is tyme to sleepe,
May poure his limbs forth on your pleasant playne,
The whiles an hundred little winged loues,
Like diuers fethered doues,
Shall fly and flutter round about your bed,
And in the secret darke, that none reproues,
Their prety stealthes shal worke, and snares shal spread
To filch away sweet snatches of delight,
Conceald through couert night.

(353–363)

These lines contain the poem's most overt references to eroticism, and eroticism, until it bears issue, is a part of Spenser's experience so personal that he explicitly denies it the publicity of answering woods and ringing Echo. He is thinking of a very human and, in Blakean terms, vegetable love, to be practiced in the "secret dark." In Blake's poem eroticism has been totally absorbed into aestheticism, into the elegance of "speak silence with thy glimmering eyes,/And wash the dusk with silver." A further dissipation of erotic heat has taken place. The warmth of "smile" has become the glimmer in the eyes which "speak silence" and the "silver dew" has become "wash the dusk with silver." This image represents Spenser's "sacred peace," and probably the moment of creation as well, but in Blake's case we stare creation's goddess clearly and coolly in the face. The face is the face of a lover, and it is described in the traditional language of paradox: "speak silence with thy glimmering eyes." The eyes are eloquent, however, because they are full of tears, and Blake emphasizes this point by translating Spenser's "sacred peace" into the "sacred dew" of the poem's last line. We must remember that the goddess is weeping, for this initiates a train of images which will lead us to "The Tyger." The tears here remind us that we are not moving away from the flesh and its pains, but in the opposite direction, for the translation of the tears of the goddess into the dew on the backs of the sheep is an unhappy naturalization. "Soon, full soon," we are told, "dost thou withdraw." The remark seems more a recognition of natural necessity than an erotic complaint, and the voice which makes it more that of ordinary shepherd than of lover. Yet the natural world develops its analogues to erotic danger—we are left with the glimmer of the goddess' eyes having gone into the lion's glare, seen through the dun forest. There is no light left in the dew, however sacred, which lies—it seems only "natural" for that time of night—on the backs of the sheep. The dews are the tears of Venus—the dew of sexual creation is the dew of "Night." This is a notion characteristic of the mature Blake, and it is interesting to find it, as well as the passions masquerading as wolf and lion, in so early a poem.

Before leaving "To the Evening Star," it ought to be remarked that the same reading, with a different emphasis, can be achieved if one concentrates on pastoralism, rather than on analysis of the hymeneal image. In this case the poem becomes an almost Ovidian series of transformations: the lover of the first stanza becomes something like a schoolmaster in the second, telling the flowers to take their timely sleep. In the third, he is an aesthete. In the last, he becomes a shepherd. The sequence of roles suggests the development of pastoralism and its historical evolution to the aestheticism of the 1890's, and hints at the relationship between the historical employment of literary modes and their inherent formal possibilities.

"NIGHT" AND THE LION OF INNOCENCE

So far we have been interested less in Blake's own language than in the language traditional to pastoralism as a whole. But since "To the Evening Star" eventually evolved into the "Night" of the *Songs of Innocence,* we are in a position to observe the relationship between the traditional language and the language of what Blake calls Innocence.

For Blake the creation of the world is simultaneous with the Fall and the Deluge. We observed a hint of this in "To the Evening Star," where the dews of creation were the dews of night. We also observed hints of another aspect of Blake's mature view of the world: at the beginning of the "Fall" there is an erotic warmth, which dissipates into the cold and distant influence which is all we have for protection after the Fall. And there is great need for protection then, because nature imitates a declined eroticism and creates a dramatic world of wolves and lambs: a cycle of hungering and devouring analogous to the cycle of passion and dependence of fallen sexuality. In language of sweet lamb and flaming tyger, Blake suggests a passionate dialectic identical with experience.

All of these hints, as the very title might suggest, are developed in "Night." There is no difficulty in identifying the language as pastoral. The second stanza begins,

> Farewell green fields and happy groves,
> Where flocks have took delight;
> Where lambs have nibbled,
>
> > (E13)

in imitation of Colin Clout's

> Adieu delightes, that lulled me asleepe,
> Adieu my deare, whose loue I bought so deare:
> Adieu my little Lambes and loued sheepe,
> Adieu ye Woodes, that oft my witnesse were.
> > ("December," 151–154)

But Colin's night is death, and his is the language of bitter experience. "Night," on the other hand, is a Song of Innocence. At the end the lion lies down with the lamb, and his "bright mane for ever, / Shall shine like the gold" (46–47). This is the language of Isaiah, and obliquely of the fourth eclogue of Virgil.

But "Night" is a very esoteric poem—in it pastoralism speaks even more obscurely than usual—and the allusions fail to explain its minute particulars. To explain these will take some time, but the effort is worthwhile for two reasons. First, "Night" is perhaps the most comprehensive of Blake's poems of Innocence, and to interpret it, therefore, is an act of critical economy. Second, as has already been noted, "Night" can tell us much about the relationship between Blake's Innocence and pastoralism more generally. The most direct way to this interpretive undertaking is by an extended quotation from Blake's best critic, Northrop Frye:

> Innocence and experience are the middle two of four possible states. The state of experience Blake calls Generation, and the state of innocence, the potentially creative world of dreams and childhood, Beulah. Beyond Beulah is Eden, the world of the apocalypse in which innocence and experience have become the same thing, and below Generation is Ulro, the world as it is when no work is being done, the world where dreams are impotent and waking life haphazard ... This is, of course, one world looked at in four different ways. The four ways represent the four moods or states in which art is created: the apocalyptic mood of Eden, the idyllic mood of Beulah, the elegiac mood of Generation, and the satiric mood of Ulro.[18]

Frye's remark "the idyllic mood of Beulah, the elegiac mood of Generation" suggests that what I have been discussing as pastoralism, especially in terms of epithalamion and elegy, would seem to encompass two of Blake's states, two of his ways of looking at the world—which Frye identifies as Innocence and Experience. This is critically convenient. And if we can identify the "way" of, for instance, Innocence, we should have something generally applicable to all of the poems identified with that state. "Spring," for example, would entail the same way of looking at the world as "Night."

In analyzing "Spring," I had something to say about the identity of the speaker of the poem, specifically that "pastoral ignorance" took the form of the concealment of a sophisticated outlook in the accents of a child, the Orphic echo lurking behind infantile rhymes. There is a tendency in pastorals toward metamorphosis, or more properly, toward "mythological condensation" (Orpheus stands behind Paris, who stands behind "a shepherd," and so on), and Blake's early "To the Evening Star" confirmed this tendency. To begin reading "Night," then, it would seem sensible to look for a narrator who seems to be pastorally ignorant, and to seek the mythological figure who stands behind him. A lyric narrator does appear in the first stanza of the poem:

> The sun descending in the west,
> The evening star does shine,
> The birds are silent in their nest,
> And I must seek for mine.

(E13)

We have a naive, or "innocent," narrator (it will be some time before we see fully who he is) who speaks with the accents of a child. But the development of the poem is such that by the end this narrator's consciousness is expressed by another *persona*, a second "I" with whom the first comes to identify himself:

> And now beside thee bleating lamb,
> I can lie down and sleep;
> Or think on him who bore thy name,
> Grase after thee and weep.
> For wash'd in lifes river,
> My bright mane for ever,
> Shall shine like the gold,
> As I guard o'er the fold.
>
> (E14)

In this case, then, the child is not the lamb, but the lion. In the discussion of "Spring" it was suggested that the narrator was not naive, not really childish, but the function of a much more complicated understanding expressed in pastoral terms. In "Night" Blake has provided us with a dramatized image of that understanding in the shape of the dream of the lion. In fact, the poem itself can be thought of as the "image" of the point of view of Innocence. To understand what the achieved consciousness represented by the dream of the lion stands for will be to understand Innocence.

One of the things for which the lion stands is a context where dependents can successfully be protected ("As I guard o'er the fold"), and in the poem this context is outlined by paradox:

> Saying: wrath by his meekness
> And by his health, sickness,
> Is driven away,
> From our immortal day.
>
> (E14)

Even "immortal day" is paradoxical, for the text makes it clear ("wash'd in lifes river") that this is an imaginative achievement, not an escape from quotidian reality.[19]

In suggesting a world in which the dependent are safe and irreconcilables are paradoxically reconciled, Blake is indulging in the commonplaces of pastoralism; his example in pastoral fictions of reconciliation was Spenser, and to examine Spenser's practice is therefore to explore the tradition of "Night." I wish to explore three instances in Spenser's version of pastoral where problems of authority and dependence are related to the question of reconciliation of opposites.

The first instance occurs in Spenser's "Febrvarie" eclogue, where the theme of ambition takes the form of a conflict between youth and age. Youth and age, then, are the "contraries" which need reconciliation, and the eclogue supplies this in the form of the fable, attributed to Chaucer, of the Oak and the Briar. This fiction appears to provide reconciliation by means of a simple moral: youth is dependent upon age for support; unsupported briars end up "trodde in the durt / Of cattell, and brouzed, and sorely hurt" (235–236). We expect intimations of order, speeches on degree, and a universe presided over by a God who understands the laws of mutual dependency. In fact we get something rather different, and stranger. The briar does direct a speech on degree to his "soueraigne, Lord," but the speech introduces issues not at all compatible with the official moral of the tale:

> Ah my soueraigne, Lord of creatures all,
> Thou placer of plants both humble and tall,
> Was not I planted of thine own hand,
> To be the primrose of all thy land,
> With flowring blossomes, to furnish the prime,
> And scarlot berries in Sommer time?   (163–168)

The language of flowers and fruit has erotic overtones, and the phrase "was not I planted of thine owne hand" strongly introduces the issue of dependence and support. The briar continues:

> How falls it then, that this faded Oake,
> Whose bodie is sere, whose braunches broke,
> Whose naked Armes stretch vnto the fyre,
> Vnto such tyrannie doth aspire?
>   (169–172)

Ambition is being figured in terms of a younger, riper lover interested in replacing an old one, but the oak's worn branches have attracted to them the idea of fire. And the briar's speech "kindled such coles of displeasure" (191) in the Lord that he runs for his axe. The implications of the briar's speech are far from clear, his phrase "whose naked Armes stretch vnto the fyre" suggesting pathos as well as contempt. Moreover, it carries strange theological overtones, for the lines are a clear allusion to the warning of John the Baptist in the wilderness of Judaea: "And now also the axe is laid unto the root of the trees: therefore every tree which bringeth not forth good fruit is hewn down, and cast into the fire" (Matthew 3 : 10). Presumably, in the gospel, this is justice, but the briar's point of view is hardly to be identified with that of John the Baptist. And the confusion in tone between contempt and pathos has its counterpart in our divided judgment of the "Lord of creatures all." He is called "Husbandman" (142) as well as "good man" (192), but he is subject to unreasonable rage. What are we to think of his judgment, of his order? Blake would call him Urizen.

Even more interesting are some further complaints of the briar to his Jehovah:

> So beate his old boughes my tender side,
> That oft the bloud springeth from woundes wyde:
> Vntimely my flowres forced to fall,
> That bene the honor of your Coronall.   (175–178)

Here the language of eroticism is expanded to include the passion of crucifixion. By means of this language, Spenser has crossed the pastoral divide between epithalamion and elegy; we have stumbled upon a likely source for the opening lines of *Lycidas*:

> I com to pluck your Berries harsh and crude,
> And with forc'd fingers rude,
> Shatter your leaves before the mellowing year.
>   (3–5)

It is curious, too, that the allusion to the Crucifixion should follow so closely, so unmistakably, after the allusion to Matthew 3 : 10. The plea of briar to lord is plainly the specious plea of upstart youth against age; it is a plea ultimately based upon the necessities of a fallen nature. Yet Spenser does three interesting things: he causes the appeal to prosper (with ultimately drastic results, to be sure); he causes the appeal to be made in unmistakably erotic language; he plants in that language allusions which outline the career of Christ, from the annunciation of John the Baptist to the Crucifixion. Thus he provides the idea of necessity with both erotic and theological analogues. If Spenser were as radical a theologian as Blake, these things would not be difficult to interpret. The range of suggested religious experience is bounded by God as absolute tyrannical dictator at the apex of a triangle (Blake's "Nobodaddy"), with the Accuser and the

Atoner at the two feet of the figure. It was Blake, in *The Marriage of Heaven and Hell*, who suggested: "the Jehovah of the Bible being no other than he, who dwells in flaming fire. Know that after Christ's death, he became Jehovah" (E35). Blake would have been especially interested to see (as perhaps he did) a theological model being implied by an erotic strategy. The difficulty with this argument is that Spenser was not so radical a theologian as Blake. And the official moral of the fable is that the briar, without oak to lean upon, has nothing to lean upon; his lord is no shepherd. Spenser must, however, have been conscious of the application of the ideas of apocalyptic accusation and martydom to the plight of his poet-hero, Colin Clout, but such consciousness as he has is masked in pastoral ignorance and a facile, reconciling moral. We simply do not know how esoteric a poem "Febrvarie" is.

Another example of Spenser's strange way with contraries is closer to "Night." This is the "Maye" eclogue. The mode of reconciliation is again moral-theological, but the contraries to be resolved are not youth and age but the related terms "craft" and "simplicitie," terms close enough to Blake's Innocence and Experience to arouse our interest. The speakers in the eclogue are "Piers" and "Palinode," both evidently older men; their articulation of the "moral" of the eclogue is in sufficiently ecclesiastical terminology to have led most critics away from pastoralism into the thickets of topical, ecclesiastical satire. But "Maye" is subtler than topical satire, and only an awareness of the ways of pastoralism—its habit of mythological condensation and taste for translation—will explain how Spenser coherently draws together the different issues in his argument.

The moral is expressed (in Greek) in two emblems which, as the gloss by E.K. makes clear, constitute a resolved dialectic:

> Both these Emblemes make one whole Hexametre. The first spoken of Palinodie, as in reproche of them, that be distrustfull, is a peece of Theognis verse, intending, that who doth most mistrust is most false. For such experience in falsehod breedeth mistrust in the mynd, thinking no lesse guile to lurke in others, then in hymselfe. But Piers thereto strongly replyeth with another peece of the same verse, saying as in his former fable, what fayth then is there in the faythlesse. For if fayth be the ground of religion, which fayth they dayly false, what hold then is there of theyr religion.   (pp. 59–60)

We notice that the two sides of this dialectic do not amount quite to craft and simplicity. The first half of the hexameter might make us think of Blake's visionary outlook (or of the cynicism of Comus); the latter reminds us of Milton's remarks at the expense of a corrupt clergy in *Lycidas*. Neither half, nor both halves resolved together, would quite prepare us for the fable said by E.K. to illustrate the principle: "what fayth then is there in the faythlesse."

The fox of this fable is not so much faithless as false. (He describes himself in terms which suggest Blake's "The Little Black Boy": "I am a poore Sheepe, albe my colour donne:/For with long traueile I am brent in the sonne"; 266–267.) And the kid is less faithful than simply innocent. Spenser, however, carefully relates this innocence both to the natural cycle of youth and age and to the sexual aspect of this cycle in particular. We are told of the kid:

> His Vellet head began to shoote out,
> And his wrethed hornes gan newly sprout:
> The blossomes of lust to bud did beginne,
> And spring forth ranckly vnder his chinne.   (185–188)

And his mother remarks:

> Now I a waylfull widdowe behight,
> Of my old age haue this one delight,
> To see thee succeede in thy fathers steade,
> And florish in flowres of lusty head.
>   (201–204)

(Blake's treatment of the same theme is in the two poems called "Nurse's Song.") The blossoms of lust constitute a theme appropriate to May, and to maying, and Palinode's description of the latter reminds us of the garlanding in the *Epithalamion*:

> Yougthes folke now flocken in euery where,
> To gather may buskets and smelling brere:
> And home they hasten the postes to dight,
> And all the Kirke pillours eare day light,
> With Hawthorne buds, and swete Eglantine,
> And girlonds of roses and Sopps in wine.
>   (9–14)

But "Maye" looks forward not to *eros* but to *thanatos*, and sexual envy of the young people by the two "men of elder witt" ("O that I were there,/To helpen the Ladyes their Maybush beare"; 33–34) leads them to discuss the wages of sin.

It is at this point in the eclogue that the reading in terms of ecclesiastical allegory becomes most grotesque, for if Piers represents the point of view of salvation by faith, Spenser would seem to be amusing himself. On the subject of a clergyman's responsibility to the children he begets, Piers remarks:

> But Shepheard must walke another way,
> Sike worldly souenance he must foresay.
> The sonne of his loines why should he regard
> To leaue enriched with that he hath spard?
> Should not thilke God, that gaue him that good,
> Eke cherish his child, if in his wayes he stood?
>
> (81–86)

Spenser's pleasure in social satire might make us think of the parallel chimney sweep poems of Innocence and Experience. In Innocence the uncared-for child is told, "So if all do their duty, they need not fear harm" (E10). But, if we assume that this advice bears a relationship to the first half of the emblem in "Maye," to the idea that the most trusting will find the most to trust, it is the teaching of Experience that

> ... because I am happy, & dance & sing,
> They think they have done me no injury:
> And are gone to praise God & his Priest & King
> Who make up a heaven of our misery.
>
> (E23)

To make up a heaven of the misery of children, of the slaughter of innocence, is to practice a perverse but human economics, and while questions of utility and economics would seem to be remote from pastoralism—which is supposed to celebrate an ideal world—exigencies still press even here, and questions of utility, we shall see, lie not very far from the center of the genre. Piers and Palinode in an eminently utilitarian way discuss the possibilities of making a heaven out of the kid's sufferings in the beast fable. Palinode is given a speech which wonderfully relates a sound economic policy for the pleasure-loving priest to letting his posterity take its own chances:

> What shoulden shepheards other things tend,
> Then sith their God his good does them send,
> Reapen the fruite thereof, that is pleasure,
> The while they here liuen, at ease and leasure?
> For when they bene dead, their good is ygoe,
> They sleepen in rest, well as other moe.
> Tho with them wends, what they spent in cost,
> But what they left behind them, is lost.
>
> (63–70)

Palinode is a good enough arguer against asceticism to have
suggested arguments to Comus, but in Spenser at least, and
as we shall see in Blake's *Thel*, the arguments about utility have
a broader scope than it was the business of Milton's Lady to
recognize. For they address themselves to the system of erotic
slavery formulated as Courtly Love. The question of the utility
of that tradition of erotic service and self-abasement is addressed
drily by Hobbinol at the end of the "Aprill" eclogue:

> Sicker I hold him, for a greater fon,
> That loues the thing, he cannot purchase.
>
> (158–159)

These arguments also address themselves to a system of dependence and preferment at court which masked itself in the language
of courtly love. This becomes clear in the relationship emerging
clearly in "Maye" between erotic and economic envy:

> Ah *Piers*, bene not thy teeth on edge, to thinke,
> How great sport they gaynen with little swinck?   (35–36)

Further, it must be remembered that envy as sophisticated as
Palinode's, craft as experienced as his, is a defense against the
slaughter of innocence which is the subject of Piers's beast fable.
In "Maye," this fact produces one of Spenser's most provocative
points. For Piers replies to Palinode's question (quoted above):

> Perdie so farre am I from enuie,
> That their fondnesse inly I pitie.   (37–38)

Pity is what we bestow on the kid in the beast fable. Palinode picks
this up in a most interesting way:

> I (as I am) had rather be enuied,
> All were it of my foe, then fonly pitied:
> And yet if neede were, pitied would be,
> Rather, then other should scorne at me:
> For pittied is mishappe, that nas remedie,
> But scorned bene dedes of found foolerie.
>
> (57–62)

In the penultimate line, Spenser seems inadvertently to be stumbling toward the relationship, so important in Blake, between pity
and necessity. We are some of the way towards the well-known
lines from "The Human Abstract":

> Pity would be no more,
> If we did not make somebody Poor:
> And Mercy no more could be,
> If all were as happy as we.
>
> (E27)

This point, deeply latent in Spenser, wonderfully clear in Blake, bring us back to the pair of emblems at the end of the eclogue, the dialectic of positions which fit together perfectly to "make one whole Hexametre." The two positions, to quote E.K., were (1) "who doth most mistrust is most false" and (2) "what fayth then is there in the faythlesse?" We are being presented with a choice between an ideal world (where suspicion is not useful) and an all-too-real one (where disguise is the rule). Interestingly, there is no room *between* the two positions for the kid, whose slaughter, and the pity it evokes, is curiously overlooked by the dialectic. In short, the middle ground between ideal and actual—and pastoral is such a middle ground—seems cruelly to have been devoured.

In the *Phaedrus* I pointed out analogous phenomena. Socrates' commitment to truth finally absorbed his responsibility for the seductive effect of his words on Phaedrus; the language of truth finally took precedence over the language of feigning, and the latter was left with the pretense that choice was unnecessary. We can see the relationship between this idea and the developing distrust of moral emotions (like pity) in the pastoral poems of Spenser and Blake, where the fiction demands at least that lion and lamb lie down together. A dialectic like the one with which we are presented in "Maye," where choice on either side kills the kid, necessitates pity, and wipes out the reconciling middle ground of pastoralism, is likely to contribute to such distrust. Blake's expression of the problem is characteristically direct: "Thus one portion of being, is the Prolific. the other, the Devouring: to the devourer it seems as if the producer was in his chains, but it is not so, he only takes portions of existence and fancies that the whole ... These two classes of men are always upon the earth, & they should be enemies; whoever tries to reconcile them seeks to destroy existence" (E39). Blake is careful here to imply rejection of the moral emotions of would-be reconcilers, for they would succeed only in falsifying the nature of the two classes; yet we must not too hastily conclude from this a willingness to accept a dualism of prolific and devourer which demands time and the slaughter of innocence. In fact, it is the tension between these two aspects of the case which represents the crux of pastoralism so far as Blake is concerned, and which explains his interest in the form.

A simplified version of this pastoral dilemma is the question: does Experience necessarily devour Innocence? If we apply this question to the concluding fiction of "Night," the answer is equivocal:

> When wolves and tygers howl for prey
> They pitying stand and weep;
> Seeking to drive their thirst away,
> And keep them from the sheep.
> But if they rush dreadful;
> The angels most heedful,
> Recieve each mild spirit,
> New worlds to inherit.
>
> And there the lions ruddy eyes,
> Shall flow with tears of gold:
> And pitying the tender cries,
> And walking round the fold:
> Saying: wrath by his meekness
> And by his health, sickness,
> Is driven away,
> From our immortal day.

(E14)

Further, the question of what happens is complicated by the question of where it happens. Are we in Generation (the visionary state which Northrop Frye associates with Experience), or are we in Beulah (Innocence)? The receipt of mild spirits "new worlds to inherit" would at first glance seem obviously to be an allegory of the transcendence of Generation—perhaps a rather childish allegory at that—but one of Blake's critics, Joseph Wicksteed, reads the passage ingeniously as a contrary allegory of birth into this world: "The angels move about in the dark world of the flesh seeking to protect innocence and control desire. But if desire breaks through their control they ... 'recieve each mild spirit new worlds to inherit.'"[20] Whatever we think of Wicksteed's sexual allegory, the language of the poem is clearly designed to defeat our enquiries, for the lion, as already noted, is "wash'd in lifes river," yet enjoys an "immortal day." I have deferred my third reference to Spenser until this point because it casts such an interesting light on this question.

The emblem to Spenser's "September" eclogue suggests a union more perfect than any available to the halves of a hexameter. The ostensible subject of "September" is the uselessness of foreign travel as anodyne for pain or solution to the problems of getting ahead, and the emblem reads, "*Inopem me copia fecit*," that is, "plenty made me poor." The application, as E.K. explains in his gloss, is to him "who that by tryall of many wayes had founde the worst" (p. 96), but E.K. also reminds us of the phrase's odd location. It belongs, in Ovid's *Metamorphoses*, to Narcissus, who is referring to the sterile fruits of a love which has transcended contraries by the simple expedient of falling in love with oneself, thereby uniting lover and love-object. The emblem, however, is oddly applied to the fiction by means of which Diggon illustrates the cunning and guile of foreigners, and the fact that cunning does not always triumph. The illustration takes the form of a tale of a shepherd (Roffy, or Roffynn), his dog (Lowder), and a cunning wolf. The wolf illustrates perfectly Socrates' principle in the *Phaedrus* that to feign the truth one must first understand it:

> Whilome there wonned a wicked Wolfe,
> That with many a Lambe had glutted his gulfe.
> And euer at night wont to repayre
> Vnto the flocke, when the Welkin shone faire,
> Ycladde in clothing of seely sheepe,
> When the good old man vsed to sleepe.
> Tho at midnight he would barke and ball,
> (For he had eft learned a curres call.)
> As if a Woolfe were emong the sheepe.
> With that the shepheard would breake his sleepe,
> And send out Lowder (for so his dog hote)
> To raunge the fields with wide open throte.
> Tho when as Lowder was farre awaye,
> This Woluish sheepe would catchen his pray,
> A Lambe, or a Kidde, or a weanell wast:
> With that to the wood would he speede him fast.
>
> (184–199)

The wolf's fate, too, is an illustration of the principle. For the shepherd finally sees through this ploy, locks the wolf *inside* the fold,

> And tooke out the Woolfe in his counterfect cote,
> And let out the sheepes bloud at his throte.
>
> (206–207)

The relevance of the couplet to the pastoral dilemma being considered here is rather startling. Metaphorically Spenser has it all ways. Insofar as the wolf has been turned into a sheep (one implication of the metaphor), innocence is again sacrificed. On the other hand, it could be argued that the emergence of sheep's blood from the wolf's throat suggests a reconcilation of these contraries, if only in death. The last point reminds us that if Spenser has accomplished an imaginative reconciliation, he has not had to falsify "reality" to do so, he has not had recourse to the namby-pamby.

Spenser's metaphor rivets our attention to pastoralism as a fiction, and reminds us of the platonic element of feigning. The perfidious disguise of the wolf is in a curious way sanctioned by the fatal machinery of justice; the creature *becomes* his disguise, just as Bottom becomes his name in Shakespeare's play. Moreover, this metamorphosis is accomplished not by magic but by means of the adoption of a position relative to others. Something like Plato's idea of the dependence of feigning upon truth seems to be implied. Further, the truth in this case includes a surprising reminder: the wolf has become the sheep because his position relative to the shepherd is identical to the sheep's, that is, he is removed from the fold to have his throat cut. This in turn serves to remind us that the shepherd's initial hatred of the wolf is founded upon the fact that from a sheep's point of view both wolf and shepherd might seem to be in the same line of work. Still, however complex the analogies and identities, there is no escaping the fact that in each case the metaphorical ceremony includes death.

Robert F. Gleckner suggests an analogous "multiple identification of the lamb, the lion, the shepherd, the Christ" in "Night." Further, he suggests a means to this identification similar to Spenser's means in "September": "The lion achieves pity by giving vent to his wrath; the lion becomes *the* Lamb by devouring the lamb."[21] But this identification is a bit too all-embracing for Blake's text, where the lion is not identical to the lamb but its protector:

And now beside thee bleating lamb,
I can lie down and sleep;
Or think on him who bore thy name,
Grase after thee and weep.
For wash'd in lifes river,
My bright mane for ever,
Shall shine like the gold,
As I guard o'er the fold.

(E14)

2. "Night," first plate

implication of the metaphor), innocence is again sacrificed. On the other hand, it could be argued that the emergence of sheep's blood from the wolf's throat suggests a reconcilation of these contraries, if only in death. The last point reminds us that if Spenser has accomplished an imaginative reconciliation, he has not had to falsify "reality" to do so, he has not had recourse to the namby-pamby.

Spenser's metaphor rivets our attention to pastoralism as a fiction, and reminds us of the platonic element of feigning. The perfidious disguise of the wolf is in a curious way sanctioned by the fatal machinery of justice; the creature *becomes* his disguise, just as Bottom becomes his name in Shakespeare's play. Moreover, this metamorphosis is accomplished not by magic but by means of the adoption of a position relative to others. Something like Plato's idea of the dependence of feigning upon truth seems to be implied. Further, the truth in this case includes a surprising reminder: the wolf has become the sheep because his position relative to the shepherd is identical to the sheep's, that is, he is removed from the fold to have his throat cut. This in turn serves to remind us that the shepherd's initial hatred of the wolf is founded upon the fact that from a sheep's point of view both wolf and shepherd might seem to be in the same line of work. Still, however complex the analogies and identities, there is no escaping the fact that in each case the metaphorical ceremony includes death.

Robert F. Gleckner suggests an analogous "multiple identification of the lamb, the lion, the shepherd, the Christ" in "Night." Further, he suggests a means to this identification similar to Spenser's means in "September": "The lion achieves pity by giving vent to his wrath; the lion becomes *the* Lamb by devouring the lamb."[21] But this identification is a bit too all-embracing for Blake's text, where the lion is not identical to the lamb but its protector:

And now beside thee bleating lamb,
I can lie down and sleep;
Or think on him who bore thy name,
Grase after thee and weep.
For wash'd in lifes river,
My bright mane for ever,
Shall shine like the gold,
As I guard o'er the fold.

(E14)

The critical question we are left with is: what in the pastoral tradition can clarify the relationship between this puzzling lion-shepherd and the context Blake calls Innocence? We have seen that the problem did not respond to analysis in terms of metaphorical geography, for the imagery of the passage is hopelessly divided between Beulah and Generation, a transcendent world and an immanent one. Here the light is golden, the flock is protected, yet the waters of life's river are on the lion, and we notice that he weeps, ominously, after his charges. Comparison to the poem's "source," "To the Evening Star," will not help either: in that poem the precipitation of the pastoral world was simultaneous with whatever fall it is that sends feral and erotic hunger into the world, but in "Night" all hunger has been satisfied. If we have not escaped from reality to a simple fairyland, what constitutes Innocence? How is the shepherd-lion, into whom merges the identity of the naive narrator, distinguished from all the other lions in the world? How is he distinguished from the Tyger?

To answer these questions we must return first to "Spring," where, it will be remembered, Innocence was a function not of childish naiveté but of a highly developed consciousness related to the mythology of Orpheus. Similarly, the fiction of "Night" dramatizes an extraordinarily complex order of consciousness, itself a record of all the puzzling ambiguities that have been discussed. The questions generated in attempting to describe that order have organized themselves in terms of a triad of characters: the lamb and the tyger (the "prolific" and the "devourer" in terms of *The Marriage of Heaven and Hell*) and the enigmatic shepherd-lion. A similar triad was noted in Spenser's "Febrvuarie," where a theological triangle was suggested with God at the apex and the Accuser and the Atoner (or devourer and prolific) at the two lower corners. It is worth recalling this because the triad becomes in Blake's hands the ultimate pastoral formula, receiving its first extended development, as we shall see, in *Visions of the Daughters of Albion*. For the moment it is enough to point out that it has already been seen in the *Phaedrus*. Socrates is the ultimate key to the "innocence" of "Night," for in the *Phaedrus* Socrates is the lion-shepherd offering to shed the golden light of spiritual emancipation on a world of real, consuming passions. Lysias in the dialogue is the tyger (not a dramatically realized role in "Night" either), and of course Phaedrus himself is the lamb. As for Socrates, perhaps we can begin to see how a state less en-

lightened than he was found it difficult to distinguish him from the tyger, the corrupter and devourer of youth.

THE ILLUSTRATIONS OF "NIGHT"

About two aspects of the lion, his tears and his position relative to lamb and tyger, more needs to be said, but it will be helpful first to define with greater precision the "location" of the final scene of the poem, the new world referred to simply as "there" in line 34. This essay commenced with a discussion of the relationship between what were called rhetorical and allegorical aspects of pastoralism. The two etchings which illustrate "Night" are depictions of the same scene, one illustrating its rhetorical effect, the other illustrating allegorical "content."

The first etching (see Fig. 2) shows the tree of nature, as always in the *Songs* entwined by a creeper (suggesting dependence and marriage), growing by the stream of life. In a hollow carved in the green bank, we see the lion at rest, his face (as nearly as we can tell) in repose, if not in fact actively pleased. There is a huge moon in the sky, against which tree branch and tendril trace themselves, and the text, the lion, and the angels (in the left margin and in the tree) are all, in the Rosenwald copy, golden with moonshine. It is worth noticing that, even though the lion is present, the etching does not "illustrate" the action of the text, but rather seems an iconographic comment on it. The illustration generally is a comment on the natural condition of the lion: he lies by the stream of experience, and over him is not only the tree but the green mound of earth; the tension inherent in the picture, and its beauty, is a function of the implied conflict between the beast's conditioned attitude and the implications of the moonlight and the angels who sport therein. The lion is couchant but not asleep, for the light from the enormous moon is very bright, bright enough in the Rosenwald copy to have obscured the stars (always symbols of a cold and circular, mechanical and Newtonian world order) and to have washed the dark a light and translucent shade of blue. This tension duplicates our doubts about the "location" of the poem's final scene, and in fact the etching is a visual image recording with great sensitivity the ambiguity we have been observing. The fact that it *is* night and the stress on natural dependence both strongly suggest that we are in Generation; the golden moonlight and the cavorting angels suggest that we are in Beulah. The expression on the lion's face, complacent but calm,

The sun descending in the west.
The evening star does shine.
The birds are silent in their nest
And I must seek for mine,
The moon like a flower
In heavens high bower;
With silent delight.
Sits and smiles on the night.

Farewell green fields and happy groves,
Where flocks have took delight;
Where lambs have nibbled, silent moves
The feet of angels bright;
Unseen they pour blessing,
And joy without ceasing,
On each bud and blossom,
And each sleeping bosom.

They look in every thoughtless nest,
Where birds are coverd warm;
They visit caves of every beast,
To keep them all from harm.
If they see any weeping,
That should have been sleeping
They pour sleep on their head
And sit down by their bed.

2. "Night," first plate

When wolves and tygers howl for prey
They pitying stand and weep;
Seeking to drive their thirst away,
And keep them from the sheep.
But if they rush dreadful;
The angels most heedful,
Recieve each mild spirit,
New worlds to inherit.

And there the lions ruddy eyes,
Shall flow with tears of gold:
And pitying the tender cries,
And walking round the fold:
Saying; wrath by his meekness
And by his health, sickness,
Is driven away,
From our immortal day.

And now beside thee bleating lamb,
I can lie down and sleep;
Or think on him who bore thy name,
Graze after thee and weep.
For wash'd in lifes river,
My bright mane for ever,
Shall shine like the gold
As I guard o'er the fold

3. "Night," second plate

keeps its own counsel in the midst of all the details we have noticed. Its enigmatic quality constitutes the visual rhetoric of the scene.

The second etching (see Fig. 3) is more obscure, less an expression of tone and emotion than a symbolic rendering of the mythology upon which the poignance of the first etching largely depends. We have the same night, symbolically the same tree and the same stream of life, but all else is quite different. The night in the background is darker than in the previous scene, and stars are visible. The tree is not a delicate affair of light, airy branches and graceful tracery, but a dense and dark green thicket, casting deep shadow. Instead of a lion, at the foot of the tree stand five figures, all evidently female. Three stand together in one group toward the background, sharing a kind of halo-effect, and the other two are closer to the foreground of the picture, so close together that they seem to be emanating from a common rootedness, and share a halo also, this—in the Rosenwald copy—more golden than that of the three-grouping. The ground beneath the group of three figures is lighter than beneath the other two, perhaps because they are less in the shadow of the tree or perhaps because the light about them and at their feet is projected from the halo around the two-grouping. One of the figures in the grouping of two is gesturing back toward the other three with extended hand, but the gesture is hard to interpret. It may be a greeting, it may be exhortatory, or the one figure may be pointing out the presence of the three to her close companion.

It is worth noticing first that this etching is the obverse of the other. This will be especially evident if we forget the details of the second etching and regard all five figures as a collective protagonist analogous to the lion-protagonist of the first picture. In the first picture the protagonist is mundane, but he and his natural world seem lit from above; in the second etching, by contrast, the world is very dark, and the only light seems to emanate from some supernatural-looking figures *within* the natural world. If we think of the two etchings in terms of Generation and Beulah, they seem to be reaching toward one another: in the first picture Beulah stands over and illuminates Generation; in the second Generation stands over and shadows Beulah.

It would be convenient to my argument to see in the groups of figures of the second etching, the three distinct figures on the left and the two conjoined on the right, allusions to the Phaedrus-Lysias-Socrates relationship and to the resolved dialectic (Spenser's perfect hexameter), respectively. Indeed, there is some truth in this. But the iconography of Blake's picture is more specialized than the traditional language of pastoralism, and the visual language of the second etching is more esoteric than that of the first. The five figures probably represent the senses, and the group of two figures to the right of the picture, growing but dividing from the same root, therefore represents the division of touch and taste into two distinct senses, increasing the total number of senses from the Blakean four to the Lockean five. The best exposition of Blake's doctrine of the senses is in Northrop Frye's *Fearful Symmetry* (pp. 280–281), but the idea is quickly explained if we think of Spenser's lamb-wolf metaphor in "September." On one level Diggon's remark was alimentary, on another metaphorical; likewise the sense of taste can be extended to include what Frye calls "mental digestion of the material world," and our failure so to digest (one way of expressing the surrender of the spirit to matter which is what Lockean psychology meant to Blake) can be symbolized by the dissolution of a higher "taste" into taste and touch as we know them. Touch is our apprehension of what is outside ourselves, and since it is the sense primarily involved in sexuality, Blake's mythology of the senses includes his attitude toward sexuality as well. Hence, the reformation of sexuality, the "improvement of sensual enjoyment" (E38), will reunite touch and taste, for then, as Frye puts it, "nothing we touch is any longer outside us."

Blake's etching seems to look forward to this restoration, as does the illustration to "The Divine Image," at the top of which the same two figures, representing the reunion of taste and sexuality, reach forward toward the praying couple. I take it that this suggests not only that the couple, as the text says, pray in their distress "to the human form divine" (E13), but that the resurrection of that form, represented at the bottom of the etching by Christ raising a couple, can be accomplished by the "virtues of delight" which an improved sensuality brings. I am assuming, then, that the gesture of taste-touch in both pictures is optimistic, a gesture in the direction of resurrection. More specifically—in the case of "Night"—although the Fall has taken place and the senses are divided, a reuniting taste-and-touch are casting their refulgence upon the ordinary and still fallen senses: sight, hearing, and smell. This refulgence suggests the possibilities of renewed vision and apprehension to these ordinary senses, a renewal which can accomplish Blake's version of the Resurrection. But it must be remembered, too, that the drama of the senses is played out within the shadow of nature.

To "locate" the poem, however, we must look at both etchings simultaneously, and to do this is to complicate simple optimism. Both illustrations seem to promise resurrection (the lion in traditional Christian iconography was used to represent the Resurrection),[22] yet the promise in each case is, iconographically speaking, qualified. The complacence and peace of the golden lion in the first illustration only emphasize the "innocence" of his obliviousness to position with respect to stream, cave, and tree—his distance from the illuminating moon. The influence of the moon is very strong, however, on the text of this first etching, for the words in the Rosenwald copy are etched across a wash of gold, and this suggests that, while the lion is "in" Generation, his dream is very much "of" the moon, that is, "of" Beulah. On the other hand (in the same copy), the final three stanzas of the poem are etched against the inky green of the tree of Generation, and the promise implied by the drama of the sense-figures is very much qualified by its context, by its position deep in the night, heavily shrouded by the tree. We cannot, therefore, in any easy, mechanical way "locate" the poem on a vertical scale of Beulah over Generation, for text and tale appear somehow to be in both places at once.

The visual language of "Night," then, only recapitulates the original ambiguity about the poem's metaphorical geography, but at least it limits our attention to one aspect of that ambiguity. For Blake's iconography—especially in the second etching—stresses a fact about the poem I have not stressed enough, that its essential subject is sexual experience. This is suggested, also, by the poem's development out of "To the Evening Star," and suggestion becomes certitude when we contemplate the identity of the lion with the collective experience of the senses in the second etching. This explains some puzzling aspects of the imagery, for example, the peacefulness of the lion within his green mound, which is a rather haunting depiction of sexual contentment. Sexual contentment, if you will, is the Beulah within Generation, and once it is clear that this is on the poet's mind we have another available approach to the relationship between satisfied lion and hungry tyger.

As a consequence of this reading, it ought to be possible to define with some precision Blake's contrary state of Experience by examining "The Little Girl Lost" and "The Little Girl Found"— poems which are also about sexuality and which employ the lion symbol—and the comparison is especially important because these poems were originally conceived as belonging to Innocence and only later shifted to Experience. But this point will have to await the explication of one or two more aspects of "Night."

THE LANGUAGE OF FLOWERS

The first stanza of "Night" concludes with the lines:

> The moon like a flower,
> In heavens high bower;
> With silent delight,
> Sits and smiles on the night.
>
> (E13)

This has been found a "ludicrous image,"[23] but seems less so when its special meaning is clear. The *Songs* contain many poems about flowers, and it is not obscure that they deal with sexual experience, Wicksteed arguing flatly for "Blake's symbolical use of flowers to signify women and their love favors."[24] So here, in "Night," the image is at least not inappropriate.

I have already referred to the two little figures in the poem's second etching who represent the distinguished but conjoined elements of Blake's unfallen sense, the tongue. The details of representation are important: both figures (as in "The Divine Image" also) emanate from the same point of ground, both seem to grow from a single pair of feet or (better) from the same rootedness. Indeed, if the figures were not human, the best analogy would be to those cloven trunks of Blakean trees, only with the trunks growing away from each other rather than entwining.

Blake's name, in his developed mythology, for this sense in its undivided state of "tongue" is Tharmas. It ought to come as no surprise that Tharmas' "eternal" occupation is as a shepherd (J., 95.16). Tharmas is also the presiding genius of Blake's pastoral state of Beulah (Frye, *Fearful Symmetry*, p. 278), and it is in Beulah, where the eternals rest from the rigor of fourfold vision, that the Fall takes place.

The relevance of this to the image in "Night" will become clear after examining another short lyric, "The Blossom."

> Merry Merry Sparrow
> Under leaves so green
> A happy Blossom
> Sees you swift as arrow
> Seek your cradle narrow
> Near my Bosom.

Pretty Pretty Robin
Under leaves so green
A happy Blossom
Hears you sobbing sobbing
Pretty Pretty Robin
Near my Bosom.

(E10)

Joseph Wicksteed went at this poem in his potentous, intuitive way, calling it "the supreme passage song between the Two Contrary States of the Human Soul. The merry sparrow, like the first laughter of the child in the 'Piper,' symbolizes Innocence, and the sobbing Robin, like the child's tears, symbolizes Experience rather then grief ... The girl 'blossoms' into experience through consummated love."[25] Wicksteed is surely correct in his assumption that the poem is an esoteric treatment of erotic experience, but his equations of Sparrow and Robin with Innocence and Experience, respectively, are too pat. As observed in "Night," tears are very much a part of the Beulah dream, and anyway the fact which Blake's text stresses is that "under leaves so green" (that is, within Generation) the Blossom is equally "happy" whether dealing with Merry Sparrow or sobbing Robin. The details of what merriness and sobbing may represent in terms of sexual experience are less important than this unshakable happiness. In short, the poem conveys the point of view of Generation, or Nature, and "pastoral ignorance" here is Nature's equanimity where the joys and sorrows of sexuality are concerned. In this there is neither indifference nor cruelty—only "innocence."

The flower, then, is both vegetable (pertaining to Generation) and sexual, and Blake pictures it in "The Blossom" etching as a sort of vegetable flame. Pictured in the crest of this flame is a circular, allegorical "progress" of tiny figures, apparently to be read in a clockwise direction. A comprehensive reading of this progress is unnecessary here,[26] but the general meaning is clear and important. The figures seem to have the same ontological status as those representing the senses in the second "Night" etching, that is, they are pictured "in" Generation, but are visionary figures (hence, most are winged): they represent a process that is going on in Generation but that is not normally seen with such imaginative clarity from within—it takes visionary eyes to see them. The progress represents the erotic growth of a soul from solitary childhood to shared love to procreation. The most interesting figure is the largest and most central, that of the winged mother, who appears to be bending over a child on her lap. What is

interesting about this figure is that she *is* winged (whereas the
cherub descending, presumably to be born into Generation, lacks
wings),[27] yet colored—in the Rosenwald copy—a distinct green
("under leaves so green"). That is, the depiction of the mother
reflects the same ambivalence about "place" (this world or the one
whence souls descend? Generation or Beulah?) that is reflected
in the two "Night" etchings. This ambivalence is reinforced by
the posture of the mother's figure; she is bent forward, protecting the dependent child on her lap, to such an extent that the
presence of the child is effectually erased, and the mother is facing
against the direction of the circular progress. Yet directly over
her head the two cherubs who represent love ecstatically embrace. In other words, Blake has loaded this tiny figure with a
remarkable weight of his doubt and ambivalent feelings about
Nature.

The center of iconographic interest, however, is the flaming
vegetable blossom which supports these figures. Wicksteed suggests that it is "a poetic and symbolic rendering of the phallus
prone and erect, a pillar of vegetable flame breaking at the crest
into multitudinous life of many happy spirits, one of which finds
its home in the lap of the happy mother."[28] Jean Hagstrum,
who has made a special study of the illuminations, while less
enthusiastically metaphorical, accepts this.[29]

That the rendering of the vegetable flame on "The Blossom"
etching is suggestive of a phallus is unmistakable, but to limit the
suggestions of Blake's visual image to this meaning is to miss its
real importance. For it is the same flame which we see driving
Adam and Eve from Paradise on the title page of the combined
issue of the *Songs*. And it is a developed version of the vegetable
flame which illuminates and borders the text of "The Divine
Image," where phallic implications are visually, if not thematically,
muffled. To track down Blake's image in terms of all these suggestions is not only to explain why Blake's moon hangs like a flower
in the night sky, but to expose in action the amazing range of the
poet's imagination.

The reader may already have noticed the visual resemblance
between the cleft flame of "The Blossom" and the representation
of Blake's dividing sense, "taste-and-touch." That this sense is
vital in Blake's theory of unfallen sexuality has already been explained; the explanation makes plain the preparedness of the
image for sexual implication. Further, this falling or fallen cloven
sense is associated in Blake's developed mythology with the

Shepherd, Tharmas, and a passage in Frye's study of Blake will explain the relationship between Tharmas and the flames driving out Adam and Eve on Blake's title page for the *Songs*. When Tharmas "falls" in Blake's myth, the sexual avenue to paradise, which Blake calls the "western gate," is closed, and Frye associates the barrier with the "great Covering Cherub" of the Bible:

> The only link left between the unfallen and fallen Tharmas is the attraction which the moon, a primary Beulah symbol, still has on the sea. The Spectre of Tharmas [Tharmas in his fallen form] thus suggests the Biblical Leviathan, the water-monster who symbolizes the tyranny of the state of nature ... But as Leviathan and Behemoth are only forms of the great Covering Cherub ... who keeps man out of Paradise, the Covering Cherub is ultimately what the Spectre of Tharmas is. The tongue which is the civilized taste of unfallen man has become the false tongue of the accusing devil, which ... continually fights against liberty and discourages hope. In the tongue-shaped flames of fallen fire ... one sees an image of this ... The flaming sword which frightens us away from Paradise is there-fore the devil's false tongue. The fact that our own tongues are moist unites the symbols of destructive fire and watery chaos. (Frye, *Fearful Symmetry*, p. 282)

Frye points to a passage on the fourteenth plate of *Jerusalem*, where Tharmas is indeed referred to as "the Vegetated Tongue even the Devouring Tongue ... Beneath Beulah: as a wat'ry flame revolving every way And as dark roots and stems: a Forest of affliction, growing In seas of sorrow" (J., 14.4–9).

The range of reference here is remarkable, but there is a biblical reference to tongues of fire—cloven ones at that—which may be just as relevant to the iconography of the *Songs*: "And suddenly there came a sound from heaven as of a rushing mighty wind, and it filled all the house where they were sitting. And there appeared unto them cloven tongues like as of fire, and it sat upon each of them" (Acts 2:2–3). This is the famous "speaking in tongues" passage, and the association with Pentecost gives Blake's blossom an opening into an area of specifically Christian pastoralism, for the crucifixion of the paschal lamb occurred the previous Pass-over; the seeds that were planted then make the later harvest, in the form of pentecostal conversions, possible.[30]

But it is not only Blake's flowers which have this surprising and versatile range of associations. Given the fact that the "scene" of "Night" is (partially) Beulah, and that Beulah is associated both with the moon and with pastoralism, the associations which would lead Blake to hang his moon in the sky like a flower seem almost inevitable. For flower symbolism is an important part of the vocabulary of English pastoralism; indeed it may be a dialect especially cultivated by the English.[31] To study Blake's employment of this symbolism against the background of Spenser and Milton is to see, again, the immersion of the poet in his models.

The importance of flowers to the courtly love conventions of blazons and posies is obvious enough, and so it is not surprising to find Spenser speaking the language of flowers in his *Epithalamion*:

> And let the ground whereas her foot shall tread,
> For feare the stones her tender foot should wrong
> Be strewed with fragrant flowers all along,
> And diapred lyke the discolored mead.
>
> (48–51)

But the impetus for the passage is at least as much the poet's own taste as any formal demand of epithalamion as such, for Spenser is recalling his "posy" to his Queen in the "Aprill" eclogue of *The Shepheardes Calender*:

> Bring hether the Pincke and purple Cullambine,
>   With Gelliflowres:
> Bring Coronations, and Sops in wine,
>   worne of Paramoures.
> Strowe me the ground with Daffadowndillies,
> And Cowslips, and Kingcups, and loued Lillies.
>
> (136–141)

This trivial point becomes important when we turn from the epithalamic to the elegiac branch of pastoral, for Milton in *Lycidas* draws on the *same* passage to urge the Sicilian muse to return and

> Throw hither all your quaint enameld eyes,
> That on the green terf suck the honied showres,
> And purple all the ground with vernal flowres.
>
> (139–141)

As J. B. Leishman points out in his study of the matter, Milton went out of his way to make this connection, for the flower passage is an afterthought.[32] Further, the demand for the passage in the fiction of the poem is doubtful (Milton tells us he is dallying with "false surmise"), for there is no corpse to strew. Finally, to quote Leishman, "the only precedent for it in classical pastoral elegy or pastoral semi-elegy is so inconspicuous that it can itself scarcely be considered as more than a hint."[33] That Milton followed up the hint in Spenser strongly suggests an important English pastoral tradition of flower imagery. Moreover, the English way with flowers was a strong unifying force on the community of imagery shared by epithalamion and elegy. Leishman recalls a passage in *The Winter's Tale* where Perdita concludes a list of flowers with the remark:

> O, these I lack,
> To make you garlands of, and my sweet friend,
> To strew him o'er and o'er!

And her interlocutor wonders, "What, like a corse?" Perdita replies,

> No, like a bank for love to lie and play on;
> Not like a corse; or if, not to be buried,
> But quick and in mine arms.[34]

But it is the community of imagery in Spenser and Milton which makes Blake's comparison of the moon to a flower less surprising, and which can serve to explain much more astonishing associations. A thorough examination of the pastoral language will even help with the leap from Milton's line "Like to that sanguine flower inscrib'd with woe" (*Lycidas*, 106: a line which goes back at least to Ovid, if not to Theocritus himself), to Blake's "In the well of sanguine woe" (E717: a line which was thrown up in the composition of "The Tyger"). One of the functions of criticism is to make the connections which are legitimate to the imagination appear less outrageous to the scholar. The following sequence of passages offers a royal road to the enlightenment which will have to be articulated more painfully in the analysis of "The Tyger."

I began with a flower passage in the erotic context of the *Epithalamion*, and moved from there to the more general language of ambition in the "Aprill" eclogue; "Aprill" led to Milton's elegy; finally we may return, logically enough, to Spenser's example of elegy in *The Shepheardes Calender*, the elegy for Dido in "November." What do we find? First, suggestively enough, exactly the same employment of refrain which we get in the *Epithalamion*, "O carefull verse" eventually turning into "O ioyfull verse" to match the assurance, "Dido nis dead, but into heauen hent" (168). Since the lady was young and beautiful, the "fayrest floure our gyrlond all emong" (75), we are not surprised to find the language of flowers:

Whence is it, that the flouret of the field doth fade,
And lyeth buryed long in Winters bale:
Yet soone as spring his mantle doth displaye,
It floureth fresh, as it should neuer fayle?
But thing on earth that is of most availe,
  As vertues braunch and beauties budde,
    Reliuen not for any good.
      O heauie herse,
The braunch once dead, the budde eke needes must quaile,
    O carefull verse.

(83–92)

I have deliberately chosen a passage which uses flowers to ask the kind of question Milton asks in *Lycidas*. Colin Clout, however, is not Milton, and his ability to turn the echoing refrain into a more hopeful sound is marginal, almost perfunctory, and Spenser uses the Dido elegy paradoxically to suggest the decay of Colin's ambitions and of his imaginative life. This purpose is reinforced by the disjunction in the passage between the fate of Virtue and Nature. The seasonal implications of the Adonis myth, the relevant archetype, are not for Spenser here, nor for Colin, and when the latter notes,

Dido my deare alas is dead,
Dead and lyeth wrapt in lead,

(58–59)

we are intended to think of poetry generally, and to remember the reference to Tityrus (Chaucer) in "June," who also lay "wrapt in lead" (89), as well as the remark in "October" that "all the worthies liggen wrapt in leade,/That matter made for Poets on to play" (63–64). When Spenser sums up in "November," he uses the pastoral conventions of flower symbolism and pathetic fallacy to construct a fiction in the wake of love-failure and the loss of ambition in a manner suggestive of Blake's in "To the Evening Star":

Ay me that dreerie death should strike so mortall stroke,
That can vndoe Dame natures kindly course:
The faded lockes fall from the loftie oke,
The flouds do gaspe, for dryed is theyr sourse,
And flouds of teares flow in theyr stead perforse.
  The mantled medowes mourne,
  Theyr sondry colours tourne
    O heauie herse,
The heauens doe melt in teares without remorse.
    O carefull verse.

The feeble flocks in field refuse their former foode,
And hang theyr heads, as they would learne to weepe:
The beastes in forest wayle as they were woode,
Except the Wolues, that chase the wandring sheepe:
Now she is gon that safely did hem keepe,
    The Turtle on the bared braunch,
    Laments the wound, that death did launch.
        O heauie herse,
And *Philomele* her song with teares doth steepe.
        O carefull verse.

(123–142)

Flowers fall, whether cultivated ambitiously for the queen's gar-land or in the beds of poets, and Spenser here completely sub-sumes grief, and almost completely indignation, in the creation of the pastoral fiction. We can describe the context, the world so produced, in terms of conventions, if we so desire. The heavens weep, the flocks hang their heads, and Philomele steeps her songs with tears. All pastoral clichés, we feel, any one of which would do to explain the disrepute into which the genre has fallen. Death implies a disjunction between nature and what we feel to be right; pastoralism, we could argue, creates an ideal, faintly silly, and unreal world where the childish conceit of pathetic fallacy assures us of the sympathy of nature.

Yet none of this is true, and we are dealing with something a lot subtler. Pathetic fallacy here does not heal the disjunction between nature and moral emotion (overlooked by "The Blos-som") but is in fact an expression of this disjunction. I suggested in "Night" an instance where events *in* Generation were observed from the standpoint of Beulah; something analogous happens here when

The flouds do gaspe, for dryed is theyr sourse,
And flouds of teares flow in theyr stead perforse.

It is a question, seemingly, of two waters using the same channel, an idea which at least qualifies the notion that pastoral easily substitutes one world for another. Even more significant, it is the waters of Beulah (Spenser's heavenly tears) rather than the waters of nature (which are dried up) that express the hole in nature. It is not natural waters which are called upon to express the poet's com-plaint, but the waters of pathetic fallacy. Moreover, these tears fall, in the second of the stanzas quoted, upon a world to which neither the term "real" nor "ideal" can be applied. It is a world of pastoralism, where the sheep and beasts both weep as if possessed by the flood bearing off Orpheus, "Except the Wolues, that chase the wandring sheepe." The exception is interesting, for the wolves perform two curious functions simultaneously. First, their precipitation into the poem as an exception implies that even Orpheus, the spirit of pastoralism, has his limits. Yet, contradictorily, their appearance as devourers of the sheep completes the pastoral fiction and definitively announces to us that we are in the pastoral world.

THE LANGUAGE OF TEARS

We instinctively associate pastoral tears with death, with elegy, but the wages of dependence are so high, and the death of all sorts of hoping so common a theme, that pastorals often shed tears even when there is no question of physical death. In the structure of *The Shepheardes Calender* Spenser introduces the elegy proper only in "November," but the thematic effect of the elegy for Dido can be seen as an extension of the more general desuetude and lamentation which begins when Colin Clout throws himself to the ground in the opening lines of the "Ianuarie" eclogue. Despite pastoral's concern with sense of loss, however, its tone usually remains a pleasurable distance short of the tragic, expressing itself, as Richard Cody remarks, by means of "a style which is neither tragic nor comic but a bittersweet alternative to either" (Cody, p. 37). The foregoing demonstration of the relationship between "To the Evening Star" and "Night," the dependence of the poems ultimately upon an erotic fiction, should make more plausible Cody's further assertion that "poetic mingling of the languages of love and death or pain and pleasure finds its first important Renaissance model in the *Canzoniere* of Petrarch, as does pastoral wordplay on landscape and soul" (Cody, p. 37). But neither pastoralism's concern with loss nor Petrarchanism, ordinarily considered, help us much with Blake's strange language of tears in the *Songs*. To explain that language we have to explain imaginative associations and leaps as radical and dramatic as Blake's leap from Milton's reference to Ovid's Hyacinth to the "well of sanguine woe" which was the Tyger's source. And in fact, for the sake of some of the most interesting weeping, we shall have to return later to "The Tyger" itself.

The thread begins, as all our threads have begun, in "Night," where there are many references to tears. We are told first of the angels, looking after the slumbers of bird and beast (and by extension of the speaker of the poem):

> If they see any weeping,
> That should have been sleeping
> They pour sleep on their head
> And sit down by their bed.

(E14)

They play the same protecting role

> When wolves and tygers howl for prey
> They pitying stand and weep.

In terms of fictional logic, there is nothing troubling here. But questions arise when the poem's lion is precipitated into one of the "new worlds" to which the text refers. For although wrath and sickness, according to the lion, are driven away "from our immortal day," there is no corresponding drying-up of tears:

> And there the lions ruddy eyes,
> Shall flow with tears of gold

The waters, like those in Spenser's "November" elegy, may have extranatural sources, but they flow freely enough. Even when lion lies down with lamb, perfect peace has its tears:

> And now beside thee bleating lamb,
> I can lie down and sleep;
> Or think on him who bore they name,
> Grase after thee and weep.

(E14)

Part of the explanation has to do with the interest Blake's age showed in feeling and sentiment, an interest which explains the somewhat antinomian pleasure Blake could take in a paradox like "Excess of sorrow laughs. Excess of joy weeps" (E36). But the almost obsessive references to tears and joy in the *Songs* cannot be explained in terms of social convention. One hopes for reasons more illuminating and more systematic.

In the case of "Night," the key to the problem, it seems to me, is the relationship between lion and lamb, and in the cases of other *Songs* analogous relationships between creator-protectors and creature-sufferers. We have already seen that dependency is an important pastoral theme; here its relationship to the poet's control of perspectives begins to emerge. Concern with this relationship, moreover, is perfectly traditional to pastoral. We can see this clearly, if eccentrically, illustrated in the very first poem of the collection, the "Introduction" to *Innocence*. "Introduction" brings together within a narrow perspective the question of the nature of the creature (the kind of poem: "Pipe a song about a Lamb") and the behavior of the creator:

> And I made a rural pen,
> And I stain'd the water clear,
> And I wrote my happy songs,
> Every child may joy to hear
>
> (E7)

Blake's version of pastoralism in this poem, although sometimes equated with a simple reconstruction in the poet's imagination of the child's outlook, is as complex as it is compact. The poem permits into view only piper and child and the song inspired by the latter, and Joseph Wicksteed has written perceptively that the disappearance of the child ("So he vanish'd from my sight") represents the poem's crisis. Wicksteed refers this disappearance to absorption, but does not see anything sinister in it: "The Child is a mere happy vision inspiring the Poet from without until he begins to work. He then cannot see the child any more for the same reason that we cannot see ourselves. The Child is now something within."[35] But the disappearance of the child, combined with details like the adaptation of reed to pen rather than to pipe accompanied by the staining of rural waters to make ink, has suggested to more than one critic a process of decline. As Robert F. Gleckner has seen it, the poem suggests a malaise both more general and radical in its implication than a coming to self-consciousness in the creation of a poem or the poet's rather technological interest in the proliferation of his works. For Gleckner the process in the poem "is characterized by restrictions upon the wild abandon of the innocents," involving "a contraction before an infinite expansion, a saddening before infinite joy."[36] But for Gleckner there *is* restoration of "infinite joy," signaled by the choice of unselfish service to mankind over an alternative not made clear in the text; this interpretation necessitates the dubious argument that within joy "mirth and tears meet in perfect harmony, each retaining its characteristic essence, yet having no identity separate from the other."[37] Gleckner's remark is dubious because it describes rather than explains, but it is interesting to discover tears at the crux of even a doubtful interpretation, and it is interesting to see them associated rather surprisingly with joy

("While he wept with joy to hear"). To provide a more thorough explanation for this phrase, we will not need to transcend the terms of Blake's texts, but we will have to see, again, how pastoral these terms are. The availability of the choice between creation and decline suggests a heightened consciousness of perspective; the ambiguity of the choice is a translation of pastoralism's traditional obsession with the twin themes of dependency and service. To go further than this will be to involve ourselves in a complex skein of references, drawing together into one knot questions of perspective, of the language of flowers, and of tears.

To begin with, we need to examine the parallels between "Introduction" and "Spring." "Spring," it will be remembered, was an Orphic poem, its childish rhymes suggestive of pastoral echoes, in which the creative spirit suffered a kind of semierotic incarnation as child playing with lamb. The child in "Introduction" asks for the piper's song again and again, and it is difficult to see the Orphism of this only if one is unconscious of the pastoral tradition, for in fact the child is making a kind of Orpheus of the Piper, as well as drawing him closer to creation, and the generalization of the Piper's song ("Every child may joy to hear") is suggestive of an Orphic fulfillment. Obviously the question of whether the lamb of "Spring" and the child of "Introduction" are identical is intriguing, and it is interesting that while there is little suggestion of eroticism in the text of "Introduction," the symbolism of the illustration—as well as of the related frontispiece to the Innocence series—does include allusions to eroticism. In the latter, for example, the child on the cloud is clearly drawing the piper's attention to a pair of treetrunks entwined in unmistakable reference to the experience of love; the poem's own etching is bordered by two pairs of entwined trunks, the interstices of which contain indistinct scenes from life in an allusion to the kind of decoration Blake might have seen in the Bedford Hours[38] (incidentally, the only sign in the *Songs* of the sort of temporal structure Spenser uses in his *Calender*), the motif constituting a sort of visual metaphor for "Generation."

This raises the question of the metaphorical location of "Introduction"—a question important in the interpretation of "Night" —and here the comparison to "Spring" is also interesting. Gleckner has written suggestively of the metaphorical implications of the gulf between piper and child, calling it "epistemological," arguing that Blake's visionary poet bridges the gulf.[39] While the gap is not treated so elaborately as the analogous geography of

"Night," we can see its relationship to pastoral dialectic and to perspective. There is the suggestion of an identical gap in "Spring" —"Nightingale / In the dale / Lark in Sky"—and we noticed already the hints there of "In what distant deeps or skies" of "The Tyger." All these instances testify to pastoralism as a reconciling mode of the imagination.

It will be remembered that in "Spring" the incarnation of Orpheus in the world of his creation was the puzzle of the poem; entrance into the world might be accompanied by loss of control over it, or by a declension (symbolized by the plight of Narcissus) into the natural order. A visionary freedom was qualified by a natural, dependent order symbolized by the assumption of dramatic or rhetorical postures. Further, the puzzle was difficult to solve by recourse to what we know of Blake's doctrines or beliefs, for it is possible to view any Fall—even Milton's more orthodox version of it—as more or less *felix*. As previously noted, a distinguished Blake critic found the case of "Spring" *felix* indeed, and the source of felicity was the idea—associated with the Christian Incarnation—of identity. Identification, as expressed in "The Lamb," indeed reflects the question of point of view:

> He became a little child:
> I a child & thou a lamb.
>
> (E9)

But another perspective on identification is presented eloquently in *Vala/The Four Zoas*. There "Nature" is Vala, the "emanation" of Luvah-Orc, and when Blake "identifies" Orc with Jesus and has Urizen crucify him on the tree of nature, he means to suggest what might be called a de facto conspiracy between Accuser and Atoner, the consequence of which is the *necessity* of both Nature and the crucifixion of impulse.

In "Introduction," the ambiguities of Generation are posed for us in a different way, and it is at this point that the *differences* between it and "Spring" become important. In "Introduction" the Orphic power of the child is measured by his ability, in vision, to inspire the piper; and if the "disappearance" of the child (which Wicksteed interprets as internalization) signals a fall-incarnation analogous to the one in "Spring," it would be puzzling to present this fall as accompanied by the release of Orphic powers within the piper, and within the fallen world generally. However, the release of these powers—if that is what is signified by the proliferation of the poet's song—also produces the mixture of laughter and tears which has prompted so much discussion. The way to understanding this mixture is via a pecular iconographic connection between "identification" (compare my own more cumbersome term, "mythological condensation") and the language of flowers.

I first pointed at a curious equivocity of merriment and tears in that most oblique poem, "The Blossom," where we seem to be in the presence of a Nature completely unconcerned by the pleasures and pains of her erotic modus operandi. The poem was an important one in terms of explicating Blake's language of flowers. The iconographic representation of the "flower" was a curious vegetable flame, and a more elaborate version of the same thing decorates "The Divine Image." And to that poem we must turn next.

"The Divine Image" is unusual among the *Songs*, for in it Blake transforms pastoral ignorance into something approaching satire, but in tone and style the poem somehow remains representative of Innocence. Its general thematic concern, indicated by the title, turns up repeatedly in *Songs of Innocence*: "And God said, Let us make man in our image, after our likeness" (Genesis 1:26). The gulf between God and man is only the widest and most ultimate example of the sort of gap we have seen before in poem after poem. In this sense, then, "The Divine Image" represents very explicitly a thematic limit, and an ultimate challenge to the reconciling power of pastoral fictions.

The poem's thematic concern enforces its structure. Its pictorial frame has already been discussed: the form of the flaming flower divides the page into two pictorial motifs, which seem to correspond in terms of "scene," or metaphorical geography, to the two plates illustrating "Night." Both motifs illustrate the same event, but from different points of view. In one we see a couple praying, about to be arrested by the dividing but connected sexual senses (one of which, in the Rosenwald copy, is colored a clear green to indicate its loyalty to Generation). The senses, the picture implies, constitute "virtues of delight" which are both human and divine. In the other pictorial motif, a Christ-figure with a halo is "raising" a naked couple. It will be noticed that the two approaches to the idea of resurrection underline the gap between transcendence and immanence which it is the business of the poem to respond to. Moreover, the division of the illustration clearly divides the poem's text as well, and underlines its structure, which is syllogistic—a three-stanza premise followed by a two-stanza conclusion. The structure of the text, then, can also be related to the principle of dialectic, to the habits of pastoral rhetoric and the ontological gap to be bridged.

One statement of the distance to be bridged is especially important, or it brings together the questions of identification and of dependency:

> For Mercy Pity Peace and Love,
> Is God our father dear:
> And Mercy Pity Peace and Love,
> Is Man his child and care.
>
> (E12)

Here, in the poetic fiction, the gap is presented in terms equivocal to theology and biology, in terms of father and son. Much of the point of the poem is Blake's awareness that man's willingness to accept this fiction can be turned against him and made a measure of his fallen condition. For acceptance of the stanza quoted *seems* to entail acceptance of the following stanza as well:

> For Mercy has a human heart
> Pity, a human face:
> And Love, the human form divine,
> And Peace, the human dress.
>
> (E12)

But in "human" practice these are abstract statements, and while man is quick to accept moral emotions in a sentimental context of dependency, he is slow to apply them in a way which would really imply the identity of God and man:

> And all must love the human form,
> In heathen, turk or jew.
> Where Mercy, Love & Pity dwell
> There God is dwelling too.
>
> (E13)

"The Divine Image" is perhaps "innocent" in that there is no hint in text or illustration that its syllogistic conclusion is contrary to the experience of social reality. Perhaps, as suggested, this is another instance of "pastoral ignorance." The words appear blandly on the page beside the figure of Christ raising the naked couple. Are we, one wonders, justified in discovering analogous suggestions of satire in *other* fictions where identification of God and man goes hand in hand with dependency? In pastoral, in other words, can we ever contemplate the lamb without at the same time contemplating the sufferance by which he lives? The question as applied to a poem like "The Lamb" is complex, but something very like what I am suggesting emerges clearly from "A Cradle Song," the setting of which is related to "Night":

> Sweet dreams of pleasant streams,
> By happy silent moony beams.
>
> (E11)

"A Cradle Song" very clearly develops the conjunction between the themes of dependency and divine identification:

> Sweet babe in thy face,
> Holy image I can trace.
> Sweet babe once like thee,
> Thy maker lay and wept for me
>
> (E12)

But it would require a considerable force of sentimentality to overlook the implications of the disparity between the poem's two illustrations and its textual lullaby. If, as Joseph Wicksteed has suggested, the first plate is a representation of the child's dream,[40] he was surely at fault for not reminding us that the dream was a nightmare, for the first plate's text is illuminated by a terribly twisted and dark vegetation which winds against a night background like seaweed. In the Rosenwald copy this foliage is in one place tinged with red in a way which suggests flesh as well as vegetation. In the second plate (see Fig. 4) a child in its cradle is protected from this representation by a heavy dark blue curtain suspended behind the cradle, and, in the foreground, by his mother, bent protectively, but severely, forward. There are clear instances in this etching of mythological condensation, for the cradle is woven of a basketlike material, and there is a white halo surrounding the infant's head. Even more significant is the figure of the mother—who seems sinister as well as protective—amply, almost redundantly gowned in a material colored the same purplish red Blake used to tinge his nightmarish vegetation on the first plate. If the infant suggests to us the Christ-child, Blake has most unpleasantly reminded us of his dependence upon the flesh in his incarnate condition. This poem, then, presents us with another version of the bridge from valley to sky, ambiguously couched—as so often— in alternative iconographic representations of Generation.

4. "A Cradle Song," second plate

But the text of the poem, more than the iconography, enforces ambiguity. Its lines,

> Smiles on thee on me on all,
> Who became an infant small,
> Infant smiles are his own smiles.
> Heaven & earth to peace beguiles,
>
> (E12)

are a nursery-rhyme version of Milton's "meek-eyd Peace" who comes sliding down in "On the Morning of Christ's Nativity":

> And waving wide her mirtle wand,
> She strikes a universall Peace through Sea and Land.
>
> (51–52)

We also find in the text a characteristic sign of Blake's having toiled with pastoral extremities, his curious language of smiles and tears:

> Sleep sleep happy child.
> All creation slept and smil'd.
> Sleep sleep, happy sleep,
> While o'er thee thy mother weep.
>
> Sweet babe in thy face,
> Holy image I can trace.
> Sweet babe once like thee,
> Thy maker lay and wept for me
>
> Wept for me for thee for all,
> When he was an infant small.
> Thou his image ever see,
> Heavenly face that smiles on thee.
>
> (E12)

Here the combination of smiles and tears signifies a remarkable commixture of the languages of dependency and identification. "All creation slept and smil'd" on the morning of Christ's nativity, yet the mother sleeps not and weeps as she makes the daring identification between her helpless child and Jesus. The effect of her tears is to suggest that the mother is not a part of the sleeping and smiling creation, but above it—herself godlike. She purchases this elevation with her tears. The succeeding stanza even more directly broaches the analogy between infant and Christ-child, but in this case it is God who weeps for the mother. Behind the metaphors of both these stanzas there lurks the idea of martydom —and it is interesting that both identifications have the effect of glorifying a mother's pains. The mother achieves this effect by means of metaphors, and the really important thing about them is that they suggest an ambiguity central to the theme of dependency. In one stanza the mother, outside creation, weeps for her child within it; in the other, the child, who is the god within creation, weeps for the mother (also within). The effect of this is to create uncertainty about whether the tears are *at* or *in* what Blake calls Generation. In the final stanza but one Blake resolves the question by writing as if it did not exist—the face of God is both weeping and smiling:

> Wept for me for thee for all,
> When he was an infant small.
> Thou his image ever see,
> Heavenly face that smiles on thee.

> (E12)

In "Introduction," where there is a similar confounding of the distinction between smiles and tears, there was the same concern for proliferation: "for me for thee for all" is related to the line, "Every child may joy to hear." But just as the piper, in the other poem, "stain'd the water clear" to communicate himself— and Blake's etching makes it clear that the waters of Generation are included in this metaphor—so the mother in "A Cradle Song" somehow insinuates the idea that the smiles of God are bound to the misery of his children. There is an even more subversive suggestion implicit here: that the Atonement, a doctrine which Blake told Crabb Robinson he abhorred,[41] is no more than tacit recognition of this idea.

We can see similar suggestions in the poem by means of which Blake's language of flowers was related to the theme of identification in the first place, "The Divine Image." For in this poem, too, the confusion of laughter and tears leaves its mark on the imagery:

> To Mercy Pity Peace and Love,
> All pray in their distress:
> And to these virtues of delight
> Return their thankfulness.

> (E12)

The idea of lip service to moral ideas is here expressed as tragic paradox: the groveling imagination of distress prays dependently to the virtues only delight can realize. Distress here is a sign of the corruption of virtues by passivity and dependence. It has already been pointed out that the iconography of the poem points to sexual delight, to that improved sensual enjoyment which the poet mentions in *The Marriage of Heaven and Hell*. Blake's prescience in associating social issues with the improvement of sensuality could hardly be exaggerated.

Indeed we are now in a position to understand pastoralism's importance even for Blake's role as social prophet. For improved sensual enjoyment will cause "the cherub . . . to leave his guard at tree of life, and when he does, the whole creation will be consumed, and appear infinite. and holy whereas it now appears finite & corrupt" (E38). The attempt to redeem human existence of which social prophecy is one instrument admits no distinction between erotic love and politics. Both, taken in any sense worth preserving, have as their aim the restoration of paradise, and to this aim dependency is equally an obstacle whether articulated in the language of courtly love, of theology, or of a corrupt social order. In "The Little Black Boy," for example, terms from the last two languages undergo conflation, and the possible fatuousness of the black boy's desire, "I'll stand and stroke his silver hair, / And be like him and he will then love me," is poignantly underlined by the illustration, which shows Christ with a shepherd's crook bent over the children in a paternal posture, himself surmounted and shaded by a tree of Generation. In the Rosenwald copy, the stream which runs at his feet, like that of "Introduction," is virtually black with pollution, its silver and black echoing the original colors of the two children.

It is worth remembering, then, that while Blake once declared his poetic intention as an "Endeavour to Restore what the Ancients calld the Golden Age" (E545), and while reminiscences or prophecies of paradise are one of the fixtures of pastoral poetry, pastoral imagery itself must not be confused with the promised land. For pastoralism is a self-conscious fiction the imaginative and analytic purposes of which are more complex than the provision of an escape from reality.

One measure of complexity, it has been suggested, is the notion of "pastoral ignorance." I have relied heavily upon this term partly in order to avoid infection by irony. The difference between the two terms is subtle, but crucial, for I would argue that the illustration to "The Little Black Boy" exemplifies the former rather than the latter term. Both irony and "pastoral ignorance," as I understand them, involve the occupation of a self-conscious rhetorical or dramatic posture, but pastoral ignorance invents an allegorical context corresponding to the role being assumed. This needs to be emphasized, for the simultaneous and self-conscious assumption of ignorance and invention must be unique to pastoralism, a function of its peculiar position midway between satire and romance. The assumption of an ironic posture is a declaration of alienation, but pastoralism provides a context for pretense and invents a world elsewhere which is a fictional response to alienation, a way of measuring and understanding it. Pastoral nonchalance is related to this point, for a failure of nonchalance betrays both alienation and the failure of invention.

It will be recognized that we have returned, after a prolonged absence, to a point with which I initiated discussion of the *Songs*. It was argued then, by means of reference to Plato's *Phaedrus*, that there was a relationship between the rhetoric and the allegorical implications of pastoralism. I discovered in Plato the Socratic idea that in order to feign truth one must understand it, an idea of great consequence for the rhetorician. To this idea can be applied what was just said about pastoral invention, and it must have been noticed that throughout the discussion of the *Songs* I have displayed a bias in favor of the language of feigning, the language of art, as against the language of Blake's supposed doctrines. In other words, confusion of fictions with theology has led, it seems to me, to persistent misrepresentations of Blake's poems, the most egregious of which can be exemplified by Kathleen Raine's notion that Blake's ultimate purpose is the expression of a traditional perennial philosophy.[42] Miss Raine, it seems to me, consistently fails to uncover in her criticism any way of distinguishing rhetorical from doctrinal intention, any mediating perspective between feigning and "truth." Pastoralism is an important element of Blake's work precisely because it is a language of mediation. This can explain why Blake so often applies techniques of perspective to the particular question of dependency. Whether we choose to grovel before a hypocritically weeping Jehovah or recognize the divinity of the human imagination is from a technical standpoint subordinate to the more general issue of a poetical language of mediation, a language subtle enough—for example— to distinguish which theological attitude is implied by "The Tyger."

Another example of the importance of language emerges from a cursory comparison of plate 99 of *Jerusalem* to the second etching of "The Little Black Boy." Both illustrations concentrate on attitudes of imploring and depending and care (the *Jerusalem* plate in fact seems to have been based upon a depiction of "The Prodigal Son");[43] both illustrate texts in which the idea of "identification" is important. Yet the two etchings have radically different allegorical significances, and the differences between them are difficult to isolate in terms of doctrine or "truth." It is not that Blake regards the black boy as simply lost in his willingness to embrace subordination, nor that he simply "approves" the embrace of Albion and Britannia (or Jerusalem). The "meaning" of both pictures is not a doctrine but an allegorical function of the *way* a mediating language is used to transcend the gap between creator and creature which that same language presented in the first place to the perceiving eye. In the case of *Jerusalem* too, we shall see, language is importantly related to the idea of pastoral.

For the moment we need not pursue this point, but may observe its analogue in a related question: why does the lion in "Night" weep? The answer, I think, is a function of the fact that the lion belongs to Beulah rather than to Eden, that he is a fictional rather than a paradisal animal, that although he suggests allegory he belongs to the pastoral world of feigning rather than to the doctrinal world of "truth." The lion is associated with Beulah and with the moon in order to remind us, respectively, that it is only in sight of the promised land and that it is golden with reflected light.

Repeatedly Blake's puzzling conflation of laughter and tears appears in conjunction with an ambivalent metaphorical geography—uncertainty about whether we are "in" Beulah or Generation. Repeatedly Blake has stressed geographical ambivalence by illustrating the same scene twice, from the standpoint of the two very different orders of vision. Gradually it ought to be occurring to us that Blake's confusion of laughter and tears is itself simply one lexical detail of an elaborate language of perspectives mediating between immanent and transcendent realms. It may, then, be that laughter and tears are allegorically identical but rhetorically distinguishable—the same thing perceived from different points of view. In *Milton*, Blake's penultimate epic, there is a striking instance, seemingly, of this. What looks like joy to Generation seems sorrow to Beulah:

Then loud from their green covert all the Birds begin their Song
The Thrush, the Linnet & the Goldfinch, Robin & the Wren
Awake the Sun from his sweet reverie upon the Mountain:
The Nightingale again assays his song, & thro the day,
And thro the night warbles luxuriant; every Bird of Song
Attending his loud harmony with admiration & love.
This is a Vision of the lamentation of Beulah over Ololon!

(31.39–45; E130)

The last two stanzas of "Night" are the achievement of a pastoral fiction, and Blake uses the figure of the lion not only to suggest final reconciliation when he lies down with the lamb but also because the lion is an obviously fabulous avatar of king, father, husband, and lover. Like Yeats's bird "set upon a golden bough," Blake's lion is an achievement of artifice, a fiction of Beulah. We have already seen that "in" Beulah he would take a very different form, the form of five tiny "human" figures—and Blake makes it very plain by the phrase "wash'd in lifes river" that, unlike Yeats's bird, the lion is not "out of nature." He is what Beulah makes of a natural child. The lion weeps, then, to remind us of these things—and that Beulah is not paradise. The lion's tears belong especially to Beulah and to Innocence. He stands for Innocence because he is a reconciling fiction but more especially because he is divided between the orders of vision which he mediates.

"THE LAMB" AND "THE TYGER"

There remains the question of what Experience is, a question holding the threads left dangling from the foregoing discussion: why the "Lyca poems" ("The Little Girl Lost" and "The Little Girl Found") were shifted from Innocence to Experience, what Experience's language of flowers looks like, what Blake makes of the elegy in his Songs of Experience. No discussion of Blake's lyrics can evade the most famous among them, and this is convenient because comparison of "The Lamb" and "The Tyger" itself involves the transition from Innocence to Experience. And since the language of tears is crucial to the analysis, comparison of the two poems is doubly convenient at this point.

It may surprise no reader of this book that there have appeared lately a number of elaborate analyses of "The Tyger"—those of Raine, Adams, Nurmi, and Grant being especially notable[44]—

sharing surprisingly little argrement among them concerning the most obvious questions about the poem: what does the tyger represent? who is the speaker of the poem? and what is his attitude toward the tyger? Yet, considering the strides forward in Blake scholarship and criticism of recent years, there ought to be some surprise at this. If I were to revive for "The Tyger" an earlier distinction between "rhetoric" and allegorical significance, it would immediately be apparent that it is the latter aspect of the poem which has received the most attention, and that with respect especially to the famous fifth stanza,

> When the stars threw down their spears
> And water'd heaven with their tears:
> Did he smile his work to see?
> Did he who made the Lamb make thee?

there is hardly the tiniest echo of the poem in the larger prophetic poems which has not been recorded, amplified, and meditated. But while these echoes have helped to draw some of the critics together on what the tyger represents, they have helped very little toward defining the speaker's attitude towards that representation. It is my assumption that the establishment of pastoralism as the most meaningful context for "The Tyger" will provide us not only with a field (in fact an ideal landscape) in which to spread out and examine the range of allusions referred to above, but also with one where "The Tyger" can be related to other poems in the same context. It seems to me that only an understanding of the medium of the poem will help us with the outstanding critical questions—which are rhetorical—and that the medium ought to make it impossible to approach the poem in isolation, especially apart from its counterpart in Innocence, "The Lamb." I will begin with "The Lamb," then, as a reminder that any successful reading of "The Tyger"—however complex that poem's implication— must arise from a vocabulary of critical assumption and technique applicable with equal illumination to the earlier poem.

Most critics have used the cryptic simplicity of "The Lamb" as a pretext for saying nothing about it, but the poem is not un-expressive, and readers of "Spring" will possess some of the vocabulary for talking about it. The poem's simplicity is not as complete as it seems, and while the interest in identification which it shares with "The Divine Image" ("He became a little child:/I a child & thou a lamb,/We are called by his name"; E9) is expressed in sacramental language, "The Lamb" is a pastoral, and we do not require access to mysteries, even childhood, to discuss it. In the pictorial language of Blake's etching, there is nothing suggestive of liturgy but much to suggest the traditional language of pastoralism.

In discussing the second etching to "Spring," I suggested a loverlike relationship between infant and lamb; likewise there is much in the "Lamb" illustration (see Fig. 5) to remind us that the same erotic tensions exist here, even if in a more resolved condition. The scene is framed by two slender saplings, each enwoven with supple vine, the heads and leaves of which entwine so regularly overhead as to suggest a kind of balance, or perfect affection, neither side being predominant over the other. Likewise, on the roof of the shepherd cottage in the background, two white doves close together suggest a happy union. In the foreground naked child and little lamb face each other, the child holding out his arms invitingly in a paternal or husbandly gesture, the little lamb stepping gently forward toward him. To remind us where we are, Blake has placed a stream in the foreground and a circular, very low, and very dense tree of Generation in the background. Between tree and stream lies a middle-sized flock of sheep, undistinguished—parallel backs and docile, cropping heads—except for two, which recline at the front of the flock, looking relaxed and off to the left, framing with their complacence the lamb who is advancing toward the child. These two remind us of the apparent parents of the lamb in "Spring." One of the most interesting features of the etching in the Rosenwald copy is its coloring: all the creatures in the foreground, the text of the poem, and especially the cottage surmounted by the loving birds, are lit in a high, almost unnatural color, while in the background of the scene, at the sides and high above the embracing trees (where the title appears), and behind the cottage, the sky is terribly livid and ominous. This stormy highlighting and cloudy blackness make a scene which is otherwise one of peace and the resolution of tension almost explosive in potential, the suggestions of imminent release and cloudburst in the coloring constituting an esoteric reminder of the sexual constituency of the scene before us. In the formal iconography of the picture, only the slightly stiff unchildlike gesture of the infant suggests the tension which is locked inside the coloring.

The "mythos" of the poem, then, is epithalamic, and all the pastoral machinery and rhetorical structure of the poem serve to

5. "The Lamb"

underline this fact. The lover's compliment contains the almost obligatory, if veiled, reference to things Orphic:

> Gave thee such a tender voice,
> Making all the vales rejoice!

(E8)

And the allusion veiled in the compliment has its traditional ringing and echoing in the achievement of love at the end of the poem:

> Little Lamb God bless thee.
> Little Lamb God bless thee.

(E9)

If one were discussing the ordinary form of epithalamion, this would constitute the nuptial conclusion to which one would apply the term, *makarismos,* "pronouncing happy."[45]

In "The Divine Image" the theme of identification of god and man was discussed ironically within the borders of one of Blake's vegetable flames, and in "A Cradle Song" the same theme was applied to mother-love and dependency. In "The Lamb" the question of "identification" again occurs in an erotic context, and this might lead us to wonder whether the question of dependency, so central to pastoralism, is important here too. The question, once asked, virtually answers itself, for the poem's epithalamic structure is designed to deal with just this question. The poem ends, as noted, on a note of epithalamic *makarismos,* but it began with the question of dependency:

> Little Lamb who made thee
> Dost thou know who made thee

(E8)

And its conclusion, it is important to see, is not only formally epithalamic, but—following the lines "He became a little child: / I a child & thou a lamb"—annihilates as well the meaning of the question. The metaphor, for a poet who professed that one way to paradise was the improvement of sensual enjoyment, is obvious enough. The celebration of erotic bliss is in Blake an unsurprising context for realizing the divinity within the human imagination. But "The Lamb," as the illustration makes very clear, is set in Generation, and it is "innocent" in that the text seems uninhibited by the contradictions between the pastoral vision of peace and what goes on in Generation. The etching makes more explicit what it is the lamb is called on to ignore, but even the suggestion of consummation registered there is blocked by an erotically un-promising cast of characters. Yet, as we regard prepubescent child and lamb, sexual "innocence" gradually yields to another idea of consummation, one more available to these oddly formal pro-tagonists. Here the less secular language of the text reminds us that, for Generation, deeply implicit in one's most heartfelt "Little Lamb God bless thee" lies the crucifixion of innocence on the tree of nature.

Northrop Frye, in his discussion of *The Four Zoas*, describes one of the theological perversions with which Blake was at war as the "adoration of the continuous martyrdom of natural life ... represented by ... the mangled body bound to the stone or dead tree as a sacrifice to the flaming Moloch in the sky" (Frye, *Fearful Symmetry*, p. 283). What troubles us about the "Tyger" is his resemblance, perhaps only apparent, to that flaming Moloch combined with the assurance of some critics that we must adopt a properly visionary attitude and admire him. Complete dis-cussion of this issue must be reserved, but it is enough here to note that David Erdman's association of Christ-militant, the Christ of the Second Coming, with the tyger may be reasonable in terms of the text he is working on (*Europe*),[46] but becomes difficult to maintain in the face of the tyger's relationship to the lamb.

A short way through the problem may be maintained by ex-amining the pastoral context of "The Tyger," for just as ex-amination of context makes it unlikely that one would admire Christ-militant for seeming about to devour Christ the lamb, so that context reminds us that "The Lamb," regarded from the pastoral point of view, is not quite about Jesus either. Rather it seems to be about "passion," and we are justified in using an upper-case "P" only if we remember that the putative "cruci-fixion" is of the self-justifying variety described by Frye, a crucifixion actually undertaken in *The Book of Ahania* and in Night VII(a) of the *Vala/The Four Zoas* manuscript. Passion, as Frye elsewhere observes (*Fearful Symmetry*, p. 401), implies passivity and necessity; in "The Lamb" the passivity of potential sacrifice on the altar of natural necessity is clearly related to sexual passion, sacrifice on the altar of the Female Will. Consequently, we will not get far with "The Tyger" unless we remember its primary (in the pastoral context) sexual connotations and its rela-tionship to the "flaming Moloch" of whom Frye speaks. I would argue, perhaps more radically, that the "deadly terrors" which Blake did not excise from his carefully revised text of the poem are at the service of the Female Will.

This argument will not make the poem more simple, but it does simplify access to a number of important questions. As already noted, "The Lamb" begins with a question, then dissolves that question—the distinctions and notions of declension upon which it was based—in idyllic *makarismos*. "The Tyger" runs its course and succeeds only in altering the emphasis of its question. "Could" in the first stanza becomes "dare" in the last: "Dare frame thy fearful symmetry?" The idea of service to the Female Will will not of itself tell us whether the alteration signifies "wonder," as Martin K. Nurmi believes, or "indignity," as John E. Grant would have it.[47] To decide this question is to decide the rhetorical tone of the poem's speaker, and decisions of this kind are among the trickiest criticism is asked to make. But in conjunction with other ideas related to the poem's pastoralism, the attempt may move us as close to certainty as we are likely to get. The first of these ideas is that while the mythos of "The Lamb" was epithalamic, that of "The Tyger" is elegiac. And a second idea is that "The Tyger" presents us with the most complex instance we have seen yet of the doctrine of feigning articulated in the *Phaedrus*.

The reconciling fiction of "The Lamb"—with its clear if troubling textual allusions to incarnation—was designed to breach an ontological gap between creator and creature, and the erotic argument of the poem dissolved the question "who made thee?" in a love which (contrary to the evidence of our ordinary state of vision, Generation) denied the existence of any gap and proclaimed the identity of creature and created. The language was the language of wedding, appropriately applied to a member of the class Blake called "the Prolific." In "The Tyger" Blake tries to apply a similar reconciling fiction to "the Devourer," to close the ontological gap between *him* and his creator. His problem was more difficult than with "The Lamb" because the Devourer means death (the primary fact posed by the question, "Did he who made the Lamb make thee?"), and form therefore dictated the language of pastoral elegy.

"The Tyger" must be unique among elegiac fictions in that it concentrates not at all on the Prolific, but strives to close the gap between Devourer and Creator. This seems less strange if we remember that argument by design is one of the problems orthodox Christian elegy has to face up to, that however carefully maintained is the poet's distinction between the fate which kills and the Christ who saves dangerous implications are possible:

So *Lycidas* sunk low, but mounted high,
Through the dear might of him that walk'd the waves.
                                                    (172–173)

"Sinking low" but "mounting high" are of course terms of a pastoral fiction, and an orthodox Christian would have no difficulty in articulating what it is about the "low" world which demands death, but a poet for whom the "Fall" was not an ontological reality but a failure of vision might be troubled by Milton's pun on "dear" and wonder whether the expense of crucifixion might not be purchasing exactly the world it was designed to transcend. In any case "The Tyger" follows a quite traditional structure insofar as it argues by design, even though its habit of undercutting each stage in its lethal logic by means of a question mark is more peculiar to Blake.[48] Among the things which make the poem so terrifying is that the argument by design produces only the subtlest of distinctions between "could frame thy fearful symmetry" and "dare frame." The fineness of distinction, which has exercised so many critics, has its counterpart in the relative stability of the speaker's attitude toward the tyger. Framed and frozen in the same world, the speaker has been hypnotized by fear and awe. But this is not to argue by design, only to succumb to it; and there is an "argument" to "The Tyger" even more disturbing than any imaginative inertia we have seen so far. It is that quite possibly the tyger is less awful than his creator.

To see this we need to examine the issues and structure of the poem clearly. Not only the animal, but the poem as well, has a "symmetry," emphasized carefully in the etching, where, in addition to other less important divisions, one branch of the dead tree beside which the tyger stands divides the poem decisively in half. These two halves, as will be seen, can to some extent be compared to the pairs of etchings which we have seen repeatedly illustrating other *Songs*, representing, despite a continuity of argument through the whole poem, distinguishable visionary approaches to the subject. This symmetry is especially worth underlining in order to suggest the relationship between stanzas 2 and 5, a relationship structurally as well as interpretively important, for too many critics have approached the fifth stanza, with its especially suggestive imagery, as "a kind of glorious digression."[49]

We may begin by looking at the second stanza. The speaker of the first half of the poem is clearly suffering from pastoral ignorance, perhaps aggravated by fear, for his uncertainty leads him to syntactic confusion in the much-discussed twelfth line: "What dread hand? & what dread feet?" Disturbing the speaker as much as fear is his inability to conceive of a creator commensurate with his conception of "The Tyger."

> What immortal hand or eye,
> Could frame thy fearful symmetry?
>
> (E24)

The confusion between spiritual and physical control possibly suggested by the uncertain "hand or eye" could be resolved in terms of artist and artifact, but the speaker can conceive of no artist commensurate with this particular artifact, especially because, as "symmetry" implies, the artifact represents an enormous range of perhaps opposed possibilities:

> In what distant deeps or skies
> Burnt the fire of thine eyes!
> On what wings dare he aspire?
> What the hand, dare sieze the fire?
>
> (E24)

The speaker literally cannot picture an appropriate God in his mind's eye. What sort of wings, what sort of hands would the god require to dare approach such a creature? "Deeps or skies" not only dramatizes the speaker's confusion but implies as well an ontological range available to his idea of the tyger greater than the range he is capable of attributing to the creator of the tyger. Despite the vagueness of "deeps or skies," we should remember that the tyger is immanent (he and the speaker are in Generation), and the creator is remote. It is at this point that Blake uses one of his interesting variations on the argument by design, using the speaker's ignorance and hesitancy to begin to implicate his idea of the god in his apprehension of the tyger. The effect is in a sense analogous to what happens in "The Lamb," to draw down the creator and make him immanent in his creature:

> And what shoulder, & what art,
> Could twist the sinews of thy heart?
> And when thy heart began to beat,
> What dread hand? & what dread feet?
>
> (E24)

The implication is, in terms of the fiction, inadvertent but no less far-reaching for that; by the end of the stanza we are not sure whose hand and feet are under discussion, or whether both appendages are attached to the same being.[50] At the same time it is clear that the references to "shoulder," "art," "twist the sinews," "hand," and "feet" together contribute to make the creator seem less remote.

The implication of the speaker's changing conception is that he seems to be making the creator either more like the tyger or more like a man. And the interesting thing about these possibilities is— given one fact—the little difference between them. That one fact is the lack of alteration, as evidenced by the repetition of the word "dread" in line 12, in the speaker's attitude toward the tyger. Fixity in fear means that the pastoral speaker in Generation cannot see beyond the terms of the pastoral fiction: he cannot conceive of a world which is not constituted according to the fiction in which he conceives—a world of lambs, a world of predators, consequently a world where dependence is necessary. Such a speaker seems left with two abhorrent possibilities: a tyger-god (that is, God can make tygers because he is one), or a man-god mesmerized by fear of his own creation.

Most Blakeans would be quick to point out that the second position would seem much the more hopeful to the poet, that he would regard the idea of tyger-god as simply delusion but might argue that the conception of man-god fearful of his own creation was halfway to the truth. At least this conceiver understands that the creation is his conceit; he simply has to be taught not to be afraid, which will tame the tyger and distinguish the flame which creates from the one which destroys. This is not what "The Tyger" is about. What "The Tyger" as a Song of Experience is about is that in Generation there is a horrifying similarity between the two "theological" positions outlined. From the standpoint of Generation, and especially from that of the Prolific in Generation, it matters little whether God is Devourer or we only conceive of him that way. In either case the imagination is imprisoned by the context in which it finds itself—by the argument from design. The relationship between Experience and pastoralism can be exposed by means of this insight, for Blake conveys his idea through the pastoral fiction of naive immersion in a form of reality than which nothing more ideal, more authentic, can be conceived. For all its terror, the world in which the tyger stalks is no less pastoral than the landscape of the other *Songs*.

To make his point, Blake accepts the tyranny of a formal convention. As long as the poem lasts, he binds himself almost as securely as his narrator to the confines of a particular conventional language and perspective. It is interesting that this point emerges in the midst of discussion of Blake's best-known poem, because it stands, as I read Blake, at the heart of what he has to say.

In *A Vision of the Last Judgment* Blake takes up the dream of eighteenth-century free-thinkers (he mentions Paine and Voltaire) of escape from terms of good and evil "to live in Paradise & Liberty." Blake embraces the dream "in spirit" but carefully distinguishes his position from that of the radicals: "You may do so in Spirit but not in the Mortal Body as you pretend till after the Last Judgment for in Paradise they have no Corporeal & Mortal Body that originated with the Fall & was calld Death & cannot be removed but by a Last Judgment while we are in the world of Mortality we Must Suffer" (E554). That sounds orthodox and sober enough for a bishop, and seems odd coming from the man who told Dr. John Trusler confidently, "I feel that a Man may be happy in This World" (E676). Much, of course, depends upon what Blake meant by a Last Judgment. In the same *Vision* he explains that "whenever any Individual Rejects Error & Embraces Truth a Last Judgment passes upon that Individual" (E551). A bit further on, corporeal reality seems only a negligible obstacle: "Mental Things are alone Real what is Calld Corporeal Nobody Knows of its dwelling Place it is in Fallacy & its Existence an Imposture" (E555). Finally, he is encouraged by enthusiasm to dismiss the "Outward Creation" as "No part of Me." And in the famous passage comparing the sun first to a disk of fire and then to a company of angels, he remarks, "I question not my Corporeal or Vegetative Eye." He does not say that the corporeal eye is "in Fallacy & its Existence an Imposture." He says simply, "I look thro it & not with it" (all E555).

At the heart of Blake's point of view lies his belief in the transforming power of the visionary imagination, imagination which always works in terms of formal particularity as opposed to mental abstraction. For Blake the Last Judgment "is an Overwhelming of Bad Art & Science" (E555). But it is unquestionably true that his passionate insistence upon the translation of truth into clearly outlined images—a belief adhered to so fiercely as to cause his dismissal of impressionistic technique—is bound to a certain equivocation where the body-mind problem is concerned. To Dr.

Trusler he wrote of the Nature he so spurns and despises in his *Vision*: "But to the Eyes of the Man of Imagination Nature is Imagination itself" (E677). I think it is not quite a solution to this equivocation or ambiguity—so clear is the evidence in his works of how tormented he himself was by it—to argue for a distinction between the claims of vision and the claims of philosophy more absolute than was available always to the poet. For to Blake's doubts about Nature—which cause him to ask "what is the material world, and is it dead?" in lines added to *Europe* (E59), and which lead Urizen even as he explores the terrible abstract abyss of his own making to plant "a garden of fruits" (E80), having been "Stung with the odours of Nature" (E79)—we can attribute his instinctive grasp of the techniques and implications of pastoralism. The pastoral world is the corporeal world transformed by the imagination, but it is not the paradise Blake says Paine and Voltaire sought. Therefore, we can see that the great crucial problems which critics adumbrate in terms of "The Tyger"—problems concerning the poet's attitude toward energy, toward revolution, and toward apocalypse—all return eventually to the problem of Nature or Generation and to Blake's pastoralism. For pastoralism, like Blake's vision, transcends corporeal reality by inventing it. The speaker of the second half of "The Tyger," who is a developed form of the speaker of the first half, seems to know this; he seems to know even that "All deities reside in the human breast" (E37). At least he has less difficulty than earlier in inventing analogies for the creative act of God to recognizable, human activity:

> What the hammer? what the chain,
> In what furnace was thy brain?
> What the anvil? what dread grasp,
> Dare its deadly terrors clasp?
>
> (E25)

God is not a tyger, however remote and tyger-ish his activities in creating the world as it is:

> When the stars threw down their spears
> And water'd heaven with their tears.
>
> (E25)

We know from lines in "Introduction" to *Songs of Experience* that this image, whatever else it signifies, refers to the world in a fallen state:

The starry floor
The watry shore
Is giv'n thee till the break of day.

(E18)

That state, rendered for us in "The Tyger" by means of the conventions of pastoralism, is a world which includes death: in addition to lambs, tygers to eat them. This causes the speaker to doubt the "humanity" of his humanly imaginable God, which is the primary meaning of:

Did he smile his work to see?
Did he who made the Lamb make thee?

(E25)

If there is not a corpse present, there is at least the imminent possibility of one in the simultaneous creation of tyger and lamb, an act which I take the syntax of Blake's text to signify was also simultaneous with the throwing down of spears and weeping. "Did he smile his work to see?" His "work" includes the fact of death, and the question, rarely seen in such explicit form, casts its shadow behind even the most orthodox versions of elegy.

Who is the speaker of the second three stanzas? Clearly he is less simple and confused than the speaker of the first three. He can more easily construct visions for his God to inhabit, and yet he cannot, any more than anyone else, escape from the visionary limitations of his pastoral world: however human his God, he is conceived a God upon whom we must depend, who has us at his mercy, remote as the terror of his creation can make him. "Did he smile" suggests a range of attitude from gloating over our terrors to smiling indulgently at the falseness of our fears. Despite the speaker's tendency to self-abandonment, however, his familiarity with the forge (stanza 4) and his access to what seem to be rather technical insights (in terms of Blake's mythology) relevant to the appearance of the world in its present form both lead us to suspect that he is no ordinary mortal, certainly not the same man who confused the appendages of God and tyger at the end of stanza 3. He appears—not to beat about the bush—to be a form of Los, Blake's *persona* of imaginative creation. This fact, however, should not cause us to leap to any conclusions concerning the speaker's outlook; he seems not to be, for instance, a very successful visionary.

Since the speaker's immediate problem in "The Tyger" is death, an appropriate interpretive *locus* is the end of Book III of

The Book of Urizen, where the just-created Urizen is identified with death:

> 11. The Eternals said: What is this? Death.
> Urizen is a clod of clay.

And we are told that

> 14. ... Los rouz'd his fires, affrighted
> At the formless unmeasurable death.

(E73)

But in *Urizen* the "rouz'd" fires are the fires of a fallen creation, and the speaker of "The Tyger" is less aware of himself as creator; certainly his arousal is uncertain. After the creation in *Urizen* and the appearance on the scene of Enitharmon and Los, we are told: "No more Los beheld Eternity" (E79). And it is perhaps at this point in his story that we take him up in "The Tyger."

We find him obsessed with death, and however much the tyger may symbolize to the visionary "the prime spiritual energy which may bring form out of chaos,"[51] to the speaker in the poem he represents death. When this is clear, something else about the imagery of the fifth stanza becomes clear: it is an instance, perfectly traditional to pastoral elegy, of pathetic fallacy:

> When the stars threw down their spears
> And water'd heaven with their tears:
> Did he smile his work to see?
> Did he who made the Lamb make thee?

(E25)

Whatever else these lines signify, their primary meaning is germane to pastoral elegy: given the fact of death (probably of the Lamb), a loss poignant enough so that Nature weeps in sympathy, can we say that the creator looks on in equanimity? Is this part of his plan? Is the same creator responsible for Adonis and the boar?

Further, there is something very odd about this image which only a knowledge of Blake's pastoral vocabulary will help explain. In the fifth stanza there is the same juxtaposition of smiles and tears so often observed in the *Songs,* especially in "A Cradle Song" of Innocence. There the mother wept while all creation and the child smiled, and this justified raising the question about authority succinctly expressed in a political context in one line from *The French Revolution*: "And can Nobles be bound when the people are free, or God weep when his children are happy?" (E291). One might wonder as well whether God can smile when his children are weeping. Moreover, the image in "The Tyger" inverts the situation in *Milton*, in "A Cradle Song," and especially in "Night." In all of these instances, an occasion for smiles in Generation was an occasion for tears "above," in Beulah, the divided ideal consciousness. If we may assume that the inversion of this situation in "The Tyger"—where Nature weeps, but the "God" on high smiles—is a "mistake," that is, a function of the speaker's pastoral ignorance (or, depending on how we read the tone of the question marks, perhaps of his duplicity), and that in fact the normal relationship between Generation and Beulah prevails, then Blake's image constitutes one of the most interesting and complex instances of the relationship, defined in the *Phaedrus*, between truth and feigning. If the normal relationship between Generation and Beulah prevails, then the God responsible for the tyger (and also for the lamb) does belong to Generation, and although he may smile at his work insofar as he is lost to it, the heavens, which are of his divided imagination, weep. This would seem to be a parody of the speaker's ostensible theology. From it there follows the realization that the present constitution of reality, according to which tyger devours lamb and the heavens weep, is entirely a creation of man's imagination (the God in Generation), of his wishing. It is a creation man "smiles to see." And it may be that the purpose of feigning in this poem is the speaker's wish to protect himself from this knowledge. Perhaps, as I have suggested, it is better to believe even terrible things of a remote and unapproachable God than to have to believe them of oneself.

To summarize, the imagination I have been talking about, in order to deal with the agony of Experience (which it senses is death) invents necessity. First the speaker invents a God of necessity and of law (Urizen), and then, to make him bearable, he invents a pastoral fiction of a pitying nature which he puts between himself and the terrible God. Dependence upon a pitying, maternal nature comforts the speaker somewhat, and so he can continue to confront both the God who smiles through tears because he knows best and the natural embodiment of God's superior knowledge and necessary authority in a creature of wonder and terror.

The tyger, then, is a creature who embodies and mediates levels of doubt and fear. As an image of nature and "natural necessity," it also embodies Blake's perplexity and ambivalence concerning the corporeal world. This is one reason why the poem, despite its difficulty, is one to which students of Blake are drawn instinctively. It is an important text, and the tyger includes a range of implication which, if traced in the prophecies and related to the mythological personages there, is impressively great.

In the prophecies, vegetable nature is Vala, an emanation or wife to Blake's figure of sexual and revolutionary energy: Luvah-Orc. Orc, as already noted, becomes in his mock crucifixion associated with natural necessity as well as with the passion of suffering, and we will shortly see another equally important link between him and the tyger. More directly, Vala in the prophecies is the great mother or "shadowy female" whom we see in *America* and *Europe* associated with Enitharmon, the emanation of Los, Blake's figure for the imagination (as opposed to reason or passion). Los's "unfallen" name, Urthona, is suggestive of possession of the physical realm. Finally, insofar as the tyger suggests law or the argument by design, he has sómething of Urizen in his nature.

Los-Urthona, Luvah-Orc, and Urizen are all indirectly implicated in "The Tyger," and it is interesting that the principal prophetic analogue for the image

> When the stars threw down their spears
> And water'd heaven with their tears,

is a passage in the fifth Night of *Vala/The Four Zoas* where Urizen is recalling his rebellion and fall:[52]

> I went not forth. I hid myself in black clouds of my wrath
> I calld the stars around my feet in the night of councils dark
> The stars threw down their spears & fled naked away
> We fell. I siezd thee dark Urthona In my left hand falling
>
> I siezd thee beauteous Luvah thou art faded like a flower
> And like a lilly is thy wife Vala witherd by winds
> (64.25–30; E337)

All three characters fall together, and it is interesting to see Blake employing his language of flowers in the same context. The lily, which he associates with Vala, is a symbol of sexual purity, and as such has its own poem in Experience; it also has an important Christian iconographical association with the Annunciation to the Virgin.

More important than the language of flowers, however, is the language of tears. In his *Book*, Urizen's tears arrive after he has explored the world which is a concretion of his rebellious fall,

and has discovered in it the terrible cycle of tyger and lamb
which we see reflected in "The Tyger":

>   ... he saw
> That no flesh nor spirit could keep
> His iron laws one moment.
>
> 5. For he saw that life liv'd upon death
> The Ox in the slaughter house moans
> The Dog at the wintry door
> And he wept, & he called it Pity
> And his tears flowed down on the winds
>
> (E80–81)

We know that Blake associates these lines explicitly with Experience, for he reworks them in Enion's "What is the price of Experience?" speech at the end of *Vala/The Four Zoas,* Night II
(36.4; E319). But Urizen's pity is not a useful emotion; it is the
sort of moral hypocrisy Blake castigates in "The Human Abstract."
This is not its first appearance in *The Book of Urizen,* for Los, from
whose side Urizen is in that prophecy torn, is terrified at the empty
spaces suggested by Urizen's possessiveness and exclusiveness,
and he weeps also:

> 6. Los wept obscur'd with mourning:
> His bosom earthquak'd with sighs;
> He saw Urizen deadly black,
> In his chains bound, & Pity began.
>
> (E76)

Pity and the sense of space, of divisiveness, assume a female form
before Los, for Blake is rendering the appearance of sexuality in
the universe, an appearance which much horrifies "the eternals":

> 9. All Eternity shudderd at sight
> Of the first female now separate
> Pale as a cloud of snow
> Waving before the face of Los
>
> 10. Wonder, awe, fear, astonishment,
> Petrify the eternal myriads;
> At the first female form now separate
>
> They call'd her Pity, and fled
>
> (E77)

The two Pity's are the same, only the second manifestation is
christened Enitharmon and "married" to Los. It is interesting

that at her first appearance she is described as "pale as a cloud of snow," which, like the lily, has associations both with purity and with death.

Enitharmon's name suggests "numberless,"[53] partly because of the tendency of nature to reduplicate itself endlessly, "consumed and consuming" by the constant need to preserve place and identity in a Urizenic world (see *Europe*, "Preludium," 5; E59). In *Europe* nature complains of natural necessity to "mother Enitharmon" in a passage which renders the problem of "The Tyger" from a different point of view:

> I wrap my turban of thick clouds around my lab'ring head;
> And fold the sheety waters as a mantle round my limbs.
> Yet the red sun and moon,
> And all the overflowering stars rain down prolific pains.
> (1.12–15; E59)

A bit later she continues:

> I bring forth from my teeming bosom myriads of flames.
> And thou dost stamp them with a signet, then they roam abroad
> And leave me void as death:
> Ah! I am drown'd in shady woe, and visionary joy.
> (2.9–12; E60)

Urizen is there with his false waters, and the "red sun and moon" may be Los and Enitharmon under the aegis of fiery passion, or Luvah; for Los is "Sol" spelled backwards, and in line 7 of the "Prophecy" he is called "possessor of the moon" (E60). (Later in the poem sun and moon are associated with Enitharmon's sons, Rintrah and Palamabron.) Again we have our fallen characters raining down prolific pains, and it is tempting to see the tyger himself as one of those "myriads of flames" nature speaks of as stamped with the signet of Enitharmon.

Europe describes by means of a sinister parody of Milton's "On the Morning of Christ's Nativity" the advent of Orc, an event important to the interpretation of "The Tyger." Orc causes ambivalent feelings in his father, who has been affected by Urizenic jealousy and fear of passion, yet his first reaction in *Europe* is that he can rest secure in the hopes represented by his son, confident even in the release of his enemy Urizen from chains. But the parody of Milton is itself ambiguous, for the advent is described in terms which simultaneously suggest a second coming and a second Fall:

Again the night is come
That strong Urthona takes his rest,
And Urizen unloos'd from chains
Glows like a meteor in the distant north
Stretch forth your hands and strike the elemental strings!
Awake the thunders of the deep.

(E60)

The ambiguity relies upon the imitation, for Milton is looking back not to an earlier Advent but to the Creation of the world itself:

Such Musick (as 'tis said)
Before was never made,
   But when of old the sons of morning sung,
While the Creator great
His constellations set,
   And the well-ballanc't world on hinges hung,
And cast the dark foundations deep,
And bid the weltring waves their oozy channel keep.

(117–124)

But for Blake, as we have seen, the creation of this Nature is a concretion of the Fall. And the appearance, or advent, of Orc—Blake's revolutionary "savior"—is perplexing because it is a function of this Creation-Fall. It is this perplexity, or doubtfulness, whether applied to imprisoning nature or to the pent-up spirit within it (compare the first stanza of Spenser's "Ianuarie") which is, I believe, the subject of "The Tyger." The Orc of *Europe*—as we shall see later—embodies no glimpse of the genuine Armageddon his terrors forecast (nor does the tyger) but is primarily a creature of Enitharmon's 1800-year dream of European history, a dream in which Blake saw Energy putting its Promethean sufferings at the service of Nature and Necessity and the Female Will. The tyger, in short, represents Orc and the Female Will in about equal portions, and the perplexity of the poem's speaker is a reflection of Los's attitude toward both: his ambivalence concerning Orc and his love-hate relationship with Enitharmon. The conjunction of associations can very accurately be traced in *Europe* and *Vala/The Four Zoas*.

If we remember to think of the flames of the tyger's burning in terms available to the other *Songs* in Blake's two series, we recall the tyger's primary sexual reference. The mesmeric effect the animal has on the speaker represents, therefore, a sexual hypnosis, an enthrallment or seduction by the Female Will. This enthrallment is precisely what is celebrated as Enitharmon's dream in *Europe*:

> Now comes the night of Enitharmon's joy!
> Who shall I call? Who shall I send?
> That Woman, lovely Woman! may have dominion?
> Arise O Rintrah thee I call! & Palamabron thee!
> Go! tell the Human race that Womans love is Sin!
> That an Eternal life awaits the worms of sixty winters
> In an allegorical abode where existence hath never come:
> Forbid all Joy, & from her childhood shall the little female
> Spread nets in every secret path.
>
> (E61)

In Night II of *Vala/The Four Zoas* Enitharmon sings an even stranger song (34.58–92; E317–318) as malevolent Queen of Heaven, the purpose of which is to "revive" Los from the periodic slumber of the sexual cycle in which she has enmeshed him, his days devoted to frustrated Desire and his nights to the death which is Jealousy. Her theme is that "The joy of woman is the Death of her most best beloved/Who dies for Love of her" (34.63–64; E317). As a kind of lunar Hecate she pays savage court to Los:

> At the first Sound the Golden sun arises from the Deep
> And shakes his awful hair
> The Eccho wakes the moon to unbind her silver locks
> The golden sun bears on my song
> And nine bright spheres of harmony rise round the fiery King
>
> (34.58–62; E317)

The pastoralism of this song will occupy us in another context; I want here only to note the unmistakable echoes of Milton's "Nativity Ode":

> Ring out ye Crystall sphears,
> Once bless our human ears,
>   (If ye have power to touch our senses so)
> And let your silver chime
> Move in melodious time;
>   And let the Base of Heav'ns deep Organ blow,
> And with your ninefold harmony
> Make up full consort to th'Angelike symphony.
>
> (125–132)

In summary, if analogies between "The Tyger" and the Prophecies are consulted, the attitude of the speaker can be compared to Los, dubious of his son and sexually mesmerized by the Female Will.

INNOCENCE AND EXPERIENCE

Since it is clear that the ambiguities represented by the tyger reflect not only immersion in Experience, but the visionary division of Innocence as well, it is perhaps time to attempt finally the distinction between the two states. The vision of Innocence, it has been argued, includes a conscious division in the form of a pastoral fiction. Innocence self-consciously maintains the gap between the lamb and the Generation which would devour him. The irony here, therefore, is the tendency of Innocence to maintain the order of reality within which the lamb stands as sacrificial victim. This irony is reflected in the tears which the lion in "Night" weeps. Experience, on the other hand, is unified, but it puts in the place of the division of Innocence a callousness to the fact of suffering. Experience is interested in giving the lie to the fiction of Innocence by declaring that the lamb is as much a part of Generation as anyone else, and eating him; it thereafter becomes necessary, unless Experience is simply to mirror the division of Innocence (which is, except for the series of question marks, the situation in "The Tyger"), to muffle the suffering precipitated in the exposure of Innocence. The distinction between and interdependence of the two orders, a "version of pastoral," is to be seen in the relationship between Enitharmon's first appearance in *Urizen* as Pity and her later embodiment of the Female Will. The logic of the relationship is made clear in Blake's visionary politics. "Can that be love," Oothoon wonders, "that drinks another as a sponge drinks water?" (E49). In *America* Boston's angel translates the question:

> What God is he, writes laws of peace, & clothes him in a tempest
> What pitying Angel lusts for tears, and fans himself with sighs
> What crawling villain preaches abstinence & wraps himself
> In fat of lambs? no more I follow, no more obedience pay.
> (E54)

Innocence and Experience are related, as we have seen, to orders of vision. In *Milton* (especially plate 15) these are rendered as orders of dream. Blake's idea is a complex one; we can simplify it by suggesting that Generation is simply a dream, but that Beulah is a dream in which the sleeper figures (as distinguished from a dream "about" ourselves, as presumably all our dreams are). This analogy includes the divided consciousness of Innocence and the unified awareness of Experience, for when we dream of ourselves we know we are dreaming; otherwise we often do not. As Blake says, "As when a man dreams, he reflects not that his body sleeps, / Else he would wake" (M., 15.1–2; E108). In other words, if the divided consciousness of Innocence becomes too acute, we "wake up" into Experience. Almost everyone has had the reluctant experience of becoming increasingly conscious—"This is only a dream"—and of waking to try, usually unsuccessfully, to put the sleeper back into the dream. Here it becomes apparent that the "reality" which holds us back from the dream is actually the sense of self. We say we "wake up," but it might be more accurate to say we "wake down." In waking we no longer "see ourselves," but it is the self which wakes us.

The essence, then, of the Beulah dream, hence of Innocence, is a peculiar consciousness: one is conscious of "oneself dreaming" but not of the self. It would be convenient simply to distinguish two kinds of self, calling one the good, real self and the other the bad, contrary self, but Blake does nothing of the kind in the *Songs*. And the ambiguity of "The Tyger" is not merely a measure of Experience, but of his unwillingness to do so. Beulah, Blake tells us in *Milton*, "is a place where Contrarieties are equally True" (30.1; E128). This is extremely unusual: in a comedy the villains suffer a change of heart before they join the wedding supper at the end; in tragedy the hero maintains his self steadfastly, but discovers that his self is incompatible with the "nature" of the universe—his self must die to remain itself.[54] (Blake despised tragedy, logically, on the grounds that it constituted ultimate slavery to the Female Will: see J., 37.29–30; E181.) Pastoralism is unique in that it reconciles without changing identities; in pastoralism the lion simply lies down with the lamb—neither loses its identity. We can see a relationship between this feature of pastoralism and the peculiar self-consciousness of the dream of Innocence.

Because the identities in pastoralism never change, pastoral fictions of reconciliation are bound to these identities. That is, the imagery of reconciliation is limited by the identities in need of reconciliation. This I have insisted upon in my interpretation of "The Tyger," and this fact explains why it is never strictly correct to speak of pastoral fictions as escapist. The golden age cannot transcend the lamb and the lion; it can only cause them to coexist. For Innocence is to dream of oneself in a fiction "of" the self; the transcending fiction is reliant for its imagery upon the order being transcended. In some sense, as I have noted, the pastoral fiction of Innocence consciously maintains the Generation self to which one succumbs, more or less unconsciously, in Experience.

The purpose of Blake's *Songs*, however, was not the multiplication of these ironies, but the clarification of a problem which can be stated in philosophical terms parallel to the literary habits of pastoralism. This is the problem broached in the *Phaedrus*, the relationship between feigning and truth, but ultimately it is a problem of transcendence. Locked into a glossary of terms, a vocabulary of fixed identities, can one transcend these identities without moving to another language? A very late addition to the Songs of Experience (1802? after mid-1805? see E722) is devoted to Tirzah, one of Blake's most terrible avatars of the Female Will, and the speaker of the poem, who like the speaker of "The Tyger" asks questions, begins:

Whate'er is Born of Mortal Birth,
Must be consumed with the Earth
To rise from Generation free;
Then what have I to do with thee? (E30)

And he concludes by asking the same question over again (another resemblance to "The Tyger"):

The Death of Jesus set me free,
Then what have I to do with thee? (E30)

I would suggest strenuously that these, like the questions of "The Tyger," are not merely rhetorical, but real questions, and that the paradoxical vocabulary of the inscription on the accompanying etching, "It is Raised a Spiritual Body" (E30), serves to underline them.

Some final remarks about "The Tyger" now become possible. We are in a position to appreciate the Renaissance pastoralists' interpretation of Orpheus as the "single voice for all the intimations of this world's beauty and the other world's that solicit a human mind" (Cody, p. 29), but Blake could see that Orpheus would cut no ice with Bacon, Newton, and Locke, neither with the science nor with the theology of eighteenth-century England. That science and that theology (for Blake virtually indistinguishable) would solve the problem of pastoral transcendence by one of two ways: by resting either upon the ultimate laws of matter or upon a completely transcendent, arbitrary, and abstract God. Blake, like Newton, came to identify these two ways of approach, and he does so in "The Tyger" to prevent the narrator from coming to peaceful terms with either.

Pastoralism, then, demands of the would-be transcendentalist an absolutism more available to consciousness, and thus more amenable to the language of art, than to the logic of philosophy. The upper and lower boundaries of this absolute realm of consciousness may be thought of respectively as the achieved song of Orpheus—the song of lover and theologian—and the concerted mourning of Nature called pathetic fallacy. Within this pastoral area, the demands made on consciousness are not felt by Blake alone, as the following example, noted by Rosemond Tuve, will testify.

In the flower passage of *Lycidas*, in the course of the catalogue, we suddenly come upon the phrase "Bid Amaranthus all his beauty shed" (149), and Miss Tuve remarks that "the sudden depth of the image is unexpected; amaranth is the deathless flower, later to be used by Milton as a symbol of the flaw-less world before the Fall, but long known as the immortal plant, that one blossoming thing whose 'beauty' is never quenched or withered."[55] Milton, "feeling the necessity of giving over to death these symbols of life-to-be-born-of-death [all the blossoms]," frankly and easily hands the immortal natural object over to the demands of his transcendentalism; he is bent on "making a connection between sacrifice and immortality born of death."[56] And since sacrifice which is *necessary*, however genuine, may not seem to have made that hole in the united fabric of God-man-and-nature upon which pathetic fallacy depends, Milton is tempted to dig the hole deeper. It is a question of consciousness and emotion, not of logic, and I would not agree with Miss Tuve "that part of the valid sense of assuagement which human beings feel in symbolic actions that assert the continuity of life despite the fact of death does disappear when the action is not possible,"[57] for the action in question, the assertion of the death of the amaranth, *is* at least imaginatively possible. If Death is going to be seen to be Life, even the deathless are going to have to die. The real difficulty of the poem, then, becomes the confluence of the imagery of pathos and the achieved consciousness of immortality, expressed epithalamically as hearing "the unexpressive nuptiall Song, / In the blest Kingdoms meek of joy and love" (176–177). In achieving that final consciousness, Milton perhaps demonstrates a suspect enthusiasm for the pit. Rosemond Tuve tries to get over the difficulty uneasily by asserting that the "bitter tides" of death "meet, and are drowned in, the full-flowing stream of symbolized life, faithfulness, creativity, eternal flowering, earthly and heavenly pity, aid, sacrifice and love."[58] Her imagery and my analysis both point to what Blake calls the Female Will.

"AH! SUN-FLOWER"

I have suggested that Experience among other things expresses Blake's sense of dismay before the fact that the language of transcendence draws upon the vocabulary of ordinary Generation and death. Pastoralism embodies this problem as does no other genre; Blake's whole perplexity can be nicely summed up in Spenser's image of letting out the sheep's blood at the wolf's throat, but Blake expresses it himself in the Song of Experience "Ah! Sun-Flower."

Before looking at this poem, it is worth considering plate 53 of *Jerusalem*, where Blake uses the figure of a sunflower in the illustration. A female figure, triple-crowned and bearing on her wings the signs of the planets and constellations, sits brooding on the blossom of a huge sunflower over some water. The depiction has proved to be an ambiguous one. In 1924 it suggested Beulah to S. Foster Damon, "mercifully veiling the Sun of Eternity from our eyes ... She is throned high above the Sea of Time and Space upon the Sunflower of the Desire for Immortality."[59] For Northrop Frye, in 1947, it represented a more ambiguous "solidified threefold Beulah-Ulro" (*Fearful Symmetry*, p. 434), that is, an embodiment of the division in Innocence. Frye's is the more correct identification, but Damon's revised opinion, in his *Blake Dictionary*, of "Vala" is also useful, for Vala—through *The Four Zoas* anyway—is the focus of the ambiguity I am discussing.[60]

Ah Sun-flower! weary of time,
Who countest the steps of the Sun:
Seeking after that sweet golden clime
Where the travellers journey is done.

Where the Youth pined away with desire,
And the pale Virgin shrouded in snow:
Arise from their graves and aspire,
Where my Sun-flower wishes to go.   (E25)

Harold Bloom suggests the poem means that "to aspire only as the vegetable world aspires is to suffer a metamorphosis into the vegetable existence."[61] But the poem is more complex than Bloom's reading would suggest, and to begin with the sunflower itself, as we have seen in *Jerusalem*, is not a simple image of vegetable existence. As heliotrope, bound to count the steps of an orb outside, it would seem an appropriate image for the abjectness and dependency of the vegetable order, but the very closeness of its attention might suggest, not passivity, but a close devotion, or even aspiration. And since flowers represent in Blake's language sexual passion, this is an important point; we remember that Enitharmon's great hymn to the Female Will in *Vala/The Four Zoas* courted Los as sun (the phrase "weary of time" is interesting in light of the fact that Los represents time in Blake's mythology), and managed to be both perfectly deceitful and strangely moving —without it Los might have fallen permanently into despair and inactivity. Further, the speaker of the poem reflects this ambivalence in his exclamatory address to the flower: we do not know whether "Ah! Sun-flower!" signifies wonder or pity.

If the latter, and this would fit with Bloom's reading, the speaker would be condescending to the sunflower's idea of paradise. Paradise, he might be saying, is an escape from time and therefore childish. Furthermore, there is a suspicious suggestion of death about the speaker's paradise. Bloom remarks, "The whole meaning of this poem is in another of Blake's descriptions of heaven, as 'an allegorical abode where existence hath never come.'"[62] It is not a great step to point out the identity of this "allegorical" death to the vegetable one.

But we should be aware from the beginning that there is here a potential trap. The language of death consists of the two phrases "Sweet golden clime" and "Where the travellers journey is done." There is nothing necessarily vegetable about the first phrase, and the second is at least surely neutral. Moreover, the latter phrase has its echo in Blake's revisions of a work originally contemporaneous with the *Songs: For Children: The Gates of Paradise* (1793). Blake's revisions, first published some time between 1805 and 1818 (E734), changed the title significantly to *For the Sexes*, and included some explanatory verses called "The Keys of the Gates," among which we read the following gloss:

> But when once I did descry
> The Immortal Man that cannot Die
> Thro evening shades I haste away
> To close the Labours of my Day
> The Door of Death I open found
> And the Worm Weaving in the Ground   (E266)

There is no need for elaborate analysis here,[63] but even without discussing what Blake means by "Immortal Man," and surely without recommending "an allegorical abode where existence hath never come," we can see in the illustration glossed a man hurrying toward his grave over the subscription "The Traveller hasteth in the Evening" (E264), suggestive of the language of "Ah! Sun-Flower."

The sunflower's image of paradise may be adequate to a miserable, vegetated creature, but the burden of Bloom's reading is that the Youth and the Virgin betray the fact that they have sunk into the vegetable realm by embracing, apparently, the same contemptible vision: "The flower is rooted in nature; the Youth and Virgin were not, but have become so."[64] I have already wondered whether the flower's emblematic nature encourages the kind of distinction between vegetable-immanence and human-transcendence which Bloom is pressing. Further, if the Youth and the Virgin are suffering from a vegetated vision analogous to the sunflower's, and if to be vegetable means to create an allegorical heaven in terms of one's own "nature," we might expect them to create paradises in terms of their own respective passions. Just as the sunflower "weary of time" creates a world where time is ended, we might expect the Youth to imagine a paradise of fulfilled desire, to cry with Oothoon "The moment of desire! the moment of desire!" (E49); and we might likewise expect the Virgin to imagine a paradise of chaste virtue released from the strain of self-imposition. (Virgin and Youth, perhaps needless to say, are "contraries," not the complementary halves of a whole; there is no question of bringing them together, here or in the hereafter, except as members of a sterile union— compare Bromion and Oothoon [before her enlightenment] bound back-to-back in *Visions of the Daughters of Albion.* Whatever the Virgin "needs," it is not the Youth, and vice versa.) In fact, both the Youth and the Virgin "aspire,/Where my Sunflower wishes to go." This imaginative identification with the sunflower's aspirations is peculiar, for everything else we are told about Youth and Virgin shows them immersed in their own imaginative limitations even to the point of death. However melodramatic the language, that the Youth has "pined away" and the Virgin is "shrouded in snow" suggests that even the vegetable circuit of the flower's imagining is closed to them. Yet finally, inspired by the sunflower, they "Arise from their graves and aspire."

This is beginning to sound more the language of wonder than of pity, but the case is still very ambiguous. I would suggest that

Blake's presentation of death in the first stanza is indeed a trap, that "the sweet golden clime / Where the travellers journey is done" is prevented from being attractive by a fear of death which is itself vegetable, that the "graves" of the Virgin and Youth are metaphorical but no less "real" for that (emblematic of slavery to the Female Will), and that their release from that Will is suggested to them *in* the natural condition by analogy to another natural creature. This is not to say that the sunflower's image of paradise is not limited, even pitiful, or that the ambiguity of the poem's opening has been completely dissipated. But it is to suggest a possibility which depends upon recognizing one's vegetable nature, and exploiting rather than rejecting it. Conceptual or imaginative asceticism is surely as reprehensible as actual denial of the flesh, and I am suggesting that Blake is acutely aware of this in "Ah! Sun-Flower." If we wanted to look ahead into the prophetic poems, we could see analogies to this poem in the merciful vegetation of souls from Beulah in the looms of Los and Enitharmon and in Los's successful struggle to accept his spectre. But we do not have to look forward to explain "Ah! Sun-Flower"; we can look back, and see the importance of the poem against the background of the pastoralism of the *Songs*. In that context the relevance of the poem to the question of transcending language is very great.

"Ah! Sun-Flower" develops a pastoral fiction in which Youth and Virgin, like the lion and the lamb of Isaiah, lie side by side safely, each retaining his identity. The paradise where this reconciliation is accomplished is no "allegorical" place but a metaphorical function of a vegetable emblem of the Female Will. The pastoral language of the poem has been so manipulated that desire, not death, is the focus of the relationship between immanent and transcendent realms. When one considers that death is in the poem, "Ah! Sun-Flower," with its jaunty air of mock-pathos, emerges as a tour de force.

"THE FLY"

Blake's pastoral nonchalance, however, is not always so gay or felicitous as in "Ah! Sun-Flower," and in "The Fly," the Song of Experience which perhaps most clearly deals with the fact that transcendence must express itself in the same language which is available to the Female Will, there is a grimness to the tone which is disturbing.

Little Fly
Thy summers play,
My thoughtless hand
Has brush'd away.

Am not I
A fly like thee?
Or art not thou
A man like me?

For I dance
And drink & sing;
Till some blind hand
Shall brush my wing.

If thought is life
And strength & breath;
And the want
Of thought is death;

Then am I
A happy fly,
If I live,
Or if I die.

(E23–24)

The etching (see Fig. 6), for one critic an illustration of the problems of living in society,[65] depicts in reality something both more general and more specific: the Female Will. This appears in two aspects. In the foreground of the picture a mother, between two dead trees of Experience, bends over to support her young (boy) child walking. Her face (in the Rosenwald copy) is dark, and the inclination of her back corresponds both to a declining limb of a dead tree and to a cloud in the background. Smothering motherhood is not the only aspect of the Female Will depicted, for behind the mother's back (and invisible to the little boy) a pubescent girl is playing the solitary half of a shuttlecock game. The implication is clear, that the child in the foreground must move from the one aspect of the Female Will to the other; he must learn to walk and eventually take up his place at the other end of the court and play the game of give-and-take with the partner already, symbolically, waiting for him. The picture, then, strongly suggests the limitation of possibility imposed on the child by his natural condition.

Like "Ah! Sun-Flower," "The Fly" poses its problem in terms of an analogy between man and some other kind of creature carried to the point of identification. One fatal result of such an "identification," as Harold Bloom rightly points out, is that it depends

6. "The Fly"

upon an implied "one law for the man as well as the fly,"[66] and involves one in acceptance of the world view promoted by that foreman of the Female Will, Urizen:

> For I dance
> And drink & sing;
> Till some blind hand
> Shall brush my wing. (E23)

But "The Fly" is unique among the *Songs* in that it is etched in two columns, the first three stanzas in one column and the two-stanza rejoinder to the right, the typographical form suggesting a dialogue with two speakers and perhaps implying two "laws." In fact we can see the last two stanzas as constituting a "reply" (this follows the pattern of the Gray ode Blake was imitating)[67] to the first three, the reply of the fly addressed in the first stanza. We assume that the speaker of the final two stanzas is in fact an interlocutory fiction of the speaker of the first, a fiction resulting from his successful identification with the fly in stanza 2. This constitutes an amusing irony, for the first speaker has killed the fly, and his fiction, therefore, succeeds in terms of imagination in bringing the creature back to life. The identification of his self with the fly's self, for all its Urizenic implication, has conferred a kind of immortality on the dead creature.

But this is irony, and the dialogue form of the poem only emphasizes the contradictions which make it a facile irony at that. It is not altogether surprising, in the case of the last stanza, that critics have been led to accept the imaginative identification of man and fly ("Then am I / A happy fly") without serious thought about its implications,[68] for such acceptance is encouraged by the rhetorical trap of the poem, although the phrase "a happy fly" might have been expected to arouse more suspicion than it has. Also suspicious is the definition of happiness compatible with death, for the analogous identification of man and fly earlier in the poem argued for the dependency of happiness upon life; it was the dependence of a common happiness upon fate's pleasure which suggested the identification in the first place. And even if we take the final stanzas of transcendence at their face value, we get the following syllogism: If consciousness is the real Life (and already I am falsifying the text, for "life / And strength & breath" is a conspicuously physical description of living), and if to be unconscious is to be dead, then I am perfectly happy whatever happens, because—it is implied—if I die, I will not be conscious of the fact. Whatever the virtue of this position, it seems at least a minor hypocrisy to address it to the corpse of a fly one has just slaughtered, and it hardly squares either with most notions of an idealist or transcendentalist position. That it may, in fact, seem to square is only testimony to the ease with which the "transcendentalist" justifies murder or its necessity.

Major irony also emerges when we see that there is another way of reading the fly's apparent expression of transcendence, his declaration of independence from death. This reading emerges when we see the relationship between "thought" in line 13 and the "thoughtless hand" of line 3. Since the resultant irony is a comment on the Female Will which dominates the poem's illustration, it must be close to the center of the poem's meaning. It also constitutes a rebuke to the "first" speaker's sentimental willingness to reduce himself to the fly's supposed subordinate status in order to pay tribute to the superiority and transcendent power of his own consciousness—which is a debased version of what Milton does in *Lycidas*, burying the deathless in order to have the pleasure of imagining their resurrection. Blake, however, seems more acutely aware than Milton is of the very real problem suggested by even a "low" imitation of elegy, the problem that in Generation a man's thoughtless hand can really cause the death of another creature, and that any dependence upon "thought" as "design" must take this into consideration. Any transcendent definition of "thought" must take into consideration the oppressive implication of vegetable thoughtlessness as well. And this the fly's rebuttal does, suggesting something like, "If my breathing depends on your thinking of me, and if your not thinking of me means my 'death,' I'm in a pretty kettle of fish in either case." In fact he will be nothing more than a "happy fly," dependent upon the speaker's consciousness for existence; without that consciousness he is "alive," but nonexistent. The argument stresses the most radical version we have yet seen of the terror of dependence upon the Female Will, of what happens when the language of transcendence speaks the lexicon of immanence.

"THE LITTLE GIRL LOST" and "THE LITTLE GIRL FOUND": THE LION IN EXPERIENCE

The last examples of pastoralism I shall examine from the *Songs* are the Lyca poems, "The Little Girl Lost" and "The Little Girl Found," and these, even apart from their great intrinsic interest, are suitable examples to end on. For one thing, as already noticed, Blake moved them from their original position in Innocence to Experience, and a rehearsal of the possible reasons for this provides a convenient pretext for summing up what we know of the poet's two contrary states. For another, the poems are profoundly related in meaning to perhaps the most comprehensive lyrics, respectively, of Innocence and Experience, "Night" and "The Tyger." An even more important reason is that the Lyca poems can clarify and deepen our understanding of Blake's relationship to traditionally pastoral modes of expression. So far, in order to stress the fact that Blake had any relationship to pastoralism at all, I have often stressed the relationship between the meanings and techniques of his poems and the themes and methods traditional to pastoralism, but Blake's relationship to tradition was always thoughtful and not slavish, and now may perhaps be the time to watch Blake stressing aspects of pastoralism certainly not inevitable to anyone possessing a sophisticated vocabulary of that kind of poetry.

We have already seen Blake apply the ambivalent language of pastoralism to the problem of transcendence of Generation. To a great extent, as centuries of rather shrill argument concerning principles of decorum among pastoralists will attest, this is a problem inherent in the very nature of pastoralism, but Blake had special concerns—the Songs of Experience are his monument to them—which accentuated it; it looms and lumps in the path of the visionary who would make the world transparent rather than invisible. But the important thing to notice here is that there existed to Blake's hand, ripe for the taking, a vocabulary perfectly adaptable to the nature of pastoralism—and traditionally so adapted—designed precisely to handle the question of transcendence. Edgar Wind remarks: "The theory that 'transcendence' is a source of 'balance' because it reveals the coincidence of opposites in the supreme One is a doctrine of such extreme dialectical nicety that it may seem strange it should ever have succeeded in firing the artistic and practical imagination of the Renaissance."[69] But however nice the doctrine, it *did* appeal to the imagination of the Renaissance, and Blake need not have known Thomas Taylor at all to have been acquainted with some of the neoplatonic doctrines of which Taylor was the pleasant respository: he need have known, as he did, only the masterpieces of the Florentine Renaissance to have acquired iconographic precedents in pastoral transcendence. We can demonstrate, further, by means of the

Lyca plates themselves, that Blake was not ignorant of this neo-platonic tradition; that he chose, pace Miss Raine and Mr. Harper,[70] to ignore or alter it is a point of interest to historical scholarship as well as to criticism.

A couple of quotations from Edgar Wind's *Pagan Mysteries in the Renaissance,* a book of enormous learning and unflagging brilliance, will serve to sketch the doctrine I am talking about, which Pico and Ficino associate with the name of Orpheus and which celebrates love as "perpetual knot and link of the universe: *amor nodus perpetuus et copula mundi"* (Wind, p. 38). To simplify a complex theology, Wind tells us: "All we must remember is that the bounty bestowed by the gods upon lower beings was conceived by the Neoplatonists as a kind of overflowering (*emanatio*), which produced a vivifying rapture or conversion (called by Ficino *conversio, raptio,* or *vivicatio*) whereby the lower beings were drawn back to heaven and rejoined the gods (*remeatio*)" (Wind, p. 37). This theme bears a close but not identical relationship to the theme of the descent of the soul into generation and subsequent return which Kathleen Raine identifies with Porphyry's *Cave of the Nymphs* and, I think wrongly, with the Lyca poems.[71] In the "triadic arguments" of Pico and Ficino (and this clearly distinguishes them from authentic neoplatonists like Porphyry and Proclus), there is a subtle lopsidedness in the direction of God, in that both "rapture by the cause" and "return to the cause" are regarded as "reverting phases," as opposed to the single "outgoing tendency" of the first cause, thought of in Judeo-Christian terms "primarily as a creator" (Wind, p. 38). There is nothing in Blake's philosophy which would lead us especially to linger on this point, but the philosophy of Pico and Ficino left its visible mark on Blake's art. The triadic argument led the Italian neoplatonists to extraordinary interest in the allegorical implications of various representations of the Three Graces. Seneca's allegorization of the Graces as "'three sundry actions in liberality' (giving, receiving, and returning)" (Wind, p. 30) was refined out of its ordinary level of ethical commonplace and adapted to the most subtle and exquisite representations of the relationship between inner harmony and transcendence. The Three Graces are traditionally *pulchritudo, amor,* and *voluptas,* and although early depictions show a fairly simple harmony among the three (being a rather literal translation of Plato's definition "Love is Desire aroused by Beauty"—Wind, p. 46—with *amor* seen from the back to indicate her as the "outgoing" mean of the other two), gradually the sense of balance was subtilized in order to emphasize the more asymmetrical harmony in keeping with the doctrines alluded to above. For *amor*—as consultation of perhaps the subtlest depiction of the relationship extant, the *Primavera* of Botticelli, will attest—is no simple mean: she harmonizes the relationship between beauty and *voluptas* even as she is supported by the one and moves in the direction of the other. There is no need to belabor all the ramifications of Botticelli's dance, for the important point here is only that Blake was aware of this tradition. We know this because of his own version of the triad, engraved for John Gabriel Stedman's *Narrative* of his adventures in Guiana, called *Europe supported by Africa & America*, 1792 (reproduced in Erdman as plate 3). Blake, presumably in order to emphasize the economic and social reality expressed by the engraving's title, stresses the inextricable and perfectly harmonious binding of the triad almost to the exclusion of everything else, and the representation is almost static. But it is possible to see in the picture nevertheless the at least vestigial *pulchritudo* (Africa), *amor* (Europe), and *voluptas* (America). *Pulchritudo* seems to be looking straight ahead as if at an onlooker; *amor*, while her head is canted at the same angle as *pulchritudo*'s, has her eyes half-closed to suggest inwardness of vision. Insofar as she looks out at all, it is, despite the angle of her head, in the direction of *voluptas*. This last figure, her hair and limbs in some disarray, has her gaze riveted on something off to the right of the picture; *amor*'s left arm is thrown around her neck, and holds her within the circumference of the triad, but the weight of *voluptas*'s body and the tug of her gaze combine to suggest a strong pull to the right in the weight of the composition. Yet, such is the arrangement of chain and linking arms and such is the effect of the head-angles, that this pull in the direction of transcendence does not disturb the balance of the whole. It is interesting that Blake has America play the role of *voluptas*, and not inconsistent with his political sympathies and myth of history, but I analyze the picture here primarily to demonstrate Blake's awareness of the principles and philosophy underlying a sophisticated technique of compositional balance.

The technique, together with its philosophical implication of harmony within transcendence, can be applied to other motifs than the Three Graces, and Edgar Wind's book is largely devoted to demonstrating just this. Important cases in point are the popular Renaissance depictions of Venus subduing Mars (Wind, pp. 89–96), which are not at all simple cases of unlikes canceling each other, but complex instances of *discordia concors*, based upon profound awareness of Venus' own threatening and martial qualities and upon the relationship between love and contrariness itself. Savanarola had medals struck for himself illustrating the argument—and it is very similar to the argument of the Three Graces —in a theological context: "The wrathful symbol of the God of vengeance whose sword or dagger hovers over the earth is not only contrasted ... with the burning love of the winged dove rising to heaven, but these are the contrary aspects of one deity: the God of vengeance is the God of love. His justice is mercy, His anger pity; His punishment itself is sent as a blessing because it purges the soul of sin" (Wind, p. 95). Expressed this way, it is easy to understand that Blake might have had misgivings about applying such a doctrine to his own pastoralism.

But the fiction of the reconciliation of Mars and Venus, in which they lie down together, has its obvious affinities with pastoralism, and would have been regarded as a version of pastoral by a contemporary. Wind cites an analogous version in the background of Titian's (probably misnamed) *Sacred and Profane Love* (also a version of the Graces):

> In the background of Titian's painting, the landscape is animated by little idyllic scenes which echo ... the theme of the *misteri amorosi*. A pair of rabbits, animals sacred to Venus (but not necessarily profane since they also attend the Madonna), relieve the heroic image of the castle on the left which is approached by a knight on horseback. In front of the lake, two riders with dogs are hunting a hare; a shepherd guards a herd of sheep; and near the edge of the painting a pair of rustic lovers engage in a passionate embrace. These three episodes, so loosely juxtaposed as if they were freely improvised and unconnected, yet carry a suggestion of three phases of life which, if they were expressed in terms of Greek mythology, would be governed by three gods—Diana the chaste huntress, Hermes the shepherd, and Venus the goddess of love. That the peaceful shepherd is placed in the centre, separating the hunters from the lovers, gives a sense of the benign protective power which mediates between passion and chastity.   (Wind, pp. 150–151)

This, Wind reminds us, is the "language of pastoral elegy" (p. 151), and, whatever the differences—which I shall insist upon— mediation between chastity and passion is not far removed from the Lyca poems, which rely so heavily upon the romance archetype Spenser uses in the *Faerie Queene*, the encounter between lion and virgin.

Edgar Wind's pictorial examples are repeated here not for the sake of thematic resemblance or distinction, but to suggest the pictorial vocabulary of Blake's magnificent third plate for the Lyca poems (see Fig. 8), a plate which, deeply informed by the language of neoplatonic pictorial conventions, deliberately seeks to criticize and parody that language. In the picture we can see echoes of all the pictorial motifs Edgar Wind discusses. Overlooking the children for a moment, we can recognize in the grouping of the three "principal" figures—the reclining nude in the foreground with her back to us, the animal reclining by her side and looking backward over its shoulder, and the lion reclining under the tree facing the viewer—a potential triadic argument, presumably on the subject of love, after the pattern of the Three Graces. Having made the suggestion, one immediately wants to overload it with observations and qualifications, but most of these must wait. Still, it ought to be pointed out immediately that the three pro-tagonists of Blake's etching suggest a circle, running in a clockwise direction (following the direction of the faces), more than the complex interdependence of the Graces. I will argue that this difference is deliberate on Blake's part and close to the heart of his meaning.

On the other hand, there is a balance to the picture suggestive of the asymmetrical harmony of the Graces; the picture is heavily weighted to the right by the two massive, intertwined treetrunks of vegetable love (a union of strength and equal parts), but some effort is made to redress the balance on the left by presenting full-length side views of both the other protagonists (and the left side, too, has two children as against one on the right), while the lion on the right faces forward, presenting a narrower view of himself. The evident suggestion of circularity, however, would leave its mark on any argument trying to balance the picture in terms of minute particulars or to identify the protagonists in terms of the Three Graces. The reclining nude would seem to be a likely candidate for *pulchritudo*, yet she is facing away from us, a position usually associated with *amor*. If the function of the lion beneath the tree(s) is analogous to that of the lion in "Night," a representation of the reconciling fiction of pastoralism, the lion could surely be *amor* also, but its position relative to the other two protagonists, balanced by them but drawing them in his direction, is suggestive of *voluptas*. The case of the third protagon-ist is even more difficult, because we have the problem of its ambiguous relationships to both nude and lion.

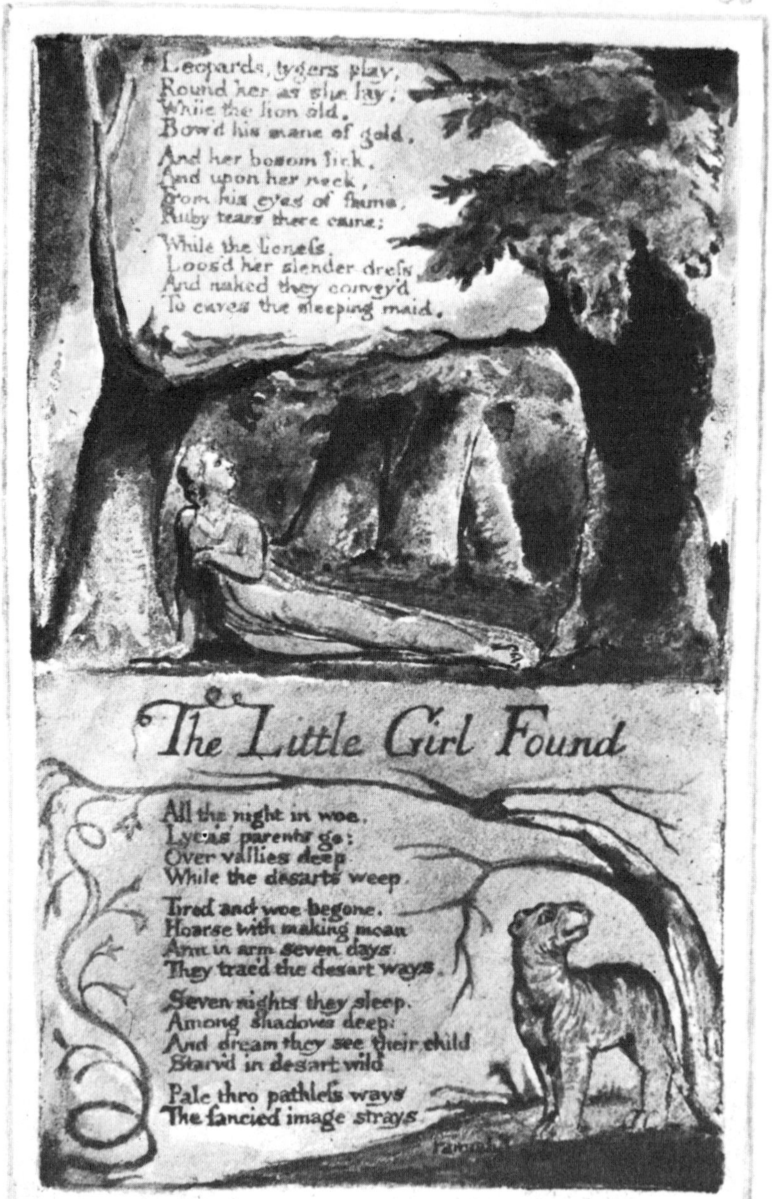

7. "The Little Girl Lost & Found," second plate

Famish'd weeping weak
With hollow piteous shriek

Rising from unrest,
The trembling woman prest
With feet of weary woe;
She could no further go

In his arms he bore,
Her arm'd with sorrow sore;
Till before their way,
A couching lion lay.

Turning back was vain,
Soon his heavy mane,
Bore them to the ground;
Then he stalk'd around.

Smelling to his prey,
But their fears allay,
When he licks their hands;
And silent by them stands.

They look upon his eyes
Fill'd with deep surprise:
And wondering behold,
A Spirit arm'd in gold.

On his head a crown,
On his shoulders down,
Flow'd his golden hair.
Gone was all their care.

Follow me he said,
Weep not for the maid;
In my palace deep,
Lyca lies asleep.

Then they followed,
Where the vision led:
And saw their sleeping child,
Among tygers wild.

To this day they dwell
In a lonely dell
Nor fear the wolvish howl,
Nor the lions growl.

8. "The Little Girl Lost & Found," third plate

But there are enough puzzles about the picture that we need not be bound by these. Another pictorial analogue, as I have suggested, is to the representations of Mars and Venus reconciled, in which case the lion plays the part of Mars and the reclining nude Venus, a role well suited to her depiction. This analogue has the advantage of explaining the presence of the children, for it is traditional in paintings of this motif to represent Venus' cherubs playing with the armor of Mars (Wind includes three examples among his plates which show this, by Botticelli, Piero di Cosimo, and Veronese: see his plates 74–76). Further, by applying a little ingenuity, we can dispose of the problem of the extraneous (for this analogue) other animal without putting an inordinate strain on the analogy. For we can identify this animal as one of the weapons of Mars or of Venus. One of the concerns of the neoplatonists was to demonstrate the *fortezza* of the goddess by portraying her with weapons as *Venus armata*. The fact that the other animal is so ambiguously depicted that we cannot be sure whether it is lion or tyger, that is, whether to associate it with Venus or Mars, only underlines the traditional conceit by which the devastations of Mars and Venus were identified.

Wind's third analogue had to do with pastoral mediation between chastity and passion; a mere glance at the etching in question, with all its odd suggestions of innocent idyll and imminent death, will suggest that this theme is close to the heart of the Lyca poems. Just as clearly, an intelligent approach to the theme will depend on greater accuracy in identifying the protagonists of the picture and their relationship than has yet been achieved here. If we remember not to define chastity narrowly (and for the neoplatonists *castitas* could play the part of *amor* among the Graces: Wind, pp. 77–79), and that its "hidden strength" over beasts is celebrated both by Milton and by Spenser, it will seem that the nude in the foreground has not been killed, or sexually "lost," but rather that she is sleeping, and sexually "found." But truly to understand the lady's passion—and what she has suffered—we must know whom she lies with; the identity of the etching's "other" animal hence becomes crucial. And it is on this point that Blake means to deprive us of certainty. In fact, we cannot even be certain of the sex of the beast. If it is a lion, then it might be female, and the "wife" of the other lion. But if it is a tyger, it may be male, and the mate, symbolically represented, of the nude. We need first, perhaps, to rehearse some of the facts about Experience and Innocence which this ambiguous creature recalls. The lion of Innocence, we said, represented a successful sexual union, and the conscious maintenance of a pastoral fiction wherein the Prolific lies down with the Devourer. The theme of union is certainly suggested by the trees over the proper lion's head, and there is nothing about the iconography to discourage our reading the other creature as his wife, especially as its head is turned attentively in his direction. Further, even without bringing the nude figure into the question, one could argue that both aspects of the theme of "Night" are illustrated because the children playing safely on the female lion's back are themselves of opposite sex, and the generous and cooperative gesture of the boy helping up the girl repeats the theme of Innocence through sexual harmony.

At least in the Rosenwald copy, however, there is good visual evidence that the "other animal" is a tyger. The creature on Blake's third plate (Fig. 8) is obviously the same creature who appears on the lower half of the second plate (see Fig. 7)—the identical facial expression and angle of the head enforce the resemblance—and the tygerishness of the latter is supported by very distinct stripes. Further, there is a distinct resemblance between the creature and Blake's etching for "The Tyger," with this important difference: that in the latter instance, the animal faces out from the dead tree which surmounts him, while on the second Lyca plate his head looks back over his shoulder at the tree. It will be remembered that this retrospective posture appears again in the third plate, where its object seems to be either the lion "husband" (if that's what he is) or the entwined trees representing sexual Generation overhead. The etching of "The Tyger," like the hesitant questions of that poem's speaker, suggests perhaps at least the possibility of passion transcending the condition of Generation, the Female Will; in the Lyca poems, the beast's eyes are fixed upon one or another emblem of that condition.

That the question of transcendence versus the sexualized condition (or Female Will) is the fundamental subject of the two poems is strongly hinted at by the first etching, where a loving couple stand beneath the ribs of a stylized tree of Generation gesturing from an embrace toward the bird of paradise floating above the tree. And since the Female Will is not a condition limited to biological females, it is not surprising that Blake should embody the ambiguities of sexualized existence in an androgynous creature. It will be recalled that the tyger in his own poem carried mythological suggestions of both sexes. As Los's son, Orc, he was masculine in gender; as seductive Enitharmon, he suggested the female. If we look again at the second Lyca plate, there is another instance of bisexualism. The plate is divided into two halves, the juncture between them coinciding with the conclusion of "Lost" and the beginning of "Found." As is so often the case in the illustrations to the *Songs*, Blake is juxtaposing here two views, or "visions," of the same scene. The upper picture, depicting the substance of Lyca's "sleep," or introduction into a sexualized Generation, shows a figure reclining beneath trees in a deep and thick *selva oscura*. The figure is clothed, almost shrouded, in a full-length gown, and presumably is another view of the nude of the third plate. But its more important parallel is to the tyger depicted immediately beneath, under the dead tree of Experience. One can see that there is no easy association of the pictures with Innocence and Experience, respectively, because both depict the individual "fallen" into the condition of Generation, or the Female Will. Both pictures seem informed by consciousness of the condition they describe, for the figure beneath the trees in the upper picture is watchful, even apprehensive; but the vocabulary of the lower illustration is drawn from the higher order of vision known as Beulah. And just as the animal there is "tyger" to the superficial gaze, yet possibly not upon closer inspection, so the figure beneath the trees on the upper half of the plate is clearly female to the casual eye, but seems increasingly androgynous on closer inspection.

An idea of the poem's three plates as triptych is gradually developing, but the sequence of illustrations moves linearly ever more deeply into the enveloping complexities and contradictions of the sexual condition. The pure, lyrical gesture of aspiration and desire in the first illustration is translated into the complex language of Blake's pastoralism in the second. The third illustration (which poses as mediating fiction) actually involves the on-looker in a bewildering maze of Nature. It is customary in pastoralism for complexity to lead to more subtle harmony, but in the Lyca poems it leads to a more complex idea of defeat—which is one way of explaining why Blake moved the poems from Innocence to Experience.

Before threading the maze, however, we need to observe in Blake's third plate two illuminating allusions to other drawings. The first is the motif of the two infants cooperating in riding the back of the "other animal." I have already discussed some of the implications of this motif, but have yet to point out that Blake uses it in two other locations: on the last plate of *The Book of Thel*, and on plate 11 of *America*.[72] The allusion is illuminating, for in *Thel* and *America* the children ride an enormous bridled serpent, representative of fallen Nature and Sexuality. Riding may represent mastery and the reversal of the process of the Fall as described in *Europe*: "Thought chang'd the infinite to a serpent" (E62). In the Lyca plate Blake alludes to this, and by emphasizing the sex of the two children (which is not apparent in *Thel* or *America*) makes the method of mastery perfectly clear. But in the prophetic versions of this motif the two children ride behind a distinctly older, female child who actually maintains the bridle in the serpent's mouth, and it is interesting to ask what happens in the Lyca treatment to this girl. Is she—a likely proposition— Lyca herself, and does the left-hand side of the third Lyca plate therefore represent a complete "version" of the *Thel-America* motif? What, then, of the right-hand side of the picture, and the child there? That child appears to be a boy, though one would be hard-pressed to say for sure. The female child mounting the tyger behind her brother appears to be quite a lot taller than he is. Has Blake simply changed the order of the three children, moving the older girl-child into the (*Thel-America*) subordinate grouping, and taking one of the younger boy-children off the back of the tyger to snuggle against the lion? If so, we can see in the Lyca plate a complex restatement of the illustration to "The Fly": the child snuggled against the lion's breast is analogous to the motif of mother-and-child; the older girl is joining, in mastery of the serpent-tyger, the game of sexual shuttlecock. Of course in the Lyca version, as befits its original setting in Innocence, there are emphatic differences from the depiction in "The Fly." Instead of brooding mother, we have the sexually more neutral and much more optimistic image of the lion; instead of Lyca ominously waiting, the boy on the tyger's back is happily taking the sexual initiative.

There is yet one other important visual allusion, this one relative to the third child of the Lyca plate, the one snuggling up to the lion. The child's gesture is one of innocent affection, yet it is qualified, rendered slightly pathetic, by the all-knowing, rather complacent expression of the lion. In the child's snuggle there is something wistful, almost loverlike. It will be remembered that in "Spring" a child played with a lamb, and we worried about the position of its hands at the animal's throat. Here we have in a sense a reversal of that position; it is the animal who is in the superior position, and the confidential gesture of the child keeps alive in our minds the potential threat. This point is underlined when we compare the illustration to plate 28 of *Jerusalem*. This plate, the source of much passionate critical and bibliographical effort, is a representation of the human situation as a giant lily; on the petals of the flower two figures embrace, variously identified, but probably Albion and Vala.[73] The plate is a complex image of man's fall into Generation; in early versions it is clear that Albion is copulating with Vala, who has thrown a net over his head. Blake later made the plate less sexually explicit, and in doing so duplicated in the left-hand figure of the two embracing exactly the sidesaddle embrace with which the child approaches the lion in the Lyca plate. Even the position of the child's hand corresponds to Albion's hand in the *Jerusalem* plate. The Lyca image, therefore, which most clearly and distinctly denotes the pastoral paradise where lion lies down with lamb, includes recondite references to the Fall, to Nature and the sexual condition, to the constant round of danger, generation, and death.

The language here is sophisticated, even learned, but it is worth insisting that the truth to which it attests owes very little to Italian neoplatonism, despite Blake's awareness of Renaissance motifs, and that there is nothing in the Lyca poems for which Blake would have needed to go to Porphyry; for his reading would have discovered all the complexity of the Lyca series in the immediate source of the poem's general theme, Book 1 of the *Faerie Queene*.

In Book 1, canto 1 of Spenser's poem, Archimago makes a two-fold sexual attack on the Red Crosse Knight's steadfastness. While the knight sleeps, a specially instructed dream from the house of Morpheus is brought him, inspiring him with lust and leading him to imagine that Una, "chastest flowre, that ay did spring / On earthly braunch, the daughter of a king" (1.1.48.4–5) was offering his lust her person. Readers of Edgar Wind's remark concerning pastoral mediation between passion and chastity will not be surprised that the false offer takes the form of falschood most suited to its purpose, the imagery of epithalamion:

> And eke the *Graces* seemed all to sing,
>   *Hymen io Hymen*, dauncing all around,
> Whilst freshest *Flora* her with Yuie girlond crownd.
>
> (1.1.48.7–9)

We have seen all of this, most recently the Graces, before. It is especially interesting to notice a connection which the false Una makes in her offer between sexuality and the need for protection: "Your owne deare sake forst me at first to leaue/My Fathers kingdome, There she stopt with teares" (1.1.52.1–2). Her statement of the connection barely stops short of lapsarian implication, and it is no wonder the knight is left "musing," but he returns to sleep and dreams of "bowres, and beds, and Ladies deare delight" (1.1.55.7).

However, survival of this onslought paradoxically makes him vulnerable to a second, which is a vision of his same Una, his own chastity having been found proof, happily copulating "In wanton lust and lewd embracement" (1.2.5.5) with someone else. What Luvah cannot accomplish, Urizen can; the knight "burnt with gealous fire" (1.2.5.6), and at dawn, the same rosy sort which Blake associates with the Fall, he departs. There ensues the game of lost and found, with all its sexual connotations intact, which underlies the Lyca poems. For Blake the rules of this game would be inextricably bound to two observations regarding the foregoing episode: the relation between sexuality, protection, and authority on the one hand; and the relationship between the knight's capacity for jealousy and his receptiveness to the lascivious dreams sent him on the other. If these observations seem unusual constructions of Spenser, one may recall Blake's remark about the Bible: "thou readst black where I read white" (E516).

On the basis of the foregoing we can make a kind of Blakean sense of Spenser's Una and the lion and apply it to the Lyca poems. The knight's initial reaction to the lady's supposed unchastity was "hasty heat": "He thought haue slaine her in his fierce despight" (1.1.50.3–4). I have already suggested a connection between this heat and the sexuality which would have seemed to Blake utterly fallen; it is not beyond the realm of possibility, then, and in fact there is ample license for this reading in Spenser's text, that the archetypal encounter between lion and virgin is a Song of Innocence founded upon and referring to Experience in canto 1; that is, the encounter represents a pastoral fiction, mediating between chastity and passion, in which dependent virgin and her devouring lion lie down together, each without losing his essential identity. Purity in this fiction is unassailable.

But there is inherent in Spenser's version of pastoral exactly the problem of pastoral transcendence which is what Experience and the Lyca illustrations are about, the fact that the language of dream is bound to define and tends to reinforce Experience in Generation. Spenser's linguistic indication of the case is very comprehensive;

Una's mastered master, her lion, is identified as her lover, her lord, and her God:

> The Lyon Lord of euerie beast in field,
>   Quoth she, his princely puissance doth abate,
>   And mightie proud to humble weake does yield,
>   Forgetfull of the hungry rage, which late
>   Him prickt, in pittie of my sad estate:
>   But he my Lyon, and my noble Lord,
>   How does he find in cruell hart to hate
>   Her that him lou'd, and euer most adord,
> As the God of my life? why hath he me abhord?
>
> (1.3.7.1–9)

Other aspects of Spenser's scene which would have spoken eloquently to Blake now become apparent. It is of interest to Blakeans that the subdued lion "lickt her lilly hands with fawning tong" (1.3.6.2), and that the encounter between the two immediately produces both pity and a flood of tears:

> Whose yeelded pride and proud submission,
>   Still dreading death, when she had marked long,
>   Her hart gan melt in great compassion,
> And drizling teares did shed for pure affection.
>
> (1.3.6.6–9)

In a following stanza we are told that it is Una's pity which finally soothes the lion, and permits Una to go on "in close hart shutting vp her paine" (1.3.8.6), pain in this case referring not to her fear but to her hurt at the loss of faith of her other lion, her other lord. There is, in other words, a curious sense in which this pastoral scene changes nothing, but simply reconciles Una to the necessity and permanence of her condition. The pastoral response of Nature itself to Una's condition raises the question Blake raises by means of the weeping stars in "The Tyger": does the pathetic fallacy signal the triumph of the imagination over Nature, or submission to the Female Will? It is interesting that Spenser's invocation of the phenomenon here utilizes a word, "redounding," which Blake is very fond of:

> Redounding teares did choke th'end of her plaint,
>   Whuch softly ecchoed from the neighbour wood.
>
> (1.3.8.1–2)

Robert F. Gleckner argues in *The Piper and the Bard* that *Tiriel*, Blake's early, ambitious, and confusing attempt to define the nature of the tyrant-father, constitutes an attempt to incarnate

the essential nature of Experience.[74] Without subscribing to all
the details of Gleckner's analysis, it is interesting that in "The
Little Girl Found" we are told of Lyca's parents:

> In his arms he bore,
> Her arm'd with sorrow sore . . .
>
> (E22)

For this motif is repeated at the beginning of *Tiriel*, when the
aged tyrant appears at his sons' gates bearing their mother in his
arms (E273). The analogy is, however, destructive of the popular
notion that Experience was not clearly formulated—whatever the
confusions of *Tiriel*—as early as 1789, and of course the Lyca
poems were originally included with the *Songs of Innocence* of that
year. Why Blake moved the poems from Innocence to Experience
is a nice question. A nicer, perhaps, is why they were included
with Innocence in the first place.

The protagonist of the first Lyca poem is not the tyrant-father,
but Lyca herself, an embodiment of the Female Will. The probable etymology of her name from the Greek for "wolf" helps to
express Blake's translation, extremely ironic in view of his reliance
upon Spenser's story of Una and the lion, of the Female Will or
"Devourer" into the less explicit language of pastoralism. Blake
has decided, upon the basis of his analysis of Spenser, that Una
represents the Devourer rather than the Prolific. There is nothing
really so very iconoclastic about this; the point, in view of
Blake's mythology of history, is almost technical. Lyca is seven
summers old, that is, in her seventh annual cycle, because the
Lyca poems deal, like *Europe*, with the seventh "Eye," or Orc
cycle, of history, the period of European history beginning with
the coming of Jesus and ending with the consolidation of religious
error in the form of deism and "natural religion."[75] Important
aspects of this Female Will-dominated period of culture are the
courtly love tradition and worship of the Virgin. Once the historical provenance of the poems is clear, analysis of their detail
becomes a possibility, for the general progress of the two poems
is a very clear fictional reflection of Blake's assumptions about
the history of the period covered. "The Little Girl Lost" begins,
as the historical period began, with prophecy and the promise of
salvation:

> In futurity
> I prophetic see,
> That the earth from sleep,
> (Grave the sentence deep)

Shall arise and seek
For her maker meek:
And the desart wild
Become a garden mild.

(E20)

The poem continues with a vision of innocence pastorally maintained in the midst of sexuality. Blake is writing under great
pressure, and the "eyes of flame" of the lion barely stop short of
apocalyptic reminder of the flaming eyes of the Word of God in
Revelation 19:12 (whose other name, "Faithful and True," might
make us think of Una).

Nevertheless, the vision concluding "The Little Girl Lost,"
as the analysis of Spenser demonstrated, represents a triumph of
the Female Will. Lyca is, no doubt, the daughter of a king, and
while her parents have lost faith in her the kingly lion appears,
closely paralleling the situation in the *Faerie Queene*:

The kingly lion stood
And the virgin view'd,
Then he gambold round
O'er the hallowd ground:

Leopards, tygers play,
Round her as she lay;
While the lion old,
Bow'd his mane of gold.

(E21)

Before examining this and its consequences further, the reader
must be reminded that between the prophecy at the beginning
of the poem and Lyca's adventure intervenes an alteration in
point of view. The prophecy is cast in the first person, and it
has been reasonable of critics, especially because of the probable
pun on "Grave the sentence deep," to think of the speaker of
these lines as Blake himself. Yet the fiction of Lyca is objectively
narrated throughout in a legendary style suited to a child's ballad;
the effect is extremely impersonal. This alteration of style is important, for it enables Blake to conceal what he knows, and we are
learning, about Lyca even as he tells her story. He conceals what
he knows because he participates in Lyca's story, initially at least,
as a fiction of Innocence. I think this is a point of great importance.
We can attach it, if we will, to Blake's affection for his master,
Spenser, or, more generally, to his large and noble emotional
capacities. Or we can attribute it to formal necessity, Blake's

genre requiring that pastoral ignorance which can mediate so well between love and irony.

Lyca's pastoral dream is a sexual fiction of Beulah. She is lying in her paradise already in the beginning of the poem, awaiting the sleep which represents sexuality and the moon of idealized vision. If her parents represent at this point not quite the tyrants of *Tiriel*, Tiriel and Myratana, "The Little Girl Lost" is nevertheless interested in the relationship between authority and corruption. Lyca's declaration of independence from her parents represents not an attempt to escape from the Female Will, but an attempt to make it good in Generation. It is the mother, who will not sleep while her daughter is away, who turns the daughter's garden into a desert in her imagination. Lyca herself is interested in realizing the garden of prophecy, and in Generation the only way to do this is to drive a wedge between the generations. The only way to achieve Innocence is to divide the consciousness which would chain one to sin. In this poem the divided consciousness is symbolized by the quotidian divisions of dark and light: day and night—emblematic of an existence half fallen—divide the generations and suggest the form of a fallen Nature. The mother must sleep while Lyca is awake, and vice versa:

> If her heart does ake,
> Then let Lyca wake;
> If my mother sleep,
> Lyca shall not weep.
>
> Frowning frowning night,
> O'er this desart bright,
> Let thy moon arise,
> While I close my eyes.

(E20)

The generations can never lie down together so long as Innocence and Experience are states of mind founded upon passion and sacrifice. As Lyca's terminology makes clear, from Experience's point of view waking means weeping, and it is no wonder, therefore, she prefers to sleep.

At this point we can begin to sketch the poems' historical reference, and at this point a parallel to *Tiriel* is important, for in that poem the aged tyrant makes an attempt, which proves abortive, to return to the "innocence" of his childhood, a false idea of innocence, really, which amounts to a vision of childish and totally dependent acceptance of things-as-they-are.[76] This is precisely what is attempted by Lyca's parents in "The Little Girl Found," a point which will lead us to the conclusion that they, rather than Lyca herself, represent the Female Will in this second poem. They follow Lyca through the desert they imagine for her seven days and seven nights, for the full period of their epoch. And they suffer dreadfully, just as Urizen, in a parallel event, suffers as he searches the full extent of his den. In the end they subvert Lyca's dream of Innocence, making out of her divided consciousness an image of necessity. They abstract from the complexities of her fiction the necessity for learning to live with tygers:

> Then they followed,
> Where the vision led:
> And saw their sleeping child,
> Among tygers wild.
>
> To this day they dwell
> In a lonely dell
> Nor fear the wolvish howl,
> Nor the lions growl.

(E22)

The reference to the historical present in the last stanza is very clear, but the interpretation of that history needs clarification. The tyger, as we learned in the poem devoted solely to it, may mean different things to different points of view. To the innocent female it means self-fulfillment, an experience which one cannot simply avoid, for the tyger avoided pursues and lies in wait for one and eventually, as Henry James understood, does one to death. But the prophetic point of view cannot be brought to accept the tyger, for that is to succumb to the Female Will and to give up prophecy in favor of things-as-they-are. This is what happens to the parents in the poem. Experience recognizes the fallen vision paradoxically implied by the pastoral fiction, Lyca sleeping beside her lion. The parents are deists in that they argue by the design of what they see: having learned to live among tygers, they cease to fear them. They live apart, apparently even from their daughter, but no doubt in their loneliness the absence of fear is some consolation. "The Little Girl Found" is, among other things, a richly comic satire of the "enlightened" outlook.

  Now that the two poems have been examined, Blake's astonishing translation of his meaning into visual terms, especially in the third plate (Fig. 8), can be fully appreciated. We see Lyca simultaneously in Beulah and in Generation, and all contradictions of her position are recorded in Blake's visual allegory. Even the pastoral dream, and this is an important insight into the nature of Experience, cannot escape the ground of its conception, and so simply runs in visual circles, futilely trying to escape or transcend itself. The eye has no refuge in Blake's picture—every pretty resting place has its own obscure but expressive suggestion of danger or corruption. The reader of the picture, like those trapped in the Orc cycle, has no ideal alternative but to read on.

Blake's decision to move the poems from their original place to Experience has its rationale in the foregoing, but I believe his decision reflects not increasing moral severity, but increasing imaginative pressure on the impulse to transcend without, like Lyca's parents, becoming trapped in the immanent. What moves us finally about the *Songs of Innocence and of Experience* is their devotion, equally passionate, to art and to truth.

PART II

The Descent into Night

TRANSFORMATIONS

When Blake wrote in "Night":

> The sun descending in the west
> The evening star does shine.
> The birds are silent in their nest,
> And I must seek for mine,
> The moon like a flower,
> In heavens high bower;
> With silent delight,
> Sits and smiles on the night,

> (E13)

he was very likely thinking of one particular evening in Milton's
Paradise Lost:

> *Hesperus* that led
> The starrie Host, rose brightest, till the Moon
> Rising in clouded Majestie, at length
> Apparent Queen unvaild her peerless light,
> And ore the dark her Silver Mantle threw.
>   When *Adam* thus to *Eve*: Fair Consort, th'hour
> Of night, and all things now retir'd to rest
> Mind us of like repose....

> (IV.605–612)

This is interesting for a number of reasons, only the least important of which is confirmation of the suspicion that "Night" is

about sexual experience; once retired, our first parents waste no time:

> ... other Rites
> Observing none, but adoration pure
> Which God likes best, into thir inmost bower
> Handed they went; and eas'd the putting off
> These troublesom disguises which wee wear,
> Strait side by side were laid, nor turnd I weene
> *Adam* from his fair Spouse, nor *Eve* the Rites
> Mysterious of connubial Love refus'd.
>
> (IV.736–743)

What must have interested Blake about this particular night is that, however simplified the rites, there were enough wedding meats to attract one important uninvited guest. The high wall of Paradise is only a single bound to Satan, who enters like a "prowling Wolfe" (183) "into Gods Fould" (192), and seeing immediately that sexuality is the very essence of Eden ("Imparadis't in one anothers arms"; 506), waits patiently to poison with the seeds of the Fall the aftermath of Eve's connubial rites. Milton's angels find Satan

> Squat like a Toad, close at the eare of *Eve*;
> Assaying by his Devilish art to reach
> The Organs of her Fancie.
>
> (IV.800–802)

Both Blake's night and Milton's have their guardian angels in residence, but beyond this depart from each other so radically that to discuss "Night" in terms of *Paradise Lost*, Book IV, is to pass beyond what we normally recognize as influence and allusion. Nothing could seem further from the dénouement of Blake's poem, with its lion and lamb recumbent together, than the sullenness of the drawn battle between Gabriel and Satan which ends Milton's book. That there does, nevertheless, seem to have been imaginative traffic between the two passages testifies to Blake's intense regard for Milton as well as to his determination to transform Milton to his own purposes.

The basis of the traffic is Blake's idea that Milton's Book IV propounds a "version" of the Fall, looked at from the sexual aspect. The feral animals who prowl the Garden would represent to Blake fallen sexuality and the fact that Man's undoing was as good as accomplished. Milton's lion *is* in fact Satan:

A Lion now he stalkes with fierie glare,
Then as a Tiger, who by chance hath spi'd
In some Purlieu two gentle Fawnes at play,
Strait couches close, then rising changes oft
His couchant watch, as one who chose his ground
Whence rushing he might surest seise them both.

(IV.402–407)

Blake would also have been interested in a remark which Satan's prey, Adam, makes while surveying his Paradise. Still "innocent," Adam notices prominently in the course of a hymn of praise to the Creator what he calls his "one easie prohibition" (433):

that onely Tree
Of Knowledge, planted by the Tree of Life,
So neer grows Death to Life.

(IV.423–425)

The remark would have seemed more than casual to Blake, who founds his ambiguous conceptions, Innocence and Experience, on awareness deeper than Adam's of how close to life grows death. With oncoming "Night," the connubial rites therein, and the insinuations of the toad, the gap will narrow to nothing; there will commence at the same moment the confluence of imageries shared by epithalamion and elegy.

Blake records some of these considerations in his poem:

I can lie down and sleep;
Or think on him who bore thy name.

(E14)

Both Lyca and Thel (and eventually Milton and Ololon) will want to lie down thus; Blake is associating sleep with fallen sexuality and entering the realm of death. But it is a bit startling to observe that the second line quoted associates contemplation of Christ's sacrifice with loss of innocence. The concluding lines of the poem may be no less subversive:

For wash'd in lifes river,
My bright mane for ever,
Shall shine like the gold,
As I guard o'er the fold.

(E14)

I have argued earlier that the speaker of "Night" undergoes a metamorphosis, his voice merging with and becoming identical to that of the lion at the end. In terms of the Miltonic analogues, this suggests that Adam in "Night" becomes identified in some sense with Satan. We could translate this suggestion simply: Adam is infected by Satan, he falls. But the lion's vision at the end of "Night" seems positive—unless terribly qualified by its appearance in a consciously maintained fiction—and this means that entrance into Generation, to be "wash'd in lifes river," is positive also. To contemplate a Satan who brings about the Fall and who also brings golden light to a fallen world is to penetrate deeply Blake's developed mythology and his reading of Milton. Blake's mythological figure who embodies aspects of both Adam and Satan is Los (in the unfallen state, Urthona). My reading of these facts will carry us eventually through *Jerusalem*. Immediately it suggests the complexity of Blake's attitude toward Generation.

In Night I of the *Vala/The Four Zoas* manuscript, Urizen (who bears some resemblance to the God of *Paradise Lost*) plans a division of the fallen world with Luvah (who bears some resemblance to Milton's Satan). The proposed division of the world between a god of repressive reason and a god of passionate energy and desire has an obvious bearing on the sexual division of Adam and Eve I have been discussing:

> Thou Luvah said the Prince of Light behold our sons & daughters
> Reposd on beds. let them sleep on. do thou alone depart
> Into thy wished Kingdom where in Majesty & Power
> We may erect a throne. deep in the North I place my lot
> Thou in the South listen attentive.
>
> (21.20–24; E307)

The lines recall Milton (see *Paradise Lost*, V. 666–693; compare IV. 782–783), and they suggest the situation in "Night." Urizen and Luvah are both willing to "smite this dark sleeper in his tent" (22.10), which recalls Satan at the ear of Eve, and when Urizen departs suddenly, as he does, he leaves the sleeper subject to "the rage of Luvah / To pour its fury on himself & on the Eternal Man" (22.36–37; E308). Urizen's defection suggests to David Erdman the Netherlands campaign of 1799,[1] but it might make us think of a Miltonic God whose protection of Adam and Eve is not as effective as it could be: Gabriel's angels arrive at the end of Book IV of *Paradise Lost* only after Satan has had a chance to deliver his message into the soft ear of Eve. How reasonable it is to think of this message in terms of the "rage of Luvah" can be seen in one of the principal metaphorical events of Blake's Night I (10.10–11.2; E301). In this metaphor Luvah assumes directly the role of Milton's Satan: rising from the heart to the brain of sleeping Humanity, he steals the horses of the Light and rises into the Chariot of Day (we recall that Lucifer is the "Son of Morn in weary Nights decline"; E266). Behind him, on Humanity's pillow, he leaves his emanation, Vala. Man's embrace of this emanation or accretion is equivalent to his Fall into what Blake calls Generation. As we shall see, these terms are more Miltonic than they sound.

The magnificent epic poem which Blake never brought to a final, publishable form was to have been called *Vala*, and it will seem logical therefore to associate the development or evolution of that manuscript, and the mental struggles to which it bears eloquent testimony, with Blake's attitude toward Generation. But if the foregoing discussion of "Night" and *Paradise Lost* points in the direction of Vala, I hope it will also have been seen to point to something even more important, the collision in Blake's imagination of Milton and the idea of transformation. For purposes of discussion it will often be necessary to deal with these two problems separately, but it cannot be emphasized enough that my purpose is to demonstrate neither that Blake is Milton in disguise nor that he is Proteus. Blake said that "Milton lov'd me in childhood & shew'd me his face" (E680), but it is Milton's conceptual importance in the development of Blake's mythology which is of concern here. That importance expresses itself through the astonishing range of transformations and metamorphoses undergone by Milton at Blake's hands (while still remaining recognizably Milton), but the controlling principle of these changes is neither influence nor Blake's astonishing agility, but what I have been calling the idea of pastoral.

I am saying, then, that having observed pastoralism to be alive and well in the *Songs*, largely with the help of Spenser, I am interested now in demonstrating its conceptual importance and developmental role in the longer poems, largely with the help of Milton. But there is a less simple, and I think more important, aspect to this.

As intensive work on Blake continues, it becomes increasingly evident how central and common to all approaches is the idea of transformation. On this common ground meet ways of reading Blake as different from each other (though not necessarily opposed) as Kathleen Raine's and David Erdman's. To read either critic is to observe the rich sea changes undergone in the pages of Blake by, say, Persephone or George III. Whether or not we want to accept a given reading ought to give way eventually to a concern for the principle of transformation itself. Northrop Frye remarks: "As I continued to work on Blake, it became inescapably clear that the kind of thinking the Prophecies displayed was normal and typical poetic thinking."[2] If we apply to the idea of Blake's imagination as a sort of universally effective transformation system Frye's idea of typicality, or normality, we come up with an idea of the poet as one who can include in his poem the whole universe of allusion. And in fact Frye, if we can trust his own genealogy for the *Anatomy of Criticism* as by Blake out of Spenser, seems to have gone on from his study of Blake, probably the best we are ever likely to have, to the idea of literature itself as a total, systematic body—the ultimate body of allusion for the ultimately allusive poet (Frye, *Anatomy*, p. vii).

The danger to this approach is that the quest for the poet's field of allusion may carry us ever further from a sense of his preferences and purposes. Frye has developed a concept of mythological *displacement* which we can use to expose this problem. Displacement is defined as "the adaptation of myth and metaphor to canons of morality or plausibility" (Frye, *Anatomy*, p. 365). Frye seems to suppose "that there is such a thing as a pure myth (archetype) the displacements of which can be traced through history."[3] The difficulty with Blake, given his universality, or archetypal quality, is to define or even identify his modes of displacement. For example, Morton Paley has recently demonstrated two instances, the illustrations to Edward Young's *Night Thoughts* and the historical apotheoses of Pitt and Nelson presented in his 1809 exhibition, where Blake's consciousness, or lack of consciousness, of displacement can be very troubling.[4] His technique in the former instance is *tacitly* to undermine Young's meaning by translating the *Night Thoughts* into a system of visual symbols the meaning of which, once understood, can be seen as a consistent attack on the values of the poem being "illustrated." The effect here is of a kind of ironic counterpoint. We have seen him doing something very similar in the *Songs of Innocence*, loading an ostensibly idyllic scene with covert reminders of physical horror. We can see him practicing similar sleight of hand in his illustrations to Ambrose Philips' imitation of Virgil, and have to contemplate his apparent willingness to accept without correction the lyric enthusiasms of Samuel Palmer—Palmer called the illustrations in his notebook "little dells, and nooks, and corners of Paradise"—despite the fact that Palmer's enthusiasms have very little if anything to do with the illustrations Blake achieved.⁵ In the case of the historical apotheoses, Blake's apparent unwillingness to descend to displacement accounts not only for the paintings themselves but as well for catalogue descriptions of them which come close to being deliberately misleading. At any rate, nothing like the "meaning" of the paintings has been publicly apparent until, thanks to the efforts of Mark Schorer, David Erdman, and Morton Paley, recent times.⁶

However, to speak of "meaning" in this connection is to beg large questions. Blake has Los say in *Jerusalem*:

Thou art in Error; trouble me not with thy righteousness.
I have innocence to defend and ignorance to instruct:
I have no time for seeming; and little arts of compliment,
In morality and virtue: in self-glorying and pride.
                                        (42.25–28; E187)

What I have been referring to as "displacement" may have seemed simply "seeming" to Blake; we must remember, moreover, that the illustrations to *Innocence* and to Philips' Virgil imitation, the *Night Thoughts* drawings and the historical apotheoses are all very much *there* for us to see. The artist himself was hardly to blame that so few have chosen to look, and there is something perverse about applying the word "tacit" to Blake's most extensive series of related paintings (the *Night Thoughts* set), 537 watercolors in all.

Nevertheless, we approach here a central problem of Blake's place in recent criticism. Geoffrey Hartman has attacked Frye's conception of displacement, arguing "not that myth is displaced but that it is historical," and that "it comes to us institutionalized from the beginning." Hartman feels that "to Frye's total myth we must therefore add a historical account of the war that myth has waged with myth." Further: "What is true of the realist is true of any writer, as Frye's own theory of displacement has shown: reality is never more than the *plausible* artifice. But in that case the notion of displacement becomes unnecessary except to indicate the direction of human credibility—credibility defining that realm in which contraries are no longer felt."⁷ Blake, as we know, was acutely conscious of the problem of plausibility:

Then I asked: does a firm perswasion that a thing is so, make it so?
He replied. All poets believe that it does ...   (E38)

Blake's awareness of the problem, and the peculiar fact that his imaginary interlocutor in this instance is the prophet Isaiah point

to an extremely high degree of historical self-consciousness. Just as
his meter is a systematically achieved function of his relationship
to the traditions of his time,[8] so his election of a prophetic function
for poetry represents similar self-consciousness to that of Thomas
Chatterton and James Macpherson. Similarly, Blake is often willing to forego "displacement" because of self-consciousness with
respect to the platitudinizing of his age. Blake's distrust of the
Augustan epigram, as John Hollander points out, was extreme:
"Epigrammatic tautology, for Blake, seems to be a kind of death."[9]
But this is the problem. Blake's creation of an alternative tradition,
of a plausibility more universally founded than that of the
Augustans, may seem to us part of his positive achievement, but
to literary history it has often destroyed all sense of his vulgar
relations and made him seem "an interruption in cultural history"
(Frye, *Fearful Symmetry*, p. 3). Blake lived in an age when the
percentage of displacement relative to original myth was very
high (as in *The Rape of the Lock*), and to reverse these proportions
was to suggest a close identification between displacement and
history itself: failure to embrace moral emotions in a sententious
time can seem the same thing as withdrawal from history. This
spurious identification has always haunted Blake criticism, and
every work which did not seem to have a definable relationship
to history (and there is much room for debate about the ones
which do) could be seen as a vacuum, drawing toward it biographical and historical information. It is no accident that Blake has
been more than usually victimized by biographical fantasists. And
even on the level of sense and sound scholarship, we can see the
danger in contemporary criticism. Kathleen Raine's criticism not
only seeks to discover meanings, but to provide a historical and
doctrinal home for the poet. Not for nothing is her major study of
Blake called *Blake and Tradition*. We can see traces of the same
problem in Erdman's criticism. David Erdman's services to Blake
scholarship are so manifold that no serious student can not be
grateful to him, and certainly his thesis that Blake's poems reflect
contemporary history is unassailable, but his anxiety to surround
each and every crux of Blake criticism with a solution based
upon responses to the progress of contemporary history needs to
be vigorously challenged. In the first edition of *Blake: Prophet
against Empire* (Princeton, N.J.: Princeton University Press, 1954)
Erdman went so far as to suggest that the *Vala/The Four Zoas*
manuscript went astray because Blake's thematic purposes were
extremely at variance with the current of history. Moreover, Blake
was attempting something *foolish*: "In *The Four Zoas* he seems to

have allowed his tune to be called by events unfolding as he
wrote. The result is as mad as the effort to play croquet in
Wonderland with living mallets and balls." My quotation comes
from the second, revised edition (1969) of Erdman's book (p. 294),
which acknowledges the very severe attack on his thesis by G. E.
Bentley, Jr., in his facsimile edition of the manuscript (Bentley
demonstrates that Erdman's approach to *The Four Zoas* is based
on inaccurate dating of the manuscript)[10] only by a footnote
appended to the passage quoted, beginning, "We cannot be sure."
Erdman's unwillingness to give in on this and many another point
relevant to *The Four Zoas* (see the discussion of Night VII(b)
below) seems in part a response to the poet's own self-conscious
and enormous repudiations, an act of painful and kind duty, like
Milton slapping flesh on the wasted frame of Urizen by the shore
of Arnon.

At any rate, we should now be in a position to see the relationship
between this question and the principle of transformation, for
even when the distance between Blake's lines and a historical
situation, or an element of what Miss Raine calls "the tradition,"
is great indeed, it is no greater than the distance between, say,
Blake and Young.

We cannot give up the transformations, for they are there. And I
do not mean to imply either that one can dispute either Miss Raine
or Mr. Erdman except on the basis of interpretations of specific
poems. But perhaps I have said enough to suggest that Geoffrey
Hartman is right in this critical instance, and that the "history"
we seek for Blake is the history of the war of myth against myth.
I believe we can find what we are looking for in the life-long
tension between Blake and Milton, but that does not mean that
Milton is Blake's myth (as Miss Raine might state this approach),
or that Milton is Blake's history—though this is much closer to the
truth. The shape of the conflict is determined by the idea of
pastoral; but it remains true that the principle of displacement in
Blake, the source at once of the world view accommodated to
Christian plausibility and of the tension with that view which gives
his work its relationship to "canons of morality," is—for the
duration of his poetical career anyway—Milton.

THE BOOK OF THEL

It will be useful at the outset to have some idea of where the
discussion is going, even if sense of direction is sometimes
achieved at the expense of statements for which justification will

only become clear as the argument develops. In addition to being useful, these remarks are necessary if we are to grasp the importance of *The Book of Thel*, dated 1789 (though David Erdman tells us the "Motto" and the last plate are "no earlier" than 1791; E713), which I take to be, for all its fragility, an important annunciation of Blake's thematic concerns. I do not mean to sound portentous here, but when we find even Northrop Frye falling into the trap reserved for so many critics by the apparent simplicity of the *Songs of Innocence*, arguing that "comment on so exquisite a poem" as *Thel* is justified only because Blake "pushed fragility so close to the line of the namby-pamby without crossing it" (*Fearful Symmetry*, p. 233), we may feel it is time to take the poem more seriously.

I hope in the first section of this study to have provided some reasons for regarding Blake's career as a type of the epic poet, following the advice of Virgil and warming up his pipes on pastorals. Further, if there is any sense to my suggestion that the themes appropriate to his pastorals are central to his imaginative and intellectual concerns, then we may expect to find an important pastoral element in his mature work. This is in fact so much the case that we can read right through Blake's career regarding him distinctly as pastoral or as epic poet. If we take the first alternative, we begin with *The Book of Thel* and end with *Milton*, the culmination of Blake's career as pastoralist. The second alternative entails beginning with the Lambeth prophecies, especially those probably intended to constitute "The Bible of Hell" (E43), and their consolidation in the *Vala/The Four Zoas* manuscript, and ending with *Jerusalem*. In rough and ready terms, then, pastoral is *Thel* to *Milton*; epic is *Vala* to *Jerusalem*.

It is reasonable to think of the first sequence as female and the second as male. Blake's pastoral realm is Beulah, a feminine and moony place where the Fall into Generation commences. It is "threefold," sexual, and associated with a mother's encircling arms (F. Z., 5.31–39; M., 30.1–7). Eden, a vision of which begins to appear on the uppermost level of consciousness at the end of *Jerusalem*, is "fourfold," above sexuality and Generation, the final visionary state into which men and women are gathered into One Man without the fallen distinctions and separations of sexuality:

> the Jewels of Light
> Heavenly Men beaming bright
> Appeard as One Man
> Who Complacent began

My limbs to infold
In his beams of bright gold
Like dross purgd away
All my mire & my clay
Soft consumd in delight
In his bosom Sun bright
I remaind.   (E684)

The term "male" applied to this state cannot, therefore, mean what it normally means, "exclusive of the female," and it is interesting that both *Vala* and *Jerusalem* are originally named after female emanations, and that both are concerned ultimately with closing the gap between man and his emanation: in the first instance healing or eliminating the veil of Generation, a process analogous to dropping the scales from the visionary eye; in the instance of *Jerusalem* separating the titular heroine from her involvement with Generation, revealing her true identity as man's liberty and the central city of paradise, and restoring her to her husband, Mankind. One can see that in this sense, despite the enormous formal differences, *Jerusalem* is a logical extension of *Vala*. One can also see that, since the great conceptual problem of Blake's version of pastoral is man's difficulty in passing through Generation, the veil of Vala, without succumbing to it, and since *Milton* deals with this problem in terms of the poet returning to Generation and accepting in a new spirit his female emanation, there is therefore no exlusive division between Blake's pastoral and epic poems so far as theme is concerned. This is of no great importance in terms of critical theory, but it is very important practically, for we will see Blake wrestling with a problem in the *Vala/The Four Zoas* manuscript, solving it in *Milton*, then restating it in *Jerusalem*.

There is another way of relating Blake's development to pastoralism. If we compare the emanations who constitute the themes of the poet's full-scale epics, we see that Jerusalem, the emanation of the Giant Albion (a "giant" in the formal sense, as Adam Kadmon of the Cabbala is a "giant form" of humanity) is less specialized in function than Vala. Vala stands for Generated Nature seen by mankind as a ground to be planted or a wife to be impregnated, the "not me" or "out there" which fallen vision fails to recognize as an emanation or projection of "me in here" and with which it falls in love, by which it is devoured. This implies that Vala is involved in the natural cycle (Blake's poem "The Mental Traveller," as Frye points out in "Notes for a

Commentary on *Milton*," details four distinct phases to this cycle corresponding to four avatars of Vala),[11] and this means that her husband, Luvah, likewise is never seen in Generation except spasmodically, as part of a cycle also. Luvah represents most generally Energy, which Blake defines as "Eternal Delight," but energy is never found without its "bound or outward circumference," which is Reason (E34). The "contraries" Reason and Energy coexist as two of the four eternal principles (or zoas) in Blake's idea of Eden, which is not at all static. Moreover, the two are "necessary to Human existence" (E34), which Blake does not distinguish from divine existence; in the history of fallen Generation they exist to one another in a progressive relationship, but it is never clear whether the progress is in the direction of Eden or simply toward repetition of cycles after biological models (See Appendix A, "A Note on the Orc Cycle"). The difference between the unfallen and fallen relationships between the principles is the result of attempted repression in Generation by Reason, a rationale for which Blake finds in Milton: "The history of this is written in Paradise Lost. & the Governor or Reason is call'd Messiah." He adds, "But in the Book of Job Miltons Messiah is call'd Satan" (E34). The remark about Milton is one which I will come back to so often that it need only be noted here. The immediate effect of repression is to drive energy underground into the forms of life (the subject of Night II of the *Vala/The Four Zoas* manuscript), whence it erupts periodically (as "Orc") with tremendous results. The pattern, commonly known as the "Orc cycle," suggests a biological cycle modeled after the relationship between Venus and Adonis (and indeed *Thel* begins with a reference to the "river of Adona"; 1.4; E3), presided over by a repressive Jove. Its most terrifying representation in Blake is his engraving 15 for the Book of Job.

When we get to Jerusalem, on the other hand, and discover that Los, the dominating figure of her poem, has an oblique but transcendent relationship to the Orc cycle, we may suspect that Blake has made the leap from Adonis to Orpheus discussed in the "Preliminaries," a suspicion strengthened when we realize that Jerusalem herself is not Nature but the Orphic aggregate of the emanations of "All Human Forms identified." It is logical to assume, therefore, that Blake's progress from the earlier to the later poem evokes consideration of pastoralism.

One more assertion of a general nature, and we will be in a position to talk about *Thel* itself. It has been suggested that there is a (not very convincing) distinction between Blake's epics and pastorals as to gender. When this notion was pursued, it became clear that we were dealing with two related aspects of the same Fall: one was repression (based upon the conflict between Energy and Reason, or Luvah and Urizen), and the other was sexual divisiveness, the separation between a subject and the object of his desire (his emanation). Eventually one comes to recognize a relationship between these two aspects of the Orc cycle and the conflict which crystallizes in the *Vala/The Four Zoas* manuscript as the "War of Urizen & Tharmas." When this conflict is first sketched for us on page 69 of the manuscript, it appears only as a statement of fallen reason's dependence upon the stuff of the world's body, something Lockean. But behind this there is something more ultimate: first, still on the fallen level, a struggle between repressive reason and the desire to dissolve into chaos; second, when we think of *unfallen* Urizen and Tharmas, a relationship between two ideals or dreams of God, one representing Right Reason and the other representing Wholeness. Tharmas represents the "combination of taste and touch" (Frye, *Fearful Symmetry*, pp. 280–281) which I suggested in the discussion of some of the *Songs* was associated with the unfallen senses; his deployment of them implies the restoration of a sexual paradise which includes the potential for an infinite amount of bringing-to-being without any of the implications of separation and death which fruition has in the fallen world. Tharmas is, moreover, a shepherd, and his realm is Beulah (see *Fearful Symmetry*, pp. 272–285). I will have something to say of the "war" later on (the phrase itself only begins to recur in Night the Eighth of *The Four Zoas*, which seems clearly to have been the last composed), but mention it here for a structural reason. Much of Blake's myth in the *Vala/The Four Zoas* manuscript can be seen as "framed" by the *emanations* of Tharmas and Urizen. That is, Night I of the poem (both the original and the "revised" versions: Nights I & II of the poem as Blake left it) ends with a lament over Generation by Enion, who is the emanation of Tharmas. As a result of the overhearing of this lamentation, Night III (originally Night II) ends with an echoing lamentation by Ahania, the emanation of Urizen, who thereafter follows Enion into the fallen world, to the limit of nonentity. This action completes the Fall, and produces what we know as the Deluge, the collapse into chaos. In Night VIII of the poem, not the last in order but the last to have been composed, we see the reverse of this process as the direction of the Fall itself begins to be reversed. First Ahania mourns Generation, and then Enion replies. Her reply, incidentally, is one of the most Orphic passages in Blake:

> As the Seed waits Eagerly watching for its flower & fruit
> Anxious its little soul looks out into the clear expanse
> To see if hungry winds are abroad with their invisible army
> So Man looks out in tree & herb & fish & bird & beast
> Collecting up the scatterd portions of his immortal body
> Into the Elemental forms of every thing that grows
> (110.3–8; E370)

Enion heals Ahania's despair, telling her,

> ... throughout the Universe whereever a grass grows
> Or a leaf buds The Eternal Man is seen is heard is felt
> And all his Sorrows till he reassumes his ancient bliss
> (110.26–28; E370)

and when we read her confession of past error:

> Once I waild desolate like thee my fallow fields in fear
> Cried to the Churchyards & the Earthworm came in dismal state
> (109.16–17; E369)

we realize that Enion here is a regenerate Thel. Her voice also bears comparison to that of the mature bard we hear in "Introduction" to *Experience* and in the Lyca poems:

> The starry floor
> The watry shore
> Is giv'n thee till the break of day.
>
> (E18)

Moreover, we hear in the complaint of her interlocutor, Ahania, the words of Oothoon, the heroine of *Visions of the Daughters of Albion*, dated 1793:

> Will you erect a lasting habitation in the mouldering Church
>   yard
> Or a pillar & palace of Eternity in the jaws of the hungry grave
> (108.11–12; E368–369; compare V.D.A., 5.41–6.1; E48)

Ahania describes sexuality in rather different terms from Enion's: "Awake the bridgegroom cometh I awoke to sleep no more" (109.21; E370).

In short, Thel is a prototype of Enion, and Oothoon, in *Visions*, a prototype of Ahania. I have already discussed why it would seem inevitable to Blake to conceive of pastoralism in terms of elegy and epithalamion. It remains only to suggest that *Thel* is an abortive elegy, and *Visions* an abortive epithalamion. The imagery they have in common is succinctly outlined in Ahania's remark quoted above.

In an early prose sketch, "The Couch of Death," in the *Poetical Sketches* (1783), a youth mourns his imminent death in tones which hang uneasily somewhere between Job and Ossian:

> My breath is loathsome, how should he not be offended? If I lay my face in the dust, the grave opens its mouth for me; if I lift up my head, sin covers me as a cloak! O my dear friends, pray ye for me! Stretch forth your hands, that my helper may come! (E432)

Blake is suggesting an equation between the condition of death and the youth's self-loathing. The mother, too, is infected:

> O my child, my child! is thy breath infected? So is mine. As the deer, wounded by the brooks of water, so the arrows of sin stick in my flesh; the poison hath entered into my marrow. (E433)

All ends well, though we are not told how or why. The youth wipes away his tears with "visionary hand" and at the last "breathes out his soul with joy into eternity" (E433). The sketch is jejune and best forgotten, but it contains some of the seeds of *Thel*.

More of the seeds, however, are to be found in the *Songs of Innocence and of Experience*. The illustrated title page of *Thel* shows a young shepherdess standing beneath the tree of generation. It is a young tree, but as Max Plowman points out, sadly bent.[12] Before her eyes the spirit of a flower is leaping joyously to sexual union with the spirit of another flower. Thel looks on sadly. The visual language of the poem is completely familiar to us, and since it is so obviously pastoral it is reasonable to expect from *Thel* an epitome of Blake's *Songs*. The language of flowers, as we have seen, is the language of sexual Experience; the language of the text,

Ah! gentle may I lay me down, and gentle rest my head.
And gentle sleep the sleep of death. and gentle hear the voice
Of him that walketh in the garden in the evening time,
(E3)

equates sexual experience, as Thel sees it, with the Fall. God walked in the Garden in the evening, so Genesis and Milton tell us, after Eve had brought death into the world, or perhaps only as Milton's Adam reassuringly remarks, "pains onely in Child-bearing" (*Paradise Lost*, X. 1051).

Most of Blake's critics make the error of talking about the poem in terms of two separate cosmological realms. Thel is con-emplating, we are told, the move from Beulah (according to Harold Bloom "a very beautiful but less than real world")[13] into Generation or Experience, a move that is inescapable in the fallen world. Having created this picture, the same critics are content to berate Thel for her cowardice in drawing back from the pains which await her, one sternly entitling his chapter on her "A Spiritual Failure."[14] It is true that Thel fails; that is what the Fall means.

It will be helpful with *Thel* if we forget cosmological models. The poem takes place in one "location": the difference between Beulah and Generation is one of outlook. Thel draws back in horror at the fallen outlook, but she cannot ultimately escape her glimpse of Experience *because* she creates it. That is, what she draws back from is a creation of her own vision. This is the central irony of the poem, one which has been unaccountably overlooked. It *is* impossible to evade Experience, and therefore Thel's de-murral is somewhat childish and futile, yet her childish and futile action is the one thing she does in the poem counter to the direction of the Fall. Lyca, we recall, only sleeps; she never wakes up in her poem. Thel may understand this.

The nature of *Thel* is one we can best appreciate via the pastoral ironies and ambiguities of the *Songs*. The second illustration to the Song of Innocence called "A Cradle Song" (see Fig. 4) shows a child, suggestive of the Christ-child, lying in a wicker cradle. The cradle is large enough for an adult, and the child is severely bound. We are puzzled by this until we realize that the cradle is also a sarcophagus and the swaddling also cerements.[15] Blake is being neither ironic nor morbid. He is concerned with two central ideas. The first is that the statement "one cannot avoid Experience" is itself an expression of the fallen outlook. The second is that we cannot *conceive* of avoiding Experience without falling into it; therefore the language by means of which we conceive Innocence is dependent upon Experience and tends to reinforce it. This means that whatever else the picture of Thel's world is like, it is not unreal. It cannot be. Thel withdraws at the end of the poem, but it is difficult to see this withdrawal unequivocally as rejection of saving vision, for the speech with which she rejects the house of Clay contains interesting insights into her condition: the valedictory of this "spiritual failure," were we to hear it from the lips, say, of Oothoon, might be interpreted as at least on the threshold of vision:

> Why cannot the Ear be closed to its own destruction?
> Or the glistning Eye to the poison of a smile!
> Why are Eyelids stord with arrows ready drawn,
> Where a thousand fighting men in ambush lie?
> Or an Eye of gifts & graces, show'ring fruits & coined gold!
> Why a Tongue impress'd with honey from every wind?
> Why an Ear, a whirlpool fierce to draw creations in?
> Why a Nostril wide inhaling terror trembling & affright
> Why a tender curb upon the youthful burning boy!
> Why a little curtain of flesh on the bed of our desire?
>
> (E6)

Inasmuch as Thel's proposed entry into Generation is sexual, her lament, "drawn," as Harold Bloom points out, "from Elizabethan conventions of erotic poetry,"[16] suggests persistence of susceptibility and perhaps eventual subsidence of resolution. It is a nice question—but an important one—whether Thel draws back *from* the vision contained in her lament, or whether that vision causes her to draw back from something else. The niceness of the question is another statement of the paradoxical complexities of Blake's view of Generation. Before examining further how Thel gets to the house of Clay in the first place, and what she says upon arrival, two technical points, one about the formal nature of the poem and the other concerned with Thel's final, mythological destination ("the vales of Har"), will be helpful.

When Thel arrives at the house of Clay, that "matron" exhorts her:

> Wilt thou O Queen enter my house. 'tis given thee to enter,
> And to return; fear nothing. enter with thy virgin feet.
>
> (E6)

The terms, we should recognize, are at least parodic of the promise of resurrection customary at the end of an elegy. If we remember, in *Lycidas*, Milton digging a grave even for the deathless amaranth, so that resurrection should be seen as a universal process, we may have more respect for Thel's distrust of Clay. Further, we may see certain sexual ambiguities in her behavior as well, at least in the symbolic terms which sex assumes in Blake's poem. That is, one of the "Proverbs of Hell" may be taken as a warning to Thel: "He who desires but acts not, breeds pestilence" (E35). But on the other hand she may be seen as rejecting all that Blake implies by the "Female Will." Finally, our consciousness of the poem's relationship to elegy may lead us to wonder about the question of pathetic responses. This too, we shall shortly see, will help us interpret the poem.

Whatever she is fleeing *from*, Thel flees in the last line of the poem to a place called "the vales of Har" (E6). One of the difficulties in working out the implications of her act stems from the fact that Har and Heva are hardly recognizable as the same figures in their two substantial appearances in Blake's work, a difficulty much multiplied because one of those appearances is in the very puzzling early prophecy, *Tiriel*. The question is a complicated one. Since *Tiriel* was unfinished and unpublished, it would seem reasonable to argue that we ought to associate the "vales of Har" with the only developed reference to Har in a *published* poem. In *The Song of Los* (1795) there is a reference to

> ... that dread day when Har and Heva fled.
> Because their brethren & sisters liv'd in War & Lust;
> And as they fled they shrunk
> Into two narrow doleful forms:
> Creeping in reptile flesh upon
> The bosom of the ground:
> And all the vast of Nature shrunk
> Before their shrunken eyes.
>
> (E66)

The assumption of reptile form accompanied by falling and shrinking, and by narrowing perceptions, is a description of the Fall of mankind into its present state, and has its parallels elsewhere in Blake (compare *The Book of Urizen*, IX.1–4; E81–82; F.Z., 42.1–17; E321–22). And the reference to the "sons of Har" two lines further into *The Song of Los* is clearly synonymous with "the sons of Man" (in his fallen state). This being the case, Thel's return to "the vales of Har" from the grave which the matron Clay has shown her in a moment of vision cannot be construed as a return to an unreal Beulah, but only as a return to ordinary fallen existence, an ambiguous retreat, perhaps, from both the horror of the grave and from the passionate intensity of her response to that horror. *Tiriel*, however, although unfinished and unpublished, has a claim on our attentions as a reference because it was composed simultaneously with or just before *Thel* (1789–1790), whereas *The Song of Los* is some five years later. And the picture of Har and Heva in *Tiriel* is responsible for the usual view that Thel unambiguously retreats from life at the end of her poem. Har and Heva (the names seem to mean, respectively, "mountain" and "Eve")[17] live in "the pleasant gardens of Har" "like two children" "playing with flowers. & running after birds they spent the day / And in the night like infants slept delighted with infant dreams" (E274). They are in their dotage. However, the relationship between "the vales of Har" (which are in the east, incidentally, not only the direction of the beginning of civilization but the direction of Luvah in the prophecies) and the lands to the west is a good deal more complicated than the relationship between ideal and "real" landscape. In fact there is nothing ideal, pretty, or "namby-pamby" about the vales or their inhabitants. And if we look at a speech toward the end of the poem, we see that Har, even in *Tiriel*, is father of a fallen mankind:

> ... when Tiriel felt the ankles of aged Har
> He said. O weak mistaken father of a lawless race
> Thy laws O Har & Tiriels wisdom end together in a curse
> Why is one law given to the lion & the patient Ox
> And why men bound beneath the heavens in a reptile form
> A worm of sixty winters creeping on the dusky ground
> (8.6–11; E281)

It is customary to think of Tiriel in Urizenic terms; here he appears—if a false god—the son of an even more mistaken god-the-father. And if Har and Heva's realm, as one may suspect, is intended as a sinister parody of an Eden which the "mistaken father of a lawless race" was never forced to leave, there is no question of it or of its inhabitants remaining unfallen, no question of their not having entered Experience. Tiriel, just before dying, rages:

> And now my paradise is falln & a drear sandy plain
> Returns my thirsty hissings in a curse on thee O Har
> (8.26–27; E282)

We know we are in the fallen world not only because of what the passage says but because of its allusion to the passage in Book X of *Paradise Lost* wherein Satan, reporting proudly to Pandemonium his corruption of mankind, hears hissing instead of applause, and shrinks himself to serpent-form, "punisht in the shape he sinnd" (516). Paradise turns to ashes, literally, in the hungry mouths of the company of snakes (*Paradise Lost*, X.504–584). Whatever Har and Heva represent, they are far from unfallen. Rather, by means of their senile and asexual paradise, Blake means to represent, not any condition *outside* of Generation, but completely complacent and satisfied immersion *in* Generation. In other words, the "vales of Har" signify the ordinary, accepting, thoughtless, fallen condition of Experience. Striking evidence for this view is provided by the eleventh of the series of drawings Blake executed for *Tiriel* (reproduced as plate 8 in G. E. Bentley's facsimile edition);[18] here we see Har and Heva asleep in each other's arms, in a bed, watched over by their nurse (or mother?), Mnetha. Har and Heva lie under a bedspread "richly patterned with flowers,"[19] a condition clearly symbolizing that they are "asleep" in Generation. We may conclude, then, that Thel's visionary conversations may illuminate the imagination of a virgin embarking upon sexual experience for the first time, but they certainly are not intended as descriptions of "a looking-glass world of talking flowers" (Frye, *Fearful Symmetry*, p. 233).

Blake's underlying concern in *Thel* is with the relationship between perception, or vision, and one's existential condition. I have already noted in "The Couch of Death" the relationship between a boy's self-loathing (expressed as sense of sin) and his horror of death. Likewise Thel, in her self-communion in the form of imaginary conversations, creates the images of Generation, of Vala, against which in the end she rebels. Among Blake's other early works which we have seen, only the lyric "Ah! Sun-Flower" from the Songs of Experience gives an adequately subtle idea of this process. The underlying thematic concern of both poems is the relationship between vision and analogy, the problem of likeness and identity. The paradoxical imaginative achievement of the lyric was the creation of a pastoral paradise capable of containing both the "youth pined away with desire" and the "pale Virgin shrouded in snow"—capable, that is, of rousing them from their metaphorical graves—after a model, the aspirations of a sunflower, as rooted in the vegetable as their frustration and self-denial. The tone of "Ah! Sun-Flower" is delicately comic, and its purpose is clearly to expose the problem I call "pastoral transcendence"— itself a division of the general problem of analogy—how, without inventing an unreal existence, "an allegorical abode where existence hath never come," can one transcend the terms of a fallen, vegetated existence? How can one depict Innocence except in terms of Experience, how do better than create the realm where lion and lamb simply lie down beside each other? We saw that Blake's purpose in "Ah! Sun-Flower" was not satire of the vegetated lovers but the creation of a fiction to expose their plight, and to make redemption of their aspirations at least imaginatively possible, and I compared Blake's fiction to Spenser's of letting the lamb's blood out of the wolf's throat.

What Thel does, on the other hand, could be compared to letting the wolf's blood out of the lamb's throat. Here two earlier remarks begin to consolidate. We cannot speak of Thel as being "in" Beulah, or of her imaginary conversations as a description "of" Beulah—conceiving of Beulah as a distinct cosmological entity from Generation—because this is entirely to miss the point of the poem. Thel is "in" Generation all right (the third line of the poem refers to "her mortal day," and the fourth to a location "down by the river of Adona") and her visions *are* innocent and childish. The point, however, is that Thel's childish visions create a Generation for her which is neither "innocent" (in the simple sense) nor childish. Blake's problem in *Thel* was not the depiction of a realm so nearly unreal as to be beyond imagery, but something more subtle and important: to depict a childish vision of Generation which neverthless contained within Innocence (in the sense of the *Songs*) the seeds of corruption and the Fall. Thel's innocent vision digs a grave for her. I have already discussed the relationship between the form of the poem and pastoral elegy; in this regard, too, we can observe the subtlety of Blake's technique. In pastoral elegy we are used to seeing all nature weep for the dead subject of the poem; resurrection dries nature's eyes. Analogously, Thel's progress through the poem is progress through various signs of natural sympathy and symbols of divine sanction. She passes from a "watry bow" (E3; in the Bible a symbol of hope and covenant with God) and "morning manna" (E4; a function of God's contract with his chosen and a sign of his favor until they get to Canaan) through fertile dew to tears. But the tears, when they come, fail to prefigure resurrection; oozing nourishing milk and oil for the child of Generation (E5), they only moisten the lip of the girl's grave, making it easier for her to slip in. In *Thel* Blake uses the conventions of elegy paradoxically—pathetic fallacy looks forward to the deluge.

Blake arranged for Thel to address herself to lily, cloud, worm, and clod of clay in the first instance because they are all associated in his mind with Luvah and Vala. It is for this reason that

analogues in the later prophecies can be suggestive. For example,
Thel's "lilly" imagines her God saying to her:

> Thou gentle maid of silent valleys, and of modest brooks:
> ... thou shalt be clothed in light, and fed with morning manna:
> Till summers heat melts thee beside the fountains and the
>   springs
> To flourish in eternal vales.
>
> (E4)

We recognize that the gentleness and modesty are important aspects of Thel's self-image, but it is interesting to see the application
of the image in the *Vala/The Four Zoas* manuscript. In Night
VII(a), the Shadow of Enitharmon communicates her vision of the
Fall of Man:

> Among the Flowers of Beulah walkd the Eternal Man & Saw
> Vala the lily of the desert. melting in high noon
> Upon her bosom in sweet bliss he fainted Wonder siezd
> All heaven they saw him dark. they built a golden wall
> Round Beulah   There he reveld in delight among the Flowers
> Vala was pregnant & brought forth Urizen Prince of Light
> First born of Generation. Then behold a wonder to the Eyes
> Of the now fallen Man a double form Vala appeard. A Male
> And female shuddring pale the Fallen Man recoild
> From the Enormity & calld them Luvah & Vala.
>
> (83.7–16; E351)

The two versions of Vala and the later, "double form" of the
"Enormity" will be explained later. It is interesting that the lily of
the valley has become "lilly of the desert," and that the passage
has its parallel to the impossibility of making any neat distinction
in *Thel*, as to place, between Beulah (where the Fall takes place)
and the Generated condition which results. It is also worth remarking that a bit earlier in the same Night, Los rebukes Enitharmon
for sexual elusiveness, complaining that the beauties of her condition seem available to everyone but her husband. He, too, speaks
in terms which make us think of Thel:

> Thy roses that expanded in the face of the glowing morn
> Hid in a little silken veil scarce breathe & faintly shine
> Thy lilies that gave light what time the morning looked forth
> Hid in the Vales faintly lament & no one hears their voice
>
> (81.35–82.3; E350)

It is an interesting lesson in the problems of perspective and point
of view in Blake to be asked to think of Thel as temptress.

However illuminating the analogues, however, Blake's Vala-images have to be seen in the first place as dramatic revelations. The conflict which makes this a drama, and not a case of static portraiture, comes out of the stresses and tensions implicit in Thel's imagery; the remarkable thing about the technique of *Thel* is not simply the revelation of the heroine's mind, but the way in which the imagery of one revelation engenders another. By this process, Thel, through expressing her Innocence, comes to express her Experience as well—and in the end to know this. Even Thel herself is finally asked to trust the tale rather than the teller of the tale.

Thel's first intimations of her condition come in the form of a soliloquy the imagery of which betrays a remarkable, undifferentiated *angst*. She is concerned with transiency ("Why fade these children of the spring?" E3), and she has forebodings of a general collapse into chaos (the idea is expressed in the *Vala/The Four Zoas* manuscript by the fallen shepherd, Tharmas), which she expresses ambiguously in terms of water and reflection. She sees herself (E3) as a "watry bow" (promising?), as a "parting cloud" (separation?), and as a reflection in a glass (reduction?), as "shadows in the water" (portending rather than reflecting?). Infants figure in her vision, but she does not explicitly develop any ideas, nor does any pattern or focus appear in her rather scatter-brained imagery of innocence: she prattles amiably but pointlessly about doves and babies and "music in the air" (E3). Only in the last three lines, when she expresses (like Lyca) the desire to sleep (in the language of the Fall in Genesis) and uses the word "gentle" four times do we see an embryonic connection between her concern about transiency and sexual anxiety. She wants to sleep "the sleep of death" (so long as it comes gently), and her sexual misgivings are deflected into concern for the fading of other innocents and into the imagery of God walking in his Garden in the evening time.

Her first imaginary conversation organizes both her vague misgivings and her imagery. She is already beginning to betray herself into the fallen outlook, but she does not know it yet. Innocence and modesty and humility and sexual anxiety are focused into the image of the pure lily of the valley. Sexuality and impermanence are the Father-God, confidently remarking, "Till summers heat melts thee ... to flourish in eternal vales" (E4). Sexuality is a flower melting before its father. (Blake's anticipation of the Freudian formulas is all the more remarkable in that he does not insist on them explicitly, but simply absorbs them into the pattern of his imagery.) The tacit implication of an Old Testament God in Thel's condition is a point I shall return to. The lily ends her speech by smiling in tears, that ominous combination of expressions which we have come to associate in the *Songs* with Urizenic pity and the Female Will.

The sexuality expressed in the image of a Father-God melting the flower may have seemed oblique to the condition of a nervous virgin, but evidently it was not muffled enough to suit Thel, for her reply to the lily attempts to shift the grounds of the argument from innocence to pure transience. She attempts a translation of what sexuality there was in the lily's speech to something more infantile; in her vision there is no phallic father, only lilies and lambs:

> O thou little virgin of the peaceful valley.
> Giving to those that cannot crave, the voiceless, the o'ertired.
> Thy breath doth nourish the innocent lamb, he smells thy
>   milky garments,
> He crops thy flowers. while thou sittest smiling in his face,
> Wiping his mild and meekin mouth from all contagious taints.
>   (E4)

Despite the explicit rejection of "contagious taints" and craving, Thel's imagery involves her in a conception of natural interdependence which will be the death of her. She remarks that the "wine" of the lily (a figure of speech which totters on the edge of oxymoron) "revives the milked cow, & tames the fire-breathing steed" (E4), which shows that she has not managed completely to dismiss sexuality from her mind. And another remark betrays that the "melting sun" is still bothering her:

> But Thel is like a faint cloud kindled at the rising sun:
> I vanish from my pearly throne, and who shall find my place.
>   (E4)

The second line echoes through Blake. In *Europe* the "nameless shadowy female" (or generated Nature) of the Preludium complains:

> O mother Enitharmon wilt thou bring forth other sons?
> To cause my name to vanish, that my place may not be found.
>   (E59)

And Enion poignantly rephrases the lament for Tharmas:

> Tho I have rebelld
> Make me not like the things forgotten as they had not been
> Make not the thing that loveth thee. a tear wiped away
> (45.24–26; E324)

But it is more important to notice that Thel's subconscious meditation of the Old Testament is coloring her imagery, for the complaint ultimately takes us back to the Book of Job (18:17): "His remembrance shall perish from the earth, and he shall have no name in the street."[20] Thel's meekness, it seems, contains its less than conscious indictment of Blake's "Accuser who is The God of This World." Blake, of course, was much more explicit than Thel:

> Tho thou art Worshipd by the Names Divine
> Of Jesus and Jehovah: thou art still
> The Son of Morn in weary Nights decline
> The lost Travellers Dream under the Hill
>
> (E266)

Thel's complaint is hardly an indictment, however, and all she succeeds in doing is calling forth the embodiment of her image, the Cloud. The Cloud associates himself explicitly with Luvah:

> O virgin know'st thou not. our steeds drink of the golden springs
> Where Luvah doth renew his horses: look'st thou on my youth,
> And fearest thou because I vanish and am seen no more.
> Nothing remains; O maid I tell thee, when I pass away,
> It is to tenfold life, to love, to peace, and raptures holy.
>
> (E4)

Blake develops the Cloud because to him it perfectly figures the veil, the obstruction to vision, which is what Luvah, or Generation, means. Further, the Cloud's language of reassurance suggests Blake's remarkable conflation of quite distinct passages in his Bible of Hell. Luvah's association with passion and the morning subtly suggests Satan; his imagery of resurrection "to tenfold life" and his wedding to a virgin (which we shall see in a moment) suggest Christianity. But Blake's language need not bear much explicitness. What is important to notice is his strategy as a dramatist. Thel has been trying to evade even what little sexual explicitness there was to be found in the language of the lily, and to deflect her thoughts to a pure consideration of impermanence. But her hypocrisy will not provide her with an escape. The Cloud speaks more clearly than the lily what is really on Thel's mind: for her Cloud does

> ... court the fair eyed dew. to take me to her shining tent;
> The weeping virgin, trembling kneels before the risen sun,
> Till we arise link'd in a golden band and never part;
> But walk united, bearing food to all our tender flowers
>
> (E4)

The Cloud's image is more insistently epithalamic than the lily's. It is to the point that Thel has not been able to evade the "risen sun" (another virgin kneels trembling before it in the "Argument" plate to *Visions of the Daughters of Albion*) and even more to the point that the dew, which is the object of the Cloud's attentions, may be indissolubly connected to the lily flower. The phrase "the weeping virgin" may suggest that Thel's imagery, despite her conscious concerns, has married the lily to someone younger than God the Father.

But Thel's consciousness trudges on its evasive way, for she picks up to develop from the Cloud's speech only the idea of bearing food, consolidating this theme with her previous picture of the lambs cropping the flowers, and producing the question of *usefulness*:

> But I feed not the warbling birds. they fly and seek their food;
> But Thel delights in these no more because I fade away,
> And all shall say, without a use this shining woman liv'd,
> Or did she only live. to be at death the food of worms.
>
> (E5)

The Cloud, of course, will proceed to tell her that to be worm-food is an honorable and useful occupation: "How great thy use. how great they blessing" (E5). But of course he is a man, and we can recognize that Thel's dilemma is especially sharp because she is a woman. For her to suffer Generation is to become Generation; insofar as her role is female it is not up to her to irrigate the desert with imagination and to impress the soil with seed, but to be irrigated and impressed. Part of her problem as a woman is that she has been conditioned to accept this role, but has been unable to cease fearing it. Thel is slightly more afraid of being used than of being useless. The haunting emblem which appears at the end of the poem illuminates her condition (as we have already seen, it illuminates the Lyca poems and *America* as well). Three children ride the back of a huge serpent, swimming forward on a vegetable sea. The foremost child is female; she rides soberly and properly, facing straight ahead, and in her hands she holds a bridle attached to the monster's mouth. The other two children appear both to be male; the foremost is reaching back to assist the other to be seated, or to play with him; their attitudes suggest frolic. As we have already seen, one can read the implications of the emblem almost endlessly.[21] Is it that Innocence, organized, can master Experience (that is, this world)? Or is it that Innocence, however genuine, must also depend upon Experience, is supported by Experience? We can isolate the same questions in the attitude of the girl rider. Does her bridle suggest mastery? I would say that it does signify at least the possibility of mastery, but that it also suggests (and here is the relevance to Thel) responsibility. The mastery is clearly there, but so is the suggestion that, as she steers, so is she all the more securely led.

The difficulty with the Serpent is to decide who is leading whom. This we saw was exactly the difficulty with argument by analogy, if the analogies are drawn from nature. Is playful sympathy with the sunflower an imaginary step forward or a giant misstep into the vegetable grave? It is the problem we have come to associate with pastoralism: Spenser could get the lamb out of the wolf, but only by killing both of them, and he was still left with a world of wolves and lambs. When the knife was passed across the wolf's throat, did the shepherd not himself become a wolf? Was he guiding or being led by the Serpent?

The paradox of Thel so far has been that when she most assumes she is leading her argument (by analogy), she is being led by it. The rest of the poem serves to clarify this fact, and to deal with the much more complicated question of whether the converse is also true: whether when Thel is following, she can be said in any sense to lead. Thel had wondered was she "to be at death the food of worms," and the Cloud forthwith calls

> The weak worm from its lowly bed, and thou shalt hear its voice.
> Come forth worm of the silent valley, to thy pensive queen.
> (E5)

In doing this, the Cloud is only following the pattern of the poem's development. Thel, in floundering away from the implication of one entanglement, lets drop an image which is developed into the sequent danger. But so far that pattern has been merely linear;

whatever serpent she has been following lies in a straight line. Suddenly, however, we discover a loop:

> The helpless worm arose, and sat upon the Lilly's leaf,
> And the bright Cloud saild on, to find his partner in the vale.
> (E5)

It must have become apparent to the cloud that Thel was not about to become his partner, but what he left her with was more than a visible emblem of her dilemma: sexuality and death in one hungry, naked, helpless form. He also left her with evidence of the circular, self-consuming pattern to Thel's rather helpless thinking, for the girl's imagery, unbeknownst to her, has returned via the sexualized cycle of generation and death to the pure lily and deposited thereon all too eloquent testimony of "contagious taint." Thel has fallen, but not in a straight line. Her imagery has discovered to her that the "catterpiller chooses the fairest leaves to lay her eggs on" (E37). Henceforward her imagery takes the bit into its mouth firmly and leads the girl on inexorably over her head into the earth. As we have seen, she is already in an important sense Experienced. What now? Is she merely following, or, since her imagery has its source in her imagination, is she leading? She enters the house of Clay and returns again. Does she fail? Or is she simply enjoying that prerogative of young people, eating her cake and having it too?

The imagery, according to its own logic, produces for Thel a Worm:

> Art thou a Worm? image of weakness. art thou but a Worm?
> I see thee like an infant wrapped in the Lilly's leaf:
> Ah weep not little voice, thou can'st not speak. but thou can'st weep;
> Is this a Worm? I see thee lay helpless & naked: weeping,
> And none to answer, none to cherish thee with mothers smiles.
> (E5)

As Harold Bloom has noticed, there is a sinister ironic invitation here: "Thel's worm is the infant image of weakness it seems, but the mother's embrace it invites will be an embrace of Experience and death."[22] However sinister it is, most critics have berated Thel for taking no notice of the invitation. Yet surely to ignore it is not a little remarkable if Thel is here passive in the hands of her own analogies.

We notice some unusual things. For the first time Thel registers surprise at the gulf between the vegetated and spiritual forms of her interlocutor. "Art thou but a Worm?" she asks. And for the first time, as if because of her awareness, her interlocutor cannot answer. Or rather it makes the ultimate, subarticulate response of Nature. "Accept, accept," it says, crying the most insistent cry known to Nature. What will be Thel's response? I take the cry of the Worm to be the annunciation of the poem's crisis, and Thel's response to be the most comprehensive indication of what, in fact, the poem is about.

Thel responds in one sense, and in another sense fails to respond. She *says* not a word (and there may be an element of wry humor in her dramatic silence: since she is, after all, having so much difficulty in contemplating *wife*, the question *mother* is understandably beyond her), but her imagination—the inexorable logic of her imagery—answers for her. Without any hesitation,

> The Clod of Clay heard the Worms voice, & raisd her pitying head;
> She bow'd over the weeping infant, and her life exhal'd
> In milky fondness, then on Thel she fix'd her humble eyes.
>
> (E5)

The logic of Thel's imagination has demanded Clay to nourish the Worm. Yet before we conclude too hastily from this that Thel is no longer a free agent, that she is being victimized, like a character in Sterne, by an automatic association of ideas, we should notice the potential freedom of her condition. Thel can continue to maintain her registration of the analogy (whether imperfect or all-too-perfect she can decide later) between Worm and infant. In her response to the Clod of Clay's speech, she speaks only in terms of the vehicle of the analogy, only in terms of Worm, and now that we are sure the word has a referent in her mind other than the interlocutor before the eye of her imagination, we can see, for the first time, that Thel is conscious of the power of the imagination. By that power Thel is introduced, if only introduced, to the franchise of the imagination. She is free enough to imagine to herself a Clod of Clay who says:

> Wilt thou O Queen enter my house. 'tis given thee to enter,
> And to return; fear nothing. enter with thy virgin feet.
>
> (E6)

If one may return to the terms of Plato with which this study was initiated, she learns the distinction between seduction by Lysias and seduction by Socrates. By virtue of awareness of imagination, after she enters she can return, flee back "unhinderd till she came into the vales of Har" (E6). Of course this last line of the poem represents a failure. Blake's last plate to *Thel* is analogous to "Earth's Answer," the rather despairing, exhortatory reply to the question posed by the bard of "Introduction" to Experience: Why wilt thou turn away? Earth answers, in part:

> Break this heavy chain,
> That does freeze my bones around
> Selfish! vain,
> Eternal bane!
> That free Love with bondage bound.
>
> (E19)

Of course Thel exemplifies "free Love with bondage bound." That is why Blake included in the speech from her grave two lines perhaps dramatically inappropriate to her consciousness, growing in awareness even as it is:

> Why a tender curb upon the youthful burning boy!
> Why a little curtain of flesh on the bed of our desire?
>
> (E6)

Perhaps this was too much for Thel to know, even in her newfound imaginative freedom, before she fled back to the ordinary un-enlightened condition of Generation (Blake erased the lines from two copies of the poem; E713), but at least she was able to flee back "unhindered." Blake may mean only that in the last analysis there *is* no one to hinder her. But he may also mean that Thel *can* return, at will, to however uninspired a condition, that she is un-marked, that she has not been drawn in—in short, that she is still a virgin (I have already noted the indications that she will not remain one forever), but a wiser one than when she began.

For this is the paradox of *Thel*, that the girl's retreat can be construed as imaginative success. Every reader must feel that her imaginative excursion, albeit only temporary, into the land of Clay finds a voice at once more serious and more authentic than any-thing we have so far seen in the poem:

> Thel enter'd in & saw the secrets of the land unknown;
> She saw the couches of the dead, & where the fibrous roots
> Of every heart on earth infixes deep its restless twists:
> A land of sorrows & of tears where never smile was seen.
>
> (E6)

It is no damage to my argument to notice that this plate seems to have been a late addition to the poem (Erdman thinks replacing an earlier version; E713), and that the voice we hear may be Blake's as well as Thel's. While it is perfectly true that Thel does not find the vision to transcend her observations of Ulro (for it makes more sense to speak of the house of Clay as that, than as Generation), her horror expresses itself in technical enough terms that we have difficulty recognizing in this speech the shy virgin who had imaginary, wandering conversations with flowers. Thel's speech concentrates on the corruption introduced to the human heart through the five senses, and it is worth recalling these lines from *The Song of Los*:

> Thus the terrible race of Los & Enitharmon gave
> Laws & Religions to the sons of Har binding them more
> And more to Earth: closing and restraining:
> Till a Philosophy of Five Senses was complete
>
> (E66)

Thel's vision is more modest, and Max Plowman is probably being too chivalrous when he argues that "by her flight [she] proclaims her perfect integrity."[23] But she is, as pedagogues say, asking the right questions:

> Why cannot the Ear be closed to its own destruction?
> Or the glistening Eye to the poison of a smile!
>
> (E6)

It is evident that Thel must enter Ulro in order to ask the questions she does, but to answer these questions from Ulro—Blake reminds us of this passionately throughout his career—is difficult indeed, and Thel's is only the first of a harrowing series of laments of Experience:

> It is an easy thing to rejoice in the tents of prosperity
> Thus could I sing & thus rejoice, but it is not so with me!
> (F.Z., 36.12–13; E319)

The Book of Thel, however, is more than lament, and its pastoralism is the structure of Blake's first narrative statement of the problem of Vala. One assumes, as I have said, that Thel returned to her questions again. In the case of Blake there is no need to conjecture.

Before passing on from *Thel,* one passage requires further comment because it expresses in so concentrated a form the problem of Vala. Since it is so much easier to recognize pastoralism in the poem in the depiction and attitudes of the *dramatis personae* and in the drift of the conversations (in the atmosphere of self-communion and the admonitions to humility) than it is in the underlying thematic preoccupations, it is useful to stress the latter aspect of the case. To do so will also be to relate *Thel* to my earlier, more general remarks, and to open up the way to relating *Thel* to poems which come later.

It will be remembered that the Clod of Clay recommends to Thel the notion that "we live not for ourselves," arguing that "he who loves the lowly" had bound her with nuptial bands, declared her the mother of his children, and given her a crown "that none can take away" (E5).[24] As we might expect, this argument appeals to Thel, and it provides her with the imaginative daring she needs in order to enter the house of Clay. She says,

> ... Alas! I knew not this, and therefore did I weep:
> That God would love a Worm I knew, and punish the evil foot
> That wilful, bruis'd its helpless form: but that he cherish'd it
> With milk and oil. I never knew; and therefore did I weep,
> And I complaind in the mild air, because I fade away,
> And lay me down in thy cold bed, and leave my shining lot.
> (E5)

The distinction between "love" and "cherish" is rather muddy, undeveloped, and sentimental (hence appropriate to Thel's dramatic character), but as stated here it contains in embryo the distinction very important to the mature Blake between the spurious God of justice (the Accuser) and a more genuine God. Therefore, the relationship between the latter conception and reconciliation to the condition of Ulro, undeveloped and unexplained as it is (the Clod says, "I know not, and I cannot know, / I ponder, and I cannot ponder"; E5), is an important preview of some of the most important themes of Blake's career. To understand the statement, we must scrutinize carefully two lines and a bit of Thel's speech: "That God would love a Worm I knew, and punish the evil foot / That wilful bruis'd its helpless form: but that he cherish'd it / With milk and oil. I never knew" (E5). The language is, of course, derived from Genesis 3:15: "And I will put enmity between thee and the woman, and between thy seed and her seed;

it shall bruise thy head, and thou shalt bruise his heel." The orthodox Christian interpretation of this passage (and interestingly, a note of Merritt Hughes reminds us, *not* the Calvinist interpretation)[25] is what we find in *Paradise Lost*. The speaker, called "Oracle," is the second person of the Trinity whom Milton enjoys thinking of as both Accuser and Mediator ("Mercie collegue with Justice"; X.59):

> So spake this Oracle, then verifi'd
> When *Jesus* son of *Mary* second *Eve*,
> Saw Satan fall like Lightning down from Heav'n,
> Prince of the Aire; then rising from his Grave
> Spoild Principalities and Powers, triumphd
> In op'n shew, and with ascension bright
> Captivity led captive through the Aire,
> The Realme it self of *Satan* long usurpt,
> Whom he shall tread at last under our feet;
> Eevn hee who now foretold his fatal bruise,
> And to the Woman thus his Sentence turnd.
>
> (X.182–192)

These orthodoxies seem bland enough, and it is only when we try to apply the biblical phrasing to Blake's passage that we see how cunningly he has subverted them. Blake's phrasing permits us to read the Worm as Adam or Nature (presumably in an unfallen condition, but in this case the terminology begs questions) and the "evil foot/That wilful, bruis'd its helpless form" as Satan. But the language encourages another reading as well: the Worm can be Satan, and the evil foot belong to Christ. That foot was punished by undergoing Incarnation and Crucifixion. In *The Marriage of Heaven and Hell* Blake makes an odd theological remark that "in the Gospel" Christ prays "to the Father to send the comforter or Desire that Reason may have Ideas to build on" (E35). Thel has been sent Desire, and in her case the integument of Desire, her "Vala," is the stinging ambiguity recorded in the phrase we have just seen. The clarification of this ambiguity was the labor of much of Blake's life.

I have already established Nights I and II of *Vala/The Four Zoas* as a *locus* for *Thel*; to examine the use Blake makes of imagery derived from *Thel* in Night II will demonstrate that I have not been making too much of implicit ambiguities, and help to establish as well the scope and importance of the question of Vala. In Night II of the manuscript, Luvah is suppressed, driven down into the natural accretions of Vala as repressed energy. Blake conveys this as Vala (Nature) melting down Luvah in a furnace, the symbol, as Frye points out, of "the natural body" (*Fearful Symmetry*, p. 253). Urizen, the Restrainer of *The Marriage*, observes and connives (for reasons which I shall examine), and when the melting down is done Blake, who never misses an opportunity to refer to Milton, has him pour off and cast from the furnaces in partial allusion to the construction of Pandemonium in Book I of *Paradise Lost*. The relevant passage, which begins with an allusion to *Thel*, is "the voice of Luvah from the furnaces of Urizen" (26.4; E311). That is, while he is being boiled down, Luvah takes the opportunity of a thumbnail sketch of human history from his vantage point. The passage is long, but worth quoting in full:

> If I indeed am Valas King & ye O sons of Men
> The workmanship of Luvahs hands; in times of Everlasting
> When I calld forth the Earth-worm from the cold & dark
>   obscure
> I nurturd her I fed her with my rains & dews, she grew
> A scaled Serpent, yet I fed her tho' she hated me
> Day after day she fed upon the mountains in Luvahs sight
> I brought her thro' the Wilderness, a dry & thirsty land
> And I commanded springs to rise for her in the black desart
> [*Till*] she became a Dragon winged bright & poisonous
> I opend all the floodgates of the heavens to quench her thirst
> And I commanded the Great deep to hide her in his hand
> Till she became a little weeping Infant a span long
> I carried her in my bosom as a man carries a lamb
> I loved her I gave her all my soul & my delight
> I hid her in soft gardens & in secret bowers of Summer
> Weaving mazes of delight along the sunny Paradise
> Inextricable labyrinths, She bore me sons & daughters
> And they have taken her away & hid her from my sight
> They have surrounded me with walls of iron and brass, *O Lamb*
> *Of God clothed in Luvahs garments little knowest thou*
> *Of death Eternal that we all go to Eternal Death*
> *To our Primeval Chaos in fortuitous concourse of incoherent*
> *Discordant principles of Love & Hate I suffer affliction*
> Because I love. for I was love but hatred awakes in me
> And Urizen who was Faith & Certainty is changed to Doubt
> The hand of Urizen is upon me because I blotted out
> That human delusion to deliver all the sons of God
> From bondage of the Human form
>   (26.5–27.18; E311; italics indicate late additions)[26]

We seem to have advanced a long way on the Clod of Clay's simple perplexity and faith, and approaching the passage from *Thel* the first thing we notice is that it is possible to read the two halves of an apparent sequence as if they were parallel in time. That is, Thel wondered, "art thou but a Worm? I see thee like an infant," and it is possible to see in Luvah's speech the separate development of both possibilities. It is worth noticing at the outset that the development of either aspect of Vala, whether Worm or Infant, seems to end in collapse; the Worm sequence concludes in the Deluge (in Blake's mythology coincident with the Creation), and the Infant sequence, if we take the additions to the passage into account, ends (from the point of view of the speaker) in the Atonement interpreted as collapse into "Primeval Chaos." Explication of the passage's symbolism, and comment on its structure, will seem to take us far from Thel's world of jejune question-begging, but the journey is necessary if we are to understand really what her questions mean.

The ultimate source of Blake's imagery is the Scriptures; the passage under consideration may derive ultimately from Ezekiel 22:20, where a vengeful God promises Jerusalem: "As they gather silver, and brass, and iron, and lead, and tin, into the midst of the furnace, to blow the fire upon it, to melt it; so will I gather you in mine anger and in my fury, and I will leave you there and melt you." But although built upon a fabric of biblical allusion, the passage, we immediately notice, takes great liberties with biblical history. For example, according to Luvah's speech, the chosen were brought through the wilderness *before* the Deluge: events in Exodus ("I commanded springs to rise for her in the black desart") precede events in Genesis. Yet clearly Luvah, in this pre-Deluge section, thinks of himself as a combination Genesis God ("O sons of Men / The workmanship of Luvahs hands") and Moses, only Blake is imagining the mission of Moses, leading his people to the Promised Land, as progressively mistaken: Moses' troubles with a backsliding, idol-worshiping people are taken as typical of his failure, and the attempt to find Canaan is equated with the progressive worship of the Natural Man. The Worm becomes a Serpent, which Moses continues to feed, until in a brilliant burst of imagery Nature becomes Leviathan itself (Blake is here reading Job in his characteristically satiric way)[27] and it takes the Deluge itself (that is, a conception of the whole world as Nature Fallen) to quench the beast's thirst. The transition from the Flood to the birth of a weeping infant is abrupt, but not inexplicable if we remember that infants are born out of a bag of waters. The speaker again cherishes Nature (this time in the form of the Infant) and again with disastrous results, only this time the speaker is not involved in a flood but denied contact: the Nature he invests with reality is, however beautiful, progressively elusive. As he fails to realize that his "natural" wife and "natural" offspring are really his emanations, they become more and more remote from him, and although he has made a paradise of his fallen nature (by falling in hopeless love with it) it is a paradise much like Spenser's Bower of Bliss, a bower which enticement finally turns into the inside of a furnace. It is worth noticing that this latter half of the passage, especially with the additions, uses traditionally recognizable pastoral imagery in an interesting way: the speaker compares himself cherishing the Infant to a shepherd nurturing a lamb—an analogy intimately related to the appearance of "soft gardens," "secret bowers of Summer," and "sunny Paradise"—but the additions show to what extent the pastoral dream has been conscious false-hood: the speaker addresses the incarnate God as Lamb with a sense of what it means to be a lamb so terrifying as to be difficult to reconcile with his role as shepherd: "we all go to Eternal Death / To our Primeval Chaos."

The most interesting aspect of the second of the passage's two phases is the question of the speaker. If the speaker of the first phase is a combination of Genesis God and Moses, who is the *persona* of the second phase: who is Luvah after the Deluge? He is still a patriarch, but one who prefers the role of deliverer to that of pseudo-Father. But he is a deliverer who has blotted someone or something out in order to save mankind, and he is one in whom love has changed to hate. Moreover, he feels that because of his deed "the hand of Urizen is upon me." In other words, we have the Satanic Christ once more. If we recognize that "I loved her I gave her all my soul" refers not only to Nature generally, but to Adam's Fall as described by Milton, and that the patriarch of mankind is Adam, one might say, satanized, we can see the affinity between this figure and Christ (the "new Adam"), who blots out the old Adam in that He suffers him to be crucified. Luvah's understanding of this last point is, from Blake's stand-point, defective, for Luvah understands the Atonement as an attempt "to deliver all the sons of God from bondage of the Human form," but Blake, characteristically, uses Luvah's ignor-ance dramatically to preserve his own profoundly ambiguous attitude toward the generated condition.

A passage analogous to this in *The Book of Urizen* (1794) under-lines the ambiguity and its accessibility to pastoralism. In *Urizen*, once the original parents, Los and Enitharmon, have appeared on earth, the Eternals are so horrified at them and at sexual organization that they resolve to build a "Tent" (the world) for them, in order that "Eternals may no more behold them" (E77). This construction is rendered in terms of the two stages, intrauterine and post-partum, of the development of Enitharmon's first-born, Orc. The intrauterine career of Orc parallels the development of Worm into Serpent which we have seen in *Vala/The Four Zoas*:

> 5. All day the worm lay on her bosom
> All night within her womb
> The worm lay till it grew to a serpent
> With dolorous hissings & poisons
> Round Enitharmons loins folding,
>
> 6. Coild within Enitharmons womb
> The serpent grew casting its scales,
> . . . .
> Many forms of fish, bird & beast,
> Brought forth an Infant form
> Where was a worm before.

(E78)

Blake seemed to know that "ontogeny recapitulates phylogeny." The worm is born a child, and, in sinister parody of Milton's "Nativity Hymn," "a shriek ran thro' Eternity : / And a paralytic stroke" (E78). Orc's appearance is disturbing enough that the Eternals secure the stakes of the Tent, thereby preventing Los from beholding Eternity any more. Orc's post-partum career is just as ambiguous. Orc grows, and his father correspondingly grows jealous, forging link by painful link a chain of Jealousy, with which Orc is chained, like Prometheus, to a rock "beneath Urizens deathful shadow" (E79). Then,

> 5. The dead heard the voice of the child
> And began to awake from sleep
> All things. heard the voice of the child
> And began to awake to life.

(E79)

The passage suggests Adonis, Orpheus, and the triumph of *eros* over *thanatos*. Whether resurrection in this case is a happy event is less certain.

In other important instances Blake muffles ambiguity and anxiety by presenting the career of Vala in terms of a historical cycle which seems tantalizingly to progress but which, eventually, like the drift of Thel's imagery, loops back on itself. His ultimate presentation of such a cycle, as I have noted, is in "The Mental Traveller" (which he never published) in which four distinct stages of cycle are distinguished but seen to drive each other like meshed cogwheels. The end of the fourth stage can be taken to illustrate how Blake could apply his doubts about Generation to historical analysis. It corresponds generally to the second stage of the process as related by Luvah in *Vala/The Four Zoas*, where pursuit of Nature as elusive female (in fact a chimera) and construction of a labyrinth is mistaken for the constructive power of civilization and progress toward enlightenment:

> Till the wide desert planted oer
> With Labyrinths of wayward Love
> Where roams the Lion Wolf & Boar
>
> Till he becomes a wayward Babe
> And she a weeping Woman Old
> Then many a Lover wanders here
> The Sun & Stars are nearer rolld
>
> The trees bring forth sweet Extacy
> To all who in the desert roam
> Till many a City there is Built
> And many a pleasant Shepherds home
>
> (E477)

The last two lines suggest Blake's England, with its urban life and proliferation of country retreats, and the reference to the "wayward Babe" should suggest Lyca, whose poems also bore reference to the poet's own time. But Blake's sense of history is complex, for although it may have been Newton who helped to roll the sun and stars nearer, "the trees bring[ing] forth sweet Extacy" suggest the Fall for "all who in the desert roam." Apparently Blake is describing a case where city planning (or, more generally, culture) recapitulates phylogeny. And again Blake compounds the Old Adam and the New, for immediately we are told,

> But when they find the frowning Babe
> Terror strikes thro the region wide
> They cry the Babe the Babe is Born
> And flee away on Every side
>
> (E477)

The Babe is saviour perhaps only in the odd Blakean sense that (like Milton's Satan) he withers Nature, but the sense of natural law is strong enough to overpower even such upstarts, and—terrifying or not—the "frowning Babe" is nailed down upon the rock by "a Woman Old."

A more specific application of the pattern of Generation to history is made in "The Argument" to *The Marriage of Heaven and Hell*, where Blake does seem to be following with some faithfulness the ordinary chronology of canonical and historical events.[28] The planting of the desert takes place in Old Testament times, and Blake suggests (by manipulation of verb tenses) the planting is a visionary process, not a process of enslavement to Nature. But then the "perilous path" is planted in actual, natural fact, and the culmination of this is the Incarnation of Christ:

> And on bleached bones
> Red clay brought forth
>
> (E33)

The Incarnation is seen as analogous to the establishment of an institutional church, which attracts "the villain" from "the paths of ease" (E33). Now we get the first reference to a serpent in the poem, for

> Now the sneaking serpent walks
> In mild humility.
> And the just man rages in the wilds
> Where lions roam.
>
> (E33)

The cycle seems to describe the process of civilized decay, that is, early austerity followed by fruitfulness followed by decadence. Whether the cycle is only going to repeat itself or lead to anything new is rendered problematic by the two lines which appear both at the beginning and at the end:

> Rintrah roars & shakes his fires in the burdend air;
> Hungry clouds swag on the deep.
>
> (E33)

Rintrah, mentioned here for the first time, is later to play an important role in *Milton*, where he is associated with the class of Reprobate, those "form'd / To destruction from the mother's womb" (M., 7.2–3), that is, like Christ. In his appearances before *Milton*, however, Rintrah is, like his father, Los, less positive a figure; in *Europe* he is one of the children of Los and Enitharmon, delegated by his mother to "Go! tell the Human race that Womans love is Sin!" (E61) and a lot of other undesirable things. His association here with hungry storms may signify revolutionary portent, but it is hard to derive much apocalyptic comfort (if there is such a thing) from this, because the same clouds on a previous occasion foretold only the driving of man out of Paradise into the "perilous path." More to the point, the references to Rintrah bracket the extremes of a cycle the exact midpoint of which is taken up by the Advent, an event, moreover, with no happy effect.

It has already been remarked that when Vala casts Luvah into the "Furnaces of affliction" Urizen watches. We are told:

> Stern Urizen beheld urg'd by necessity to keep
> The evil day afar, & if perchance with iron power
> He might avert his own despair.
>
> > (25.42–44; E310)

The "evil day" is of course one of the last, after which Hell will be permanently sealed; the *locus classicus* for the despair of Satan would be for Blake Book IV of *Paradise Lost*, where the demon, "onely supream / In miserie" (91–92), makes his way in agony to the bower of Adam and Eve. It is interesting that Blake associates Urizen, presiding genius of the Worm-Infant passage just examined, with *necessity*, for Satan, just before he makes for the ear of Eve (the situation in "Night") justifies his evil deed by remarking, "Honour and Empire . . . compells me now to do what else though damnd I should abhorre" (390–392). And Milton remarks:

> So spake the Fiend, and with necessitie,
> The Tyrants plea, excus'd his devilish deeds.
>
> > (IV.393–394)

This point is worth insisting upon, and not merely because it takes us back to Blake's "Night," where, repeatedly, we started. The crux of my analyses of imagery has been, again and again, ambiguous Vala as conflux of Old Adam, New Adam, and Satan. And it is important to be reminded that this conflux is profoundly dependent upon Milton, not only so that we will begin to see the importance of *Milton* in Blake's career, when we come to it, but also in order to distinguish in Blake between theological originality and reaction against Milton (see Appendix B, "Blake as Radical

Christian"). For one of the most interesting visual instances of Thel's question "Art thou a Worm? image of weakness" is to be seen in the magnificent Crucifixion in Blake's series of water-colors after *Paradise Lost* (see Fig. 9). In this case the "image of weakness" is the crucified body, and we can see that the Worm is nailed to the same cross.

But the first thing to be noticed about Blake's painting is, for all its iconographic concentration, its faithfulness to Milton's text. The figure of admonitory angel on the left is Michael, sent by Milton's God with Cherubim to dispossess Adam and Eve of Paradise, after telling Adam the history and eschatology of life. Michael puts Eve to sleep (remarking to Adam, "As once thou slepst, while Shee to life was formd"; XI.369) in her bower, and ascends a mount of vision with Adam. In Blake's painting, we see Eve asleep beneath the cross. Michael's recital, when he comes to the Crucifixion, is very particular, and we can see that Blake is following him to the letter. Michael tells Adam:

But to the Cross he nailes thy Enemies,
The Law that is against thee, and the sins
Of all mankinde, with him there crucifi'd,
Never to hurt them more who rightly trust
In this his satisfaction ...

(XII.415–418)

And he is even more specific about Adam's enemies:

... this act
Shall bruise the head of *Satan*, crush his strength
Defeating Sin and Death, his two maine arms.

(XII.429–431)

The serpentine shape and the heads which lie defeated at the foot of Blake's cross, nailed to it by the same nail which passes through the feet of Jesus, are Sin and Death. Blake has created a fearful symmetry of Christ's outstretched arms on the cross above and the defeated heads on either side of the foot below, suggesting an hourglass shape like Yeats's gyres, but in doing so he has remained very faithful to Milton's description of Sin and Death. Sin is

... Woman to the waste, and fair
But ended foul in many a scaly fould
Voluminous and vast, a Serpent armd
With mortal sting ...

(II.650–653)

9. "Crucifixion," *Paradise Lost*

On her breasts are visible the faces of her dogs, born of incestuous union with her son. We can see nothing of Death with any certainty except the head, and this too accords with Milton's description of a shape "that shape had none" (II.667). We are told only that "what seemd his head / The likeness of a Kingly Crown had on" (II.672–673). To the left of the crucifix stands Michael, pointing to the cross with a gesture of grand admonition. He is helmeted and carries a spear, but, says one commentator, "it would be difficult to find a more benign figure."[29] This too would accord with Milton's textual instructions, which also distinguish between the angel's military mission and his emotional attitude. "From the Paradise of God without remorse drive out the sinful Pair," God tells Michael, but "all terror hide. If patiently thy bidding they obey, dismiss them not disconsolate" (XI.104–105; 111–113). Blake's Adam (who is naked, although Jesus wears a loincloth on the cross) stands to the right, his head turned up with an expression of humble adoration, his hands pressed together before his breast in the familiar gesture of prayer. Presumably Blake is illustrating his speech in *Paradise Lost* which begins,

> O goodness infinite, goodness immense!
> That all this good of evil shall produce,
> And evil turn to good; more wonderful
> Then that which by creation first brought forth
> Light out of darkness!
>
> (XII.469–473)

Or perhaps he has just discovered, in Michael's phrase, "a paradise within thee, happier farr" (XII.587). The expression and attitude of the Christ are serene and untormented.

I have insisted upon minute faithfulness to the letter and spirit of Blake's original because a complete interpretation of the picture is impossible without such insistence. Yet there is more to this picture than might have met Milton's eye, and the quickest way to see what more there is is to compare it with plate 76 of *Jerusalem* (see Fig. 10), which makes more open and explicit what is implicit here. In the *Jerusalem* plate a very similar Jesus, also wearing a loincloth (and one insists upon this because of Blake's remark "Art can never exist without Naked Beauty displayed"; E272), is crucified upon a tree, rather than a cross. Immediately we think of Orc in the *Vala/The Four Zoas* manuscript (or of Fuzon in *The Book of Ahania*) persuaded by Urizen to undergo crucifixion on the tree of Nature and Mystery (F.Z., 81.1–6; E349; *The Book of*

10. *Jerusalem*, plate 76

Ahania, III.6; E86). In these mock crucifixions the part of crucified is played by a figure representing Desire, and Urizen wants the crucifixion as an expression of natural necessity. This, it is his tyrannical purpose to assert, is what is always going to happen to desire, and the corpse on the tree (a source of pestilence in *Ahania*) becomes a monstrous emblem of Nature under Urizen:

> He knew that weakness stretches out in breadth & length he
> knew
> That wisdom reaches high & deep & therefore he made Orc
> In Serpent form compelld stretch out & up the mysterious tree
> He sufferd him to Climb that he might draw all human forms
> Into submission to his will . . .
>
> (81.2–6; E349)

The emblem of the crucifixion, then, can easily be distorted into something pestilential, and adoration of Christ on the cross amount to worship of natural necessity, or Satan (see Frye, *Fearful Symmetry*, pp. 400–401). But this clearly is not what is going on in *Jerusalem*. There the Adam-figure (in this instance Albion) is adoring Christ not with piety but with a dance of gladness. He is naked, and his posture a variation on the exultant "Glad Day" posture, discussed eloquently by David Erdman as an emblem of the new man risen from slavery, triumphing like the sun over his batlike spectre and the bound chrysalis from which he has emerged (see Erdman, pp. 10–11; plate 1). Beneath an engraving of "Glad Day" made in 1800 or later, Blake subscribed the lines:

> Albion rose from where he labourd at the Mill with Slaves
> Giving himself for the Nations he danc'd the dance of Eternal
> Death.
>
> (E660)

Erdman notes: "Albion's facial expression must be read as that of one offering himself a living sacrifice" (p. 10). Evidently we are far indeed from the Urizenic vision of the sacrifice, but are dealing with something no less strange. I will discuss Blake's phrase "Eternal Death" later on, but for the moment it will suffice to take it as meaning "in Generation." Therefore, in the *Jerusalem* plate two images of sacrifice are face to face, one an emblem of torture, the other of joy, met together in Generation. The crucified Christ here is no image of pestilence for Albion; likewise Albion's glorious celebration of his condition is a mirror-image of acceptance of sacrifice. If we look closely at the picture, we suddenly see that the face of Albion and Jesus are related, that Blake's plate is only a very complex understanding of his early insight "God becomes as we are, that we may be as he is" (*There is NO Natural Religion*; E2).

We are now in a position to apply to the *Paradise Lost* illustration two very different (but related) ideas of the Crucifixion, but to do so will be to see how essential to Blake's meaning is the primary Miltonic terminology. The result of the examination will be a poignantly ambiguous image of the Generated condition, an image significantly related to the idea of pastoral.

Jean H. Hagstrum refers casually to the images at the foot of the cross as Urizen and Vala.[30] If we remember Blake's lines on the Crucifixion in *The Everlasting Gospel*,

> And thus with wrath he did subdue
> The Serpent Bulk of Natures dross
> Till he had naild it to the Cross
>
> (E515)

Hagstrum's is a reasonable enough interpretation. One can reinforce it by remarking that the face of the female figure, with its blind eyes, is reminiscent of one of Blake's most horrifying representations of Orc,[31] and that the crown on Death's head has five points—surely an oblique reference to Blake's association between the empire of death and the "natural" philosophy of the five senses. Another interesting visual analogue is the well-known drawing on page 27 of the *Vala/The Four Zoas* manuscript, where the figures are a skeletal, ancient Luvah (under the Urizenic dispensation) balanced against a sexually blooming, lascivious Vala (her veil is clearly over them both). The drawing illustrates the relationship between Luvah and Vala as described in "The Mental Traveller" by the line "And she grows young as he grows old" (E475). A glance at the two figures will confirm that they share the same face.

A further glance at the *Paradise Lost* painting will reveal that all the figures there share the same face. If we add to this the fact that the body of sleeping Eve lies, not *on* the ground, but *in* it, and that perspective cuts off the top of the cross over Christ's head, so as to reinforce its resemblance to a tree, we may suspect that the best name for that one face is Luvah. That is, we are looking at the Crucifixion very much from the point of view of Generation. But the reader should be cautioned against overturning the immediate visual terms of the picture, which are Miltonic, for just as Blake is not here giving us *Jerusalem*, plate 76, he is not giving us the crucifixion of Orc either.

Having gone this far into the picture by means of Blake's own mythology, we can go a bit further, taking our cue from a remark of Northrop Frye's: "Man is ... a Luvah or form of life subject to two impulses, one the prophetic impulse leading him forward to vision, the other the natural impulse which drags him back to unconsciousness and finally to death" (*Fearful Symmetry*, p. 259). We can allocate these two impulses to the two sides of Blake's picture, associating them roughly with a right way and a wrong way of looking at the Crucifixion, associating the forms of Luvah with Blake's four zoas. To look at the picture this way is to see on the left (resting his weight upon his left foot)[32] a Urizenic Luvah: the expression not benign but pharisaic, the headgear and spear suggesting the Roman centurion who pierced Christ's side. It is to see on the cross a passive, neutral Luvah, a veiled emblem of patience. The poles of existence to which his suffering bears reference are suggested by the parallelism between the outstretched arms of the cross and the two interdependent heads bound within the serpent's folds at the foot. Finally, we can look at Adam as a version of Los-Urthona, stepping forward onto his right foot (the spiritual one) and looking at the sacrifice with a gaze of adoration. The base of the whole composition is Eve, obviously a form of Vala here, but it will be helpful for our purposes if we think of her as a Thel who has accepted the house of Clay.

At this point we must return to Miltonic terminology, and ask how we are to interpret Adam's simple reverence toward the cross. Blake shows Adam resting upon his right foot, and there is a very great contrast between his attitude of pure devotion and the merely exemplary use made of the cross by Michael. Is Adam worshipping natural necessity, or is he groping, however uncertainly, toward the visionary understanding represented by *Jerusalem*, plate 76? The more we compare the two pictures, the more poignant their relationship becomes. The *Jerusalem* plate, more openly doctrinal, has its ambiguities: joyful acceptance of life, what some critics recommend to Thel, is a mirror of agony and sacrifice of the self. But the poles of the ambiguity are openly expressed, the joy of Albion's dance, the agony of the face on the cross. How are we to describe the visual language of the *Paradise Lost* painting? I think we may recognize in this a familiar question, and begin to get some inkling of the importance of Milton to Blake.

We need a richer critical term than "displacement" to describe the effect we are talking about. It is not irony or satire. Blake is commenting on, but not sneering at the Miltonic vision. By scrutinizing the picture we can see in it a response to Thel's agony which transcends moralizing but which is addressed very specifically, as we see from the depiction of Eve, to her condition. What makes this illustration poignant next to the *Jerusalem* illustration is its stillness, its enigmatic containment of possibilities. The focus of these possibilities is the two faces turned toward each other, the faces of Adam and Jesus. They are the same face, and seeing this we can understand the relevance of Blake's image, with its reliance upon Milton, to *Thel* and the idea of pastoral. Pastoralism, I have suggested, raises in its acutest form the problem of transcendence. Adam's paradise within will ultimately depend upon his apprehension of the fallen world without, and his reverence for a crucified God who is his own identical image is perhaps the ultimate representation of this fact. There is nothing like an answer to the pastoral dilemma in the *Paradise Lost* watercolor, but as we pass our eyes from left to right across it, we cannot help but notice a visual progress toward an ever clearer representation of the "human form divine." The visual direction of the faces is toward Adam's simple reverence, which is strong enough to balance the more overt gesture of the didactic Michael. The *Paradise Lost* watercolors are dated about 1807, when Blake was well into the work of his maturity,[33] and so one can hardly in any chronological sense describe his career as the progress from this painting to *Jerusalem*, plate 76. But as images of the "idea of pastoral," these two representations of the Crucifixion are significant benchmarks indeed.

AMERICA AND *EUROPE*

David Erdman refers in passing to "A Song of Liberty" as an "epithalamium of the new republic" (Erdman, p. 189). It is only a chance remark, but one which raises a number of important issues. The "Song" is appended to a work called *The Marriage of Heaven and Hell*, and it would be pleasant to regard its emphatic conclusion as one of the fruits of consummation: "Empire is no more! and now the lion & wolf shall cease" (E44). But in fact the "Song" begins with Orc (Luvah in Generated form) being delivered from his mother, the "Eternal Female," which seems a subject for a different kind of poem. Indeed the imagery of the "Song" is more related to elegy than to epithalamion, for Orc is cast down by the jealous starry king (Urizen) like Lycidas into the western sea. (It is worth remarking that Orc's first appearance, which prompts an exhortation to the "citizen of London," the Jew, and the African, should be associated with the "sinking sun"; E43.) He resurrects, still like the sun, in the east (France perhaps), but it is not clear from the "Song" that this natural recurrence, for all the revolutionary fervor with which it is greeted, does anything to displace the "starry king" of the west, surrounded by the sullen, faded fires of his imperial court. If the "starry king" is in England, and the "son of fire" has appeared in Paris, Blake's position as an Englishman—expressed in imagery as natural as it is political—might imply some qualification of the "sunny confidence" which has been discovered in *The Marriage* (Erdman, p. 189).

One speaks here of imagery, rather than of relationship to political events or of political radicalism. For, while it is perfectly reasonable to think of Blake as responding to current affairs, there is very little evidence in his imagery of waxing and waning radicalism. A host of assumptions about Blake's politics have been attached to interpretations of the poems in which Orc prominently figures, notably *America* and *Europe*, but as interpretations alter such assumptions are very vulnerable. For example, Blake's "faith" in the revolutions of America and France has tended for a number of critics to be a quantity roughly equivalent to his "faith" in his mythological character Orc (Luvah generated). As "faith" in Orc comes to be called into question by events in the prophecies, equivalent political opinions are extrapolated. A crisis of confidence in revolutionary apocalypse is hypothesized to explain Orc's crucifixion scene in *Vala/The Four Zoas*. Morton Paley is one of the most decided exponents of this point of view, and his conclusion from it is a clear and absolute distinction between the kind of apocalypse (historical) to which the poet looks forward *through* the Lambeth prophecies (to 1795) and the kind of apocalypse (eschatological) to which he looks forward thereafter.[34] But an examination of the imagery of the poems calls any such absolute distinction into question, and will replace it with the concerns most recently represented to us in terms of the crucifixion of Luvah in Blake's illustration of *Paradise Lost*.

If we have to choose between imagery of epithalamion and of elegy, and if we find the distinction between the two surprisingly difficult (as a version of the question of history versus eschatology), we are only dealing with a problem familiar to us from *Thel*. There the agonized fears of a virgin demanded elegiac forms, and in

Visions of the Daughters of Albion a wedding which is prevented
by rape and obdurate jealousy refers demonically in a repeated line
of its chorus to Spenser's *Epithalamion*. The complex of imagery
may seem curious, but it was plain enough to Milton to constitute
a pastoral commonplace. When Eve comes to Adam to tell him for
the first time of her sin, he has in his hand a garland of flowers
appropriate for the epithalamic crowning of a Harvest Queen, and
while Eve talks,

> From his slack hand the Garland wreath'd for *Eve*
> Down dropd, and all the faded Roses shed.
>
> (IX.892–893)

To point the image, Milton has Adam ask,

> How art thou lost, how on a sudden lost,
> Defac't deflourd, and now to Death devote?
>
> (IX.900–901)

Similarly, we can trace most of the ambiguities related to Orc in
Blake's reading of Milton.

To begin with it will be remembered that when Thel looked
into her grave, she saw "where the fibrous roots / Of every heart
on earth infixes deep its restless twists" (E6). In the "Preludium"
to *America* (1793), the "shadowy daughter of Urthona" (an early
form of Vala) uses precisely the same image to describe the onset
of the American Revolution:

> On my American plains I feel the struggling afflictions
> Endur'd by roots that writhe their arms into the nether deep.
>
> (E51)

The daughter's sexual affliction, however, is real, not imagined, for
"red Orc," having attained the age of fourteen years, has risen to
impregnate her. Blake manages to make the event sound both
happy and portentous:

> Round the terrific loins he siez'd the panting struggling womb;
> It joy'd: she put aside her clouds & smiled her first-born smile;
> As when a black cloud shews its light'nings to the silent deep.
>
> (E50–51)

Since Orc, as already noted, is more force than human, his
athletic surfacings in the world of Generation assume in differing

places different forms, "In Mexico an Eagle, and a Lion in Peru ... a Whale in the South-sea" (E51; images suggesting ferocity), but in his dual roles of "terrible boy" (E51) and "a serpent folding / Around the pillars of Urthona" (E50), we can recognize a more threatening, pubescent version of the Infant-Worm who so puzzled Thel. The daughter of Urthona finds a voice, and cries:

> I know thee, I have found thee, & I will not let thee go;
> Thou art the image of God who dwells in darkness of Africa.
> (E51)

Blake is only by the way using Africa to suggest the outbreak of repressed phallic energy,[35] for the primitivism he associates with the name has nothing to do with racist cliché. "Africa" for Blake is Egypt, and the section of *The Song of Los* devoted to the continent begins with Adam, passes through Jesus (who receives "A Gospel from wretched Theotormon"; E66), and ends with Newton and Locke, Rousseau and Voltaire on the eve of the American Revolution. The daughter, then, may be saying simply: "I know that you are what God looks like in the fallen world." Her next line complicates the image of tygerish, apocalyptic God which this conjures up: "And thou art fall'n to give me life in regions of dark death." The line, to be sure, suggests the Incarnation of a Savior; it should also suggest Eve's fallen attitude, in *Paradise Lost*, toward Satan. And indeed the concluding lines of the paragraph suggest less the first or second coming of Christ than complete apprehension (as opposed to vegetated acceptance in the vales of Har) of the fallen condition:

> O what limb rending pains I feel. thy fire & my frost
> Mingle in howling pains, in furrows by thy lightnings rent;
> This is eternal death; and this the torment long foretold.
> (E51)

"Thy fire & my frost" are contraries, and for this reason it seems hardly possible (unless we argue that the "Preludium" has no bearing on the political implications of the poem) to suggest that the contraries apply only to the soul, and not at all to social conditions after the advent of Orc.[36] Fire and frost suggest Orc and Urizen (especially their magnificently realized confrontation in Night VII(a) of *Vala/The Four Zoas*), but they also suggest the

revised version of Nature which the Creator brings into being in
Paradise Lost as suitable to fallen man:

> The Sun
> Had first his precept so to move, so shine,
> As might affect the Earth with cold and heat
> Scarce tollerable, and from the North to call
> Decrepit Winter, from the South to bring
> Solstitial summers heat.
>
> (X.651–656)

The phrase "This is eternal death; and this the torment long
foretold" suggests plainly an Eve coming to terms with the fallen
condition. We have already seen that "eternal death" is a key
phrase in Blake; the daughter's rape in the "Preludium" is almost
indistinguishable from giving birth (her womb pants and struggles, and the joy of consummation is rendered in the phrase,
"smiled her first-born smile"; E51), and it is interesting that
Adam and Eve, a little puzzled that the death foretold them does
not descend immediately, put a similar construction on childbirth.
Adam remarks,

> wee expected
> Immediat dissolution, which we thought
> Was meant by Death that day, when lo, to thee
> Pains only in Child-bearing were foretold,
> And bringing forth, soon recompenc't with joy,
> Fruit of thy Womb.
>
> (X.1048–1053)

One could hardly ask for a closer analogue to the "first-born
smile." The question of Blake's attitude to the American Revolution seems, therefore, to have as much to do with Milton as with
historical events.

Blake probably borrows more imagery from Book II of *Paradise
Lost* than from any other location, and it is no accident that this
book relates the delegation of Satan as Hell's ambassador to the
new world, his passage through the Gates of Hell and past his
offspring, Sin and Death, through the Abyss ("the Womb of
Nature and perhaps her Grave"; 911) and finally to Earth. Blake
did not need to be reminded by his critics who Satan was, but it is
true that his vision of Satan as Desire (and hence one of the
eternal contraries) concentrates on this book, no doubt because
most of the evidence for Milton's lurking sympathy lies here

too. The first thing we hear Satan say is, "I give not Heav'n for lost" (14), and it is clear that resolution not to accept the condition of Hell struck responsive chords in Blake. Beelzebub's great speech advocating active resistance to God inspires a similar speech by Los in *Jerusalem* (compare *Paradise Lost*, II.310ff. to J., 38.12ff.; E182). Most poignant of all, perhaps, is Satan's response to ambassadorial honour,

> for on whom we send,
> The weight of all and our last hope relies,
>
> (II.415–416)

for Milton himself, when he returns to "Eternal Death" in Blake's epic, is similarly a last hope for mankind, and Blake's casting of the poet thus is an expression of gratitude and affection. "By mingling expressly personal utterances with the epic narrative in *Paradise Lost*," we are reminded by M. H. Abrams, Milton "solicits critics to seek him in other passages not written in the first person."[37] Thus, when we hear Satan saying to Sin, his daughter,

> I come no enemie, but to set free
> From out this dark and dismal house of pain,
> Both him and thee, and all the heav'nly Host ...
>
> (II.822–824)

it is difficult not to be reminded of lines in the noble invocation to light at the beginning of Book III,

> Thee I re-visit now with bolder wing,
> Escap't the *Stygian* Pool, though long detaind
> In that obscure sojourn.
>
> (III.13–15)

And it is difficult, too, to avoid relating a further autobiographical detail to Satan's career:

> ... thee I revisit safe,
> And feel thy sovran vital Lamp; but thou
> Revisit'st not these eyes ...
>
> (III.21–23)

These references are only commonplaces in what is now familiar as a standard argument of Romantic critics (for the insight was by no means limited to Blake),[38] but Blake's response to the commonplaces was unique: I suggested above that the journey of Satan for

Blake concentrates imagery confounding the first and second coming of Christ with complete apprehension of the fallen condition. Blake makes Milton a character in a poem, causes him to repeat in his own person the journey of his character, thereby leading him to apprehension not only of the fallen condition but also of the tendency of his metaphysics to maintain it:

> I in my Selfhood am that Satan: I am that Evil One!
> He is my Spectre! in my obedience to loose him from my Hells
> To claim the Hells, my Furnaces, I go to Eternal Death.
> (M., 14.30–32; E107)

Blake's idea is much more complex than the simple, emotional satanism often equated to his position by the unsympathetic, and the apprehension which the character Milton attains is more than sentimental sympathy for the underdog. Los, who sees the poet's coming, identifies it in no uncertain terms:

> He is the Signal that the Last Vintage now approaches
> Nor Vegetation may go on till all the Earth is reapd
> (M., 24.42–43; E119)

Milton, then (or one may say Milton) embodies a point of the utmost importance to the interpretation of *America*, the idea that *by* "apocalypse" Blake means the total apprehension of the fallen condition. It is in light of this fact (and the imagery of the poem) that we must judge Blake's attitude toward the revolutions of his time (an attitude more fundamental than his obvious and unchanging delight in the overthrow of tyrannical political and religious institutions). In a remarkable letter of 1800 he expresses his metered gratitude to John Flaxman for soothing him through the revolutionary period:

> The American War began. All its dark horrors passed before my face
> Across the Atlantic to France. Then the French Revolution commenc'd in thick clouds.
> And My Angels have told me that seeing such visions I could not subsist on the Earth,
> But by my conjunction with Flaxman, who knows to forgive Nervous Fear.
>
> (E680)

"Nervous Fear" is a phrase curiously bare of any political implication, but it is perhaps an appropriate phrase with which to greet revolutionary events understood to signify not merely apocalyptic hopefulness but "eternal death" and the "torment long foretold" as well. Blake actually added to these expressions of Miltonic justice the following lines from *America*:

> The stern Bard ceas'd, asham'd of his own song; enrag'd he
>   swung
> His harp aloft sounding, then dash'd its shining frame against
> A ruin'd pillar in glittring fragments; silent he turn'd away,
> And wander'd down the vales of Kent in sick & drear
>   lamentings.
>
> (E51)

These lines, traditionally assumed to constitute some sort of recantation, have proved a puzzle to critics concerned to prove that Blake has not fallen out of sympathy with the Revolution so early in his career. The lines were on Blake's original plate, however, and were subsequently *erased* (which is opposite to the procedure we would expect if they represented a change of heart), and there is little solace for historical critics either in that the lines were erased from all but the *first* and *last two* editions of the poem (E724). It is surely worth pointing out that if the lines were intended merely as recantation (and Blake could more effectively have recanted by simply melting the plates), they would more logically appear at the end than in the "Preludium." It is also worth pointing out that they have their specific literary analogue in Colin's breaking his pipes at the end of "Ianuarie," the first eclogue of *The Shepheardes Calender*. Hence, David Erdman's ingenious explanation ("The gesture may be chiefly against the English terror, if Blake, in traditional bardic fashion, is shattering his harp rather than play it in slavery"; Erdman, p. 286) may be too sober. There is further impetus for considering the pastoral parallel in that the harp-shattering bard may turn up, again defeated, at the end of the poem, his distressing condition being his share in the pestilence of England's attempt at counter-revolution:

> Hid in his caves the Bard of Albion felt the enormous plagues.
> And a cowl of flesh grew o'er his head & scales on his back & ribs.
>
> (E56)

If the two bards, at the beginning and the end, are identical, this latter description of his response to events overseas (or across the

Channel) casts a strong ironic light on any interpretation (including the following) of the apparent recantation.

The recantation theory is based upon the assumption that the bard of the "Preludium" (probably Blake himself) came to feel that the prophecy was too *optimistic* (and since the war in America was over, and Louis XVI had already been guillotined when *America* was ready for sale, this optimism is said to be aimed at the futility of Pitt's attempt to crusade against a revolutionary France: see Erdman, p. 201). It may be, however, that the reverse is true: Blake, in smashing his harp, was not attempting to erase his text, but to suggest how hard it was to bear his awareness of apocalypse as Fall.[39] In other terms, Blake may be expressing even more clearly than in his lyric the agonies of living with divinely sanctioned tigers. Or, to put the matter in still another way, by his pastoral gesture Blake expresses the strain imposed upon him by the "idea of pastoral." The important question, then, is not whether Blake believed the revolutions in France and America to portend apocalypse (the evidence of *America* and *Europe* exists to suggest that he was at least prepared to act as if he did), but what he believed apocalypse portended. The answer to this question is something roughly equivalent to expression of the ambiguities of Generation.

This idea is at least very useful for an appreciation of the imagery of *America*. It is customary, for instance, for critics to stress the fervor and apocalyptic hope of Orc's great speech beginning, "The morning comes, the night decays, the watchmen leave their stations" (E52). Yet it is not to undermine the effect of that speech to notice that it is a dramatic utterance, delivered by a character in a context. Its speaker is introduced thus:

> The Spectre glowd his horrid length staining the temple long
> With beams of blood; & thus a voice came forth, and shook the temple
>
> (E52)

Blake's special technical meaning for the term "Spectre" (the function of a divided and "natural" existence, later to be identified, in the case of Urthona, with the time-bound will; see Frye, *Fearful Symmetry*, p. 292) *may* still lie in the future, but it is interesting that a contemporaneous notebook poem presents in the most forceful terms a relationship between the ejaculations of a similarly conceived Orc and agonized awareness of a fallen condition:

I saw a chapel all of gold
That none did dare to enter in
And many weeping stood without
Weeping mourning worshipping

I saw a serpent rise between
The white pillars of the door
And he forcd & forcd & forcd
Down the golden hinges tore

And along the pavement sweet
Set with pearls & rubies bright
All his slimy length he drew
Till upon the altar white

Vomiting his poison out
On the bread & on the wine
So I turnd into a sty
And laid me down among the swine

(E458)

The enormous contradictions implicit in Orc's American imagery are systematically explicable. Albion's Angel asks him,

> Art thou not Orc; who serpent-form'd
> Stands at the gate of Enitharmon to devour her children?

(E52)

and we recognize a clear reference to Revelation 12:4, to the
dragon who stood before the "woman clothed with the sun"
(though that is an odd role for Enitharmon—unless Blake is thinking of her husband's name), ready to devour her child as soon as
she is delivered of it. But Orc in his reply agrees to an identification
with Satan even as he insists upon his apocalyptic function:

The terror answerd: I am Orc, wreath'd round the accursed
   tree:
The times are ended; shadows pass the morning gins to break.

(E52)

A bit further into the prophecy, imagery of Revelation becomes
inextricably entangled with images derived from *Paradise Lost*,
Book II, where Death's incest with his mother, Sin, produces
dogs, who (their mother complains):

To mee, for when they list, into the womb
That bred them they return, and howle and gnaw
My Bowels, their repast.

(II.798–800)

Blake boldly identifies his "rebel form that rent the ancient Heavens" with the "Devourer of thy parent," and it seems to be Sin (rather than the woman clothed with the sun) who is Orc's mother, a Sin identified with the serpentine, or fallen, form of Nature:

> And where the mothers milk? instead those ever-hissing jaws
> And parched lips drop with fresh gore; now roll thou in the
>   clouds
> Thy mother lays her length outstrech'd upon the shore beneath.
> (E53)

Clearly this Orc is not on either "side" in a revolutionary conflict (though he may portend apocalypse), but is simply the force and nature of the antagonism. Hence, while the conflict is raging, it is absolutely impossible, on the basis of imagery, to distinguish between the antagonists. Both are Orc. Here, for example, is the opening description of "Albion's wrathful Prince":

> A dragon form clashing his scales at midnight he arose,
> And flam'd red meteors round the land of Albion beneath[.]
> (E51)

Just so, in *Urizen*, we are told of Orc: "The serpent grew casting its scales" (E78). When the thirteen "Angels" who are Albion's representatives in the New World decide to throw in their lot with the American patriots, they tear off their robes to the "hungry wind" (the same wind which blows in the "Argument" to *The Marriage*) and stand beside "Washington & Paine & Warren" (E54). We are told:

> And the flame folded roaring fierce within the pitchy night
> Before the Demon red, who burnt towards America,
> In black smoke thunders and loud winds rejoicing in its terror
> (E54)

David Erdman identifies the "Demon" reasonably as "not Orc but one of Albion's 'punishing Demons' or redcoats" (Erdman, pp. 26–27). But Blake uses exactly the same phrase for the spirit of revolution later, explaining how Urizen was "Hiding the Demon red with clouds & cold mists from the earth" (E56). At the poem's end, the Urizenic forces

... slow advance to shut the gates of their law-built heaven
Filled with blasting fancies and with mildews of despair
With fierce disease and lust, unable to stem the fires of Orc;
But the five gates were consum'd, & their bolts and hinges
    melted
And the fierce flames burnt round the heavens, & round the
    abodes of men

                      (E56)

The most important gate, perhaps, is the one associated with the loins (see the "gate of Enitharmon" referred to above), and Blake means here the "improvement of sensual enjoyment" to which he refers in *The Marriage* (E38). More generally, as Northrop Frye puts it, "the poem ends with a vision of the imagination bursting through the senses until the chaos of earth and water that we see begins to dissolve in fire" (*Fearful Symmetry*, p. 206). But we shall miss half Blake's point if we miss the reference to Hell's Gates in *Paradise Lost* ("So wide they stood, and like a Furnace mouth / Cast forth redounding smoak and ruddy flame"; II.888–889), through which Satan passes to this world. For Blake, apocalypse is indeed the "Marriage of Heaven and Hell."

For the frontispiece to *America* Blake reworked an early painting, *War*, and for *Europe*, dated 1794, he reworked related paintings of *Famine* and *Plague*.[40] Within the context of revolutionary history, it makes sense to think of *America* and *Europe* as studies of "War" and "Peace," respectively. The associated paintings, as well as the historical research of David Erdman (pp. 210–225), make it clear that the "peace" is pestilential, the central, historical section of *Europe* referring to a period in England of war scares and anti-Jacobinism, in fact no peace at all but that phase of war which is referred to by political hypocrites as "keeping the peace." The irony of *Europe*, as we might expect from its theme, is more complex than that of *America* (as complex, in fact, as that of the Lyca poems, and Enitharmon's sleep of 1800 years in *Europe* is only a historically particular version of Lyca's sleep), and the imagery of the poem is correspondingly under more elaborate control, the principal element of which is manipulation of a cunning historical cycle. This cycle, like the paradoxical imagery of *America*, relies upon confusion of three events: the coming of Satan to earth in *Paradise Lost*, the first coming of Christ (also rendered by allusion to Milton in a parody of the "Nativity Hymn"), and the second coming. The period between first and second coming is the dream of Enitharmon, a period in which England's pestilential response to the appearance of new light in France is taken as a type of history's perversion of Jesus and as type of the Fall in general. Blake's imagery displays clearly the relationship in his mind between the landscape of "The Tyger,"

> Thought chang'd the infinite to a serpent; that which pitieth:
> To a devouring flame; and man fled from its face and hid
> In forests of night ...
>
> (E62)

and the world of the Enlightenment:

> Then was the serpent temple form'd, image of infinite
> Shut up in finite revolutions, and man became an Angel;
> Heaven a mighty circle turning; God a tyrant crown'd.
>
> (E62)

Making allowances for irony, we can see Shaftesbury and Newton in these lines.

However, despite the more elaborate imagery and mythological framework, the underlying thematic concern of *Europe*, again dependent for its expression upon allusion to Milton, is the same as that of *America*—the conflation in Generation of the imagery of Fall and Apocalypse. The prefatory twenty-four-line poem added to two of the extant copies of the poem may be "lyric after-thought," as David Erdman suggests (Erdman, p. 264), but it nevertheless comes close to being an expression of what is really on Blake's mind. Evidently alarmed by the extent to which his doubts might betray him as a pessimist, Blake tries in a fanciful *jeu d'esprit* to lighten the tone of his poem. Blake plays the part of naif (which could hardly have been a comfortable role), and the Fairy, after a prefatory exhortation to the improvement of sensual enjoyment, settles down to answer the naif's question: "Then tell me, what is the material world, and is it dead?" (E59). The Fairy promises, if primed with "a cup of sparkling poetic fancies" to show the naif "all alive the world, when every particle of dust breathes forth its joy" (E59). But the demonstration, while it sometimes manages to sound demonically cheerful, does not really dispel the gloom.

The gloom is presented to us in the first instance by the "Preludium," mainly a soliloquy by the "nameless shadowy fe-male" who "rose out of the breast of Orc" (E59: that Orc should be lover in *America* and parent power in *Europe* is not surprising if one remembers the various interdependent appearances of Vala and Luvah outlined in "The Mental Traveller") to register a complaint cognate to complaints we have already heard from Enion and Thel:

> O mother Enitharmon wilt thou bring forth other sons?
> To cause my name to vanish, that my place may not be found.
>
> (E59)

Here fear of Generation is related in a way which should by now seem familiar to consummation at the hands of an Orc. But the consummation to which the "shadowy female" refers is clearly not periodic but incessant, "consumed and consuming!" (E59), being the normal state of the tygerish "seventh Eye" of history (associated with Jesus). The "Preludium" is not, then, "an oracle of the second coming of Christ" or even "of the Armageddon of 1793" (Erdman, p. 265), but an account of the pseudo-peace which accepts the Tyger and the Female Will as part of the Eternal Plan. Nature is in agony, and achieves its fallen, shadowy, and watery form trying to shelter from the Urizenic, starry tears which rain down here as they do in "The Tyger":

> I wrap my turban of thick clouds around my lab'ring head;
> And fold the sheety waters as a mantle round my limbs.
> Yet the red sun and moon,
> And all the overflowing stars rain down prolific pains.
> Unwilling I look up to heaven! unwilling count the stars!
> Sitting in fathomless abyss of my immortal shrine.
> I sieze their burning power
> And bring forth howling terrors, all devouring fiery kings.
>
> (E59)

The "red sun and moon" are related later in the poem to two of the children of Enitharmon, Rintrah and Palamabron (who represent the fallen, equivocal contraries Wrath and Pity); the stars belong to Urizen, and both the reference to counting the stars and the suggestion of one-to-one correspondence between fallen stars and "fiery kings" suggest Urizen's identification with Satan as the dragon whose "tail drew the third part of the stars of heaven, and did cast them to the earth" (Revelation 12:4). This becomes an important link to the imagery of the prophecy proper.

I have already suggested that *America* concludes with a "marriage" of heaven and hell. The "Preludium" to *Europe* also includes references, both recondite and comic, to erotic alliances (or at least attempted ones). The essential imagery here is terribly concentrated:

> I bring forth from my teeming bosom myriads of flames.
> And thou dost stamp them with a signet, then they roam abroad
> And leave me void as death:
> Ah! I am drowned in shady woe, and visionary joy.
>
> And who shall bind the infinite with an eternal band?
> To compass it with swaddling bands? and who shall cherish it
> With milk and honey?
> I see it smile & I roll inward & my voice is past.
>
> > She ceast & rolld her shady clouds
> > Into the secret place.
>
> > (E60)

The "Preludium," not merely a prelude to action, constitutes a reflection in mythological form of the thematic core of the poem, and the truest sign of apocalyptic "quickening," or gathering intensity, is that Nature, usually dumb, has found a voice. The sexual collision with Orc (and this was also the case in *America*) is in this sense both apocalyptic and Orphic. Analysis of the imagery will show that it is not fanciful to associate the speaker's newfound voice with the Serpent's in *Paradise Lost* and with Milton's Eve.[41] Even more to the immediate point is that in the stanzas quoted the language recapitulates the problem of Generation as presented in Blake's earlier poems. The first of the two stanzas contains an unmistakable reference to *Visions of the Daughters of Albion* (1793), and the second recapitulates the crisis of *Thel*, in its last line underlining the connection between that poem and "A Cradle Song":

> Smiles on thee on me on all,
> Who became an infant small,
> Infant smiles are his own smiles.
> Heaven & earth to peace beguiles.
>
> > (E12)

I will pursue these suggestions in the order of their appearance in the poem.

In *Visions*, after the heroine, Oothoon, has frankly declared her love for Theotormon (whose name suggests "tormented by God") by plucking a flower of Leutha (even as Blake's Fairy plucks flowers in the preface to *Europe*), she is rent ("My virgin mantle in twain"; E44) by Bromion, a character associated with Urizen. I take this "rending" to be a psychological or spiritual event, rather than merely a physical rape, and I take Bromion in one sense to be Theotormon's "spectre" (as, say, Iago is in a sense Othello's spectre),[42] and therefore I understand that the relationship between Bromion and Theotormon (who is associated with both the sea and with tears) is an early version of the "war" between Urizen and Tharmas in *Vala/The Four Zoas*. Oothoon is identified as the "soft soul of America" (E44; so that we expect the poem to have a relationship to the prophecy *America*), and the upshot of the "rape" (or so Bromion mistakenly thinks) is reduction of that soul to the code of fear which Bromion represents. Blake associates the fall of Oothoon into the imaginative condition of Bromion with the practice of slavery:

> Thy soft American plains are mine, and mine thy north & south:
> Stampt with my signet are the swarthy children of the sun.
>
> (E45)

The "shadowy female" of *Europe* is, then, on the first level complaining that Enitharmon is doing to her children (children of the sun, of Blake's vision of "Africa") what Bromion thinks he does to Oothoon. Even more important, especially with reference to the 1800-year period Blake is surveying, is the allusion in the next line to "shady woe" and "visionary joy," for when we see in *Visions* Oothoon and Bromion bound back-to-back in the cave of Theotormon, we are seeing one of Blake's enduring visions of the fallen condition, a vision described in *Milton* as "the Contraries of Beulah ... beneath Negation's Banner" (M., 34.23.; E133). The Negation is Theotormon, "shady woe"; Oothoon is one of the Contraries, and she represents very poignantly, as we shall see, "visionary joy." The point is that Negation and Contrary can never interact, can never marry, and so the remark "I am drowned in shady woe, and visionary joy" (which is a bit more specific than the "nervous fear" of Blake's letter) contains its hopeless imagery of unconsummated marriage.

When we read, next, the female's question, "And who shall bind the infinite with an eternal band? To compass it with swaddling bands?" if we recognize the allusion to *Thel*, we can see that this imagery too has to do with marriage. The "eternal band" is, on the level of allusion, a wedding band, and the "shadowy female" is asking (among other things), "Who is to be my bridegroom?" The next tendency of her imagery, motherhood and nurture (a mother, notice, who swaddles her child), simultaneously suggests the encompassing of Eternity which takes place according to orthodox views in the Incarnation and the tendency of the "shadowy female" to assume the posture of the sinister vegetable mother of "A Cradle Song."

But there is another, entirely comic answer to the female's question, an answer not related to *Thel*, for the person who can *bind* the infinite and *compass* it in baby clothes is, on another level, Newton, who indeed does make an appearance at the end of the Prophecy blithely to blow the trumpet of the Last Judgment. Well might eternity smile at the female's conceit, and it remains only to point out that when she retires under clouds "into the secret place," she is enacting an allusion to *Paradise Lost*. "Shady woe" and "visionary joy" suggest Milton's Eve as well as Theotormon and Oothoon; it is certainly Eve who remarks, after eating the forbidden fruit:

> Experience, next to thee I owe,
> Best guide; not following thee, I had remain
> In ignorance, thou op'nst Wisdoms way,
> And giv'st access, though secret she retire.
> And I perhaps am secret; Heav'n is high,
> High and remote to see from thence distinct
> Each thing on Earth.
>
> (IX.807–813)

I have already observed, in the course of analyzing "The Tyger," Blake's parody in *Europe* of Milton's "Nativity Hymn" (see also Erdman, pp. 266–267),[43] where the parody is used to accomplish the confusion of Fall, first and second comings:

> Again the night is come
> That strong Urthona takes his rest,
> And Urizen unloos'd from chains
> Glows like a meteor in the distant north
> Stretch forth your hands and strike the elemental strings!
> Awake the thunders of the deep.
>
> (E60)

Blake, as already noted, is imitating stanzas 10 and 13 of Milton's great ode, but it is more to the point in this context to remember that the night "that strong Urthona takes his rest" is the evening of *Paradise Lost* celebrated in "Night," and that Urizen, loose and glowing in the distant north, is the approaching Satan. Los calls for music ("Awake the thunders of the deep"), and although it is a robust music we can see that it is suitable for celebrating the natural, feral pleasures of the long night of Nature. (There is exactly analogous music in Enitharmon's hymn—celebrating a cognate occasion—in *Vala/The Four Zoas*, and David Erdman is surely wrong in regarding it here as Los's revolutionary warning to "the people": Erdman, p. 267.) Indeed, the alarming thing about Los's response to memory is his failure to regard repetition of the Fall as anything he need do anything about, even though his language reflects the fact that he used to be "Urthona" (earth owner) and is now "Los" (loss). But this is only one of his failures to understand: even as he provokes impending war with Urizen by arousing the envy of his sons, he complacently contemplates binding (we remember the shadowy female's concern with bind-ing) "all the nourishing sweets of earth / To give us bliss" (E60). Los's response to the sinister Advent is a mindless embrace of his fallen condition; as in the corresponding passage in *Vala/The Four Zoas*, he is mesmerized by a song of this fallen world. He is even hypocritical enough to urge Orc, his son, to rise, promising to crown his head with garlands—but only because he sees Orc as already bound.

These ideas applied to Blake's parody of Milton make that parody seem rather bitter, but Blake evidently felt bitter about a song which associated the return of the age of gold (135) and of Truth and Justice (141) with the Advent, only to conclude:

But wisest Fate sayes no,
This must not yet be so,
   The Babe lies yet in smiling Infancy,
That on the bitter cross
Must redeem our loss;
   So both himself and us to glorifie:
Yet first to those ychain'd in sleep,
The wakefull trump of doom must thunder through the deep.
                         (149–156)

Blake records his divergence from this sentiment not only in the ambiguities of his Advent, but in the rather raw comedy of his Last Things as well:

The red limb'd Angel siez'd, in horror and torment;
The Trump of the last doom; but he could not blow the iron tube!
Thrice he assay'd presumptuous to awake the dead to Judgment.

A mighty Spirit leap'd from the land of Albion,
Nam'd Newton; he siez'd the Trump, & blow'd the enormous blast!
                         (E63)

The joke at Newton's expense is obvious enough (see Frye, *Fearful Symmetry*, p. 254); the allusion to *Paradise Lost* is subtler, but perhaps even funnier:

> Thrice he assay'd, and thrice in spite of scorn,
> Tears such as Angels weep, burst forth: at last
> Words interwove with sighs found out thir way.
>
> (I.619–621)

In Milton's poem the emotion-choked speaker is Satan, making his first address to his fellows after the Fall. Blake's "Trump of the last doom" is the annunication of Satan's resistance to God's designs.

The sun, in Milton's ode, "with-held his wonted speed, and hid his head for shame" (79–80) before the Advent; Blake sardonically uses the extra time for a prolonged account of the daughters of Enitharmon and their dreadful revels. But morning does eventually come, and when it does "terrible Orc" leaves the "heights" of Enitharmon and reappears "in the vineyards of red France" (E65). A crisis impends, one which will make use of "furious terrors," "golden chariots," lions and tygers who "couch upon the prey & suck the ruddy tide" (E65). Everything we have seen about the poem calls into question any simple optimism about this crisis, and indeed we notice that the reappearance of Orc is not quite the end of the poem. For we read,

> Then Los arose his head he reard in snaky thunders clad:
> And with a cry that shook all nature to the utmost pole,
> Call'd all his sons to the strife of blood.
>
> (E65)

Those who wish to extract a "hopeful" apocalypse from *Europe* must concentrate on these lines. The suggestion of "snaky thunders" makes it clear that Los is still "fallen," and there is nothing *in* the poem (perhaps only the poem itself) to explain what has roused Los from his lethargy. There is no hint of what he will do, and nothing to suggest that what he does will be anything more than involvement in the ghastly cycle of Orc and Urizen. But Los's act is the first remotely to suggest departure in the poem from cycle and ironic repetition, and I think we may take it as a hint of Blake's new direction in the works to follow.

VISIONS OF THE DAUGHTERS OF ALBION AND *VALA*

In *Europe* we saw that Enitharmon was the presiding spirit of a fallen nature, constantly "Devouring & devoured" (E60). The poem concluded with a long expression of her Female Will as she called her children, representative of sexual secrecy, jealousy, and pestilence, to preside over Europe. Her final exhortation is to Orc ("give our mountains joy of thy red light"; E65), but as we have seen, she has mistaken the date, and Orc has business in France. In the revisions to the second "Night" of *Vala/The Four Zoas* Blake concentrates his expression of Enitharmon as Female Will into a magnificent and terrifying hymn or ode, which is one of the greatest glories of the manuscript (see 34.58–92; E317–318). Enitharmon has been torturing Los with unfulfilled desire and jealousy, summing up in her relationship to Los the sexual aspects of the Fall of the Eternals in Beulah. That fall is expressed (in the first four Nights) as the sexual separations of Enion and Ahania from their respective husbands, and Enitharmon has been entertaining herself by assuming the forms of both and attempting to arouse Los sexually. When he responds, she accuses him of unfaithfulness. Finally he is nearly done to death by her torment, and the purpose of the hymn is to revive Los in order to preserve the world order which their "marriage" represents. One of the song's most telling aspects, as we have already seen, is its transformation of the music of the spheres as expressed in Milton's "Nativity Hymn" to express the outlook of the Female Will. The hymn, like Los's evocations at the beginning of *Europe*, is essentially Orphic epithalamion, and there is more than one suggestion of Spenser in it. In the first stanza we encounter that pastoral cliché the echo ("The Eccho wakes the moon to unbind her silver locks"; E317— which takes us back to "To the Evening Star"), and there is a phrase repeated in the first two stanzas ("bears on my song") reminiscent of the *Prothalamion*. But the song is almost too strange to remind us of anything; a Pindaric ode (as the eighteenth century understood such things), it manages beautifully to be both grand and antiquely stiff.

As a sort of female Orpheus Enitharmon speaks words that evoke a vision of the universe as sexual cycle dependent on jealousy and torment. The central stanza includes a reference to sexual consummation as the deeps lift up a "rugged head" and lose it with a cry in "infinite humming wings" (E317; compare

Spenser's *Epithalamion*, 357–363). Enitharmon is seducing Los, and so she dwells lovingly on these wings, the sparkling after-thoughts of sexual pleasure:

> Arize you little glancing wings & sing your infant joy
> Arize & drink your bliss
> For every thing that lives is holy for the source of life
> Descends to be a weeping babe
> For the Earthworm renews the moisture of the sandy plain
> (E317)

Again we are shocked to discover the Incarnation at the heart of what Enitharmon represents; again we see Blake recapitulating his earlier poems. The reference to the concerns of *Thel* is unmistakable in the last two lines quoted. The first two-and-a-half lines are quoted directly from *Visions of the Daughters of Albion*, being the final lines of Oothoon's magnificent oration on behalf of imaginative freedom and the improvement of sensual enjoyment: "I cry, Love! Love! Love! happy happy Love! free as the mountain wind!" (E49).

The remark "Arise you little glancing wings ... For every thing that lives is holy!" occurs, then, in two remarkably different contexts, and this fact is a reminder of our central problem, the ambiguities of the Generated condition. For Oothoon is a form of Generation, of course, but Blake's expropriation of her sentiment for Enitharmon's hymn no more constitutes a sneer at her than does his translation of the ecstatic song of the lark in *Milton* to a "Vision of the lamentation of Beulah" constitute a sneer at the expense of that creature (M., 31.28–45).[44] Oothoon is not an object of the poet's scorn, but she does represent for him his dilemma. In analyzing that dilemma in *Visions* Blake suggests the direction of its solution, a fact which is most easily exposed if we pursue the parallels between the earlier poem and Night III of the *Vala/The Four Zoas* manuscript.

I have recorded at some length the registration of Blake's attitude toward Generation in the person of Orc, and I have briefly wondered whether Los (Blake's Adam) was not, for all his participation in Enitharmon's world, going to represent a more positive attitude. It is interesting to see, at the beginning of Night III, Urizen torment himself at the prospect of a figure in whom we cannot distinguish Los from Orc:

> O bright [*Ahania*] a Boy is born of the dark Ocean
> Whom Urizen doth serve, with Light replenishing his darkness
> (38.2–3; E319–320)

And it is interesting to observe that the only defense of which Urizen can conceive is a kind of incarnation in reverse, in which the principles of Nature (Luvah and Vala) are planted in Los and Enitharmon:

> ... yet I must serve & that Prophetic boy
> Must grow up to command his Prince but hear my determind Decree
> Vala shall become a Worm in Enitharmons Womb
> Laying her seed upon the fibres soon to issue forth
> And Luvah in the loins of Los a dark & furious death
> (38.6–10; E320)

It is evident from the imagery that Orc is meant, but it is odd to have him referred to as "Prophetic boy," since Los is "Eternal Prophet" in *Urizen* and *The Book of Los*. And the boy born of the "dark Ocean" (Tharmas) is also Los. Evidently a new sort of conflation is under way in Blake's imagination.

More immediately pertinent is Ahania's response to Urizen's anxiety, her attempt to persuade him to trust in the "Eternal One" and to "Resume thy fields of Light" (E320). She first upbraids him,

> Why didst thou listen to the voice of Luvah that dread morn
> To give the immortal steeds of light to his deceitful hands
> (39.2–3; E320)

and the substance of her accusation becomes, in *Milton*, the basis for the myth in the Bard's Song where Palamabron (Blake in the personal allegory) hands over his harrow for the day to Satan (the part played at Felpham by William Hayley). Ahania then relates to Urizen a version of the Fall in which Man, after Luvah has risen into the porches of the mind, is seen to fall in love with "a sweet entrancing self delusion, a watry vision of Man" (40.5; E320). This image recurs later in the Night when Urizen casts out Ahania, despite her advice, telling her, "thou hast risen with thy moist locks into a watry image" (43.17; E322). In each case one suspects that Blake is thinking of Eve, first shown to us in *Paradise Lost* (IV.453–465) admiring herself in water, and Urizen's language as he casts Ahania out suggests Adam's bitterness toward Eve after the Fall as well as a fear of tenderness and sexuality:

> Shall the feminine indolent bliss. the indulgent self of weariness
> The passive idle sleep the enormous night & darkness of Death
> Set herself up to give her laws to the active masculine virtue
> (43.6–8; E322)

Urizen's sensibility is also reflected in Blake's drawings for the Night, which depict the Fall as about equal parts of horror and idolatry of sex.

Here is where the links between Enitharmon's hymn, Oothoon, and Ahania's vision are forged. The "rape" of Oothoon by Bromion results in the visual grouping we have already observed, Bromion and Oothoon bound back-to-back in his cave ("terror & meekness"; E45), Theotormon wearing the threshold "hard with secret tears" (E45). Oothoon's response is at first masochistic and self-abasing:

> Oothoon weeps not: she cannot weep! her tears are locked up;
> But she can howl incessant writhing her soft snowy limbs.
> And calling Theotormons Eagles to prey upon her flesh.
>
> I call with holy voice! kings of the sounding air,
> Rend away this defiled bosom that I may reflect.
> The image of Theotormon on my pure transparent breast.
>
> (E45)

The ironies (based upon the career of Milton's Eve) are less important than the fact that self-abasement is here complicated by sexual response; as Harold Bloom suggests, Oothoon's writhings are presumably venereal.[45] Enitharmon, to conclude her hymn of sexual resurrection in *Vala/The Four Zoas*, soothes Los with the following sentiments, drawing on similar ideas:

> O I am weary lay thine hand upon me or I faint
> I faint beneath these beams of thine
> For thou hast touchd my five senses & they answerd thee
> Now I am nothing & I sink
> And on the bed of silence sleep till thou awakest me
>
> (E318)

The last three lines would do for a summary of Ahania's career as described in Night III. And indeed, in Ahania's account of man "Idolatrous to his own Shadow" (his God a watery reflection of the principle of repression), we discover the same language which Enitharmon uses:

> O I am nothing when I enter into judgment with thee
> If thou withdraw thy breath I die & vanish into Hades
> If thou dost lay thine hand upon me behold I am silent
> If thou withold thine hand I perish like a fallen leaf
> O I am nothing & to nothing must return again
> If thou withdraw thy breath behold I am oblivion
>
> (40.13–18; E321)

Blake again illustrates the connection between religious self-abasement and consciousness of sexual affliction by means of allusion to Milton's Adam and to Job:

> ... futurity is before me
> Like a dark lamp. Eternal death haunts all my expectation
> . . . .
> And Luvah strove to gain dominion over the Eternal Man
> They strove together above the Body where Vala was inclos'd
> And the dark body of Man left prostrate upon the crystal
> pavement
> Coverd with boils from head to foot. the terrible smitings of
> Luvah
>
> (41.7–16; E321)

Urizen's mistaken, watery self-worship eventually engulfs the world, for his dismissal of Ahania completes the Fall in Beulah (the subject of the first four Nights of the manuscript), breaks the "bounds of Destiny," and initiates the Deluge. The universes of Blake's four mythological protagonists are ruined, and there is a noise premonitory of the Last Things. But just as Melville's *Pequod* has its one survivor, so the fallen ocean floats its one survivor from the past (Los and Enitharmon are "generated" into the fallen world):

> But from the Dolorous Groan one like a shadow of smoke
> appeard
> And human bones rattling together in the smoke & stamping
> The nether Abyss & gnashing in fierce despair. panting in sobs
> Thick short incessant bursting sobbing. deep despairing
> stamping struggling
> Struggling to utter the voice of Man struggling to take the
> features of Man.
>
> (44.14–18; E323)

This character is Tharmas, in his fallen state identified with the flood. Tharmas is very relevant to an investigation of Blake's pastoralism, for as we have seen his eternal occupation is shepherd, and he is associated with Beulah, the pastoral realm where "Contrarieties are equally True." In Night I of the manuscript, an incredible thicket of revisions and corrections, we see the process of the Fall and the creation of Generation initiated by the sexual union of Enion and the spectrous or fallen ego of Tharmas. The union itself is of a piece with the feral but barbarously beautiful sexuality celebrated in Enitharmon's hymn; Tharmas' threats—

the initiatory stages of this union—bring *Paradise Lost* to mind, an accusatory Adam or a threatening Satan:

> Art thou not my slave & shalt thou dare
> To smite me with thy tongue beware lest I sting also thee
> ·
> This world is Mine in which thou dwellest that within thy soul
> That dark & dismal infinite where Thought roams up & down
> Is thine & there thou goest when with one Sting of my tongue
> Envenomd thou rollst inwards to the place of death & hell
> She trembling answerd Wherefore was I born & what am I
> A sorrow & a fear a living torment & naked Victim
>> (a deleted passage—with many corrections unre-
>> corded here—E741–742; or, more accessibly, 6.27–
>> 37 in the Bentley facsimile transcript)

The interesting reference to "that dark & dismal infinite where Thought roams up & down" can be traced in *Paradise Lost* to an unheroic Belial, urging acceptance of Hell and finding resistance to God too risky,

> ... for who would loose,
> Though full of pain, this intellectual being,
> Those thoughts that wander through Eternity,
> To perish rather ...
>> (II.146–149)

Indeed, one of Belial's projections of a worse fate is very suggestive of Tharmas' condition in Night III:

> ... for ever sunk
> Under yon boiling Ocean, wrapt in Chains;
> There to converse with everlasting groans,
> Unrespited, unpitied, unrepreevd,
> Ages of hopeless end; this would be worse.
>> (II.182–186)

But an even better analogue (seasoned with the lugubrious spices of Job; see 28:12 and 28:20) is from Blake's own *Visions*:

> Tell me where dwell the thoughts forgotten till thou call them
>   forth
> Tell me where dwell the joys of old! & where the ancient loves?
> And when will they renew again & the night of oblivion past?
> That I might traverse times & spaces far remote and bring
> Comforts into a present sorrow and a night of pain
> Where goest thou O thought? to what remote land is thy flight?
>> (E47)

The speaker is Theotormon, whose relationship to Tharmas is worth insisting upon.

Looked at in one way, *Visions of the Daughters of Albion* (dated 1793) is merely a restatement of the familiar mythological conflict between repressive Urizen (whose name is evoked for the first time in *Visions*) and irrepressible Luvah (represented in this case by the female "emanation," Oothoon). But in the development of Oothoon's "husband," Theotormon—and to a lesser extent in the development of Bromion, her "lover"—Blake achieved an important imaginative breakthrough. Even here there is no violation of "the unusual organic consistency of Blake's symbolism" (Frye, *Fearful Symmetry*, p. 205), for Theotormon (as well as Tharmas) develops a selected aspect of the earlier Tiriel, but in terms of the role Blake was planning for Los Theotormon is a new kind of character, neither simply repressor nor simply repressed. It would be difficult to exaggerate the importance of this (and it may seem we are doing so when we recollect how relatively few lines Blake assigns to Theotormon in *Visions* and how shadowy his depiction is), and we get some hint of the implications in the *Vala/ The Four Zoas* manuscript when Theotormon's counterpart there, Tharmas, first encounters Los. In the earlier Lambeth books, Los's energies were completely subsumed by Urizen: Los's creation is seen as a way of holding Urizen in check (see *Urizen*, IV, and *The Book of Los, passim*). In *Vala/The Four Zoas* Los meets Tharmas on the eve of his great work of creation/containment, declaring (as we might expect):

> Our God is Urizen the King. King of the Heavenly hosts
> We have no other God but he thou father of worms & clay
> (48.15–16; E325)

But despite this it is Tharmas, initiating what Blake comes to call the "war" between himself and Urizen, who directs Los from this point on. Therefore it is Tharmas, and his earlier correspondent, Theotormon, who must now receive our best attention.

As is so often the case with Blake's sensitivity to formal causes, if one can discover the signs of genre (however buried or transformed), this is a help in determining intention. As already noted, *Visions* is threaded by the recurrent line, "The Daughters of Albion hear her woes. & eccho back her sighs" (E45), surely a broad enough hint of the *Epithalamion*. The hint, however, enforces an irony, because, although *Visions* seems designed only as a showcase for Oothoon's imaginative breakthrough from masochistic reflection of her husband to ecstatic celebrant of Urizen's folly ("thy labour vain, to form men to thine image"; E47), the "marriage" is in no real sense ever consummated. Oothoon is "in" Vala, in a generated condition, but Blake, who was the author of her very moving imaginative revelations, was not satisfied with this explanation for her ultimate domestic failure to reach Theotormon. A rough approximation of Blake's understanding of the reason for the failure would be "doom in the human heart," but his analysis of this idea in terms of the three protagonists of *Visions* is extraordinarily obscure even by Blakean standards. One reason for this is surely a multiplicity of thematic motives—sexual, political, and spiritual—combined with the failure to consolidate these themes into one unified pattern of imagery. Blake makes an attempt at the beginning of the poem to relate the failure of the "marriage" to the failure of America's aspirations by summing up both in the image of slavery (see Erdman, pp. 226–242). The image is successful enough as a vision of the institutional idea of marriage, and it is useful as a metaphor for explaining some aspects of Oothoon's initial sado-masochistic relationship to Theotormon (see the illustration to plate 9), but it is less useful when applied to Theotormon's fundamental failure to respond to Oothoon (on the political level, England's total inability to realize the implications—so far as "policy" was concerned—of what was going on in America). Hence, in one of the poem's most striking illustrations (plate 4) we see Oothoon, chained by the foot inside one of Theotormon's green waves, which rises like a licking tongue of flame over the shore where he sits, unseeing, sunk in despair. We can explain Oothoon's manacles in terms of "slavery" (or, more comprehensively, in terms of her being bound to the vegetable condition), but it is the relationship between the metaphor and Theotormon's despairing indifference which is the difficult crux of the poem.

The most definitive statement of this crux (illustrated in the frontispiece, which is often printed as the last page of the poem) comes early in the text. The character Bromion, who in the fiction of love triangle plays the part of "lover," rends Oothoon, and then Theotormon himself is rent. The fact that the same language is used in each case (compare 1.17 to 2.3; E45) tells us that ordinary sexual rape is not meant (though that may be included in the case of Oothoon), but a more psychological or spiritual sense of division and self-loathing. Presumably to be "rent" by Bromion or by his stormy terrors is to be reduced to the position of Tharmas and Enion at the beginning of the Fall in *Vala/The Four Zoas*, here described by Enion:

> Once thou wast to Me the loveliest son of heaven—But now
> Why art thou Terrible and yet I love thee in thy terror till
> I am almost Extinct & soon shall be a Shadow in Oblivion
> Unless some way can be found that I may look upon thee & live
> Hide me some Shadowy semblance. secret whispring in my Ear
> In secret of soft wings. in mazes of delusive beauty
> I have lookd into the secret soul of him I lovd
> And in the Dark recesses found Sin & cannot return
>
> (4.19–26; E298)

It is notable that Theotormon's response to being rent is to put Oothoon in a secret place where he cannot see her; and with her he puts his "terror," Bromion:

> Then storms rent Theotormons limbs; he rolld his waves around.
> And folded his black jealous waters round the adulterate pair
> Bound back to back in Bromions caves terror & meekness dwell
>
> (E45)

This image has to be seen as a complicated psychological metaphor. The cave "belongs" to Bromion, but its establishment is in the imagination of Theotormon. What this means is that both Bromion and Oothoon are aspects of Theotormon's imagination, and a measure of the complexity of the metaphor—looked at as an example of psychological analysis—is that Theotormon has bound the two aspects of his imagination "back to back" (presumably in order to preclude sexual relations between them), but that one of the aspects is itself responsible for the "cave" in which he can be bound. The point, then, is that Bromion is an active, in some sense constructive agent within Theotormon (the relationship between the three characters is the standard one we see elsewhere in Blake as subject, emanation, and spectre: see Frye, *Fearful Symmetry*, pp. 72–73), and Blake not altogether convincingly tries to render this in terms of a Bromion who is a raping slave-agent who hands his charges (women in general), once they are impregnated, over to a deaf and sterile overlord for legal protection and respectability.

The imagery may be problematic, but Blake's imaginative achievement, which surely helped unleash the extraordinary and moving exuberance of Oothoon, was great. Bromion, as critics seemingly never tire of pointing out, is Urizenic, but the only important reason for pointing this out is to notice that for the first time Blake makes the Urizenic imaginative condition an aspect of a larger, "parent power." And Bromion is not entirely Urizenic either; it ought to have been noticed more than it has that his speech outlining the Urizenic position places question marks at the ends of statements, for Bromion, like Thel, is on the verge of enlightenment, and the most important reason that he cannot pass out of his cave is that Theotormon occupies the threshold and refuses to budge. Bromion's questions, like Oothoon's sexual overtures, are addressed to Theotormon, but the latter remains deaf. This, however, should not blind us to the possibilities inherent in the questions:

> Ah! are there other wars, beside the wars of sword and fire!
> And are there other sorrows, beside the sorrows of poverty!
> And are there other joys, beside the joys of riches and ease?
> And is there not one law for both the lion and the ox?
> And is there not eternal fire, and eternal chains?
> To bind the phantoms of existence from eternal life?
>
> (E47)

Bromion's "terror," moreover, is a more volatile response than Urizen's to the fact that "no flesh nor spirit could keep / His iron laws one moment" (E80), but it is also more susceptible to change. In fact, if we try to find a character in Blake analogous to Bromion, devoted to Urizen but constructive in his own right of a containing world, the only character who remotely fits the description is Los, and it is interesting to see that Blake himself makes this association when he has Los, in *Milton*, relate his four sons (of whom Bromion is the fourth) to the four eternal zoas (M., 24.9–12; E118). It is also interesting that when Blake portrays Bromion as tottering on the edge of enlightenment he permeates his language with oblique allusions to the temptation of Eve in *Paradise Lost*. As a man gropes through Experience toward some kind of imaginative renewal, Blake is anxious to relate his insight (and his failure to make an impression on Theotormon) to an expression of his falling:

> Thou knowest that the ancient trees seen by thine eyes have
>   fruit;
> But knowest thou that trees and fruits flourish upon the earth
> To gratify senses unknown? trees beasts and birds unknown:
> Unknown, not unperceivd, spread in the infinite microscope,
> In places yet unvisited by the voyager. and in worlds
> Over another kind of seas, and in atmospheres unknown.
>
> (E47)

This is an extraordinary, subtle speech. Bromion, as his remark about the microscope shows, has interested himself in science, and Northrop Frye has pointed out the connection between his Urizenic prejudices and his belief in "an unthinkably mysterious and remote world beyond his reach" (*Fearful Symmetry*, p. 239). But, since he is stationed in Theotormon's mind and is under the impetus of his dim divination that the Urizenic outlook is not the only one, his attraction to that "remote world beyond his reach" can only be regarded as a good thing. Yet it is a good thing, like Oothoon's glorious speech in praise of sexual liberation, undeniably qualified by a fallen condition. Blake has loaded Bromion's intimations of a better life with echoes of Eve's speech in *Paradise Lost*:

> But say, where grows the Tree, from hence how farr?
> For many are the Trees of God that grow
> In Paradise, and various, yet unknown
> To us, in such abundance lies our choice,
> As leaves a greater store of Fruit untoucht,
> Still hanging uncorruptible, till men
> Grow up to thir provision ...
>
> (*Paradise Lost*, IX.617–623)

It is good to know that the fruit is "uncorruptible," and that Bromion is growing up to its provision, but his speech surely also refers to a more ominous remark of Eve's, made just before she falls:

> For good unknown sure is not had, or had
> And yet unknown, is as not had at all.
>
> (IX.756–757)

The essence of experience, whether fallen or unfallen, must be realization, and the motto of *Visions* is "The Eye sees more than the Heart knows" (E44). In this case the eye belongs to Oothoon

(and partially to Bromion); the unknowing heart is Theotormon's. As long as it remains that way, despite her insights Oothoon
as emanation will remain, like Enion and Ahania in *Vala/The Four
Zoas*, "a solitary shadow wailing on the margin of non-entity"
(E49).

If we look at the depiction of Bromion in the frontispiece to
Visions and compare it to the ninth of Blake's engravings for the
Book of Job, we find that Eliphaz, Job's friend who cannot help
believing that Job has somehow deserved his calamities, and who
had a vision of God as image of terror ("Then a spirit passed
before my face; the hair of my flesh stood up"; Job 4:15) is in
fact Bromion. This would suggest a close relationship between Job
himself, before his enlightenment, and Theotormon; indeed the
latter speaks a language weighted down with echoes of Job:

> Tell me what is the night or day to one o'erflowed with woe?
> Tell me what is a thought? & of what substance is it made?
> Tell me what is a joy? & in what gardens do joys grow?
>
> (E46)

Theotormon is passive, and his imagination remains obdurately
resistant to Oothoon. But his peculiar metaphysical maunderings
reveal an odd paradox about his mental state. Theotormon is not,
in the active sense of Urizen, closed; the despair in the power of
intelligence with which he insulates himself from new experiences
is based upon a metaphysics which leaves him curiously open to
them. He huddles into himself like a child because he thinks
disturbing thoughts may come at him, under their own steam, so
to speak, from the outside at any time; likewise he believes that
he has no control over his own thoughts, and that they escape
from him into the publicity of the outside air like vapor. He is
at least incapable of that sort of hypocrisy which requires insight
into form.

So far in this study I have approached the ambiguities of
Generation from the side of Generation. In the *Vala/The Four
Zoas* manuscript, Blake approaches Generation from the side of
Eternity, the first four Nights of the poem being premundane.
The same ambiguities prevail in either case, but to approach
them from the other side of the metaphorical divide, so to speak,
is to be reminded of interesting isues. Blake is often said to be
a humanist, but if that term has any religious content it is
qualified by the same idea of pastoral which prevents him from

being transcendentalist in any ordinary sense. This is clearly
apparent at the outset of Night IV of the manuscript, where
Los and Enitharmon discover themselves after the deluge as
Adam and Eve fallen. The destruction of the "bounds of Destiny"
has cast down Enitharmon for the time being from the world
represented by her hymn, and she is wildly bitter with Tharmas
therefore, but Los is foolish enough to declare himself (to Tharmas)
God:

> And Los remains God over all. weak father of worms & clay
> I know I was Urthona keeper of the gates of heaven
> But now I am all powerful Los & Urthona is but my shadow
> (48.18–20; E325)

Blake will have nothing of a humanism based upon the fallen condition, and Tharmas "doubts" (perhaps the source of his name)
and weeps red tears (like Orc, but also like the lion in "The Little
Girl Lost"). Tharmas has a clear grasp at least of the principles of
chaos, and he aims to maintain his control over it. Enitharmon
declares her allegiance to Urizen as architect of the fallen world,
and Tharmas abruptly acts. We may see his act as constituting a
development from Theotormon's passivity, and Blake's imagery
makes it clear that it is of *Visions* he is thinking. First Tharmas
declares his authority over the waters, and then:

> So Saying in a Wave he rap'd bright Enitharmon far
> Apart from Los. but coverd her with softest brooding care
> On a broad wave in the warm west. balming her bleeding wound
>
> O how Los howld at the rending asunder all the fibres rent
> Where Enitharmon joind to his left side in griding pain
> (49.4–8; E326)

His act painfully recreates Adam and Eve in the fallen world; it is
also a reconstruction, as the imagery makes clear, of the domestic
situation in *Visions*. Blake develops the image of sterility into the
idea of a painful divorce, but it is clear that Tharmas, Los, and
Enitharmon correspond to Theotormon, Bromion, and Oothoon
in the earlier poem. It can be seen that with great rapidity Blake is
revising his myth; Los will conclude Night IV by rebuilding the
world and, as before (in *The Book of Urizen*), that rebuilding
will be seen simultaneously as the "binding" of Urizen and the

creation of man's current physical form. But henceforth Los's activities will have to be seen in relationship to Tharmas as well as to Urizen. In itself there is nothing very hopeful in this, unless it be the possibility of a showdown between Urizen and Tharmas. Tharmas, like Theotormon, has lost sight of his emanation, and despairs of finding her, but he has at least developed Bromion's inkling that Urizenic repression stands in his way. His despair is in one sense absolute, for he believes that "The Eternal Man is seald never to be deliverd" (51.15; E327), and that (as he remarks to Urizen) "Thy Eternal form shall never renew my uncertain prevails against thee" (51.19), but his commitment to what he calls "Eternal Death" contains at least a reserve of strength:

> And I what can I now behold but an Eternal Death
> Before my Eyes & an Eternal weary work to strive
> Against the monstrous forms that breed among my silent waves
> (51.26–28; E328)

Tharmas applies to his emanation, Enion, the same peculiar metaphysics which Theotormon expressed in terms of intellectual being in general; in emotional terms Tharmas experiences a sense of chaos and loss which Blake expresses with moving power. It is the farthest opposite of the pastoral state where man carries the image of paradise within the careful simplicities of the human heart:

> O fool fool to lose my sweetest bliss
> Where art thou Enion ah too near to cunning too far off
> And yet too near. Dashd down I send thee into distant darkness
> Far as my strength can hurl thee wander there & laugh & play
> Among the frozen arrows they will tear thy tender flesh
> (45.1–5; E323)

The important thing is that the resolution which Tharmas is able to recover from his chaotic imagination is still significantly a function of the "idea of pastoral";[46] moreover, it is an important enough resolution to contain within itself all the seeds of Blake's later poetry. In terms of visionary activity Tharmas is absolutely fallen, but he is no less absolutely committed to making something of the "elements" of his fallen condition, of Eternal Death; and the terms of his commands to the "Spectre of Urthona," however founded upon the will to power and however driven by despair, are nevertheless the terms of an ultimate choice:

I will compell thee to rebuild by these my furious waves
Death choose or life thou strugglest in my waters, now choose
   life
And all the Elements shall serve thee to their soothing flutes
Their sweet inspiriting lyres thy labours shall administer
                                                  (52.1–4; E328)

It is not simply the Orphism here which reminds us of Tharmas'
relationship to pastoralism, but much more his commitment to
life ("Now choose life") on the terms of death.

Tharmas is in a spectrous condition, and he issues his orders
to a new character, the "Spectre of Urthona," precipitated by the
forcible "rape" of Los from Enitharmon. The Spectre is in a sense
a further reduction of Los (already reduced from Urthona), yet
there is another reminder of the habits of pastoralism in the fact
that the newly humbled Spectre can recognize the truth more
clearly than Los could:

Tharmas I know thee. how are we alterd our beauty decayd
But still I know thee tho in this horrible ruin whelmd
                                                  (49.27–28; E326)

And there is a most important hint of Blake's future direction in
Tharmas' application of the Spectre to the essential choice of life
in terms of the fallen elements, for henceforth Blake will begin
to apply the problems attendant upon the "idea of pastoral" to the
relationship between Los and his Spectre. And there is another
hint of things to come in Tharmas' speech:

Go forth said Tharmas works of joy are thine   obey
   & live
So shall the spungy marrow issuing from thy spinterd bones
Bonify. & thou shalt have rest when this thy labour is done
Go forth bear Enitharmon back to the Eternal Prophet
Build her a bower in the midst of all my dashing waves
Make first a resting place for Los & Enitharmon. then
Thou shalt have rest.
                                                  (49.15–21; E326)

The work of the Spectre, the work of Generation, will largely take
the form of bearing Enitharmon "back to the Eternal Prophet,"
that is, of healing the separation which is the basis of sexuality,
that separation which first appears in Blake as Bromion and
Oothoon bound back-to-back in the imagination of Theotormon

and which thereafter becomes a dominating concern of his work through *Jerusalem*. Further, in the "bower" which the Spectre is exhorted to build we dimly glimpse Los's Golgonooza (the name suggests both "Golgotha" and "new zoa"), the holy city of archetypes and art, the foundations of which are laid in *The Four Zoas* and which is so important in *Milton* and *Jerusalem*.

The final accomplishment of Tharmas' commitment to Eternal Death will be Blake's final, unorthodox version of the Atonement, and his solution to the problem of the spectrous self and the separated emanation will be "forgiveness of sins," but the Christian terminology should not be allowed to disguise the fact that Blake's great theme remains throughout the one we are approaching from the vantage point of pastoralism. Its development through *Milton* will occupy the next section. For the moment, however, it should be noted that Tharmas' commitment to the realm of Eternal Death releases in Blake a flood of hope and optimism, expressed most patently in pastoral terms in Night IX of his manuscript.

Here, in the course of the Apocalypse, Luvah finally appears in unfallen form; his first act is to call forth Vala, or Generation, and she runs gloriously forward to take her place in a pastoral fantasia which entertains the sleepers on the Couches of Beulah for 150 lines. She appears as a shepherdess serving her master, Luvah:

> I walk among his flocks & hear the bleating of his lambs
> O that I could behold his face & follow his pure feet
> I walk by the footsteps of his flocks come hither tender flocks
> Can you converse with a pure Soul that seeketh for her maker
> (127.31–34; E381)

After singing a beautiful song of pastoral responses, she falls asleep, her head pillowed on a ram. Luvah passes, sees her, and commands:

> Let a pleasant house arise to be the dwelling place
> Of this immortal Spirit growing in lower Paradise
> (128.29–30; E382)

Vala finds her beautiful house, leaves it to go up to her flocks, bearing in her lap fruits and flowers. She finds a clear spring, and, like Eve, beholds herself:

And her bright hair was wet with the waters She rose up from
    the river
And as she rose her Eyes were opend to the world of waters
She saw Tharmas sitting upon the rocks beside the wavy sea
                       (129.15–17; E383)

It is most important to notice that, even in this vision, Blake is
careful to respect the terms of Generation. Tharmas is mourning,
just as we have seen him mourn before, for lost Enion. Vala prays
for him, and at first there is no response. But when she returns to
her house, she finds two children by the door beneath the trees.
They are Enion and Tharmas, reborn as children, and as the sun
sinks Vala takes them inside and puts them to bed. Every detail
of this account is a lyric recapitulation of a condition of Generation.
In the morning Vala finds the two children acting as we would expect them to act in Vala. Enion is eluding Tharmas in Vala's
garden, and Tharmas complains:

O Vala I am sick & all this garden of Pleasure
Swims like a dream before my eyes but the sweet smelling fruit
Revives me to new deaths I fade even like a water lilly
In the suns heat till in the night on the couch of Enion
I drink new life & feel the breath of sleeping Enion
But in the morning she arises to avoid my Eyes
Then my loins fade & in the house I sit me down & weep
                       (131.1–7; E384)

We can hear echoes of old acquaintances in these lines, Eve in
the first two, and Thel in the third. Vala's solution to the children's
problem is simply, despite their doubts, to lead them together.
We are told:

Thus in Eternal Childhood straying among Valas flocks
In infant sorrow & joy alternate Enion & Tharmas playd
Round Vala in the Gardens of Vala & by her rivers margin
                 (131.16–18; E384–385)

To change "Eternal Death" into "Eternal Childhood" is of course
no solution to the problem of Generation, but the charm and easi-
ness of this little fiction, with which Blake entertains his Eternals,
is perhaps a sign that he was confident of having found one.

MILTON AND *THE FOUR ZOAS*

As Blake's career progressed (in the sense of accomplishment),
his poems did not become any simpler; one of the more minor
mysteries of *Milton* is that, although the extant poem is in two

books, and although "Finis" is written at the end of the second, the title page of the two latest and most revised copies (on paper watermarked 1815) reads "a Poem in 12 Books." To make the mystery greater, we know that "12" was the number originally inscribed on the title page (dated 1804). David Erdman, whom I am following here (E727–728), has suggested that twelve books was to have been the original form for the "Sublime Allegory" based upon Blake's "Spiritual Acts" while he was in residence at Felpham (see the letters to Thomas Butts of April and July 1803),[47] and that when Blake actually got around to completing the poem in its two-book form (probably, Erdman suggests, after his 1809 exhibition) he carefully erased the "1" before the "2" of "12." The question is complicated by our general uncertainty about Blake's dates, and certainly by the fact that Blake was working on *Vala/The Four Zoas* at Felpham. Blake had also originally projected twenty-eight chapters on the 1804 *Jerusalem* title page (there are only four to the completed poem), but after erasing this he never revived the sign of his early enthusiasm; why, then, did he restore the "1" to "12" in the two late copies of *Milton*? Was it merely, as Erdman suggests, rather defiantly to commemorate his original plan? There is surely no reason to discount the theory for the *original* discrepancy which relies upon early enthusiasm; Blake, after all, engraved his title page a good five years before getting to the text. But I would like to suggest that the *revival* of "12" on his *Milton* title page is a reflection upon the *Vala/The Four Zoas* manuscript, oblique notice of the poet's awareness that the latter would never be revised into publishable form. The "12" (the "1" is not only restored but emphasized by stippling; E728) on the two late copies refers to the two books of *Milton* plus the ten Nights of the unfinished *Four Zoas*.[48] The evidence for this view is internal: a study of the relationship between the revisions of the manuscript, especially Nights VI through VIII, and *Milton*. Especially important is the relationship between *Milton* and Night VII(b).

That the *Vala/The Four Zoas* manuscript in a sense "demands" the epic *Milton* is a function of two facts: (1) that *Milton* is the thematic consummation, or fulfillment, of the concerns evident in *Vala/The Four Zoas* and (2) that those concerns in the first place are defined largely by means of oblique allusions to *Paradise Lost*. One example—because it is so central to all three of Blake's epics—will make clear what I mean. When Urizen, at the end of the fifth Night of *Vala/The Four Zoas* announces his intention to

"Explore these dens" (that is, the world created by Los's binding of Urizen), we recognize that Blake is expanding on an account of the same exploration in the eighth chapter of *The Book of Urizen* (E80–81), a despairing exploration the principal fruits of which were Urizenic pity and "The Net of Religion." But if we look ahead into the future, we see that Urizen's journey is also the prototype of analogous ones in *Milton* and *Jerusalem*: the poet John Milton's return to Eternal Death from the mazes of his false heaven in *Milton* and the exploration and illumination of Ulro by Los which is the subject of the *Jerusalem* frontispiece and a central image of the poem (Erdman, p. 469). The terms of Urizen's annunciation are also important:

> I will arise Explore these dens & find that deep pulsation
> That shakes my caverns with strong shudders. perhaps this is
>   the night
> Of Prophecy & Luvah hath burst his way from Enitharmon
> When Thought is closd in Caves. Then love shall shew its
>   root in deepest Hell
>
>   (65.9–12; E337)

The last two lines refer to the birth of Orc (and incidentally constitute a comment on the situation in *Visions*), but I am more concerned for the moment with the reference to "Prophecy." Again the importance of Miltonic allusion in Blake is evident, for the "prophecy" in terms of *Paradise Lost* is of the New World Satan will corrupt (II.344–351), and we recognize (as subsequent imagery will confirm) that Satan's journey to earth is the prototype of all Blakean expeditions. The last line quoted, with its consciousness of the mechanism of repression, tells us why this is so. In *Milton* Los, observing the descent of John Milton, recognizes the allusion to *Paradise Lost* (see Frye, "Commentary," p. 133), can make no distinction at first in his imagination between Milton and Satan, and grows desperate. Here we get another reference to "Prophecy":

> At last when desperation almost tore his heart in twain
> He recollected an old Prophecy in Eden recorded,
> And often sung to the loud harp at the immortal feasts
> That Milton of the Land of Albion should up ascend
> Forwards from Ulro from the Vale of Felpham; and set free
> Orc from his Chain of Jealousy, he started at the thought
>   (M., 20.56–61; E114)

The release of Orc from the Chain of Jealousy has of course a bearing on the theme of sexual separation, but it also relates to Blake's vocabularies of revolution as apocalypse and of Generation. We may suspect a new articulation is being formulated of the revolutions in France and America, and that seems to be exactly what Blake is driving at in the following passage:

> But Milton entering my Foot; I saw in the nether
> Regions of the Imagination; also all men on Earth,
> And all in Heaven, saw in the nether regions of the Imagination
> In Ulro beneath Beulah, the vast breach of Miltons descent.
> But I knew not that it was Milton, for man cannot know
> What passes in his members till periods of Space & Time
> Reveal the secrets of Eternity.
>
> (M., 21.4–10; E114)

What appeared to all men as a "vast breach" (revolutionary upheaval) was the descent of Milton. It needs to be emphasized, however, that this new articulation represents a development and intensification of Blake's earlier versions of eighteenth-century cataclysm; the utilization of the figure of Milton may seem eccentric, but it represents a cleaving to the source of the imagery by means of which Blake expressed earlier versions. This is not a new departure, but a development. As Milton descends into "the Sea of Time & Space," Blake tells us he first saw him "in the Zenith as a falling star" (M., 15.46–47; E109), and we remember that in *Europe* the apocalypse dawned with Urizen glowing comet-like in the north, also by way of allusion to Milton. If we consider the assemblage, in Blake's imagery, of the ideas of Milton, Satan, revolution, apocalypse, and Orc, we can see that Blake is only dealing more directly than before with the ultimate expression of the problem of Generation: apocalypse as Fall. We have already seen Los identify the poet's descent as "Signal that the Last Vintage now approaches" (M., 24.42); when Milton reaches Blake at Felpham, he is

> Descending perpendicular, swift as the swallow or swift;
> And on my left foot falling on the tarsus, enterd there;
> But from my left foot a black cloud redounding spread over
>   Europe.
>
> (M., 15.48–50; E109)

We have seen this said before, though less directly; what *is* new is the idea that the descent of Milton himself may dissolve the "black cloud . . . over Europe" and enable light to penetrate the thicket of Blake's doubts. The form that dissolution and penetration will take is a reminder that the problem of revolution was for Blake always an aspect of the more general problem of Generation. Orc has hope, it seems, of release from the Chain of Jealousy, by which metaphor Blake suggests that the idea of renewal is going to be expressed in terms of a sexual rapprochement. This looks forward not only to the relationship between Milton and Ololon (his emanation), but as well to the giant image of apocalypse as the "marriage" of Albion to his emanation (and idea of Human Liberty), Jerusalem. Also new in *Milton* is the fruit of marriage; Milton's "breach" of the realm of Eternal Death is also the consummation of his marriage to Ololon, and its immediate effect upon the character "Blake" is a reminder of the natural basis of these metaphors, for

> . . . all this Vegetable World appeard on my left Foot,
> As a bright sandal formd immortal of precious stones & gold:
> I stooped down & bound it on to walk forward thro' Eternity.
> (M., 21.12–14; E114)

In *Milton*, as we shall see, the "marriage" is directly a function of the rebirth of Generation in the imagination of Los.

To get to this point is a long journey through the *Vala/The Four Zoas* manuscript, but it is a journey somewhat eased by the fact that Milton's poems are usually the most reliable road map. In order to explore his dens, Urizen, at the beginning of Night VI, has to cross a river into the new, fallen territory. He is opposed by three fateful sisters, who turn out to be his daughters. The general resemblance to the situation in *Paradise Lost*, Book II, where Satan has to pass his offspring, Sin and Death, in order to get through the Gates of Hell, has been noticed (E875); the Miltonic passage, much transformed, is also an element of the crisis of Blake's Night VII(a). It is also worth noticing the relationship between this scene and another, by the shores of Arnon, in *Milton*.

In *Vala/The Four Zoas* the three sisters represent aspects of Generation. One, "clad in shining green" (67.17; E338), is associated with the mount which supports Eden and which underground divides the river of Paradise into four parts (see *Paradise Lost*, IV.223–246). Another is associated with the "Saphire Fount" through which, Milton tells us, the waters of the sacred river flow into Paradise (*Paradise Lost*, IV.237–240). However, in the *Vala/The Four Zoas* instance the fountain ominously attracts the water rather than pouring it forth. This would seem to be emblematic of a sinister woman, or of the Female Will; Vala in Night VII(b) has both blue eyes and "sapphire shoes" (93.1; E396). The third and eldest sister is the most forbidding of all; like Tharmas she is associated with running water, and her name (like that of the whore, Mystery, in the Book of Revelation) is written on her forehead.

There is a remarkable development of the encounter with these three in *Milton*;[49] this time Milton himself is making the (return) journey, and he is opposed by the single figure of Urizen. Urizen attempts to distort the meaning of Milton's apocalyptic return by baptizing him as a false Messiah with Jordan water; Milton resists by attempting to fill the concavities of Urizen's wasted body with Succoth clay, making of him a "new Adam" (see Frye, "Commentary," p. 134):

> ... when with cold hand Urizen stoop'd down
> And took up water from the river Jordan: pouring on
> To Miltons brain the icy fluid from his broad cold palm.
> But Milton took of the red clay of Succoth, moulding it with
>   care
> Between his palms; and filling up the furrows of many years
> Beginning at the feet of Urizen ...
>
> (M., 19.7–12; E111)

Even the enlargement of the idea of the waters of Generation to include the constructive stuff of earth is not surprising, for Urizen's daughters in *Vala/The Four Zoas* also make bread to sustain Orc (79.25–38; E348). *Milton* speaks, it will be noticed, a new, much more complex and compactly biblical language than most of the *Vala/The Four Zoas* manuscript; what is new about this language, with its ironic approach to the ideas of baptism and the "new Adam," is its developed ability to manage Blake's old ambiguities about Generation.

The most interesting *locus* for studying these ambiguities in the old language are the two Nights VII of *Vala/The Four Zoas*. Here we can see most clearly Blake's dependence upon Milton and the corresponding development of ideas upon which *Milton* is based. Once across the river, Urizen finds himself in a landscape already apocalyptic:

> . . . tygers roam in the redounding smoke
> In forests of affliction. the adamantine scales of justice
> Consuming in the raging lamps of mercy pourd in rivers
> The holy oil rages through all the cavernd rocks   fierce flames
> Dance on the rivers & the rocks howling & drunk with fury
> The plow of ages & the golden harrow wade thro fields
> Of goary blood the immortal seed is nourishd for the slaughter
> (77.9–15; E346)

The imagery is important, and I will return to it. Orc is lying in the midst of the landscape, howling, and apparently Enitharmon has managed to restore her reign of jealousy and terror, for Orc's

> Pulse after pulse beat on his fetters pulse after pulse his spirit
> Darted & darted higher & higher to the shrine of Enitharmon
> (77.21–22; E346)

Los is present, too, for "Los felt the Envy in his limbs like to a blighted tree" (77.27). The reference to envy tells us that we are back in the world of "Night," that is, of *Paradise Lost*, Book IV, where Satan is consumed by envy of Adam and Eve "Imparadis't in one anothers arms" (IV.506), and it is interesting to see how Blake this time involves both Orc and Los in the scene, for the emotion is a function of repression (Urizen and Orc), but it is Los (playing here the role of Adam) who feels its force. Beneath Urizen's heel the Tree of Mystery, based upon the tree in *Paradise Lost* from which Adam and Eve gather their figleaves after the Fall (IX.1101ff.), takes root, and Urizen begins the melancholy seduction of Orc which will end, as we have seen, with the crucifixion of Orc upon its branches. Blake had absorbed the Miltonic division between heat and light,[50] and there is a reflection of "darkness visible" as Orc mounts his cross: "Despising Urizens light & turning it into flaming fire" (80.45; E349). The luring of Orc to the Tree of Mystery is, however, only one aspect of the temptation which is the subject of Night VII(a).

In Night IV, as we have seen, Tharmas set the Spectre of Urthona to the work of creation, that work being synonymous with the binding, or containment, of Urizen. Los and the Spectre worked together, using Urizen's old furnaces, and Los took the opportunity (the Spectre participating only against his will) to chain Enitharmon even as he chained Urizen (53.5–19; E329). Now that Urizen has once again gained control of Orc in Night VII(a), Enitharmon is free to practice her torment, and as Orc is crucified she and Los reenact the cycle of enticement and jealousy until they are both virtually empty of vitality. At this point, Blake begins to work out a second aspect of his temptation scene. The Spectre of Urthona reappears, and with him this time a spectrous Enitharmon as well, called her "shadow." They see each other

> Beneath the tree of Mystery which in the dismal Abyss
> Began to blossom in fierce pain shooting its writhing buds
> In throes of birth & now the blossoms falling shining fruit
> Appeard . . .
>
> (82.18–21; E350)

Los and Enitharmon remain moribund, but the Spectre begins to woo the Shadow beneath the tree:

>   . . . he wept & he embracd
>   The fleeting image & in whispers mild wood the faint shade
>
>   Loveliest delight of Men. Enitharmon shady hiding
>   In secret places where no eye can trace thy watry way
>   (82.26–29; E351)

The "hiding in secret places" here suggests Milton's Satan (who enters Paradise for the Temptation by a "watry way": see *Paradise Lost*, IX.69–76), but the imagery of the passage as a whole suggests Blake is combining Books IV and IX of *Paradise Lost*, the temptation occurring as Adam and Eve lie asleep, in their dreams. The dream seduction of Shadow by Spectre is a curious affair. The Spectre begins by reminding us of the imagery of *Europe*. He knows that Enitharmon was shocked and "rent" by the birth of Orc "from thy sweet loins of bliss" (82.32; E351), and he promises her next time (perhaps partly by way of ironic reference to *Paradise Lost*, X.1051–1052) a painless birth "in sweet delusion" (82.35). They while away the time before coitus like young people at a dance, telling each other where they come from; this means we are given two more accounts of the Fall of the Eternals, from their respective points of view, each account ending with a resolve to blame Vala for the Fall and to punish her by subjecting her to the fiery embraces of Orc. It is a solution which suggests not the hopeful theory but the hopeless practice of revolution, as it seemed to Blake. The accounts of the Fall are peculiar, but they are important to review for the narrative patterns they suggest. The Shadow's version begins by reminding us of *Thel*:

Among the Flowers of Beulah walkd the Eternal Man & Saw
Vala the lilly of the desart. melting in high noon
Upon her bosom in sweet bliss he fainted
(83.7–9; E351; see Thel, I.19–25; E4)

But as the pattern develops, we think more of *Visions of the Daughters of Albion*:

There he reveld in delight among the Flowers
Vala was pregnant & brought forth Urizen Prince of Light
First born of Generation. Then behold a wonder to the Eyes
Of the now fallen Man a double form Vala appeard. A Male
And female shuddring pale the Fallen Man recoild
From the Enormity & calld them Luvah & Vala. turning down
The vales to find his way back into Heaven but found none
(83.11–17; E351)

The Man who cannot find his way back suggests Theotormon, whose first offspring is a Urizenic Bromion, and whose second is a terrifying image of the divided sexes. The image of a divided Luvah and Vala, presided over by Urizen as elder brother, is the precipitate of this account. The Spectre has a more vivid memory, in his account, of events closer to the present, of the enclosure of Los and Enitharmon in the arteries of Generated life, and of their birth into this world as "infant woe" and "infant terror" (84.16–23; E352). He stresses, however, not the separation of the sexes into Luvah and Vala, but a separation of another, more spectrous kind:

My masculine spirit scorning the frail body issud forth
From Enions brain In this deformd form leaving thee there
Till times passd over thee but still my spirit returning hoverd
And formd a Male to be a counterpart to thee O Love
Darkend & Lost In due time issuing forth from Enions womb
Thou & that demon Los wert born
(84.24–29; E352)

These two accounts of the Fall, then, clearly develop the two aspects of a fallen "separation" which will occupy Blake's imagination for a long time to come. The Spectre's withdrawal from life is especially important, because it develops eventually into Blake's mature vision of Satan.

The Shadow and Spectre have as their immediate aim the punishment of Generation, but when they mate they paradoxically produce a new, doubly fallen Vala, the birth of whom from the body of sleeping Enitharmon is even more painful than was the birth of Orc. Moreover, the newborn infant

> ... burst the Gates of Enitharmons heart with direful Crash
> Nor could they ever be closd again the golden hinges were
>   broken
> And the gates broke in sunder
>
> (85.13–15; E353)

Again Blake is referring closely to Milton. The birth of the re-newed, doubly fallen Vala is based upon Milton's description of Sin's delivery of Death in *Paradise Lost* (II.778–785), and the opening of the Gates refers to the opening of Hell's Gates by Sin (II.879–889). Even the new Nature is based upon Milton; we have already seen the radical alterations which God makes in Nature after the Fall in Book X (651ff.). When Blake's gates "sunder," we are told "their ornaments [are] defacd." When Adam eats Eve's apple in Book IX of *Paradise Lost*, we are told that "Nature gave a second groan" (1001), and Adam thereafter re-marks:

> Bad fruit of Knowledge, if this be to know,
> Which leaves us naked thus, of Honour void,
> Of Innocence, of Faith, of Puritie,
> Our wonted Ornaments now soild and staind.
>
> (IX.1073–1076)

Again we see that by means of allusions to Milton, Blake is loading the image of a new Vala with all the ambiguity of the old. But surely the breaking of the gates of Enitharmon's heart may also be a hopeful omen, suggesting that she is open to pity at long last and can never return to the ways of courtly love and sexual torment. And things now seem to be happening, too, for we are told of the new Vala,

> ... a Cloud she grew & grew
> Till many of the dead burst forth from the bottoms of their
>   tombs
>
> (85.17–18; E353)

We can begin to see the action of *Milton* in the distance, but it is very unclear whether the resurrection of the dead here (a resur-rection, note, *downward*) is a good thing or an epiphany of horror.

The Spectre of Urthona himself, according to Blake's original intentions, saw nothing untoward, for "The Spectre smild & gave her Charge over the howling Orc" (85.22; E353); and it is not much help to us that Blake later changed "smild &" to "terrified," adding in the next line: "Then took the tree of Mystery root in the World of Los." At this point in the narrative we. are at the end of Night VII(a), except for the very late additions. If we ignore these additions, we find that the narrative continues directly on into Night VII(b) as Blake originally set it down (he later changed the order of pages). For this reason, but also for much more important ones, it is to Night VII(b) we must turn next.

Night VII(b) of *Vala/The Four Zoas* (manuscript pages 91–99) has probably been more the victim of that natural critical inertia which besets any study than any other considerable passage in Blake. The critical damage produced by this inertia, however, has been more substantial than is usually the case. The manuscript Blake left has two Nights titled "First" (which, as G. E. Bentley, Jr. points out, bothered no one because there was no Night marked "Second")[51] and two Nights marked VII. Since the title page declares there ought to be nine Nights in all, the traditional temptation for critics was to get rid of one of the Nights VII, arguing that the other must have been written to replace it. (S. Foster Damon, however, holds out for the view that each version "lacks some essential episode which is found in the other. Blake undoubtedly intended to blend the two, but he did not.")[52] Received critical opinion until very recently was probably closest to the idea expressed in 1947 by Northrop Frye that VII(b) was "certainly earlier" (though Frye goes on to associate its contents with *Jerusalem*), suggesting that something burst upon Blake's imagination to occasion the rewriting of VII(b) to make VII(a) (Frye, *Fearful Symmetry*, p. 298). David Erdman makes a similar assumption, though he is following not Frye, but the Sloss and Wallis edition.[53] In 1956, however, H. M. Margoliouth, in his edition of *Vala* (an edition which tries insofar as possible to separate a *Vala* layer of text from a later *Four Zoas* layer) reminded scholars that, except for obviously late additions, the narrative of VII(a) flows continuously into VII(b).[54] This fact of course hinted that the long-held assumption that VII(b) was composed prior to VII(a) needed to be reexamined, as did the idea fostered by received opinion that the two versions were somehow thematically opposed to each other. (Harold Bloom, as late as the third printing of Erdman's text, 1968, remains committed to the view that it is not "fair" to read VII(a) and VII(b) as an "intentional sequence, in that order. VII(a) in at least some respects is an imaginative advance on VII(b)." See E876.) Margoliouth's hint was developed into a death knell for received opinion by G. E. Bentley's facsimile edition of the poem, which demonstrated conclusively on the basis of stitch marks on the manuscript that VII(b)—as VIII and IX—had to be considered later than VII(a).[55] In a section of his edition called, "*The Four Zoas* and the Critics," Bentley devoted what might be called the lion's share of his space to an attack on Erdman's reading of the poem in *Blake: Prophet against Empire* (1954).[56] This attack is of interest to us mainly because Erdman, in addition to being a critic of Blake, is also one of the poet's two most authoritative editors. This means that Erdman's enormously energetic attempts to salvage as much of his reading as possible from Bentley's demonstration that it was based on a wrongly edited and inaccurately dated text colors Erdman's presentation of *The Four Zoas* in his edition of Blake's poems. Erdman cannot make VII(b) go away, but his removal of it out of serial order to a place at the back of the text includes the assumption, as he says, that it was "supplanted . . . but not discarded" (E739). Erdman's edition offers no critical evidence for this view (though it would find support in Harold Bloom's commentary), and even his critical study of Blake leaves it unclear why he remains so committed to this aspect of the case (pp. 295–296 of *Blake: Prophet against Empire* are relevant) unless by way of general resistance to Bentley. He does offer evidence (I think questionable: see Appendix C) of a "link" between VII(a) and VIII, but even if this evidence were stronger the removal of a whole Night from the text on its basis would be an editorial procedure open to question.

I, however, am taking the view that VII(b) belongs in Blake's text where he left it not because of lack of evidence to the contrary, but because of the Night's conceptual importance in terms of the development of Blake's ideas about Vala (Generation). In terms of this problem VII(b) says something vital about the development of Blake's ideas which none of the other Nights say. As "prophecy," in Blake's special sense of relationship of canonical event to historical event, it recapitulates and develops the idea of *Europe*, itself a seminal work. Moreover—and much more important— ideas which occurred to the poet in the course of its composition are the genesis of *Milton*, which was probably originally to have formed a section of the longer poem.

In working through VII(b) I want first to follow the Night, for reasons which will be apparent, in order of composition. Echoes of the *America* "Preludium" have been noted in the first pages of VII(b),[57] but no one has to my knowledge pointed out the very close general resemblance to *Europe* (which, as we have seen, absorbs the "historical" burden of *America* in its central episodes). *Europe* begins with an apocalyptic appearance upon the basis of which Orc is told confidently (since he is bound) to rise. Likewise at the beginning of VII(b) Orc is confidently invited to rise by the incarnation of Vala, who assumes that he will be bound by her, his wrath absorbed by her meekness (91.5; E395). (To anticipate a point it is worth pointing out here that this neutralization will not work, and that the separation of wrath and meekness thereby implied is one basis for the Rintrah-Palamabron myth of *Milton*, a myth which also owes its ultimate beginnings to *Europe*.) At the end of *Europe*, after Orc has appeared in France, rousing his lions and tygers (compare Orc in VII(b); 91.15) under critical circumstances which invest the act with almost unbearable ambiguity, we read:

> Then Los arose his head he reard in snaky thunders clad:
> And with a cry that shook all nature to the utmost pole,
> Call'd all his sons to the strife of blood.
>
> (E65)

Night VII(b) ends with a passage beginning:

> Los reard his mighty stature on Earth stood his feet. Above
> The moon his furious forehead circled with black bursting
> thunders
> His naked limbs glittring upon the dark blue sky his knees
> Bathed in bloody clouds. his loins in fires of war where spears
> And swords rage where the Eagles cry & the Vultures laugh
> saying
> Now comes the night of Carnage now the flesh of Kings &
> Princes
>
> (96.19–24; E393)

Once the similarity has been seen, we can concentrate on the differences, applying them especially to the new incarnation of Vala who appeared in VII(a). As one reads the Night, the most important issue to keep in the back of one's mind is the prophecy in *Milton* of the release of Orc from the Chain of Jealousy.

The union with which VII(b) begins is another error analogous to what the crucifixion of Orc in VII(a) stands for, "the consolidation of tyranny and mystery" (Frye, *Fearful Symmetry*, p. 299). Indeed this instance of error is much purer than the corresponding event in *Europe*, for here Vala is newly, doubly fallen, here she is not "drown'd in shady woe, and visionary joy" (these are conditions she will apply to Tharmas) but confident of her ability to swamp Orc's fire and devour him. This "purity" of error has the effect of focusing the reader's attention upon the question of Generation; surely if Vala is to triumph as an epiphany of fallen error, and if Blake is going to repudiate her error, he is going to run the risk of falling himself into the repressive pattern of Urizen and Orc. This is another aspect, then, of the idea of pastoral; to see Vala from the apocalyptic point of view is to relive *Thel*, and to fall oneself. But as the union with Orc takes place, with results that are on the whole predictable, we notice some subtle and unexpected differences which promise hopefulness with respect to Generation.

At the beginning things happen much as we might expect. Vala is sadly mistaken; Orc immediately recognises her "Pity and meek affection" as the "arts of Urizen" (91.11; E395), and she only manages to promote his most fiery appearance to date, for he is "jealous that she was Vala now became Urizens harlot" (91.14; E395). In terms of the prophecy in *Milton*, we see Blake practicing his accustomed irony, but here more focused than in *Europe*. For in VII(b) Orc has definitely broken his chains ("The hairy shoulders rend the links free are the wrists of fire"; 91.17), even if, as yet, he hardly seems free of jealousy. Immediately after his epiphany, we again see the familiar with new eyes. For there is an enormous cataclysmic war, and "blood / From east to west flowd like the human veins in rivers" (92.6–7; E396), from the direction of Luvah—in terms of Blake's spiritual geography— toward Tharmas, the fallen body (for a different reading, see Erdman, p. 326). But this time "war" more clearly corresponds to Los's call to the elements to celebrate a night of peace in *Europe*: the motive is stated perfectly clearly—"Stop we the rising of the glorious King" (91.30)—and the first thing we notice about this is the implication that he *is* still rising. The second thing we notice is that the elemental gods, in terms of whose wrath the crucifixion of Luvah is reenacted as the betrayal of history (92.9– 16; E396), and whose war inspires the sons of Urizen to change "all the arts of life ... into the arts of death" (93.21; E396), have a surprisingly clear view of what Vala represents in terms of the war:

> Now now the Battle rages round thy tender limbs O Vala
> Now smile among thy bitter tears now put on all thy beauty
> Is not the wound of the sword Sweet & the broken bone
>   delightful
> Wilt thou now smile among the slain when the wounded
>   groan in the field
>
> (92.34–37; E396)

The elemental soldiers are demonically fighting "for" Vala to stop the rising of Orc; this is one of Blake's clearest and most terrible metaphors for apocalyptic suffering.

Then, most abruptly:

> Orc rent her & his human form consumd in his own fires
> Mingled with her dolorous members strewn thro the Abyss
> She joyd in all the Conflict Gratified & drinking tears of woe
> No more remaind of Orc but the Serpent round the tree of
>   Mystery
>
> (93.21–24; E397)

The imagery of the Serpent, which I have already analyzed at length, only serves to underline a continuing dilemma: is this an epiphany of error? or a move in a new, more hopeful direction? The terms of the prophecy have been fulfilled; Orc has risen, but the soldiers who, disappointed, leave the battle with "lamentations mourning & weeping" (93.31), seem to have been robbed of their apocalyptic conclusion. We seem to have come closer than before to clarifying the problem of Generation, but still no closer to solving it.

To understand Blake's next move, it is necessary to recognize in "Orc rent her" the allusion to *Visions of the Daughters of Albion*, and to see that in the next few pages Blake is reworking that earlier poem. The reworking will seem at times to cast a dark light on Oothoon (whose role will be assumed by Vala), but Oothoon's vision, however darkened, will here be put to its most important conceptual use. Tharmas appears, as usual looking for his lost Enion, and we suddenly realize that Blake is going to rework the relationship between Tharmas and the Spectre of Urthona (Night IV) in terms of *Visions*. Tharmas of course assumes the role of Theotormon, and Bromion will be played by Orc. Tharmas' commitment to "Eternal Death," first suggested to us in Night IV, is here going to be reinterpreted and developed in terms of Vala and Orc. The analogy Blake is making is dependent upon our understanding that the "rape" of the female which initiates the *Visions* represents a conscious fall into the divided condition of Generation, and this consciousness bears some of the responsibility for what happens to Bromion and Theotormon. The demonic battle *for* Vala *against* the rising of Orc is a good account of what Bromion and Oothoon bound back-to-back within the imagination of Theotormon represent. And insofar as this imaginative condition represents a "vegetation" of Theotormon, Oothoon is not innocent of responsibility. In fact even Oothoon's enlightened vision, depending as it does upon a generated condition within the cave of Bromion, is "innocent" only in the special sense of the *Songs*, where Innocence is related to a divided consciousness, one part of the mind (as in "Mad Song") turning its back on the other. But her vision does have the important effect of countering Theotormon's motions toward despair. Blake expresses this idea in VII(b) in terms of the Shadowy Female

> . . . making Lamentations
> To decieve Tharmas in his rage to soothe his furious soul
> To stay him in his flight that Urizen might live tho in pain
> (93.35–37; E397)

Tharmas' complaints should remind us sharply of Theotormon:

> . . . all delight
> And life appear & vanish mocking me with shadows of false
>   hope
> Hast thou forgot that the air listens thro all its districts telling
> The subtlest thoughts shut up from light in chambers of the
>   Moon
> (94.8–11; E398)

The answer to Tharmas' problem is that his emanation, Enion, is not elusively "out there" before him, but inside his own breast, and that if he can find the power to forgive her supposed sins she will reappear to him. We have already seen that this reunion is brought about very deviously in Night IX, not through forgiveness of sin but by the expedient of having Enion and Tharmas reborn as children out of Vala. Vala's immediate response to Tharmas' complaint is to lie, but her lie (like an analogous one in *Jerusalem*; see plate 81, and, for text, 82.17–21; E236–237) in the end proves prophetic. She begins:

Tharmas. The Moon has chambers where the babes of love lie
  hid
And whence they never can be brought in all Eternity
Unless exposd by their vain parents. Lo him whom I love
Is hidden from me & I never in all Eternity
Shall see him
(94.12–16; E398)

She goes on to blame the other emanations for secreting her Orc
away, and concludes,

              . . . for tho I have the power
To rise on high Yet love binds me down & never never
Will I arise till him I love is loosd from this dark chain
(94.21–23; E398)

Tharmas realizes the trap she is setting him, and that only his continuing wrath and despair—consciousness of the fall—stand
between the world of chaos and its complete absorption by Urizen.
And we know that Vala is simply lying, for we have already seen
her attempt to prevent the rising of Orc. Nevertheless, Vala's lie
is of enormous importance because for the first time she acknowledges the real existence of a realm within the human, fallen
imagination which is outside her control. Blake was quick to take
advantage of her concession, and in *Milton* and *Jerusalem*, using
a succession of odd names—the Spaces of Erin, Golgonooza,
Bowlahoola, Allamanda—he was to move into the accommodation
Vala here provides the whole work of imaginative redemption.

But the chambers of the moon belong to an addition (94.12–26;
E398), and Blake's first attempt was to work in the direction of
redemption through Oothoon's ecstatic vision of the possibilities
avilable even in Generation. The Orphism latent in Oothoon
becomes more apparent in the reworking of her vision for Vala:

And she went forth & saw the forms of Life & of delight
Walking on Mountains or flying in the open expanse of heaven
She heard sweet voices in the winds & in the voices of birds
That rose from waters for the waters were as the voice of Luvah
Not seen to her like waters or like this dark world of death
Tho all those fair perfections which men know only by name
In beautiful substantial forms appeard & servd her
(94.37–43; E398)

In this passage Blake opens up new possibilities for Generation
by putting Vala to the task of realizing in substantial form "perfections which men know only by name." It sounds as if Blake is

edging away from the "idea of pastoral" toward an idea of radical transcendence, but this is not the case. Blake's language *will* shortly display a new hospitality to Christian terminology, but any idea of the poet's "renovated Christianity"[58] has to include the fact that the purpose of Vala's visions can be seen in their result: "Wood & subdud into Eternal Death the Demon Lay" (94.54; E399). Tharmas is being lured ever further into "Eternal Death"; if this be Christian renovation, then Blake's radical Christianity is dependent upon the idea of pastoral.

So far are we from any traditional notion of transcendence, in fact, that the reader may fear he is again about to be plunged into the abyss of Blake's ambiguous attitudes toward Generation. But this is not the case, even though what happens could be identified as yet another epiphany of error. Once Tharmas has been "wood & subdud," the daughters of Beulah awake to discover a "horrid sight of death & torment" (95.4; E399). Vala has consolidated into a dreadful accretion of vegetation and flesh which Blake calls "Polypus," and the daughters find this thing attached to their pastoral realm as firmly as a sucker to a rock. The imagination may be upon the point of death, and we remember that the first line of the Night placed us "in the Caverns of the Grave & Places of human seed" (91.1; E395). But there is a reminder of reassuring words on the tombs:

And all the Songs of Beulah sounded comfortable notes
Not suffring doubt to rise up from the Clouds of the Shadowy
    Female
Then myriads of the Dead burst thro the bottoms of their tombs
Descending on the shadowy females clouds in Spectrous terror
Beyond the Limit of Translucence on the Lake of Udan Adan
These they named Satans & in the Aggregate they namd Them
    Satan
                                                    (95.9–14; E399)

It ought suddenly to occur to us that Blake has once again worked us back to the crossroads where he so often stands, and that we are seeing another instance of the enormous importance to Blake of Milton. For the passage before us is another reinterpretation of the coming of Satan to this world in *Paradise Lost*. Satan is being reinterpreted in terms of the sexual attraction for humanity of Generation. The daughters of Beulah suffer no doubts as the souls of the dead tumble down into the female Polypus, but we may have doubts. Urizen, when he sees what is happening, interprets it as a great *coup*:

The time of Prophecy is now revolvd & all
This Universal Ornament is mine & in my hands

(95.4–5; E392)

For the moment we need not comment on his mistake. What is important to notice is the conjunction of Milton, Milton's Satan descending, the commitment to "Eternal Death" (even in the horrible form of the Polypus), the reference to the fulfillment of prophecy (Orc has been released from chains, even if this is not Urizen's understanding), and Urizen rushing forward as Satan descends. There is no question but that this crisis, in Night VII(b), represents the genesis of *Milton*. If we compare the language of Satan's descent in VII(b) to Blake's account of the descent of Milton in *Milton*, our certainty is reinforced:

Like as a Polypus that vegetates beneath the deep!
They saw his Shadow vegetated underneath the Couch
Of death . . .

(M., 15.8–10; E108)

And further on:

Onwards his Shadow kept its course among the Spectres; call'd
Satan, but swift as lightning passing them, startled the shades
Of Hell beheld him in a trail of light as of a comet
That travels into Chaos: so Milton went guarded within.

(M., 15.17–20; E108)

It should be clear, also, why finally it was Milton who had to descend to usher in the Last Judgment. From Blake's point of view, Milton's vision had made of Generation a realm of Eternal Death; as summed up in his character, Satan, the Miltonic purpose

Is to impress on men the fear of death; to teach
Trembling & fear, terror, constriction; abject selfishness

(M., 38.37–38; E138)

A better spiritual purpose is

. . . to teach Men to despise death & to go on
In fearless majesty annihilating Self, laughing to scorn
Thy laws & terrors, shaking down thy Synagogues as webs

(M., 38.40–42; E138)

The only way this can be done finally is to break the chain of repudiation and rejection which underlies the metaphysics of "Negation" upon which Milton's view of reality was based in the first place, and this means that Milton must tear himself away from his false heaven and accept the "Eternal Death" which is the real function of his vision. To do so is to enter a "void" outside of real existence, but a void which "Becomes a Womb" (M., 41.37–42.1; E142). "Eternal Death" turns out no longer to be the realm of the Polypus and death (which belong to "Ulro"), but the imaginative space of Los's imagination:

> The Sky is an immortal Tent built by the Sons of Los
> And every Space that a Man views around his dwelling-place
> Standing on his own roof, or in his garden on a mount
> Of twenty-five cubits in height, such space is is his Universe;
> And on its verge the Sun rises & sets. The Clouds bow
> To meet the flat Earth & the Sea in such an orderd Space:
> The Starry heavens reach no further but here bend and set
> On all sides & the two Poles turn on their valves of gold.
>   (M., 29.4–11; E126)

In *Anatomy of Criticism* (p. 119) Northrop Frye defines an apocalypse as "the imaginative conception of the whole of nature as the content of an infinite and eternal living body which, if not human, is closer to being human than to being inanimate." I think it can be seen that in the passage from *Milton* Blake—for whom the eternal body would always remains emphatically human—is trying to tell us what the world would look like from an almost apocalyptic point of view. *Jerusalem* goes further in that the whole poem, as an entire form, is an apocalyptic analogy, but the idea of the "Tent built by the Sons of Los" is what the whole of nature can look like to the imagination in the fallen world. Hitherto in Blake we have seen apocalyptic consciousness coterminous with an almost desperate awareness of the universe as fallen; here we have that vision in a sense inside-out: apocalyptic vision coterminous with the world before one's eyes seen as unfallen universe. In either case apocalypse includes what I have been calling the "idea of pastoral," the idea that the ordinary world of extensive, fallen vision includes the imaginative wherewithal for that world's intensive, visionary transformation.

We have been moving awfully quickly, however, into Blake's imaginative future, and this should not be allowed to conceal the fact that when Blake originally set VII(b) down—judging by the

confusions, inconsistencies, and rearrangements of the manuscript
—he must still have been in considerable doubt about whether he
was transforming the world of "Eternal Death" into Heaven or
into Hell. The idea of the descent of the Polypus (and the
attendant chain of considerations leading to *Milton*) came to
interrupt the plan for what was probably going to constitute the
"Preludium" to a final apocalyptic war (perhaps even, as G. E.
Bentley suggests, a "titanic war among the Zoas"),[59] the subject
of Night VIII. This war was going to be initiated by the rising of
Los, which comes at the end of VII(b) in its original order, exacer-
bated into action by a preceding epiphany of error. Considerations
of *Milton* and Polypus aside, something like this makes sense of
Blake's original ordering of pages for the Night. After the epiphany
of Vala as Polypus, Urizen, on the strength of what he takes to be
victory, erects a new temple "in the image of the human heart"
(95.33; E392). A slip of the pen shows it to be modeled upon the
idea of Pandemonium (96.19; E393). Then Los rises, and in
initiating war reveals that Orc, who was consumed earlier, is still
on the scene, apparently unaltered (97.24; E394). Presumably he
must reappear in order that Enitharmon may reveal, too late, a
corresponding enlightenment to that of her husband, for she tells
Orc,

> I put not any trust in thee nor in thy glittring scales
> Thy eyelids are a terror to me & the flaming of thy crest
> The rushing of thy Scales confound me thy hoarse rushing
> scales
> And if that Los had not built me a tower upon a rock
> I must have died in the dark desart among noxious worms
> (97.28–32; E394)

But her cry is futile in the event, for the Serpent has the last
word as the book was originally set down. He undergoes one final,
terrible metamorphosis, and appears as a priestly "Prester Serpent" (98.30; E395), joining with Los in calling for a holy war in
which his principal weapon will be the "Seven Diseases of Man"
(98.27). And Enitharmon herself is sucked down into a world of
vegetation, here called "Existence," which strongly suggests the
Polypus:

> So Enitharmon cried upon her terrible Earthy bed
> While the broad Oak wreathed his roots round her forcing his
> dark way
> Thro caves of death into Existence
> (98.7–9; E394)

One could argue, then, that so far as the implications of Generation go, things are still pretty bleak at the end of VII(b), especially if we do not think very deeply about the implications of the descent of the Polypus. In fact the only hopeful sign is that at the end, during the vegetation of Enitharmon and the account of the Prester Serpent, Los remains conspicuously aloof—a sign perhaps that Blake wishes us to understand him as being offstage, occupied with a more visionary approach to the impending war. But at the end of VII(b), in handwriting difficult to distinguish from that in preceding lines, Blake wrote, "Then follows Thus in the Caverns of the Grave &^{c} as it stands now in the beginning of Night the Seventh" (E762). This suggests that Blake, almost as soon as he finished writing, decided to rearrange the pages. The new beginning comes just at the juncture we have discussed, where the Polypus descends as Satan and is welcomed by Urizen. According to the new order, then, VII(b) begins with Urizen announcing his triumph and constructing Pandemonium. Then Los rises (apparently in response) and announces the beginning of war, Enitharmon is vegetated, and *then* Orc and the "nameless shadowy Vortex" merge; there is a great explosion and conflict leading to the final rending of Orc and to the apotheosis of Vala as the Polypus descending into Generation. The new order suggests that Blake had finally made up his mind about the descent of Vala into "Eternal Death," for, coming as it does at the climax of the Night, the descent of the Polypus must imply either the absolute defeat of Los's "rising" or its implementation. Either we are to understand the epiphany of error to constitute the final defeat of whatever is represented by Los's rising, or we must take it as a fulfillment, however paradoxical. If the latter is the case (as I believe), then Blake had already started to make the series of connections which would lead, eventually, to *Milton*. By the time Night VIII was written, Blake was certainly suggesting a positive attitude toward both the "shadowy Vortex" and its descent into "Eternal Death":

Then Los beheld the Divine vision thro the broken Gates
Of Enitharmons heart astonishd melted into Compassion &
   Love
And Enitharmon said I see the Lamb of God upon Mount Zion
Wondring with love & Awe they felt the divine hand upon them
For nothing could restrain the dead in Beulah from descending
Unto Ulros night tempted by the Shadowy females sweet
     (99.15–20; E357; lines 15 and 16 later altered: E758)

The descent is still described as "delusive cruelty" (99.21), reminding us that we have not left the world of Thel and seductive
appearances completely behind, but the reference to the "divine
hand" and the hopeful interpretation put upon Enitharmon's
broken gates (they were broken giving birth to Vala) combine to
suggest some motion in the direction of *Milton*. Night VIII is a
war Night (Blake still had not disentangled the idea of apocalypse
from the imagery of war), and it contains yet another epiphany of
error to shock the visionary into action, but the extent to which
Blake sensed another direction even as he worked is revealed in a
couple of lines a bit further into VIII:

> Los builds the Walls of Golgonooza against the stirring battle
> That only thro the Gates of Death they can enter to Enitharmon
> (101.40–41; E359; numbered 101.35–36 in the Bentley ed.)

Here Los's imaginative work is not only apart from the war, but
in a sense opposed to it; even more interesting is the fact that here
death (that is, entry into Generation; "birth" from our point of
view) has become an adjunct to the work of the imagination. We
get another glimpse of the same connection between the imagination and "Eternal Death" in one of the very late additions to
VII(a). This begins with a beautiful description of the work of
Golgonooza:

> And first he drew a line upon the walls of shining heaven
> And Enitharmon tincturd it with beams of blushing love
> It remaind permanent a lovely form inspird divinely human
> Dividing into just proportions Los unwearied labourd
> The immortal lines upon the heavens till with sighs of love
> Sweet Enitharmon mild Entrancd breathd forth upon the Wind
> The spectrous dead Weeping the Spectres viewd the immortal
>   works
> Of Los Assimilating to those forms Embodied & Lovely
> In youth & beauty in the arms of Enitharmon mild reposing
>   (90.35–43; E356)

Blake is obviously working toward a union of Generation and the
Imagination. But it is ominous in VII(a) that the drawing and
weaving of Spectres into vegetated form is a comfort to Orc.
Surprisingly we are told:

> But Los loved them & refusd to Sacrifice their infant limbs
> And Enitharmons smiles & tears prevaild over self protection
> They rather chose to meet Eternal death than to destroy
> The offspring of their Care & Pity
>   (90.50–53; E357)

This represents a commitment to Tharmas rather than to Urizen, and both Tharmas and the Spectre of Urthona are comforted. But the imagination's determination to preserve its children from the world of Orc and the equation of this determination with the willingness to "meet" Eternal Death is surely suggestive of *Milton*. And so is the fact that the first two children are Rintrah and Palamabron.

According to the myth of *Milton*, Los in Golgonooza regulates with his hammer a world organized into three "Classes":

> The first, The Elect from before the foundation of the World:
> The second, The Redeem'd. The Third, The Reprobate &
>   form'd
> To destruction from the mothers womb: follow me with my
>   plow!
>
> (M., 7.1–3; E99)

To these three classes Blake assigns in the poem his three characters, Satan (the Elect), Palamabron (the Redeem'd), and Rintrah (the Reprobate). The terms for the classes are ironically chosen to be misleading in accordance with the distorted outlook of a fallen world, but they are a development of the triangular relationship of *Visions*. The Elect (Satan, the part played at Felpham by Blake's earnest patron-tormentor, William Hayley) can be related to the position of Theotormon in *Visions*. In *The Song of Los* Theotormon is associated with the perversion of Jesus' gospel (3.23–24; E66), and in *Milton* the Elect are the audience for and demanders of the Crucifixion of Christ, understood in terms of legal exaction rather than in terms of love:

> For the Elect cannot be Redeemd, but Created continually
> By Offering & Atonement in the crue[l]ties of Moral Law
> (M., 5.11–12; E98)

The Elect are never capable of visionary enlightenment, and they only exist at all by devouring the fruit growing on the Tree of Mystery—which is a way of saying that Satan in order to live feeds upon Orc crucified. The latter is the role played in *Visions* by Oothoon—and I have already commented upon the fact that Oothoon in a sense feeds Theotormon's condition. In *Milton* this part is taken by Rintrah, who is, however, slightly different from Orc or Oothoon as sacrificial victim. Rintrah represents wrath and energy—as do his predecessors—but he is in no sense a function of reaction against repression; rather he represents "those form'd to destruction / In indignation" (M., 8.34–35; E101). Like Elijah in the Bible (with whom he is associated: see 9.8; E102), he embodies disinterested, righteous wrath (Frye, "Commentary," pp. 129–132). Blake associates him with one side of his divided nature, and more especially with his beloved dead brother, Robert. Finally, there is the class of the Redeem'd—those ordinary mortals caught between the demands of Generation and of Vision. Another son of Los, Palamabron, takes this role, associated with Pity as Rintrah is with Wrath; at Felpham Blake associated his own position relative to Satan (Hayley) with Palamabron's.

A fuller rationale for the name of Blake's third class, the Reprobate, is related to the reinterpretation of Milton's idea of the Atonement implicit in the return of Milton to "Eternal Death." For the Redeem'd are

> ... redeem'd from Satans Law, the wrath falling on Rintrah,
> And therefore Palamabron dared not to call a solemn Assembly
> Till Satan had assum'd Rintrahs wrath ...
> (M., 11.23–25; E104)

The myth conveys here a very complicated dramatic situation, and at the same time an ingenious theory of the Crucifixion. Essentially, Blake is attempting to portray a world which is absolutely fallen but which does not necessitate the involvement of the generated individual (Palamabron) in the cycle of repression and sacrifice. We begin, then, with a Satan "not having the Science of Wrath, but only of Pity" (9.46; E103), that is, incapable of righteous indignation (because incapable of vision) but capable of the sort of Urizenic "Pity" which is a socially prized emotion and which is fed by and demands the Orc cycle. Then Palamabron is wronged by Satan, and wants to call him to justice before an Eternal Council. But he senses that to do so will be to risk involvement in the Satanic law of exaction and sacrifice, which would make his imagination a function of Satan's. So he waits until Rintrah appears, and Rintrah rages with righteous indignation at Satan. At this point the council is called, and the eternals pass judgment upon Rintrah. Here is where the new interpretation of the Atonement begins:

> And it was enquir'd: Why in a Great Solemn Assembly
> The Innocent should be condemn'd for the Guilty? Then an
> Eternal rose

> Saying. If the Guilty should be condemn'd, he must be an
>   Eternal Death
> And one must die for another throughout all Eternity.
> Satan is fall'n from his station & never can be redeem'd
> But must be new Created continually moment by moment
> (M., 11.15–20; E104)

And the Reprobate Rintrah does recreate Satan in that the latter, once the judgment has gone against Rintrah, feels encouraged by the judgment to vent his "righteous indignation" on Palamabron (Hayley loses his temper with Blake; see Frye, *Fearful Symmetry*, p. 329), thus, in a sense, becoming more "like" Rintrah. In terms of the personal allegory, Blake and his overbearing patron at Felpham have been metaphorically made "brothers"—if brothers who quarrel—Satan-Hayley has been forced to give up some of his pious hypocrisy, and Blake (even if society does not recognize him as the victor) has been redeemed from accepting the sacrificial role Hayley was planning for him. In Book Two of *Milton* we see this theory reenacted in terms of John Milton and Satan. Milton has come to recognize in Satan his Spectre (just as Blake came to recognize the unredeemable, Satanic aspect of the man Hayley as *his* Spectre), and rather than try to annihilate Satan (by "covering" him and becoming a "greater in thy place"; 38.29–32; E138), he attempts to "recreate" him by giving up his "self" to him. The relationship Milton has in mind is like that of the notebook lyric "My Spectre around me night & day" (E467): that is, Milton will become the "Body" of Satan, and Satan will play the role of Spectre, circling around the body waiting to pounce and devour it. But, Blake tells us, he cannot devour his new body because it is himself ("if he touches a Vital,/His torment is unendurable"; 39.19–20; E139), and so he "howls round it as a lion round his prey continually" (39.21). The image of the lion who does not devour his prey takes us all the way back through Blake to "Night."

It can be seen that the real importance of the Rintrah-Palamabron-Satan myth in *Milton* is not merely Blake's reinterpretation of the Atonement, but as well the redemption of Palamabron from the Orc cycle. For the ceaseless alternation of energy and repression, Blake substitutes what he calls "Separation," a key conception in both *Milton* and *Jerusalem*. And Palamabron is not redeemed from separation. When the eternal judgment falls upon Rintrah, and Satan feels encouraged to assume Rintrah's wrath, he accuses Palamabron of ingratitude and other vices. As he rages, in a remarkable image, he turns opaque before his auditor's eyes, revealing the existence in his bosom of "a vast unfathomable Abyss" (9.35; E102). He grows increasingly opaque until he is "covering the east with solid blackness" (9.40), and by this time Rintrah can stand it no longer and tries to protect Palamabron:

> Rintrah rear'd up walls of rock and pourd rivers & moats
> Of fire round the walls: columns of fire guard around
> Between Satan and Palamabron in the terrible darkness.
> (M., 9.43–45; E103)

This is a repressive act like any other, and the landscape Rintrah succeeds in amassing should remind us of Hell and the construction of Pandemonium in *Paradise Lost*. But at least Palamabron himself has not been drawn into Satan's game. The outcome is in any case unfortunate enough:

> And Satan not having the Science of Wrath, but only of Pity:
> Rent them asunder, and wrath was left to wrath, & pity to pity.
> He sunk down a dreadful Death, unlike the slumbers of Beulah
>
> The Separation was terrible ...
> (M., 9.46–49; E103)

Blake is making the point that henceforth, in the fallen world, Palamabron will easily be led to believe he has more in common with Satan (the "Science of Pity") than with Rintrah: the tension between Orc and Urizen has been translated into the separation of Rintrah and Palamabron. The reference to "rending" reminds us of *Visions*; again, just as in *The Four Zoas*, Night VII(b), the allusion leads to the descent of Satan into the fallen world. This time the event is interpreted for the reader with more assurance:

> Then Los & Enitharmon knew that Satan is Urizen
> Drawn down by Orc & the Shadowy Female into Generation
> (M., 10.1–2; E103)

If we attempt to trace the idea of "Separation" back into the *Vala/The Four Zoas* manuscript, we find ourselves working back through Night VII(b) to the two versions of the Fall related in VII(a) by the Shadow of Enitharmon and the Spectre of Urthona. The version narrated by Enitharmon's shadow, it will be remembered, suggested a pattern of relationships (Urizen fallen and

Luvah divided into sexes) derived from *Visions of the Daughters of Albion* and the Orc cycle. We have just observed how this pattern of relationships is transformed into *Milton* in such a way as to rechannel the energies of the Orc cycle into the division between Pity and Wrath. This rechanneling, however, has not absorbed any of the energy of sexual strife, and we remember that the Orc cycle has a Luvah-Vala aspect as well as an Orc-Urizen aspect. It is to the aspect of Generation which involves Blake's attitude toward the Female that we must turn now, and it is in this connection that the version of the Fall told by the Spectre of Urthona becomes important.

According to his own account, the Spectre of Urthona came into the world in the first place by way of resistance to the generated condition. In the late additions to Night VII(a)—even after Los has become reconciled to him—he still refers to his engenderment in terms of "separation," and seems, moreover, apologetic:

> Urthonas Spectre terrified beheld the Spectres of the Dead
> Each Male formd without a counterpart without a concentering
>   vision
> The Spectre of Urthona wept before Los Saying I am the cause
> That this dire state commences I began the dreadful state
> Of Separation & on my dark head the curse & punishment
> Must fall ...
>
> (87.30–35; E355)

The articulation of separation in sexual terms (men without women) suggests a more positive role for the Female to play in Blake's mythology than any we have seen so far. The same thing is suggested in Night VII(b), where Enitharmon's "chambers of the Moon" inaugurated the theme of the saving spaces of the imagination. But Enitharmon only stumbled upon the conception via a lie, and the event which concludes her career in VII(b)—her transfixion by the roots of the Oak of sacrifice—does not hold out much hope from her quarter. Indeed, this is the problem. In the additions to Night VII(a) Los is reconciled to his spectre (85.32–86.8; E353–354), but reconciliation to Enitharmon proves more difficult. Los reaches to embrace his emanation, but she "fled & hid beneath Urizens tree" (87.1; E354); thereafter the function of the obedient spectre is the one suggested in the first place by Tharmas in Night IV,

Being a medium between him & Enitharmon But This Union
Was not to be Effected without Cares & Sorrows & Troubles
Of Six thousand Years

(87.27–29; E355)

The conflicts of history are now translatable into two distinct
but related "separations." The first separation (no doubt related
to Blake's apprehension of his own character)[60] is the "terrible"
separation of Wrath and Pity. This leads to the descent of
Satan (in the form of the Polypus) into Eternal Death, and
demands the saving, creative descent of Milton (also Jesus and
Albion) in order to renovate Eternal Death. The other separation,
owing much to Blake's reading of Milton's Adam and Eve, is
after the model of the enduring sexual tension between Los and
Enitharmon. The two sorts of separation can be related to Blake's
idea of Adam and Satan as the merciful limits, respectively, of
contraction and opacity (see the late passage in *The Four Zoas*,
Night IV, 56.17–22; E331), and they are related to each other as
intimately as the idea of the Polypus is related to the chambers of
the moon in *The Four Zoas*, Night VII(b). Plate 31 of *Jerusalem*
(35 in the Stirling order)[61] has as its subject Albion undergoing the
journey of John Milton in *Milton*:

Albion goes to Eternal Death: In Me all Eternity.
Must pass thro' condemnation, and awake beyond the Grave!

(J., 31.9–10; E176)

The text on this plate is a narrow ribbon dividing an illustration
above from one below. Above we see Albion floating face down
through fire toward Eternal Death. His position is cruciform, and
there are stigmata on his hands and feet. In the picture below,
Los is lying asleep, and Enitharmon is being born, like Eve,
out of his left side. Her face is turned radiantly upward, and we
see that the flames through which Albion is descending above
emanate from this sexual division below. Once we have seen the
relationship between top and bottom, and that the illustrations are
a unity, we can see too that the plate presents a renovated version
of the idea of apocalypse as fall, for the sexual division at the foot
of the page is a total form of history.

And while the descent of the Polypus and the myth of Rintrah
and Palamabron may have absorbed the tensions of the Orc cycle,
Blake's doubts and ambiguities concerning Generation live on in
terms of the separation of Los and Enitharmon. For insofar as

Enitharmon represents the Female Will in Generation, Los's giving himself to Enitharmon would represent Eternal Death in a new and entirely unfortunate sense: the death of the imagination. But without the Female Los is powerless in Generation, for he can desire nothing, his spectre can will nothing, without the female space which provides body and form, the realization of will and desire. Henceforth, the problem of Generation is for Blake the problem of the female: the conundrum of *Jerusalem* is the apparently insoluble bond between two females, Vala and Jerusalem. We will hear very little of Orc, and Los will control his spectre (though the agony of their conflict, representing as it does all the pain of Blake's heroic endeavor as an artist, is nearly unbearable), but he will often be unable to control his animus against women:

> What may Man be? who can tell! but what may Woman be?
> To have power over Man from Cradle to corruptible Grave.
> There is a Throne in every Man, it is the Throne of God
> This Woman has claimed as her own & Man is no more!
> Albion is the Tabernacle of Vala & her Temple
> And not the Tabernacle & Temple of the Most High
> O Albion why wilt thou Create a Female Will?
> To hide the most evident God in a hidden covert, even
> In the shadows of a Woman & a secluded Holy Place
> That we may pry after him as after a stolen treasure
> (J., 30.25–34; E175)

(After considering the phrase "the most evident God" we may decide that to say we hear little of Orc in *Jerusalem* is inaccurate. We do hear about him in a new way.)

We may begin with a vision of the Fall as frankly female.

> The nature of a Female Space is this: it shrinks the Organs
> Of Life till they become Finite & Itself seems Infinite
> And Satan vibrated in the immensity of the Space! Limited
> To those without but Infinite to those within: it fell down and
> Became Canaan: closing Los from Eternity in Albions Cliffs
> (M., 10.6–10; E103)

But even in the face of such evident severity, even before the Finite and the false Canaan, the reader should remember and take comfort in the "idea of pastoral." The narrator of Andrew Marvell's "The Garden" tells us, "Stumbling on Melons, as I pass,/Insnar'd with Flow'rs, I fall on Grass" (39–40), yet he rescues the imagination necessary for "Annihilating all that's made / To a green Thought in a green Shade" (47–48). And while Enitharmon's imagination is shown to be producing, not only one, but a host of doubtful children, it may be that this is part of an imaginative plan more ambitious, even greener than Marvell's:

> First Orc was Born then the Shadowy Female: then All Los's
>   Family
> At last Enitharmon brought forth Satan Refusing Form, in vain
> The Miller of Eternity made subservient to the Great Harvest
> That he may go to his own Place Prince of the Starry Wheels
> (M., 3.40–43; E97)

The scope of Blake's ambitions for a myth of the female, and also the nature of the problem he was trying to solve, is suggested first in *Milton* by the great speech of Leutha which ends the Bard's prophetic song at the beginning of the poem. It is a remarkable, almost incredible speech, for within a bare hundred lines it translates into the language of the Female problem not only the Rintrah-Palamabron-Satan myth, but Blake's interpretation of *Paradise Lost* and a thumbnail version of his whole theory of human history as well. The vales of Leutha were where Oothoon turned aside to pluck the flower of sexuality in *Visions*, and in the penultimate plate of *Europe* (14.9–14) she appears as a daughter of Enitharmon in her *belle dame sans merci* aspect as the "lureing bird of Eden" and a "sweet smiling pestilence!" (E64). By a brilliant irony Blake associates her sexual manifestation of the Fall with the arc of the Covenant in Genesis (9:8–17), since for Blake the Flood and the creation of life in its fallen aspect are the same event. In *Milton* Blake develops this association, but associates Leutha also with Milton's Sin, the emanation of Satan (see M., 12.38–39; E105; and compare *Paradise Lost*, II.760).[62]

The purpose of Leutha's speech is to explain the all-important role of the female in the terrible "separation" of Rintrah and Palamabron. Leutha begins by frankly declaring her responsibility ("by my suggestion / My Parent power Satan has committed this transgression": 11.35–36; E104), for she says, "I loved Palamabron." Presumably Blake on the level of personal allegory is explaining the genuine admiration which Hayley's creative, emanative side had for him (Elynittria's consequent jealous repulse of Leutha may also refer to Catherine Blake's attitude toward Hayley when he was being especially warm to her husband), but Blake's application of personal history transcends the local, for in a brilliant image Leutha complains of Elynittria:

> For her light is terrible to me. I fade before her immortal beauty.
> O wherefore doth a Dragon-form forth issue from my limbs
> To sieze her new born son? Ah me! the wretched Leutha!
> (12.1–3; E104)

By means of the enormously daring allusion to the dragon of Revelation (12:1–4), Blake makes of the squabbles at Felpham an apocalyptic image. His development of the allusion is equally brilliant, and draws in, as if by the way, *Paradise Lost*. Since the direct approach will not work with Elynittria, Leutha enters Satan's brain, stupefying the "masculine perceptions" (12.5) (one can see behind this image a Hayley becoming increasingly loving and effeminate, and an increasingly suspicious Catherine Blake)[63] until Palamabron is weak enough to pity Satan and let him drive the Harrow of mercy for one long, eternal day. At noon, when Satan rests, Leutha wants to play the part of Elynittria and give succor to the horses which drive the harrow (that is, presumably, to soothe the driving power of Blake's graver), but the horses see Leutha as the rainbow, which they associate with the Flood, and begin to rage. Satan, in order to control the horses, sets the Urizenic gnomes

> . . . to curb the horses, & to throw banks of sand
> Around the fiery flaming Harrow in labyrinthine forms.
> And brooks between to intersect the meadows in their course.
> (12.17–19; E105)

We are back in the landscape in which Urizen finds Orc in Night VII(a) of the *Vala/The Four Zoas* manuscript, that "Cavernd Universe of flaming fire" in which we saw before the "plow of ages & the golden harrow" (77.6–15; E346). Leutha recognizes the allusion to the construction of Pandemonium even as she completes the reference to Revelation:

> The Harrow cast thick flames & orb'd us round in concave
> fires
> A Hell of our own making. see, its flames still gird me round[.]
> Jehovah thunder'd above! Satan in pride of heart
> Drove the fierce Harrow among the constellations of Jehovah
> Drawing a third part in the fires as stubble north & south
> (M., 12.22–26; E105)

The language here is enormously concentrated, and the bare reference to "north & south" includes all the wars of Luvah and Urizen. There ensues much ill-feeling and recrimination in the vicinity of the harrow; even the gnomes curse Satan for his foolish hypocrisy, and when Leutha appears to them in *propria persona*, to spur them on, they "call'd me Sin, and for a sign portentous held me" (12.39; E105). It is a portentous sign because the sense of sin consolidates Satan's fallen position. When he returns home, Elynittria is furious with him for having diverted the harrow of pity into the fields of burning rage, and so she and her singing women go out satirically to fête Satan with "wine of wildest power" (12.43; E105). Satan, as we are told elsewhere, "fainted beneath the artillery" (5.2; E97), and decided to beat a retreat from the warm work of creation. His retreat takes the form of self-condemnation and the assumption of holiness, following up the hint of the gnomes:

> Wild with prophetic fury his former life became like a dream
> Cloth'd in the Serpents folds, in selfish holiness demanding
>   purity
> Being most impure, self-condemn'd to eternal tears, he drove
> Me from his inmost Brain & the doors clos'd with thunders
>   sound
>   (12.45–48; E105)

At this point Leutha begs for pity on Satan:

> O Divine Vision who didst create the Female: to repose
> The Sleepers of Beulah: pity the repentant Leutha. My
> Sick Couch bears the dark shades of Eternal Death infolding
> The Spectre of Satan. he furious refuses to repose in sleep.
>   (12.49–13.2; E105)

In psychological terms, it will be noticed that the "separation" mirroring that between pity and wrath has been accomplished in Satan's imagination. His spectrous and his emanative halves are divided, even as the Spectre of Urthona stands between Los and his emanation, and the result is he cannot rest. It is interesting, too, that in her final summing-up Leutha identifies herself as "the Spectre of Luvah the murderer of Albion" (13.8–9; E106).

But although things look very dark at this point, and Satan seems condemned forever to be a wandering spectre, there is suddenly a change, no less related to the question of the Female than what we have seen so far. Leutha suddenly realizes that

"Enitharmon had / Created a New Space to protect Satan from punishment" (13.12–13; E106), and so she rushes and hides in Enitharmon's tent. The spaces which we have seen before as the "chambers of the moon," emanative spaces, here reappear, and we suddenly see that these spaces are going to contain human history, including Generation, for an Assembly ratifies "the kind decision of Enitharmon & gave a Time to the Space, / Even Six Thousand years" (13.16–17; E106). The Seven Eyes of Blake's theory of history are rehearsed (the image derives from Zechariah 3:9),[64] and the two "limits" of Satan and Adam (opacity and contraction). What is especially interesting about this sequence, apart from its nerve and velocity, is that it ends with an account of the Female as Body of Death, in which the imagery involves allusions both to Satan and to Jesus:

> For then the Body of Death was perfected in hypocritic
>   holiness,
> Around the Lamb, a Female Tabernacle woven in Cathedrons
>   Looms
> He died as a Reprobate. he was Punish'd as a Transgressor!
>   (13.25–27; E106)

The idea is less dialectical than it sounds, and Blake quickly reveals that he has on his mind, not the orthodox Atonement, nor even any annihilation of the Body through Sacrifice, but only the imaginative breakthrough we have seen already: when Palamabron can recognize Satan as his brother, redeemed from the wrath of Satan by Rintrah,

> The Elect shall meet the Redeem'd. on Albions rocks they
>   shall meet
> Astonish'd at the Transgressor, in him beholding the Saviour.
> And the Elect shall say to the Redeemd. We behold it is of
>   Divine
> Mercy alone! of Free Gift and Election that we live.
>   (13.30–33; E106)

But it is the following line which gives the game away, for it tells us on what point the "Elect shall meet the Redeem'd": "Our virtues & Cruel Goodnesses have deserv'd Eternal Death." That is, in this version of the Atonement, the Lamb takes up a position within the Body of hypocritic holiness, and we can see again that Blake is primarily interested in the Crucifixion as an emblem of human suffering carefully cultivated and maintained and perpetuated by our fallen idea of goodness. For the Atonement Blake substitutes the epiphany of God as breaker of the law of Jehovah's virtue, and it is in the development of this epiphany of the Reprobate that the Female becomes terribly important. For it is the sexual separation between Satan and Leutha—dramatized when Satan locks Leutha out of his mind as "Sin"—which is the perfection of "hypocritic holiness." This holiness is in turn equivalent to Jehovah's law. Finally, in terms of the most redeeming metaphor of all—and one with enormous consequences so far as the imaginative redemption of Generation is concerned—hypocritic holiness is the Body of Death. This is not an occasion for nailing a body to a cross—neither one's own nor anyone else's—but an occasion for Rintrah to make himself wrathfully manifest, not destructively but as a creative lawbreaker, recreating Satan in his own image. That is, the Body of Error is "Burnt up the Moment Men cease to behold it" (E555), and we can see the relationship between this epiphany of the Reprobate and Blake's eschatological remark that "whenever any Individual Rejects Error & Embraces Truth a Last Judgment passes upon that Individual" (E551). It would seem, then, that in the characterization of Rintrah in *Milton* Blake resolved much of the pastoral ambiguity attaching to Orc and the Tyger, reserving it for his myth of the Female. The epiphany of God as outlaw, designed to concentrate the distinction between the visionary and the natural man of hypocritic holiness, is a positive—but paradoxical—achievement of the Female.

If the positive achievement of the Female is a function of desire, there is still the possibility of a less fortunate achievement, a function of the Female's assumption of the role of delusory rest or dreamy wish-fulfillment—the passive aspect of the Female which makes Beulah liable to attachment by the Polypus (see Frye, *Fearful Symmetry*, p. 234). This side of the case is reflected in the conclusion of Leutha's dream, for once Leutha has hidden herself in Enitharmon's tent, Elynittria at long last relents, takes pity on her, and brings her "to Palamabrons bed" (13.38: Catherine Blake acquiesces in the "seduction" of her husband by Hayley's "good side"). Blake uses this unhappy mythical event to explain his invention, in Lambeth, of the spiritual enemies of mankind:

> In dreams she bore the shadowy Spectre of Sleep, & namd him Death.
> In dreams she bore Rahab the mother of Tirzah & her sisters In Lambeths vales . . .
>
> (13.40–42; E106)

"Tirzah & her sisters" refers to the five brotherless daughters of Zelophehad (Numbers 27:1); the fact that there were five of them (corresponding to the number of the fallen senses) and that they were the first female recipients of an inheritance from the male line made them convenient symbols for the Female Will. (There is a Song of Experience, "To Tirzah," where she is called "Mother of my Mortal part"; E30.) Rahab is "the emblem of earthly political tyranny (Egypt, Babylon, the English state church) and of spiritual tyranny as well, any supposedly Christian church's claim to exlusive salvation."[65]

MILTON AND *JERUSALEM*

The dramatic action of *Milton* has been succinctly described as follows:

> At the end of Book One, the whole objective world is seen as a creation of Los, and is thereby transformed into a responsive emanation, the Beulah described at the opening of Book Two, from whence Ololon the milky way descends, like the angels descending Jacob's ladder (M.39:35). The emanation retreats from anyone who seeks her in the outside world, but appears when the natural perspective is reversed; hence the paradox that although the object of Milton's journey is to seek Ololon, Ololon in fact seeks him.   (Frye, "Commentary," p. 136)

All we need to know beyond this is that Satan in the poem is identified both with the character in *Paradise Lost* and with the poet John Milton's spectre, and that the reunion of Milton with his emanation at the end of the poem in fact involves all three characters and constitutes a resolution of the difficult and tense relationship we have seen defined in terms of Los, Enitharmon, and the Spectre of Urthona. Since that relationship has been used in Blake to define the form of human history, the resolution of all difficulties implies the end of history. Hence, when Milton descends into vegetated Ulro (the Polypus), a part of him is left behind on a couch in Eden: this sleeping part is his immortal aspect, and as Milton descends it gets up and begins with difficulty to walk, an act suggestive of imminent resurrection. It is supported by the "Seven Angels of the Presence," that is, by representatives of the seven "Eyes" of history, and the fact that all seven are present, even Jesus, suggests that Milton is an "eighth" (15.3–7; E108): his resurrection means the end of all cycles, the end of history itself. We are about to experience an apocalypse and Last

Judgment. But phrases like "apocalypse" or "Last Things" are meaningless, especially the former, unless they convey to us in a language we can understand the form of what is meant, and we must look at the conclusion to *Milton* in terms of language and form. In order to acquire a sense of direction, we may reflect upon the fact that *Milton* even in its title conveys the depth of Blake's interest in the history of his vocabulary—his successive readings of the poems of Milton. Moreover, the great act of the conclusive second book of the poem is the redemption of man's emanative life, the Female. When we recall that the "form" of Blake's apocalypse is finally the female form of Jerusalem ("The Emanation of The Giant Albion"), the importance of this redemption emerges.

The last section concluded with a consideration of the relationship between an epiphany of God as Reprobate and the role of the Female in perfecting hypocritic holiness. In the paradox of this positive female achievement we recognize another form, a transformation, of a notion we are familiar with: the idea of apocalypse as total awareness of the fallen condition. This idea has been examined in terms of "Generation" and as made manifest in the extraordinary ambiguity of the imagery—most of it derived from Milton—used to present Orc's fiery and periodic manifestations as would-be savior there. The ambiguity, in turn, has been discussed in terms of Blake's faithfulness to the idea of pastoral, the idea— underlined by the poet's constant recourse to pastoral imagery and themes—that the fallen world must supply the language and forms for the imaginative resurrection of reality. If we consider what happens to Ololon in Book Two of *Milton*, that she is imaginatively renovated, that she nevertheless goes to "Eternal Death," and that her marriage to Milton is finally consummated, we can see that the "idea of pastoral" in *Milton* is realized by the final and ultimate coalescence of the imageries of elegy and epithalamion—the two forms which would have seemed inescapably pastoral to Blake. The idea of transformation, which inaugurated the second half of this study, is beginning to resurface, and it is now clear that the consummation of Ololon is only the culminating instance of the complex interaction in Blake of Miltonic language and pastoral forms. Even in less crucial instances we can observe the same transforming imaginative force at work. A few examples will have to suffice.

Milton is often remarked to be pastoral in the vulgar sense that it contains idyllic pictures of nature, notably the passionate hymn to the lark and flowers near the beginning of the second book. The lark

> ... leads the Choir of Day! trill, trill, trill, trill,
> Mounting upon the wings of light into the Great Expanse:
> Reecchoing against the lovely blue & shining heavenly Shell:
> His little throat labours with inspiration; every feather
> On throat & breast & wings vibrates with the effluence Divine
> All Nature listens silent to him & the awful Sun
> Stands still upon the Mountain looking on this little Bird
> (31.31–37; E129)

It is a song of "natural" resurrection, and in that sense illustrates as closely as any passage in Blake the "idea of pastoral." When we get to the flowers, there is an Orphic dance, and we do not need to be reminded of the usual connotations of flowers in Blake to guess that it is epithalamic:

> And Flower & Herb soon fill the air with an innumerable Dance
> Yet all in order sweet & lovely, Men are sick with Love!
> (31.61–62; E130)

The relationship between these songs and the career of Ololon is obvious. Less obvious is the meaning of the conclusion to each song: "Such is a vision of the lamentation of Beulah over Ololon" (31.45 and 31.63). Blake is really less interested here in point of view than he is in the fact that the weeping daughters of Beulah are frankly mistaken; they do not see that Ololon is headed toward consummation and fulfillment: to them she is headed toward the Polypus and Eternal Death. Again we have a conflation of elegy and epithalamion, here underlined by the fact that the chorus of Beulah reminds us of the epithalamic sighs of the daughters of Albion in *Visions* as they looked toward Oothoon.

This fact could enforce exactly the same ambiguity about Ololon's descent that we saw developed previously concerning Orc's periodic appearances in Generation. Blake seems about to develop just such ambiguity in one instance in *Milton*, but he uses the occasion finally for one of his most strongly positive interpretations of Ololon—and for an oddly comic tribute to Milton. When Milton goes to Eternal Death, he makes a track (the subject of a diagram on plate 33; E132) through the void and the Polypus analogous to Satan's journey through the realm of chaos to nature in Book II of *Paradise Lost*. It will be remembered that in Book X of Milton's epic, Sin and Death, sensing their parent power's success in the New World, pave a highway over Chaos "To make the Way easier from Hell to this World to and fro" ("The Argument" to Book X). When Ololon descends in Blake's epic, we see her enacting the role of Sin and Death:

> O how the Starry Eight rejoic'd to see Ololon descended!
> And now that a wide road was open to Eternity,
> By Ololons descent thro Beulah to Los & Enitharmon.
>
> For mighty were the multitudes of Ololon, vast the extent
> Of their great sway, reaching from Ulro to Eternity
> Surrounding the Mundane Shell outside in its Caverns
> And through Beulah. and all silent forbore to contend
> With Ololon for they saw the Lord in the Clouds of Ololon
> (35.34–41; E134–135)

Blake acknowledges, not without irony, the enormous influence of Milton on his whole system both in the tenor and the vehicle of his metaphor, but the rejoicing of the "Starry Eight" (the seven angels plus Milton's immortal remnant) and the last line assure us that this time Blake has left real ambiguity behind.

Before commenting on the last line quoted above, it is worth noticing that Milton's track (and Ololon's highway therefore) enter the Mundane Egg from the quarter of the East and South, that is, intersecting the fallen universes of Luvah and Urizen. This is just one of the ways Blake accomplishes the transformation of his old concern with the Orc cycle into new terms without relinquishing his interest in either Miltonic vocabulary or pastoral forms. We have already been exposed to the materials of an analogous transformation, from "The Tyger" to the consummation of Ololon, for each passionate appearance, uniting *eros* and *thanatos*, finds fulfillment in a rain of lamentations from above. We see still another analogous transformation in Book II's most striking pastoral motif. Blake is developing the optimistic idea that "There is a Moment in each Day that Satan cannot find," arguing that Ololon's descent to Los and Enitharmon occupied such a moment (35.42–47; E135). Then he makes an analogy between the visionary ability to find the one "moment" and the inconspicuous Wild Thyme, pungent beyond its humility:

> The Wild Thyme is Los's Messenger to Eden, a mighty Demon
> Terrible deadly & poisonous his presence in Ulro dark
> Therefore he appears only a small Root creeping in grass
> Covering over the Rock of Odours his bright purple mantle
> Beside the Fount above the Larks nest in Golgonooza
> Luvah slept here in death & here is Luvahs empty Tomb
> Ololon sat beside this Fountain on the Rock of Odours.
> (35.54–60; E135)

Harold Bloom suggests that "as a purple flower on Luvah's rock of sacrifice, the Wild Thyme recalls the traditional pastoral emblem for the death of a young man or god" (E840). Here Blake uses the motif to suggest the resurrection of Luvah through the agency of Ololon, just as the descent of Milton was seen as fulfillment of the prophecy about the release of Orc from the "Chain of Jealousy." But we mistake Blake's meaning if we assume the passage implies a simple equation between Luvah and Christ, an equation which implicates the orthodox conception of the Atonement. Here is another case where we must treat Blake's renovated "Christianity" with some care, because the paradoxical truth is that the appearance of orthodox-sounding terminology in the *Vala/The Four Zoas* manuscript (see especially the identification of Luvah and Christ in Night VII(b); manuscript page 92) signals Blake's identification of the orthodox ideas of Crucifixion and Atonement with the circular sterility of the Orc cycle. The empty tomb of Luvah signals not merely the resurrection of the body, but the disappearance as well of the old form of Luvah as an imaginative force in Blake's world.

At this point, then, just this side of apocalypse, the questions of transformation and of the renovation of the Female coalesce, for as we have observed the "Starry Eight" see the Lord in the "Clouds of Ololon," and Ololon therefore is not merely a function of the transformation of the Atonement into an Epiphany of the Reprobate, but the agency of that process. The contrast at this point with Milton is very pointed, for God says in *Paradise Lost*:

> He with his whole posteritie must die:
> Die hee or Justice must; unless for him
> Som other able, and as willing pay
> The rigid satisfaction, death for death.
>
> (III.209–212)

Blake causes Ololon to repudiate this idea with great firmness:

> And Ololon said, Let us descend also, and let us give
> Ourselves to death in Ulro among the Transgressors.
> Is Virtue a Punisher? O no!
>
> (21.45–47; E115)

Coincidentally Milton must be absolutely repudiated as well, for his is the idea. As this is accomplished by "the Divine Family," Ololon's role as conductress of the savior is made crystal clear:

                                                  Obey
The Dictate! Watch over this World, and with your brooding
    wings,
Renew it to Eternal Life: Lo! I am with you alway   ˙
But you cannot renew Milton he goes to Eternal Death

So spake the Family Divine as One Man even Jesus
Uniting in One with Ololon & the appearance of One Man.
Jesus the Saviour appeard coming in the Clouds of Ololon!
                              (21.54–60; E115)

The translation of the language of Milton upon which this
accomplishment depends must be examined carefully. Ololon is
referred to indifferently as "she" or "they." The latter pronoun
refers to the fact that Ololon (the name is derived from a Greek
verb which in Homer means to cry to the gods in praise or thanks-
giving, or from the cognate noun meaning "an effeminate, dis-
solute person") is "sixfold," a composite of Milton's three wives
and three daughters. In addition she embodies the poet's impact
upon the world, and if we put these aspects of Ololon's nature
together, we can see her as the total *object* of Milton's desire. What
Blake is saying is that Milton's *desire* only succeeded in bringing
to the world the Orc cycle: the savior descended as Satan, bringing
on his heels a Urizenic god. The oscillation of Satanic Hell and
Urizenic Heaven, using the world as a fulcrum, suggests the
metaphor of the scales of justice which demand the Crucifixion
and Atonement. But where Desire failed, the Object of Desire can
succeed. We saw that the sons of Los, understandably enough,
were alarmed by the descent of Milton, for they saw him as Satan.
But when Ololon descends, it is a different matter:

For Ololon step'd into the Polypus within the Mundane Shell
They could not step into Vegetable Worlds without becoming
The enemies of Humanity except in a Female Form
                              (36.13–15; E135)

We can see in these lines the genesis of the symbol so important
in *Jerusalem*, the almost inextricable embrace of Jerusalem and
Vala. This embrace, so distressing to the visionary Los, is at the
root of all Blake's poetic thinking; it embodies the idea that the
fallen world, the "veil" before our eyes, is nevertheless—insofar
as it is female—capable of containing our salvation. This does not
mean that it is not also capable of containing our disaster, and

Ololon is acutely aware of the role of sexuality in the Fall. She says to Milton:

> Is this our Femin[in]e Portion the Six-fold Miltonic Female
> Terribly this Portion trembles before thee O awful Man
> Altho' our Human Power can sustain the severe contentions
> Of Friendship, our Sexual cannot: but flies into the Ulro.
> Hence arose all our terrors in Eternity!
>
> (41.30–34; E141–142)

Neverthless, the "Feminine Portion" can also be the agent of salvation.

Blake's demonstration of how this is so takes us back to his radical interpretation of the Atonement. It also underlines the relationship between his "root" idea and pastoralism, for the renovation of mankind through Ololon takes us back to the two halves of the pastoral argument in Blake—*The Book of Thel* and *Visions of the Daughters of Albion*. I am referring of course to Ololon's "consummation." She asks Milton,

> O Immortal! how were we led to War the Wars of Death
> Is this the Void Outside of Existence, which if enter'd into
> Becomes a Womb? & is this the Death Couch of Albion
> Thou goest to Eternal Death & all must go with thee
>
> So saying, the Virgin divided Six-fold & with a shriek
> Dolorous that ran thro all Creation a Double Six-fold Wonder!
> Away from Ololon she divided & fled into the depths
> Of Miltons Shadow as a Dove upon the stormy Sea.
>
> (41.36–42.6; E142)

In the questions of the first three lines, and in the shriek, we recognize Thel, the difference being that Ololon commits herself finally, and not provisionally, to Eternal Death. But we must remember that Ololon is not sacrificing herself, that is, not crucifying herself, but committing herself to sexuality. The division she undergoes, and the separation of the "Six-fold wonder" is simultaneously an allusion to the divisions of *Visions* and an allusion to the loss of her virginity, for her marriage to Milton is finally being consummated. The dove who flies into the depths of the stormy seas (Milton as Eternal Death) is a brilliant emblem of her loss of virginity, the innocent dove losing itself in the flood of the fallen world, but it is also an allusion to the same passage of Genesis whence the image of Leutha as arc of the Covenant was derived. Again Blake uses the image creatively, for in Genesis the dove fails to return because it has found dry land. As well as being a sexual symbol, the plunge of Blake's dove is a reminder that for him there is no such thing as dry land. More to the point is the relationship between both Ololon's dove and Leutha's bow and the idea of the Covenant between God and man. For Blake, as we have seen in his use of the rainbow image, the Covenant is the fallen condition made manifest as law, and it is in terms of the idea of law that we can begin to discern in Leutha (whose name might be derived from the Greek verb meaning to loosen clothes or to dissolve a legal obligation) *and* Ololon the two halves of one enormous metaphor. Leutha's female contribution to salvation was related to the epiphany of God as Reprobate; hers was the accomplishment in her husband of that hypocritic holiness which Blake associated with the lamb. Ololon is in a sense a lamb who is *not* a body of hypocritic holiness, and her giving of herself to sexuality, like the appearance of Rintrah, is a repudiation of hypocrisy and law with apocalyptic implications.

It was insisted above that Ololon's passionate embrace of sexuality was by no means patience of crucifixion; it can now be seen that Blake is developing an astonishing inversion of that rejected metaphor. For the implication of his metaphor is that the blood of Christ comes from Ololon's maidenhead when she breaks the law. Ololon's blood becomes the "Garment" (the vegetated body or veil) of Christ made manifest as the formal shape of human history: Ololon herself becomes the Ark (like Beulah and all aspects of emanative life associated with the moon) to bear mankind up upon the flood of fallen reality:

> Then as a Moony Ark Ololon descended to Felphams Vale
> In clouds of blood, in streams of gore, with dreadful
>   thunderings
> Into the Fires of Intellect that rejoic'd in Felphams Vale
> Around the Starry Eight: with one accord the Starry Eight
>   became
> One Man Jesus the Saviour. wonderful! round his limbs
> The Clouds of Ololon folded as a Garment dipped in blood
> Written within & without in woven letters: & the Writing
> Is the Divine Revelation in the Litteral expression:
> A Garment of War, I heard it namd the Woof of Six Thousand
>   Years
>
>   (42.7–15; E142)

The force and brilliance of Blake's imagery beggar the imagination, and it seems a pity to belabor them with critical insistence. Perhaps enough has been said to negotiate my argument that *Thel* and

Visions initiate a long pastoral argument in Blake. It should also be clear that the strange relationship in Ololon between sexuality and the blood of the lamb can be traced back very clearly into *Songs of Innocence and of Experience.* When I argue that "The Tyger" is essentially a pastoral poem showing the visionary imagination caught between the Orc cycle on one hand and the Female Will on the other, it can be seen that the pastoralism of which I speak provides the formal argument of *Milton.* In short, Ololon embodies the idea of pastoral.

The first obstacle the reader finds in the way of *Jerusalem* is a poetical language not only complex and rich but extraordinarily dense and economical as well. For example, it takes considerable experience of Blake's writings to "translate" a rather simple-sounding declaration like the following (the act is attributed to "Bath"): "A triple octave he took, to reduce Jerusalem to twelve" (37.4; E181). The meaning is that Bath institutionalized religion and thereby destroyed its meaning; Bath created the three principal religious holidays of the Jewish calendar (octaves), and thereby reduced the idea of Jerusalem, which ought to be universally available, to the conception of twelve tribes of the chosen. If it be objected that this is wantonly obscure language, one can point out that the obscurity takes a "form" which is determined in the metaphorical depths of Blake's concern: thrice eight is twenty-four, and half twenty-four is twelve—Blake is shaping obscurity according to his conception of "Separation," a conception important enough to have determined the division of Ololon at the end of *Milton* (Ololon was "multiplied" in division, however, rather than "reduced") and indeed to constitute the argument of Chapter 2 of *Jerusalem* from which the statement was taken. The relevance to Ololon will be apparent later. I make the point here to emphasize the fact that in *Jerusalem* language to an extraordinary degree *is* form. Blake himself makes essentially the same point by way of a wry apology for the rather cacophonous result of his superimposition of the map of the Holy Land upon the geography of England:

(I call them by their English names: English the rough
    basement.
Los built the stubborn structure of the Language, acting against
Albions melancholy, who must else have been a Dumb despair.)
                                                        (J., 36.58–60; E181)

Blake's English may seem to the reader as stubborn a structure as one would wish for, but we will miss the point of its uncompromising toughness, of what Northrop Frye calls its "prickly shell" (*Fearful Symmetry*, p. 380), if we fail to understand its identity with the compliant, emanative, female spaces of the imagination in which Blake imagines his hero constructing saving remnants of Albion's vision of Eternity. In *Jerusalem* we find Blake's supremely expressive epic statement founded upon the assumption that Word and Woman are in some sense one "form." At the end of the poem, Woman, City, and Poem emerge together as the one ultimately articulated emanative word of a speaker who includes in his human, apocalyptic body "All Human Forms identified" (99.1; E256).

Before going any further with this idea, it will be necessary to distinguish strictly between the *structure* of the poem and the "forms" of which Jerusalem is the supreme statement. The structure of the poem is notoriously difficult, but perhaps not quite as forbidding as it has been made to seem.[66] What makes the structure difficult is fundamentally Blake's handling of his "canonical history." Blake's theme is always the same, the Fall into Nature and the Raising by Vision. But in *Jerusalem* for the first time he develops his theme as a four-part "drama" (see Frye, *Fearful Symmetry*, p. 357), in which each "act"—itself part of a larger dramatic movement—has its own distinct development in terms of theme and unifying image. There is nothing very complicated about this, but as the drama takes shape and a sense of crisis emerges, Blake relates the rising urgency of the poem to his earlier development of crisis in *Vala/The Four Zoas*. Hence, there is a rough analogy between Chapter 1 of *Jerusalem*, which deals with the Fall, and the first four, premundane Nights of *Vala/The Four Zoas*. Chapters 2 and 3 of the later poem follow roughly the dramatic action of Nights VI–VIII of *Vala/The Four Zoas*, the imaginative crisis represented by the two Nights VII being especially important. Chapter 4 of *Jerusalem* develops an apocalypse out of the extreme opposition between the ideas of error and of vision according to a process which suggests to most critics a dialectic[67] or an inversion.[68] The historical aspect of this drama, as extrapolated from *The Four Zoas* as well as from references within the poem itself, suggests a "history" in which Chapter 1 deals with the first two "Eyes" of history, down to the Deluge; Chapter 2 deals synoptically with the third "Eye" down to modern times (from Genesis to the eighteenth century), but as the subtitle, "To the Jews," suggests, concentrates on Old Testament history as a "type" of degeneration; Chapter 3, now that the "limits" Adam and Satan have been set, deals with the seventh or "Jesus" Eye, focusing especially on the development of Deism and "Natural Religion" as the culmination of error; and Chapter 4, an apocalypse, is set in the eternal now of apocalyptic vision. What makes the structure of the poem difficult is that the "history" I have been rehearsing is only available to the imagery in *dramatic* terms. That is, all idea of history as "chronology" has been abandoned, sacrificed to the development of an archetypal dramatic evolution. Hence, the same events often occur in all four chapters of the poem, refashioned to accord with the development of a pattern of conflict rather than adjusted to any temporal scheme. Thus, to give a simple example, on plate 12 of the poem Los complains that his emanation is separating from him (12.7–9; E153), and of course his whole heroic career in history is based upon the assumption of this separation, and yet in Chapter 4 on plate 86 we read: "His Emanation separates in milky fibres agonizing" (86.39; E243). History as a category has been entirely absorbed by dramatic form, and in this we can see the perfection of Blake's labors to marry canonical and political history in his "prophecies," *America* and *Europe*. It is noteworthy that this perfection is really an aspect of language, for it frees Blake to compose his complex historico-dramatic polyphony of the sons of Jacob as analogous to the sons of Albion, a polyphony producing the dense language already noted. It can be seen that in terms of such a language, to place Norfolk, Suffolk, and Essex in the "Gates of Reuben" (16.43–44; E159) is not only an identification defiant of chronology but a dramatic utterance.

Having observed a relationship between structure and language, we can now return to the quite distinct question of language and *form. Jerusalem* is nothing if not a self-conscious poem, and the distinctness of questions of structure from questions of "form" is reflected and dramatized in the text of the poem itself as a series of odd terms—the Spaces of Erin, Dinah, Divine Similitude, Analogy, Canaan—all of which concretize the power of metaphor either as a female form or as a shape within which the imagination can work. *Jerusalem* as a poem is not organized around these "spaces," which appear irregularly, but it is in a sense "formed" in terms of the tenor—the metaphorical effect—for which these spaces are the vehicle. As we have just seen, history has in *Jerusalem* no chronological structure (only dramatic relevance), but it does have "form" by virtue of the fact that it appears in the most important of the imaginative spaces, the Halls of Golgonooza:

> All things acted on Earth are seen in the bright Sculptures of
> Los's Halls & every Age renews its powers from these Works
> With every pathetic story possible to happen from Hate or
> Wayward Love & every sorrow & distress is carved here
> Every Affinity of Parents Marriages & Friendships are here
> In all their various combinations wrought with wondrous Art
> All that can happen to Man in his pilgrimage of seventy years
> (16.61–67; E159)

Indeed, history's formal appearance in the Halls of Golgonooza or one of the other imaginative "spaces" is the only thing which can save it from the darkness of the Polypus and render it viable to the power of saving vision. The power which shapes the sculptures in Los's Halls is therefore for Blake the essential, saving power of vision, and its identification becomes a matter of importance. I think we can identify this power, and the "spaces" which it makes available to form, with a peculiar metaphorical effect—not unique to *Jerusalem* but existing to a degree of high development therein—which is itself a development of the "idea of pastoral." It is worth remarking, before explaining this idea, that the ultimate accomplishment of the metaphorical effect of which I speak is to destroy the distinction, common to so many of our inherited mental categories, between "imagination" and "reality." Any expression of such an accomplishment is likely to attract to itself versions of pastoral.

We can get some idea of this metaphorical effect by glancing back at earlier works of Blake's career. There, too, we observe poems as structurally "difficult" as *Jerusalem*—but in those cases, because the poems happen to be brief, critics are not often troubled by this aspect of them. We saw in *The Book of Thel*, for instance, a poem difficult to unify according to the standard Romantic criteria, a poem in which the metaphorical tendency of an argument looped suddenly back on itself, like someone taking a stitch. *Visions of the Daughters of Albion* likewise has an asymmetrical structure, and at the heart of this poem we discovered the cave of Bromion within the haunted imagination of Theotormon: the essence of the psychological metaphor, it was argued, was that the cave was manufactured *by* Bromion *within* the mind of Theotormon. We notice that in both poems a "form" equivalent to the power or effect of a metaphor is generated within the text.

In neither case does the form so generated constitute a structure for the poem—it does not constitute an exoskeleton covering the whole body of the text (as a snail shell covers the whole body of the snail)—but there is in both cases an obvious sense in which we can say that the form "shapes" the poem, however asymmetrical or disunified the poem's *structure*.

Both *Thel* and *Visions* figured largely in the discussion of the idea of pastoral, and it is pastoralism which offers the clearest examples of and best explanations for the effect under discussion here. Marvell's poem "The Garden," to which I have alluded before, illustrates it perfectly, and makes clear the relationship between the metaphorical effect and the distinction endemic to pastoral fictions between a natural, "real" world and a transcendent, "imaginary" world. We remember Marvell's account of the Fall into Nature ("Stumbling on Melons, as I pass,/Insnar'd with Flow'rs, I fall on Grass"; 39–40), and his suggestion of the mind's ability to create

> transcending these,
> Far other Worlds, and other Seas;
> Annihilating all that's made
> To a green Thought in a green Shade.
>
> (45–48)

The essential impetus of the poem's dramatic fiction is love-complaint, and so after the speaker's soul has achieved a state transcending the flesh ("Casting the Bodies Vest aside"; 51) and has plumed itself in a paradisal tree (52–56), there is no little irony in his imagining Eden *before* the creation of woman:

> Such was that happy Garden-state,
> While Man there walk'd without a Mate:
> After a Place so pure, and sweet,
> What other Help could yet be meet!
> But 'twas beyond a Mortal's share
> To wander solitary there:
> Two Paradises 'twere in one
> To live in Paradise alone.
>
> (57–64)

The tension in the poem between "reality" and "imagination" comes to a head in this stanza in terms of the barely comic collaboration of the idea of the Fall and the speaker's reaction against woman. But it is the resolution of the tension which especially concerns us:

How well the skilful Gardner drew
Of flow'rs and herbes this Dial new;
Where from above the milder Sun
Does through a fragrant Zodiack run;
And, as it works, th'industrious Bee
Computes its time as well as we.
How could such sweet and wholsome Hours
Be reckon'd but with herbs and flow'rs!

(65–72)

Marvell begins by returning from Eden to Nature, boldly involving the form of Nature's largest mechanism, the Zodiac—and
the natural driving force this would symbolize to the Renaissance
imagination—in a simulacrum of flowers. The miniaturization of
form is itself a charming imitation of a pastoral habit, but it only
moves a very little way toward resolving the tension between
natural and ideal upon which the poem depends. But suddenly,
within the minimizing simulacrum, a bee appears, and begins to
move from flower to flower within the floral zodiac. The first
metaphorical idea behind this appearance is that the bee represents a miniaturization—a minimalization—of the temporal
force within the zodiac which pursues the poet in the flesh. But
the movements of a bee are irregular, and uninfluenced by the
horological shape of the garden, and so we see that by the bee
in the floral simulacrum Marvell is figuring a new *form* of time,
"sweet and wholsome Hours." Pastoralism has enabled the poet to
create out of Nature a form of time less "Natural"—less compact
of the fateful necessities of a fallen, sex-driven existence—than
the form we are used to experiencing. It is first important to
recognize that this creation is entirely dependent upon the prior
habit of pastoralism to rest upon the formal ambiguities of "real"
and "ideal." And it is important, second, to recognize that in the
moving bee and the floral zodiac Marvell creates less an idea or an
image than the *experience* of a new form of time as the force of a
metaphor impinging upon the imagination of the reader. I think
it makes sense to speak of this impact on the mind in terms of a
form actively filling a mental space, and to suggest that this
space—which has no influence on the very regular *structure* of the
poem—is in an important sense the poem's form. It is an arena,
circumscribed by the workings of a bee, which finally encompasses
all the metaphorical energies of the poem, where the Fall into
Nature and the transcendence of Nature alike achieve an inte-
grated formal possibility. It is to Marvell's lyric very much what
"Jerusalem" is to *Jerusalem*.

The effect of metaphorical form, I have suggested, depends upon a prior exposition of the ambiguities of the idea of pastoral. If I am correct in my assumption that the idea of pastoral is a central concern of Blake's earlier works, then it follows that the Halls of Golgonooza and all those other "spaces" wherein metaphorical form makes itself felt are likely to be founded upon allusions to the poet's earlier work. In a very real sense the "form" of *Jerusalem* is something which cannot be appreciated without a prior appreciation of Blake's other works. It is the final function of the idea of transformation upon which I have relied so often. This is in fact true even when the idea of pastoral and of the imagination's space is only very obliquely alluded to. For example, plate 10 of Chapter 1 (an interpolated plate) is the culmination of an agon between Los and the Spectre of Urthona which is itself representative of the "theme" of the chapter, the division in the generated heart between vision (represented by the building of Golgonooza) and "the land of death eternal" (13.30; E155). The agon depends upon allusion not in the sense that it recalls previous quarrels (though it may do that), but in the sense that the *form* of the quarrel is an allusion:

Los cries, Obey my voice & never deviate from my will
And I will be merciful to thee: be thou invisible to all
To whom I make thee invisible, but chief to my own Children
O Spectre of Urthona: Reason not against their dear approach
Nor them obstruct with thy temptations of doubt & despair[.]
(10.29–33; E152)

We cannot understand the passage unless we recognize the underlying allusion to a Miltonic God and his attitude toward Satan and his creatures—and the more mediate allusion to Blake's criticism of that attitude. But we will not understand the passage either until we appreciate how Blake has transformed the emotional content of these allusions into a *form*, assumed to be the substance of the fallen world. In other words, Blake is not using the allusions merely as dramatic comment on Los's posture relative to his Spectre (though we may feel the critical function of allusion has not entirely been submerged either), but as models constituting the form reality assumes in Generation. The paradoxical effect of this method (when the allusions are recognized), even when the forms are fallen, is of a world in all its minute particulars and obdurate density available to the imagination. The conclusion of this passage is moving evidence. The Miltonic model has produced a Los (on the model of "God") and a Spectre (on the model of "Satan") who must endure the agony of alienation. The Spectre complains passionately, "the Almighty hath made me his Contrary / To be all evil" (10.56–57; E152), and he weeps pitifully at his merciless condition. But the allusion to Milton has produced a form of reality, not a psychological condition subject to immediate revision, and so we are told that Los wiped his Spectre's tears "but comfort none could give! or beam of hope" (10.61). This is not a function of Los's attitude, but of the way things are. Drama has become form, and the poignance of the form is augmented when we realize that Blake is here allegorizing the conflict in his own psyche between his visionary nature and the engraver-husband who had to earn his daily bread. The passage continues with Los driving the Spectre (as his agent) to the building of Golgonooza. Los

> compelld the invisible Spectre
> To labours mighty, with vast strength, with his mighty chains,
> In pulsations of time, & extensions of space, like Urns of Beulah
> With great labour upon his anvils[;] & in his ladles the Ore
> He lifted, pouring it into the clay ground prepar'd with art;
> Striving with Systems to deliver Individuals from those
>   Systems;
> That whenever any Spectre began to devour the Dead,
> He might feel the pain as if a man gnawd his own tender
>   nerves.
>
> (10.65–11.7; E152–153)

Again we have a primary allusion to the construction of Pandemonium in *Paradise Lost* and a secondary allusion to Blake's reading of Milton's Satan. On the level of allusion the passage embodies Blake's familiarly ambigous Satan, but the passage really does not function on that level. Rather it makes out of allusion an imaginative, metaphoric form of reality—in this case the reality of pain experienced in Generation in the conflict with one's spectrous self. But the form is not available unless we recognize the allusions. When we do, the turnabout of Miltonic terminology is sufficiently startling: Milton's Pandemonium (so Blake believed) was a metaphorical, fictional function of the failure of Milton's imagination to come to grips with certain aspects of reality; here, in *Jerusalem*, Pandemonium is a "real form" which has been made totally available to the imagination.

But, as I said, the idea of pastoral was only obliquely available (in terms of the ambiguous Satan) to this passage. Earlier in this study we have seen the idea of pastoral most vividly expressed in terms of a painful marriage of heaven and hell, a marriage conceived in Miltonic terms and later consummated by the character John Milton and by Ololon, in Blake's penultimate epic. To pursue the imagery of that marriage through *Jerusalem* will be to see most clearly the idea of pastoral expressing itself in metaphorical form.

JERUSALEM

Chapter 1

The opposed images of the first chapter of *Jerusalem* are, as Northrop Frye suggests (*Fearful Symmetry*, p. 357), Golgonooza (the Halls of archetypal vision) and Babylon (the function of fallen vision, equivalent to Fallen Nature and the "Wastes of Moral Law"; 24.24). The architecture of each place is a function of the curiously direct language of sentiment which is part of Blake's late manner. Here is Golgonooza:

> The stones are pity, and the bricks, well wrought affections:
> Enameld with love & kindness, & the tiles engraven gold
> Labour of merciful hands: the beams & rafters are forgiveness:
> The mortar & cement of the work, tears of honesty: the nails,
> And the screws & iron braces, are well wrought blandishments,
> . . . .
> The cielings, devotion: the hearths, thanksgiving:
> Prepare the furniture O Lambeth in thy pitying looms!
> (12.30–38; E154)

Here, by contrast, is Babylon:

> The Walls of Babylon are Souls of Men: her Gates the Groans
> Of Nations: her Towers are the Miseries of once happy
>   Families.
> Her Streets are paved with Destruction, her Houses built with
>   Death
> Her Palaces with Hell & the Grave; her Synagogues with
>   Torments
> Of ever-hardening Despair squard & polishd with cruel skill
> (24.31–35; E168)

The idea of making forms out of metaphors is less important than the fact that both places are made out of the same sort of stuff. That this is so leads us to the central problem of this chapter, the fact that Vala and Jerusalem are inextricably bound together in Generation. The emanation of the unfallen Albion is here securely embraced by the opaque flesh. The question put to Jerusalem is not only the central question of this chapter, but perhaps the central question in Blake as well:

> Vala is but thy Shadow, O thou loveliest among women!
> A shadow animated by thy tears O mournful Jerusalem!
> Why wilt thou give to her a Body whose life is but a Shade?
> Her joy and love, a shade: a shade of sweet repose:
> But animated and vegetated, she is a devouring worm.
> (11.24–12.3; E153)

The puzzling interrelation of Vala and Jerusalem produces not only the psychological need to make a clear distinction between them but the formal necessity as well of a world wherein such a distinction can be made. We have already observed that the formal model for such a world is the outlook of Milton solidified. We see this very clearly when we observe Los in the process of distinguishing his visionary identity from his generate self:

> O thou Negation, I will continually compell
> Thee to be invisible to any but whom I please, & when
> And where & how I please, and never! never! shalt thou be
>   Organized
> But as a distorted & reversed Reflexion in the Darkness
> And in the Non Entity: nor shalt that which is above
> Ever descend into thee: but thou shalt be a Non Entity for ever
> And if any enter into thee, thou shalt be an Unquenchable Fire
> And he shall be a never dying Worm, mutually tormented by
> Those that thou tormentest, a Hell & Despair for ever & ever.
> (17.39–47; E160–161)

Los's psychological necessity has called forth allusions to Milton (the "distorted . . . Reflexion in the Darkness" is ultimately Blake's reading of Milton's Satan as Man in the Hell of his own making) not as expressions of need but as formal, metaphorical models for the world in which need makes itself felt. The last three lines of the passage contain a remarkably compressed expression of the relationship of Los to the Orc cycle, but it is important to notice, too, that they translate that relationship into a "form" of reality in which Los finds himself.

In the phrase "nor shalt that which is above / Ever descend," the reader must have noticed an allusion to the conclusion to *Milton*, suggesting that Los's necessities are framed according to the model of reality he sees, which is provisional. Toward the end of Chapter 1 we get a fully developed allusion to the marriage of Milton and Ololon which illustrates perfectly the translation of

metaphor into form, and the availability of all realities to the power
of imagination suggested by the translation. The interweaving of
life and death suggested by the embrace of Jerusalem and Vala is
in psychological terms said to cause the discouragement and fall
of the Giant Albion. As he falls, in an amazing metaphor he
withdraws *into* his own body, and the rivers which are his arteries
supply the waters of this fallen world (19.36–47; E163). On the
Thames he finds Jerusalem and Vala assimilated, borne up by a
"Lilly of Havilah" (perhaps the illustrative subject of the revised
version of plate 28),[69] and the three together converse about the
Fall. The condition of Jerusalem corresponding to the fixed
condition or form of the fallen world is that she cannot fall completely enough to escape the torment of being reminded of her
former condition. She is addressing Vala:

> I cannot put off the human form I strive but strive in vain
> When Albion rent thy beautiful net of gold and silver twine;
> Thou hadst woven it with art, thou hadst caught me in the
>   bands
> Of love; thou refusedst to let me go: Albion beheld thy beauty
> Beautiful thro' our Love's comeliness, beautiful thro' pity.
> The Veil shone with thy brightness in the eyes of Albion,
> Because it enclosd pity & love; because we lov'd one-another!
> Albion lov'd thee! he rent thy Veil! he embrac'd thee! he lov'd
>   thee!
> Astonish'd at his beauty & perfection, thou forgavest his furious
>   love:
> I redounded from Albions bosom in my virgin loveliness.
> The Lamb of God reciev'd me in his arms, he smil'd upon us:
> He made me his Bride & Wife: he gave thee to Albion.
> Then was a time of love: O why is it passed away!
> (20.29–41; E164)

The dependence of this passage upon the account, at the end of
Milton, of the consummation of Ololon's marriage to Milton will
be obvious without detailed comparison. What is especially remarkable is Blake's adaptation of the division of Ololon, the
metaphor of sexual consummation which produced the Thel-like
virgin dove (committed at last to the dangerous water of Generation) as well as the "wife" to Milton. In this version of the image
psychological considerations have been made subordinate to the
formal model of reality. The essence of the model is a twofold
division symbolized by the virgin Jerusalem and the Lamb of God
on one hand opposed to the consummated marriage of Vala and
Albion on the other. The image, in other words, not only "accounts

for" the Fall (as did the myth of Albion falling in love with the Vala Luvah left upon his pillow in the *Vala/The Four Zoas* manuscript), but also gives to the Fall formal substance. That the same imagery can produce other forms will be the burden of the examination of the rest of the poem. Finally it will be seen that all the forms can be summed up under the one name Jerusalem, which is also the name of the poem.

Chapter 2

The second chapter of *Jerusalem* is organized around the ideas of Law and of the Family, the principal institutions of the fallen world. The connection between the two ideas is articulated through Blake's reading of the Bible, the Old Testament of which (as Blake read it) recorded the fallen experience as the adventures of a "family" of twelve sons whose "wisdom" is inherent in a conception of law. (The New Testament is shaped according to "forms" analogous to those in the Old, for example, the twelve Disciples corresponding to the twelve sons of Jacob, exemplifying a "new law." See Frye, *Fearful Symmetry*, pp. 370–371.) There are twelve sons of Albion, who embody his error and who are "divided" so that each has his embattled female emanation. This makes twenty-four offspring in all, and if we add to their number the four "ungenerated" sons of Los (Rintrah, Palamabron, Theotormon, and Bromion), we get twenty-eight, a number Blake associates with the cathedral cities of Britain, calling them "friends" of Albion. These "friends" are also fallen, but as Albion's family they are willing to enlist themselves under Los to try to reverse the direction of the Fall. So far as vision is concerned, they are ambiguous figures—hopeful but untrustworthy. As such they embody the troubling relationship between Jerusalem and Vala already examined, and one of the two leading sons (see 38.55; E183), Bath, expresses Albion's dilemma with great clarity:

> But Albions sleep is not
> Like Africa's: and his machines are woven with his life
> Nothing but mercy can save him!
>
> (40.24–26; E186)

(The reference to "Africa" is to "the enslavement in Egypt, and the release under Moses.")[70]

Bath absorbs the same problem in his own make-up, and for reasons which will quickly be apparent he is worth a digression. Blake chose Bath to express the ambiguities of the fallen condition because the city of his name is both a cathedral city and a monument to the frailties of the flesh. But there is more to it than this: the two leading sons of Albion are Hand (who represents, roughly, fallen Reason, and therefore corresponds to Urizen in the myth of the four zoas) and Hyle (who represents, roughly, fallen "Nature"—the name may come from the Greek word for matter, as well as from "Hayley"—and corresponds to Luvah-Orc in the earlier myth). Blake once isolates Bristol and Bath from the names of the other cathedral cities in a way which suggests a correspondence to Hand and Hyle (38.55). This would mean that Bath is a form of Orc also, and this hint is illuminated by the odd identification "Bath who is Legions" (37.1; E181), for there is an unmistakable reference here to the episode of the Gadarene swine in the Bible, probably to the version in St. Mark. There the account of the man possessed by evil spirits, who identifies himself as "Legion," sounds very much like an account of the sufferings of Orc:

> 4. Because that he had been often bound with fetters and chains, and the chains had been plucked asunder by him, and the fetters broken in pieces: neither could any man tame him.
> 5. And always, night and day, he was in the mountains, and in the tombs, crying, and cutting himself with stones.
>
> (Mark 5:4–5)

There are two other events in the fifth chapter of St. Mark from which this account was taken. After Christ leaves "Legion," he passes through a crowd, and a woman touches his garment thinking to be healed. Her wound is interesting: it is "an issue of blood twelve years" (5:25). Also interesting is Christ's reaction to being touched, for although the woman does not make herself known, "Jesus, immediately knowing in himself that virtue had gone out of him, turned him about in the press, and said, Who touched my clothes" (5:30). Blake would have been interested in the number twelve in this passage, and in the fact that the woman touched the garment, not the man. Further, the issue of blood and the reaction of Jesus to being secretly touched suggest, respectively, Generation and the Female Will, both of which are absorbed presently by the woman's "faith" (5:34), which is identified as the real healer. Finally, the chapter concludes with a third episode: the resurrection of a virgin twelve years old (5:41–43). Again we have a reference to twelve years, and it is worth being reminded that when Ololon descends into the Polypus in *Milton* she appears as a twelve-year-old virgin in Blake's garden (M., 36.17; E136). In short, Bath, by the devious route of Blake's Bible, takes us right back to the complex of imagery at the end of *Milton*. Blake makes a more direct use of this imagery, not once but twice, in Chapter 2 of *Jerusalem*.

The first time he employs it, the formal force of the allusion is indirect, having been absorbed into a passionate indictment of the idea of Law. In this case it is Albion who rehearses the descent, declaring, "I die! I go to Eternal Death!" (35.16; E179). In this case the declaration is a function of despair, and there is nothing at all hopeful about it. Then Albion asks for an Atonement, an epiphany of his own vision of Law, in a way which underscores Blake's association of the two terms with a despairing, fallen outlook:

> Will none accompany me in my death? or be a Ransom for me
> In that dark Valley?
>
> (35.19–20; E179)

Los's answer achieves certainty, but produces nevertheless a division of his soul:

> Los answerd, troubled: and his soul was rent in twain:
> Must the Wise die for an Atonement? does Mercy endure
>   Atonement?
> No! It is Moral Severity, & destroys Mercy in its Victim.
>
> (35.24–26; E179)

This Descent and Division are, however, formally productive only in the sense that they proliferate and reproduce themselves in the psychic make-up of all the "friends." These are divided just as Los is divided (and Blake returns to the terminology of pity and wrath to make the point), and their sense of division has its correspondent to the idea of Atonement, for they are unwilling to descend to their spectrous aspects—they are unwilling to imitate Milton—and so look forward helplessly to a savior:

> If we are wrathful Albion will destroy Jerusalem with rooty
>   Groves
> If we are merciful, ourselves must suffer destruction on his
>   Oaks!
> Why should we enter into our Spectres, to behold our own
>   corruptions
> O God of Albion descend! deliver Jerusalem from the Oaken
>   Groves!
>
> (38.8–11; E182)

Blake's subsequent reliance upon the imagery of *Milton* is more developed, taking us back not only to *Milton* but to the origins of *Milton* in *The Four Zoas* as well. Satan is seen in Chapter 2 legalistically as a "Reactor," and the principle is established that we cannot look forward to visionary renewal until Satan (who has hid himself "thro envy"—43.9—recalling Book IV of *Paradise Lost*) is revealed, until a place has been prepared for him. The preparation of a place in Eternal Death is suggestive of the sepulcher prepared for Christ, and indeed Satan is in this passage identified not only with the subject of the Orc cycle but as well with the Christ of the Atonement:

> Albions Reactor must have a Place prepard: Albion must Sleep
> The Sleep of Death, till the Man of Sin & Repentance be
>   reveald.
> Hidden in Albions Forests he lurks: he admits of no Reply
> From Albion: but hath founded his Reaction into a Law
>   (43.11–14; E189)

From this general condition of fallen waiting, two alone escape, "two Immortal forms" (43.28) who are our old friends "the Emanation of Los & his / Spectre" (44.1–2; E191) from Night VII(a) of the *Vala/The Four Zoas* manuscript. The evolution of the idea of *Milton* is rehearsed in a very few lines. The Spectre and Enitharmon (Blake does not here retain the distinction from *The Four Zoas* between Enitharmon and her "shadow") "had been on a visit to Albions children" (44.6), and are apparently unaware how bad things are in the fallen world. When they see how things are, they attempt to weave the doubly fallen, "second" Nature as a refuge:

> And they strove to weave a Shadow of the Emanation
> To hide themselves: weeping & lamenting for the Vegetation
> Of Albions Children: fleeing thro Albions vales in streams of
>   gore.
>   (44.6–8; E191)

The streams of gore remind us of Ololon, and it is surely no accident that in a few lines we come upon this image:

> They saw the Sexual Religion in its embryon Uncircumcision
> And the Divine hand was upon them bearing them thro
>   darkness
> Back safe to their Humanity as doves to their windows.
>   (44.11–13; E191)

The first line refers simply to the relationship Blake saw between fallen, Natural Religion and the mysterious cult and law of chastity. A few lines on we get an explicit connection between the "Rocky Law of Condemnation" (rocky because solid and dead) and the Miltonic "double Generation" (44.37). The last lines of the passage follow inevitably and look forward to the formal application of the imagery:

> Albion hath enterd the Loins the place of the Last Judgment:
> And Luvah hath drawn the Curtains around Albion in Vala's bosom
> The Dead awake to Generation! Arise O Lord, & rend the Veil!
> (44.38–40; E191–192)

The period of the clarification of error, while a place is being prepared for Satan and while man has simply in his divided being to wait, is given in Chapter 2 an ironic identification and structure: it is the Scriptures ("a Couch of repose, / With Sixteen pillars"), organized around the sixteen books of the Old and New Testaments most important to Blake (48.4–12; E194). But the structure of history is given further formal attention in the last plates of the chapter, which describe in imagery now familiar to us the "separation" of Jerusalem from Albion. The psychological and moral rationale of this separation is clear. Now that Albion has succumbed to despair and been laid to rest in the grave of life, his emanation must be rescued from "Eternal Death" and a refuge must be prepared for her, lest the emanative life too

> . . . become an Eternal Death, an Avenger of Sin
> A Self-righteousness: the proud Virgin-Harlot! Mother of War!
> And we also & all Beulah, consume beneath Albions curse.
> (50.15–17; E198)

The "separation" has two stages. First, as Albion sinks into death, his emanation has to leave Beulah and follow him into the grave. Once there, she reacts to "Eternal Death" by violently trying to escape from Albion's breast; the danger here is that she is, in her terror, "struggling to put off the Human form" (48.49), and a place must be prepared lest she disappear altogether. The reader will notice the similarity between this "separation" and the tale told by Jerusalem in Chapter 1 in terms of Albion's having pierced the veil of Vala, but in this instance the virginal Jerusalem is taken to the refuge prepared for her rather than to the embrace of the Lamb. The equation between the Lamb in Chapter 1 and the Refuge of Chapter 2—even if only implied at this point—becomes important later on.

When Jerusalem descends out of Beulah, we are told that all the Daughters of that place:

> Wept for their Sister the Daughter of Albion, Jerusalem:
> When out of Beulah the Emanation of the Sleeper descended
> With solemn mourning out of Beulahs moony shades and hills:
> Within the Human Heart, whose Gates closed with solemn
>   sound.
>
> (48.22–25; E195)

(The reference to Jerusalem as the "daughter" of Albion should not be disturbing. As emanation she is indifferently "wife" or "daughter"; see Frye, *Fearful Symmetry*, p. 392.) We recognize in the metaphor an inversion of the image in Night VII(a) of the *Vala/The Four Zoas* manuscript, where the new incarnation of Vala descended from Enitharmon and "burst the Gates" of her heart "with direful Crash" (85.13; E353). The interesting thing about the two versions of the image is that, in psychological terms, they signify the same thing: commitment to Generation. But the emphasis of the *Four Zoas* version is almost exclusively psychological—the breaking of the Gates signifies a new openness to certain emotions. The emphasis of the later version of the image—while the literal signification is the same, that henceforth Jerusalem is securely devoted to Generation—has an entirely different force and a formal purpose. We are being told not merely that Jerusalem cannot now get back to Beulah, but that Generation itself has its Gates closed. In other words—and this meaning is entirely dependent upon our recognizing the allusion in these lines—Generation now wears the female aspect of the virgin. We are reminded of a phrase from an earlier plate, "Arise O Lord, & rend the Veil" (40.40), and the passage from St. Matthew undoubtedly referred to, where we are told that when Jesus gave up the ghost, "the veil of the temple was rent in twain from the top to the bottom" (Matthew 27:51).

"The Emanations of the ... Friends of Albion / Concenter in one Female form" (48.27–28; E195), named Erin (for in *Jerusalem* Blake systematically begins to associate Ireland with liberty), and Erin prepares a "space" for Jerusalem even as, in *Milton*, Enitharmon prepared one for Satan. The "Refuge" takes the form of history, all "eight thousand and five hundred years" of it (48.36), and I have already suggested an association between this expanse of time and the Lamb. We expect history, then, to encompass legal exaction of the Atonement, the Body of Hypocritic Holiness, and to associate this with the aspect of the Female Will which expresses itself in the cult of purity. But the spaces of Erin are a refuge from the Fall, not an expression of it, and so the allusions to earlier ideas have to take on a new metaphorical force. The "formal" description of the space is interesting:

> With awful hands she took
> A Moment of Time, drawing it out with many tears &
>   afflictions
> And many sorrows: oblique across the Atlantic Vale
> Which is the Vale of Rephaim dreadful from East to West,
> Where the Human Harvest waves abundant in the beams of
>   Eden
> Into a Rainbow of jewels and gold, a mild Reflection from
> Albions dread Tomb.
>
> (48.30–36; E195)

The imagery here, as in so much of *Jerusalem*, is remarkably syncretic and compressed. The Vale of Rephaim is variously translated as "valley of ghosts" or "valley of giants."[71] It is, Frye tells us, "where the Israelites fought the Amalekites" (*Fearful Symmetry*, p. 368), and so Blake's "Human Harvest" may refer to this slaughter. More probably, though, Blake associates the name with a passage in Isaiah where the prophet threatens the "glory of Jacob":

> And it shall be as when the harvestman gathereth the corn, and reapeth the ears with his arm; and it shall be as he that gathereth ears in the valley of Rephaim.
>
> (Isaiah 17:5)

Blake identifies the valley with the "Atlantic Vale," where, according to *America*, the lost Atlantis was located, from the summits of which "you may pass to the Golden world" (E54). The "Harvest" may, then, be an oblique reference to the flooding over of the Vale during the Deluge ("Human Harvest waves abundant") or—if we think of *America*—to the overwhelming of the American Revolution. If we pursue the American context of the imagery, there is another interesting fact: the reference to the Rainbow (reminding us of Leutha in *Milton*) recalls the title page of *Visions of the Daughters of Albion*, where Oothoon is dashing across the waves of the Atlantic Vale (Theotormon's reign) pursued presumably by Bromion (there is a Urizenic figure in the heavens) beneath a rainbow. Further, on the last plate of *Milton*, there is a reference to "Oothoon ... weeping oer her Human Harvest" (42.32–33; E142). We have already seen that the rainbow is an ambiguous image for Blake; it is trebly ambiguous here, for it is jeweled (Blake often associates precious stones with the Covering Cherub)[72] and seen as a "Reflection from Albions dread Tomb." In the creation of the Refuge Blake has not shrunk from the ambiguities and doubtfulness of generated history, but the unifying center of the imagery is the idea of Oothoon—the vision which can be achieved even from inside the Orc cycle. What is remarkable is the way Blake translates his metaphorical implications into a space "oblique across ... from East to West" in which to place his heroine. Since that space is also our history, Blake's formal definition of it makes history's "many tears & afflictions" available to the imagination. The first fruit of this accomplishment is the distinction implicit here between our history and the Death Couch of Albion.

Chapter 3

I remarked earlier that the limits of the Fall, Satan and Adam, are established in Chapter 2. Once this has been done, and the danger of slipping over the edge entirely into nothingness obviated, man can devote himself with relative safety to the clarification and contemplation of error. Indeed, this can become a positive duty, and the idea of "separation" can similarly accumulate positive connotations: the top of the poem's first plate of text has "SHEEP" engraved on one side and "GOATS" on the other (plate 3; E143). Blake sets himself to the work of clarifying error with his customary vigor, much of his energy being consumed—we are not surprised to observe it—in anathematizing Vala and Rahab, particularly identified in this chapter with each other (70.31). Some of the poet's sexual observations in this chapter are, for a pre-Freudian, startling indeed ("I must rush again to War: for the Virgin has frownd & refusd": 68.62; E220), and the mastery of psychological motive combined with an equally great grasp of sociological insights give the poem a contemporary sound. For example, Rahab is defined as

A Religion of Chastity, forming a Commerce to sell Loves,
With Moral Law, an Equal Balance, not going down with
    decision
Therefore the Male severe & cruel filld with stern Revenge:
Mutual Hate returns & mutual Deceit & mutual Fear.
(69.34–37; E221)

The ease with which Blake articulates and intertwines the different levels of such a complex observation is impressive. Even more so is his ability to involve in the passage an aspect of the imagery we have been concerned with:

> Hence the Infernal Veil grows in the disobedient Female:
> Which Jesus rends & the whole Druid Law removes away
> From the Inner Sanctuary: a False Holiness hid within the
>   Center,
> For the Sanctuary of Eden. is in the Camp: in the Outline,
> In the Circumference: & every Minute Particular is Holy:
> Embraces are Cominglings: from the Head even to the Feet;
> And not a pompous High Priest entering by a Secret Place.
>   (69.38–44; E221)

Jesus does not "rend the veil" in Chapter 3, but the structural principle and central metaphor of the chapter is probably what is signified by the odd phrase "the whole Druid Law." Blake associates the Druids with the patriarchal Jews ("Abraham, Heber, Shem, and Noah"; see plate 27), and the good work of the law in question is probably that particularized in the following passage:

> The Infinite alone resides in Definite & Determinate Identity
> Establishment of Truth depends on destruction of Falshood
>   continually
> On Circumcision: not on Virginity, O Reasoners of Albion
>   (55.64–66; E203)

Circumcision, for Blake, brings together two ideas: it is a symbolic introduction to sexuality (and therefore an attack on the cult of purity and secrecy), and it is an emblem of separation, of distinction from others.[73] The last aspect will concern us first, for it is the subject of one of the most curious and ambiguous plates of the chapter. In plate 55 there is an Assembly of the Eternals recalling the conclave of angels in Book II of *Paradise Lost*, and the "synod" in Heaven in Book XI (67–83). The purpose of Blake's Assembly is this: some of the Eternals, having observed Los "still retain his awful strength" in Generation—clearly here Los corresponds to Milton's Satan—resolve to descend "and see these changes!" (55.5; E202). (We may suspect that we are reading about the descent of the Dead into the Polypus, attracted by the "renewed" Vala, but that suspicion is not immediately relevant.) An objection to the descent is raised by some among the Eternals: "What have we to do with the Dead?"—that is, the generated—they wonder (55.6), and they recall that all are equals in heaven; none are "chosen" or "separated," for the Eternal Man walks among them,

> Forbidding us that Veil which Satan puts between Eve & Adam
> By which the Princes of the Dead enslave their Votaries
> Teaching them to form the Serpent of precious stones & gold
> To sieze the Sons of Jerusalem & plant them in One Mans
>   Loins
> To make One Family of Contraries: that Joseph may be sold
> Into Egypt: for Negation; a Veil the Saviour born & dying
>   rends.
>
> (55.11–16; E202)

The argument is good enough so that the combatants call on "him who only Is" (55.17) to make a decision, the process of which looks very like the portents of the Last Things. The decision, when it comes, is suitable to the crisis state which is the subject of Chapter 3. No decision is declared for one side or the other; the decision *is* the crisis—or its ratification—and we are told simply: "Then far the greatest number were about to make a Separation" (55.30). When it comes, the separation takes a form familiar to us:

> And they Elected Seven, calld the Seven Eyes of God;
> Lucifer, Molech, Elohim, Shaddai, Pahad, Jehovah, Jesus.
> They namd the Eighth. he came not, he hid in Albions Forests.
>
> (55.31–33; E202)

The purpose of all this, we are told later, is

> To decide Two Worlds with a great decision: a World of
>   Mercy, and
> A World of Justice: the World of Mercy for Salvation
>
> (65.1–2; E214)

If we now back up a bit, we can see that what Blake seems to be saying is that the world now and again works itself into a crisis stage, where error has to be clarified and a radical distinction made between "two worlds." The metaphor for this distinction is circumcision, simultaneously an attack on virginity and the accomplishment of the evident separation.

I mentioned before that when the Assembly of Eternals calls for a decision, no decision is explicitly given. Separation itself seems to be the "decision." This symbolizes the fact that the distinction represented by circumcision is seen not as something ethically desirable but merely as a formal function of the state the world is in. We shall see shortly how this is, but separation exists in the world as the one thing which stands between that world and its annihilation. To ignore this fact, and to approach the idea of circumcision from the standpoint of ethical exhortation, is to make of it just another necessary evil. Looked at as part of the religion of necessity, circumcision becomes a form of sacrifice, and indeed sacrifice is exactly the ruling passion of the world presided over by Rahab and Tirzah. The relationship between circumcision and sacrifice explains some of the odd imagery of the chapter:

> Go Noah fetch the girdle of strong brass, heat it red-hot:
> Press it around the loins of this ever expanding cruelty
> Shriek not so my only love! I refuse thy joys: I drink
> Thy shrieks ...
>
> (67.59–62; E219)

The rite is even applied, in a sacrificial way, to the *head* of the fallen Albion (which lies in Verulam, the seat of Francis Bacon):

> The Twelve Daughters in Rahab & Tirzah have circumscribd
>   the Brain
> Beneath & pierced it thro the midst with a golden pin.
>
> (67.41–42; E218)

Indeed it seems to be the Jewish rite specifically, and not merely sacrifice in general, which determines the "form" of one of Blake's most astonishing metaphors for the fallen world:

> The Heavens are cut like a mantle around from the Cliffs of
>   Albion
> Across Europe; across Africa; in howlings & deadly War
> A sheet & veil & curtain of blood is let down from Heaven
> Across the hills of Ephraim & down Mount Olivet to
> The Valley of the Jebusite.
>
> (68.19–23; E219)

We can relate this passage to the Harvest imagery of Chapter 2, for an angel of the Lord, who punishes David for his transgressions to the tune of seventy thousand men, is seen standing "by the threshingplace of Araunah the Jebusite" (II Samuel 24:15–16).

Another recurrent image involves Los in the creation of a form dependent upon the metaphor of sacrifice. The sons of Jacob are cut off from the Polypus in order to be "separated" and sent to their place in Canaan. In the midst of this relation, we come upon the following:

> I see a Feminine Form arise from the Four terrible Zoas
> Beautiful but terrible struggling to take a form of beauty
> Rooted in Shechem: this is Dinah, the youthful form of Erin
> (74.52–54; E228)

Blake's identification of Dinah as "the youthful form" of Erin, creator of the redemptive spaces in Chapter 2, is in itself a poignant comment on the form assumed by the Fall in Chapter 3. Dinah's story is told in Genesis 34. Dinah is a daughter of Jacob who is violated by Shechem, "one that is uncircumcised." Her brothers feel the dishonor keenly, but Shechem truly loves Dinah, and his father petitions Jacob to accept a marriage. A condition is established which potentially vitiates the idea of "separation" upon which circumcision is based; it is suggested that not just the groom but all who want to join in the larger community symbolized by the marriage practice the rite of circumcision. This is agreed to and done, yet while the men are recuperating from the operation two of Dinah's brothers beset them and "slew all the males" (Genesis 34:25). It is the separation symbolized by this grisly tale that Blake takes—in the world of Deism and Natural Religion—as an undeveloped type of the saving space of the imagination.

Chapter 4

Separation, even when applied to the world in its most fallen form of circumcision, has emerged in *Jerusalem* as the avenue to the restoration of vision. Blake's application of the idea in Chapter 4 bears an interesting comparison to the technique of Chapter 3. There the idea of separation was applied to an idea which had, in a sense, two sides: one side was "circumcision" and the other was "sacrifice." As realized in the beautiful but terrifying figure of Dinah, Blake's technique fostered all possible ambiguities shared by the two sides of his idea but depended ultimately on the possibility of making an absolute distinction. The reader had to be counted on to derive from the story the idea of the separation of Mercy from Justice—rather than, for example, the idea of the separation of the mercilessly just from everyone else (which seems to be the moral of the story as originally told in the Bible). Blake was confident the reader would make no mistake because his reference focused upon Dinah as a beautiful woman. She was, no doubt, also compliant, and Blake expects the reader to set her in his imagination against all those awful priestesses of chastity who abound in the chapter. He had also included a long fantasia on Mary the mother of Jesus which made clear that he regarded the story of the Annunciation as an allegory of the unfaithful wife forgiven (plate 61; E209–210), and he probably expected us to associate the story of Mary with the more ambiguous case of Dinah: in the latter case forgiveness, which rends the veil, is out of the question, so we must satisfy ourselves with circumcision. This reminds us that circumcision had a sexual significance for Blake, and tells us something new about the way he built and used ambiguity. I have suggested that the distinction between the sacrifice demanded by Rahab and the "circumcision" demanded by Dinah had finally to be absolute, but we have seen that Blake, in his account of the former, constantly suggests the latter. Sacrifice had a tendency to be expressed in terms of circumcision. As sacrifice became more and more prevalent, more and more of the world found itself metaphorically included in the rite of circumcision. If we draw back from the third chapter now, and look at it as a whole—especially as a piece in a larger structure—we can see how circumcision functions *in the poem* as an imaginative rite of preparation. It is not merely a provisional distinction, hard-won from a fallen reality: if we look at Chapter 3 as a stage in a process, circumcision functions as formal preparation of the world for the assumption of visionary manhood in Chapter 4.

Corresponding to Circumcision/Sacrifice in Chapter 3, we have in the following chapter Consummation/Atonement (in Blake's special sense of the latter). Blake's technique in the later chapter is exactly analogous to that of the third, especially in that metaphors associated with the idea of consummation suggest the form of the world looked at from the point of view of Atonement. But here there is a difference: the structure of Chapter 3 ultimately rested upon the fact that a line could finally be drawn between circumcision and sacrifice; in Chapter 4 no corresponding line can be drawn between Consummation and Atonement, or, more accurately, as we look toward such a line it recedes infinitely into the distance. This accounts for the feeling expressed by Northrop Frye that "suppression of crisis" is the key to the poem *(Fearful Symmetry*, p. 358). It would be more accurate to suggest that by Chapter 4 everything *but* crisis has been suppressed, giving "crisis" the rather special meaning of "translation of metaphor into form." It may have been noticed in my comments on Chapter 3 that

I talked a lot about circumcision, less about sacrifice; this reversed the proportions of the chapter, which talked a lot about sacrifice, less about circumcision. My proportions were critically correct, however, because I was stressing the "imaginative form" of sacrifice—a form which is the ultimate point of the chapter. Looking at Chapter 4 in analogous fashion, we sense that in terms of sexual consummation (based upon *Milton*) Blake is really talking about the Atonement (in his special sense), that consummation dictates the metaphorical form of the Atonement. But as we work our way through the chapter, we never come to a line where "consummation" ends and "Atonement" begins. We do come to a Vision, but that is another matter. The odd thing is that when we get to this point the crisis has become the form of the Vision, and Atonement never materializes. Christ simply disappears from sight. This is, if you will, the epiphany of the idea of separation. It is also, as we shall see, the final expression of the idea of pastoral.

To follow the chapter with these remarks in mind is to be prepared for a fiction which reiterates most of the stages of Blake's development bound to the problem of Generation and the idea of pastoral. A proem concludes:

> For Hell is opend to Heaven; thine eyes beheld
> The dungeons burst & the Prisoners set free.
> (E231)

We are plunged into a crisis with Cambel and Gwendolen, the emanations of Hand and Hyle, intent upon perfecting themselves as types of the Female Will. "Humanity the Great Delusion," it is declared, "is changd to War & Sacrifice" (82.42; E237):

> So saying: She drew aside her Veil from Mam-Tor to Dovedale
> Discovering her own perfect beauty to the Daughters of Albion
> And Hyle a winding Worm beneath *her Loom upon the scales.*
> *Hyle was become a winding Worm*: & not a weeping Infant
> Trembling & pitying she screamd & fled upon the wind:
> Hyle was a winding Worm and herself perfect in beauty.
> (82.45–50; E238; italics indicate cancellations)

We are back to the imagery of *Thel*, with Gwendolen taking the part of Clay. Her beauty having been perfected, man has been perfectly reduced to worm. The nadir has been reached, and there is now nothing left for Gwendolen to do but to begin

... her dolorous task of love in the Wine-press of Luvah
To form the Worm into a form of love by tears & pain.
(82.75–76; E238)

The crisis suggests the ending of one Orc cycle and the beginning
of another, but there is a sign that this is in fact the end of the
seventh cycle, and so the beginning of the end (82.56). On the
basis of this sign Los undergoes the descent into the Polypus. He
enters the loins (the place of the Last Judgment) and tells Albion:

Corrup[t]ability appears upon thy limbs, and never more
Can I arise and leave thy side, but labour here incessant
Till thy awaking!
(83.1–3; E238)

Then, in a beautiful passage, he goes down from his refuge,
Golgonooza:

... Los arose upon his Watch, and down from Golgonooza
Putting on his golden sandals to walk from mountain to
  mountain,
He takes his way ...
(83.75–77; E240)

We are reminded of the passage in *Milton* where Nature appeared
to Los as a sandal, a vehicle (M., 21.12–14; E114). We have not
given up the idea of imaginative space, however, for the daughters
of Albion, who need room in which to nurture the Worm into a
form of love, take a lie uttered previously by Gwendolen ("But
if you on Earth Forgive You shall not find where to live": see
plate 81; E236), and the lie

grew & grew till it
Became a Space & an Allegory around the Winding Worm[.]
They namd it Canaan & built for it a tender Moon
(84.32–85.2; E241)

This has erotic as well as imaginative connotations, and soon we
are told, "Jerusalem & Vala cease to mourn" (85.15).

Los has found a new imaginative vigor, and as he works he
sings a sort of hymn to Jerusalem in which he sees her "Wingd
with Six Wings" (86.1; E242). When, later, he associates her
"extreme beauty & perfection" with the twelve tribes of Israel
(86.16–17), we recall the sixfold Ololon and her division. Los
also remarks that he sees the New Jerusalem "Clear as the rainbow" in her wings (86.21).

This passage culminates with the assurance "Nor can any consummate bliss without being Generated / On Earth" (86.42–43; E243), and now when Enitharmon, aroused to jealousy by the hymn to Jerusalem, *divides*, we can see that this time the division is in fact the metaphorical "form" of the assurance. In a recapitulation of their post-lapsarian Generation, Los and Enitharmon appear "like two Infants wandring" (86.62; E243). Not everything is recapitulation, however, for the imagery here is much more pointed and economical than anything we have seen so far. This, for example, is the summit of Enitharmon's role as Female Will (the east is the direction of Luvah):

> His rage or his mildness were vain, she scatterd his love on the
>   wind
> Eastward into her own Center, creating the Female Womb
> In mild Jerusalem around the Lamb of God.
>   (88.51–53; E245)

The reader probably does not need to be reminded that the idea of the Lamb out of Jerusalem is not a simple reference to the Incarnation; the "Lamb" is the body, associated with hypocritic holiness, into which Jesus descends—its derivation from Jerusalem reflects back onto her association with Vala.

At this point the Covering Cherub is finally revealed, and we are told two interesting things about him, first that "His Head dark, deadly, in its Brain incloses a reflexion / Of Eden all perverted" (89.14–15; E245), and second that Jerusalem resides in the midst of his "devouring Stomach" as in a tabernacle (89.43; E246). We assume that Blake means she is there in the same sense that Eden is in his head, a suspicion strengthened when we read:

> A Double Female now appeard within the Tabernacle,
> Religion hid in War, a Dragon red & hidden Harlot
>   (89.52–53; E246)

This double female draws down the dead, just as the second Vala did in the *Vala/The Four Zoas* manuscript. The epiphany of evil ends with a passage descriptive of the veil of Generation which needs to be rent, relying on the language of pastoral elegy:

>   a Veil & Net
> Of Veins of red Blood grows around them like a scarlet robe.
> Covering them from the sight of Man like the woven Veil of
>   Sleep

Such as the Flowers of Beulah weave to be their Funeral
   Mantles
But dark! opake! tender to touch, & painful! & agonizing
To the embrace of love, & to the mingling of soft fibres
Of tender affection. that no more the Masculine mingles
With the Feminine. but the Sublime is shut out from the Pathos
In howling torment, to build stone walls of separation,
   compelling
The Pathos, to weave curtains of hiding secrecy from the
   torment.

                           (90.4–13; E247)

All would now seem to be ready for a glorious sexual consummation (the "Sublime" and "Pathos" can be identified, on the basis of *A Descriptive Catalogue*, with Tharmas and Luvah—see E533—and so Blake has managed to involve in the "veil" his "war" of Urizen and Tharmas from *The Four Zoas*), but in fact when it comes it is unrecognizable as a consummation. If we consider the situations of the various female emanations as Blake approaches his apocalypse, we can see that he could not have been entertaining the idea of conveying it by a sexual metaphor. I have not said much in my analysis of *Jerusalem* about the ambiguities of Generation, nor followed up the embrace of Jerusalem and Vala. But we can see that in Chapter 4 Jerusalem is in very peculiar straits: she is in the devouring stomach of the Covering Cherub in one reference; in another she is the virgin vehicle of the female womb around the Lamb of God. In short, we can associate her two conditions with the succinct phrase of Los: "A Vegetated Christ" (the Satanic Body of Holiness with the "Double Female" Virgin—"Religion hid in War"—inside) "& a Virgin Eve" (90.34; E247). The only possibilities available to the sexual mechanism, at this point, would seem to be to extricate a virgin from Christ, or Christ from a virgin. To realize either possibility, the sexual mechanism would have to become other than what it is. Nor can much be hoped for from Enitharmon; as the poem draws to its term, she becomes increasingly jealous of Los's creative power ("Then thou wilt Create another Female according to thy Will": 92.12; E250), and Los informs her: "Sexes must vanish & cease / To be, when Albion arises from his dread repose" (92.13–14; E250). Vala is not on the scene as a personage; she is, of course, the Veil referred to earlier, but all the interest in her as a "character" has been transferred to Cambel and Gwendolen. All of this makes *Jerusalem* look at the moment like a poem without a heroine, but things are not quite so simple.

Instead of a consummation (in any recognizable form) we get what seems to me one of the most remarkable metaphorical developments in literature. The act or vehicle of this metaphor is simple enough; interpretation of the vehicle is bewilderingly complex. At the climactic moment—the moment when we have been led to expect a "consummation"—"Jesus appeared standing by Albion as the Good Shepherd/By the lost Sheep" (96.3–4; E253). Albion sees in Jesus "the Universal Humanity" (this language is very important) and "his Form/A Man" (96.5–6). But Jesus is clothed in a "form" of fallen history which Albion recognizes—even as Los was led to recognize his spectre in *The Four Zoas*—as his fallen Self:

> I behold the visions of my deadly Sleep of Six Thousand Years
> Dazling around thy skirts like a Serpent of precious stones &
>   gold
> I know it is my Self . . .
>
> (96.11–13; E253)

At this point Jesus expresses himself in rather orthodox language, offering to die for Albion: "Thus do Men in Eternity/One for another to put off by forgiveness, every sin" (96.18–19; E253). What actually happens at this point is that Los does nothing to prevent the drawing nigh of the Covering Cherub, who is allowed to come between Jesus and Albion, dividing them and concealing Jesus from sight. It is apparent that Blake could have composed this scene either in terms of Jesus' *descent* into the Polypus, or as the "birth" of the Lamb out of Jerusalem (in which case Jerusalem, from her husband's point of view, would no longer be a virgin—like Enitharmon in *The Four Zoas* after her gates were broken), but Blake in fact sacrifices all these suggestions to the simple idea of interposition, or "separation." The actual phrase he uses, "divided them asunder" (96.29; E253), takes us back to *Visions of the Daughters of Albion*. On the basis of this division, Albion is so afraid for his friend (not for himself) that his hope revives and he throws himself into a fourfold frenzy of visionary activity. In his Vision, the Four Zoas are restored to their unfallen condition and proceed imaginatively to restore reality.

In order to understand the tenor carried by this vehicle we have to backtrack. We have seen that Albion sees in Jesus "the Universal Humanity." We are also told: "And the Divine Appearance was the likeness & similitude of Los" (96.7; the language shows how conscious Blake is of a metaphorical strategy). To understand the point we have to realize the distinction in the poem between "Universal" characters (like Albion, Jesus, or Ololon)—who have a corporate identity—and generated, individual characters, like Los. Los himself regards this distinction as important:

> Los cries: No Individual ought to appropriate to Himself
> Or to his Emanation, any of the Universal Characteristics
> Of David or of Eve, of the Woman, or of the Lord.
> Of Reuben or of Benjamin, of Joseph or Judah or Levi[.]
> Those who dare appropriate to themselves Universal Attributes
> Are the Blasphemous Selfhoods & must be broken asunder[.]
> A Vegetated Christ & a Virgin Eve, are the Hermaphroditic
> Blasphemy, by his Maternal Birth he is that Evil-One
> And his Maternal Humanity must be put off Eternally
> Lest the Sexual Generation swallow up Regeneration
> Come Lord Jesus take on thee the Satanic Body of Holiness
> (90.28–38; E247)

Los's point is not that to be an individual is *less* than to be a universal (for it is in their "Individual Identities" that men are immortal: M., 32.23–24; E131), but merely that "universals" are corporate "forms," and that the identification of one's individuality with a universal form is really a disguise for the identification of the fallen, exclusive Self with an impregnable tabernacle of holiness. In short, it is to make of the Self the Anti-Christ. While we are on the subject of Los's opinions, it is useful to be reminded, in the face of so much talk about Blake's "renovated Christianity," of their heterodoxy. Divine Worship, for Los, "is honouring his gifts / In other men: & loving the greatest men best"; "there is no other / God than that God who is the intellectual fountain of Humanity" (91.7–10; E248). The basis of this religious idea is in fact intellectual ("Go! put off Holiness / And put on Intellect": 91.55–56; E249), and Los's application to the problem posed him by his spectre is his primary religious obligation:

> Thus Los alterd his Spectre & every Ratio of his Reason
> He alterd time after time, with dire pain & many tears
> Till he had completely divided him into a separate space.
> (91.50–52; E249)

Yet—and this is why we digressed—Los *does* become identified with a Universal. And in the climactic passage of the poem. What does this mean?

We have to backtrack again, this time to recall that the fallen world in Chapter 4 is being kept afloat in a space called Canaan, a metaphorical space built around the statement:

> In Heaven the only Art of Living
> Is Forgetting & Forgiving
> Especially to the Female
> But if you on Earth Forgive
> You shall not find where to live.
>
> (E236)

It is the second, coordinate clause, said to be a "falsehood," which supports Canaan. Falsehood or not, the fact remains that Los (and by extrapolation Blake) believed the statement to be largely true. We know from "The Everlasting Gospel" that Blake largely understood forgiveness of enemies to be a form of moral cowardice, an attribute of what he calls "creeping Jesus" ("He who loves his Enemies betrays his Friends"; E510), and Los expresses similar notions just before the climax of *Jerusalem*:

> It is easier to forgive an Enemy than to forgive a Friend:
> The man who permits you to injure him, deserves your
> vengeance.
>
> (91.1–2; E248)

The point, which is relevant to understanding the metaphorical "form" of Canaan, is that to refuse to forgive is for Los analogous to circumcision in Chapter 3; it is a way of maintaining an important distinction.

We are now in a position to understand the *Jerusalem* version of the Atonement. Los assumes the posture of a Universal. What "happens" is merely what happens in the additional pages to Night VII(a) of the *Vala/The Four Zoas* manuscript. Los forgives. This act has three aspects. In terms of Los as an individual, forgiving means to assume the Satanic Body of Holiness, to embrace the Anti-Christ. This is the Sacrifice. From Albion's corporate point of view, Albion sees in Jesus "the likeness & similtude of Los." This accomplishes for him the metaphoric identification of the individual as the "Universal Humanity" which is God. Finally, there is a third point of view, related to the sexual aspect of "forgetting & forgiving": Los's assumption of the Satanic Body of Holiness is made manifest as the passing of the Cherub between Los and the corporate form of mankind: "So saying the Cloud overshadowing divided them asunder" (96.29). In the first chapter of the poem, a "cloud" is the usual image for Vala (see especially 5.46–53; E147)—as indeed it symbolizes Vala in the iconography of the *Songs*; if we care to define sexuality, then, as the interposition of Generation between Albion and the perception of Jesus as the similitude of an individual, then we may regard him as undergoing a sexual experience. But it is a sexual experience the sexuality of which is totally symbolic.

Sexuality as understood by mortals is a function of threefold vision; Albion by the sacrifice of his friend is inspired to call his emanation ("Awake! Awake Jerusalem!") and proceed to fourfold vision. We got to this point by contemplating the tension (in the drama of Los and Albion) between deathless individuality and a universal form. There are two ways through this tension: one is to suggest an individual form in which universals are identified. Los associates this way with vegetation and the Anti-Christ. When he takes this way himself—to move Albion to renewed vision—we can see that his act is a metaphorical "form" of the idea of Atonement suggested in *Milton*: the epiphany of the Reprobate. The other way round is to define a universal form in which all individuals are identified (as themselves: see Frye, "Commentary," p. 107). A universal form *in* which all individuals are identified is the logical extension of the pastoral landscape. The Four Zoas, risen in Albion's imagination, first create a "space":

> Creating Space, Creating Time according to the wonders
>   Divine
> Of Human Imagination, throughout all the Three Regions
>   Immense
> Of Childhood, Manhood & Old Age.
>
> (98.31–33; E255)

It will be noticed that all idea of a two-level reality, of an Eternity opposed to a Generation, has been dropped. Within the space we get a form:

> All Human Forms identified even Tree Metal Earth & Stone. all
> Human Forms identified, living going forth & returning
>   wearied
> Into the Planetary lives of Years Months Days & Hours
>   reposing
> And then Awaking into his Bosom in the Life of Immortality.
>
> (99.1–4; E256)

It may be objected that this is not a form, only a description of our world. As such, of course, it is the ultimate expression of the idea of pastoral, which makes out of this world *the* world. But the last line of the poem makes of the description a form which at least corresponds to the metaphoric power of the poem before us: "And I heard the Name of their Emnations they are named Jerusalem" (99.5). Albion's Vision finally swallows Blake's poem and makes of it, not a universal thing, but a universal form—a "likeness & similitude."

It is evident that the paradoxical intercourse between universal and individual I have been describing is the final instance and transformation we have to discover of "Blake's Night." For, as suggested at the very beginning, the interposition of the Covering Cherub, of the darkness of Generation, between Albion and Jesus—and more particularly the joyous acceptance of this sacrifice by the Divine Imagination in Los—is Blake's final version of the idea of pastoral. The complexity of that idea—whereby the human imagination must simultaneously apprehend reality as fallen and as capable of transcendence—is very great in the last pages of *Jerusalem*, but there is no difference in kind from the many analogous realizations of the idea in pages of Blake which we have already seen. The obscure sexuality latent in the relationship between Albion and the Covering Cherub in *Jerusalem* is of a type with the sexuality of the lyric, "Night," and with the attraction between the generations of dead and the Polypus in *Vala/The Four Zoas.* Just so the Incarnation and Atonement are for Blake analogous to Milton's consummation of his marriage to Ololon and to his acceptance of Eternal Death. We are dealing, then, with an order of consciousness first represented to us in this study by the dream of the lion in "Night," finally and most fully represented by the character Los in *Jerusalem.* For this consciousness wedding song and death song—the two sorts of consummation and access to paradise—are related by an apprehension passionate enough for the Last Things. It has been my aim here to identity and clarify the relationship between this apocalyptic awareness and the idea of pastoral.

The first part of this study concluded with an examination of the third illustration for the Lyca poems. We found there that the eye, impelled restlessly by the ambiguities of the Generated condition, was forced around the picture ceaselessly in a kind of planetary circle. The poem was painful partly because the reconciling vision suggested, however satirically, by the text had produced no corresponding visual resting place. Now that we know enough to associate the lion in that illustration with Satan and with Los—and have seen how these two characters finally come together in *Jerusalem* at the point of the imagination's final reconciliation to reality—we can understand that the visual circularity of the Lyca illustration is a type of the planetary circle specified in plate 99 of *Jerusalem*. Ultimately it is the idea of pastoral which leads us to understand these images as forms of Eternity rather than of the sterile repetitions of Generation.

APPENDICES
NOTES
INDEX

APPENDIX A

A Note on the Orc Cycle

One quite strenuous disagreement among Blakeans has had to do with the nature of the poet's character Orc: whether from the first he was conceived as complementary and obverse to Urizen, or whether his relationship to the latter character was an afterthought on Blake's part, only arrived at after the poet had in some sense "changed his mind" about the force which Orc represents. For example, it has been suggested by critics interested in the relationship between Orc and Blake's supposedly changing attitude toward the revolutions in America and France that Orc is originally benign, or at worst ambivalent, and that his involvement in a systematic and compromising Orc cycle (the term is Frye's) only comes with the *Vala/The Four Zoas* manuscript. What Morton Paley says is strictly true: "In the Lambeth books, as we have seen, Orc had alternate human and serpent forms, an expression of his ambiguity. In *Vala* the forms are not alternate but successive."[1] But I think Paley's emphasis on differing narrative forms, if it is being used to rescue an "original" Orc more positive than the conception in *Vala/The Four Zoas*, may be misconceived. The problem is a complex one, but constancy with regard to the sources and employment of Blake's imagery suggests that the complexity is never merely a function of the poet's historically determined *uncertainty* about Orc.

The alternate serpent of the Lambeth poems is surely among other things Milton's Satan, and enough has been said about him as bringer of light and agent of the Fall (not alternate but coincidental functions) to suggest that Milton, more than revolutionary fervor and misgiving, controls his depiction there. I suppose the crucial case, where, argues Paley, alternation becomes succession, is in Night VII(b) of *Vala/The Four Zoas*. Orc undergoes a consuming coital embrace with Vala, only to reappear horribly as "Prester Serpent." We notice that the direction of the Fall begins to change, however, and wonder whether Paley's remark that Orc loses, together with his "human form," his "regenerative capacity" is really responsive to the case.[2] Even more interesting is the image Blake uses to describe the embrace of consummation:

> she embracd his fire
> As when the Earthquake rouzes from his den his shoulders
> huge
> Appear above the crumb[l]ing Mountain. Silence waits around
> him
> A moment then astounding horror belches from the Center
> The fiery dogs arise the shoulders huge appear
>
> (91.5–9; E395)

For this is an echo of the following speech of Tiriel:

> Earth thus I stamp thy bosom rouse the earthquake from his den
> To raise his dark & burning visage thro the cleaving ground
> To thrust these towers with his shoulders. let his fiery dogs
> Rise from the center belching flames & roarings.
>
> (5.4–7; E279)

Tiriel here is a type of Urizen (and of Job), and although there is some uncertainty about the date of *Tiriel*, there is general agreement that it is early, the latest suggestion being 1790.[3] At least by that date, then, this evidence strongly suggests, the interpenetration of Orc and Urizen in Blake's imagination was clear. To me, at any rate, the evidence of such interpenetration calls into question the idea of an Orc whose evolution is, primarily responsive to contemporary history. Indeed for me it calls into question an Orc who changes substantively at all.

APPENDIX B

Blake as Radical Christian

A most interesting case for Blake as radical Christian is made by Thomas J. J. Altizer in his often brilliant study *The New Apocalypse: The Radical Christian Vision of William Blake* (East Lansing, Mich.: Michigan State University Press, 1967). Altizer's book is a case, it seems to me, where correct or very suggestive conclusions are arrived at via a misleading critical method. Blake's criticism of Milton has led many to false conclusions about his stance, beginning with Swinburne's "satanic" Blake. Altizer finds in Blake a radical, apocalyptic vision, founded upon an anticipation of the Hegelian dialectic and resulting in a "Vision [which] ... effects a true reversal of the opposites ... that, in negating the opposites, unites them by making possible their transition into one another, thus effecting not an abolition of the opposites but a genuine *coincidentia oppositorum*" (p. 215). Hence, "Satan finally becomes manifest as the 'Human Form Divine' when He dies for man and thus becomes united with Jesus or Jerusalem," and "the Incarnation and Atonement [are] dual symbols of a single kenotic process" (p. 207). Finally, as we might expect, the penultimate plate of *Jerusalem* shows "the consummation of the initial union between Satan-Albion and Jesus-Jerusalem ... Blake's final depiction of a Christian and apocalyptic *coincidentia oppositorum*" (p. 208). There is much that is suggestive here, but there is more of Hegel than of Blake in it. The best distinction between Blakean and Hegelian dialectic is Peter Fisher's: "Hegel supposed that his dialectic *mirrored process* and could therefore be applied to it; Blake saw process as the interplay of the contraries."[1] Hegel's idea of spirit would surely have seemed a vacuum to Blake, and Blake's "Reasoning Negative," as Fisher points out, "could not unite the contraries in a higher synthesis."[2] There is neither room nor need here for a full-scale critique, but Altizer seems fundamentally to go astray only when he applies to Blake extra-Blakean terminology, and the nature of this error can be conveniently summed up by examining Blake's relationship to Milton; Blake often sounds *logically* paradoxical when all he is in fact doing is applying irony to Milton's conceptualizations. Thus, references to "Satan" have to be thoroughly scrutinized to determine whether Blake's own or Milton's conception is in Blake's mind, and this need extends even to allusions to Satan when the latter is not mentioned by name; that is, when they are attached to names in Blake's original mythology. Altizer does not sufficiently ponder the implications of the fact that fully realized kenotic incarnation is practiced for the first time in Blake by the character "Milton," rather than by Jesus, and the meaning of Generation involves not merely revision of Miltonic orthodoxy but the minute particulars of that act as interpreted in the Bard's Song in *Milton*, 1.24–13.45.

APPENDIX C

The Four Zoas: Nights VII

Night VII(a) of *The Four Zoas* originally ended on MS p. 84 (part of a stitched grouping; see the Bentley ed., pp. 193–196, for an exhaustive description of the MS), to which were added— perhaps at distinct dates—*first* MS pp. 85–86 (a leaf of the same kind of paper Blake had been using for much of the MS, proofs for his *Night Thoughts* engravings), and *second*, pp. 87–90, written on the back of another engraving, *Edward and Elenor*, which was then folded and cut in half (except for two sentences of prose the only text is on 87 and 90, 88 and 89 being taken up—with the exception noted—by an impression of the engraving). On MS p. 100 (the second page of Night VIII), Blake wrote the words "Los stood &^{c}," with lines indicating the need for an insertion between lines 1 and 2 of the page. Erdman (E758) has evolved an interesting theory (accepted by Morton Paley)[1] explaining this. Erdman argues that Blake wrote pp. 87 and 90 "as a sequence" (that is, as I understand him, without having decided where the sequence was to fit into the finished manuscript). At this point p. 90 began not with the present first line, "So Enitharmon spoke trembling & in torrents of tears," which appears above the plate-mark—Erdman arguing on this basis that it was added later—but with the second line, "Los sat in Golgonooza in the Gate of Luban where." The second word of this line, "sat," is over an erasure (not noted by Bentley, even though the erasure is clearly evident in the photograph of the page), and Erdman suggests the original word—which seems to end with a "d"—was "stood." On this basis Erdman argues that after pp. 87 and 90 were written as a sequence, Blake decided to fit p. 90 into p. 100 (this, says Erdman, would require merely changing "the phrase 'Into his hands' that begins 100.2 into 'In his hands' in the antepenultimate line of p. 90"). But, Erdman says, Blake then decided against this insertion, decided to "tighten" the sequence by adding the present line 1 to p. 90 (at the same time, for reasons which are not clearly developed—Erdman says "to round out the tale"—Blake is said to have added lines 26 and 27—32 and 33 by Bentley's count—to p. 99), and added the tightened sequence to VII(a).

Before dealing with the conclusions Erdman draws from his theory, it ought to be pointed out that, on the basis of physical evidence alone, Erdman's theory is extremely suppositious. For example, it is assumed that Blake wrote two pages as a sequence, decided against this, but in returning later to his original plan found it necessary to "tighten" his sequence (the aspect of this which involves altering "stood" to "sat" perhaps has more merit, as we shall see). Much more damaging to Erdman's argument is his connection between the antepenultimate line of p. 90 (beginning "In his hands") and the second line of p. 100 (beginning "Into his hands"). For Erdman does not point out that the antepenultimate line of p. 90 is the *eighth* line of an additional passage to that page which is written sideways very close to the margin and in bolder handwriting than that of the rest of the page. The "fitting" of p. 90 into p. 100, then, as a thematically related unit, more or less ready to be plugged in, becomes less likely when we see this. Further, if we reproduce the last *four* lines of the additional passage to p. 90,

Startled was Los he found his enemy Urizen now
In his hands. he wonderd that he felt love & not hate
His whole soul loved him he beheld him an infant
Lovely breathed from Enitharmon he trembled within himself

it seems highly unlikely that Blake would want to break off the passage after the first two lines. Los's feeling of reconciliation to Urizen is obviously the principal point, and it seems on the face of it unlikely that Blake would have submerged the emotional emphasis of the passage by lopping off the last two lines. Finally, the very unusual reconciliation of Los and Urizen seems very much in keeping with the equally unusual reconcilation of Los to the Spectre of Urthona, which happens on p. 85—suggesting that when the additional lines to p. 90 were written, Blake had already associated them with earlier additions to VII(a).

Erdman could salvage a very suppositious argument, however, by arguing simply that the whole sequence *was* written with VII(a) in mind, but that Blake nevertheless later tinkered with it with an eye to inserting p. 90 on p. 100—the real strength of his argument being the thematic resemblance between Golgonooza activities on both pages—and one is impelled to argue with Erdman not because his argument is not interesting but because on its basis he concludes: "This bit of masonry, which cements VII(a) closely to VIII, seems to indicate a time when Blake considered VII(b) as abandoned (or moved)." Here Erdman is on shaky grounds indeed, and one can only conclude that he is, on the basis of his very questionable evidence, overcommitted to the received assumption that VII(b) must in some sense be opposed to VII(a). I have tried to provide evidence in the text for assessing the importance of VII(b) to Blake's argument, but it needs to be pointed out that in general arguments of thematic relationship are questionable grounds for removing all the text *between* the points being related out of serial order. Anyway, to "move" a text is not at all the same thing as "abandoning" it. In other words, there are lots of possibilities.

One of these possibilities relates to a question already noted: if p. 90 originally began, "Los stood" (as Erdman believes), why did Blake, in the course of alterations, find it desirable to change "stood" to "sat"? The change seems to imply that "standing" is important in Los's case, and we recall that Los stands up, very importantly, in VII(b). Can it be that Blake changed "stood" to "sat" because he did not want to show Los standing until after his important rising—recapitulating an analogous event in *Europe*—in VII(b)? If we look again in detail at the passage where Blake indicated an insertion by the words "Los stood &^{c}," we discover other references to VII(b). In quoting the passage, words lined out by Blake will be italicized, words added in smaller handwriting will appear in parentheses:

> . . . they descend away from the Daughters of Beulah
> And enter Urizens temple Enitharmon pitying & her heart
> Gates broken down. they descend thro the Gate of Pity
> The broken heart Gate of Enitharmon *which joins to Urizens temple*
> *Which is the Synagogue of Satan* She sighs them forth upon the wind
> Of Golgonooza Los stood *at the Gate* recieving them
> (For Los could enter into Enitharmons bosom & explore
> Its intricate Labyrinths now the Obdurate heart was broken)
>
> (100)
>
> From out the War of Urizen & Tharmas recieving them

Into his hands. Then Enitharmon erected Looms in Lubans
    Gate
And calld the Looms Cathedron in these Looms She wove the
    Spectres
Bodies of Vegetation

> "Los stood &^{c}" is inserted between the first two
> lines of p. 100.

We should notice first that there are clear references in this passage
both to VII(a)—the Gates of Enitharmon—and to VII(b)—
Urizen's temple. And we cannot argue either that Blake was
trying to eliminate references to VII(b), for he lets the plain reference to Urizen's temple stand, while eliminating "which joins to
Urizens temple / Which is the Synagogue of Satan"—a rather
technical description. Also he lines out one reference to Enitharmon's gate, which, we should notice, leaves Los "standing" more
emphatically. Finally, the first line of p. 100 refers to "the War of
Urizen & Tharmas." The imagery of VII(a), which is organized
around the idea of temptation, contains no war references of any
kind; nor are there any references to "war" in the passages of
Night VIII preceding the reference. But we *do* get war in VII(b),
and in the course of it both Tharmas and Urizen make
important appearances. Therefore, is it not possible that Blake's
revisions and marginal instruction quoted above suggest that he
was planning to incorporate VII(b)—changing the order once
more, perhaps, in order to begin with Los's visionary rising—into
the body of Night VIII? (G. E. Bentley, Jr., has suggested that
VII(b) broke off from VIII in the first place, but differing styles
make it hard to believe it broke off from the version of Night VIII
we have. See his edition, p. 163.) This would explain at least why
Blake let a plain reference to "Urizens temple" stand, but lined
out a technical description of the temple which would make little
sense until the reader had been exposed to the material of VII(b),
why he tried to underline "Los stood" by lining out "at the Gate,"
but then registered his dissatisfaction with the result by putting
the all-important phrase—indicative of an important new phase of
the narrative—in the margin. He lined the insertion between lines
1 and 2 of p. 100 not because he had any piece of material that
would exactly "fit" there (like a piece in a jigsaw puzzle) but because the "descent of the Polypus" (in his mind the conclusion or
climax of the previous Night) accorded with "From out the
War . . . recieving them."

I hasten to add that this is a completely suppositious argument, too, and since Blake did not finish his poem both Mr. Erdman and myself will have to live in final ignorance of Blake's intentions. He left us with a chaotic manuscript, containing two Nights VII. If my argument has any validity beyond Mr. Erdman's in terms of physical evidence (as opposed to critical argument), its superiority rests upon its respect for what Blake left—that chaotic manuscript with two integral, not alternative, Nights VII.

NOTES

Preliminaries

1. Harold Bloom, "The Pastoral Image," in *Blake's Apocalypse* (Garden City, N.Y.: Doubleday & Co., 1963), pp. 36–62.

2. Northrop Frye, "Literature as Context: Milton's *Lycidas*," in *Fables of Identity* (New York: Harcourt, Brace & World, Harbinger Books, 1963), pp. 119–120.

3. Hallett Smith, *Elizabethan Poetry* (Cambridge, Mass.: Harvard University Press, 1952), p. 8.

4. Northrop Frye, *Anatomy of Criticism* (Princeton, N.J.: Princeton University Press, 1957), p. 119. Hereafter referred to in the text as Frye, *Anatomy*.

5. The interested reader should consult Erdman's review of G. E. Bentley's edition for a careful listing of textual inaccuracies: "The Binding (et cetera) of *Vala*," *The Library*, 5th ser., 19 (1964), 112–129.

Part I. The Dream of the Lion

1. William Nelson, *The Poetry of Edmund Spenser* (New York and London: Columbia University Press, 1963), pp. 31, 33.

2. Donald Dike, "The Difficult Innocence: Blake's Song and Pastoral," *ELH*, 28 (1961), 353–375, and George Mills Harper, "Apocalyptic Vision and Pastoral Dream in Blake's *Four Zoas*," *South Atlantic Quarterly*, 64 (1965), 110–124. Also see Bloom, *Blake's Apocalypse*, pp. 36–62.

3. See especially Vivian de Sola Pinto, "William Blake, Isaac Watts, and Mrs. Barbauld," in *The Divine Vision*, ed. Vivian de Sola Pinto (London: Victor Gollancz, 1957), pp. 65–88. For the possible influence of

Charles Wesley's *Hymns for the Nation*, see Martha Winburn England, "Blake and the Hymns of Charles Wesley," in *Hymns Unbidden*, by Martha Winburn England and John Sparrow (New York: The New York Public Library, 1966), pp. 43–112. For bibliographical information concerning Blake's illustrations for works by Mary Wollstonecraft, see G. E. Bentley, Jr., and Martin K. Nurmi, *A Blake Bibliography* (Minneapolis, Minn.: University of Minnesota Press, 1964), items 402 and 421.

4. William Empson, *Some Versions of Pastoral* (Norfolk, Conn.: New Directions, 1960), pp. 27–52.

5. Northrop Frye, "Introduction," *Blake : A Collection of Critical Essays* (Englewood Cliffs, N.J.: Prentice-Hall, Spectrum Books, 1966), p. 2, referring especially to Robert F. Gleckner's "Point of View and Context in Blake's Songs," reprinted on pp. 8–14 of the same volume.

6. A. Parry, "Landscape in Greek Poetry," *Yale Classical Studies*, 15 (1957), 29; cited in Richard Cody, *The Landscape of the Mind* (Oxford: Oxford University Press, Clarendon Press, 1969), p. 10.

7. Werner Jaeger, *Paideia : The Ideals of Greek Culture*, trans. Gilbert Highet (Oxford: Basil Blackwell, 1939–1945), II, 189. Hereafter this work is cited in the text as Jaeger.

8. C. H. Herford, cited in *The Minor Poems*, vol I of *The Works of Edmund Spenser : A Variorum Edition*, ed. Charles Grosvenor Osgood and Henry Gibbons Lotspeich (Baltimore: The Johns Hopkins Press, 1943), p. 267.

9. A. E. Taylor, *Plato*, 4th ed. (London: Methuen & Co., 1937), p. 300.

10. Hazard Adams, *William Blake : A Reading of the Shorter Poems* (Seattle: University of Washington Press, 1963), p. 226.

11. Ibid., p. 227.

12. Ibid., p. 228.

13. J. B. Leishman, *Milton's Minor Poems*, ed. Geoffrey Tillotson (London: Hutchinson, 1969), p. 267.

14. Thomas M. Greene, "Spenser and the Epithalamic Convention," *Comparative Literature*, 9 (1957), 222.

15. A. Kent Hieatt, *Short Time's Endless Monument* (New York: Columbia University Press, 1960); Hieatt, "The Daughters of Horus: Order in the Stanzas of *Epithalamion*," in *Form and Convention in the Poetry of Edmund Spenser*, ed. William Nelson (New York and London: Columbia University Press, 1961), pp. 103–121.

16. "Spenser and the Epithalamic Convention," p. 223.

17. Important articles on the *Calender* include: Mary Parmenter, "Spenser's Twelve Aeclogues Proportionable to the Twelve Monthes," *ELH*, 3 (1936), 190–217; A. C. Hamilton, "The Argument of Spenser's Shepheardes Calender," *ELH*, 23 (1956), 171–183; R. A. Durr, "Spenser's Calendar of Christian Time," *ELH*, 24 (1957), 269–295; and S. K. Heninger, Jr., "The Implications of Form for *The Shepheardes Calender*," *Studies in the Renaissance*, 9 (1962), 309–321.

18. Northrop Frye, "Blake's Treatment of the Archetype," in *Dis-*

cussions of William Blake, ed. John E. Grant (Boston: D. C. Heath and Co., 1961), p. 9.

19. The phrase "wash'd in lifes river" might itself suggest paradox. The primary connotation is sexual, but W. H. Stevenson has pointed out the probable allusion to Revelation 22:1–2 (*The Poems of William Blake* [London: Longman, 1971], p. 68). The language compounds Blake's ideas of Generation and of Beulah.

20. Joseph Wicksteed, *Blake's Innocence and Experience* (London, Toronto, and New York: J. M. Dent, 1928), p. 129.

21. Robert F. Gleckner, *The Piper and the Bard* (Detroit: Wayne State University Press, 1959), p. 124.

22. George Ferguson, *Signs and Symbols in Christian Art*, 2nd ed. (New York: Oxford University Press, 1955), p. 20.

23. Adams, *William Blake*, p. 294.

24. *Blake's Innocence and Experience*, p. 122.

25. Ibid., p. 125.

26. Ibid., pp. 127–128.

27. This is one of the cruces of the illustration which there is no time to discuss fully in the text. In fact the illustration is ambiguous—I think deliberately—and we cannot tell whether the descending cherub is wingless or not, for it is facing the viewer, and its wings, if any would be hidden away on its "back side."

28. *Blake's Innocence and Experience*, p. 125.

29. Jean H. Hagstrum, *William Blake: Poet and Painter* (Chicago and London: University of Chicago Press, 1964), p. 82.

30. William Smith, *A Smaller Dictionary of the Bible* (London:John Murray, 1870), p. 424.

31. See Leishman, *Milton's Minor Poems*, pp. 301–302.

32. Leishman's whole discussion of the flower passage is worth consulting: *Milton's Minor Poems*, pp. 299–313.

33. Ibid., p. 299.

34. IV.iv.127–133. Cited in ibid., p. 301.

35. *Blake's Innocence and Experience*, p. 81.

36. *The Piper and the Bard*, p. 84.

37. Ibid., p. 88.

38. See Hagstrum, *William Blake*, pp. 31–33.

39. *The Piper and the Bard*, p. 89.

40. *Blake's Innocence and Experience*, p. 100.

41. G. E. Bentley, Jr., ed., *Blake Records* (Oxford: Oxford University Press, Clarendon Press, 1969), p. 337.

42. See *Blake and Tradition* (Princeton, N.J.: Princeton University Press, 1968).

43. Anthony Blunt, *The Art of William Blake* (New York and London: Columbia University Press, 1959), p. 81; plate 49.

44. Kathleen Raine, "Who Made the Tyger?" *Encounter*, 2, no. 6 (June 1954), 43–50; Hazard Adams, "Reading Blake's Lyrics: 'The

Tyger,'" in Grant, ed., *Discussions of William Blake*, pp. 50–63; Martin K. Nurmi, "Blake's Revisions of *The Tyger*," *PMLA*, 61 (1956), 669–685; John E. Grant, "The Art and Argument of 'The Tyger,'" in Grant, ed., *Discussions of William Blake*, pp. 64–82. A long note in Morton Paley's *Energy and the Imagination* (Oxford: Oxford University Press, Clarendon Press, 1970), pp. 39–40, is a useful survey of "Tyger" criticism.

45. Greene, "Spenser and the Epithalamic Convention," p. 222.

46. David V. Erdman, *Blake: Prophet against Empire*, 2nd ed. (Princeton, N.J.: Princeton University Press, 1969), p. 265. Hereafter cited in the text as Erdman.

47. Nurmi, "Blake's Revisions of *The Tyger*," p. 680; Grant, "The Art and Argument of 'The Tyger,'" p. 75.

48. Harold Bloom, whose approach to "The Tyger" is something like my own, also discusses the "argument from design"; *Blake's Apocalypse* (Garden City, N.Y.: Doubleday & Co., 1963), p. 138.

49. The phrase, but not quite the attitude, belongs to Grant, "The Art and Argument of 'The Tyger,'" p. 73.

50. Grant notices the indeterminacy of reference, but makes something different of it: "The Art and Argument of 'The Tyger,'" p. 70.

51. Adams, "Reading Blake's Lyrics: 'The Tyger,'" p. 63.

52. Cited most recently in ibid., p. 58.

53. S. Foster Damon, *William Blake: His Philosophy and Symbols* (1924; reprint ed., Gloucester, Mass.: Peter Smith, 1958), p. 69. Hereafter cited as Damon.

54. These remarks are heavily indebted to the discussion of comedy and tragedy in Northrop Frye, *Anatomy of Criticism* (Princeton, N.J.: Princeton University Press, 1957), pp. 163–185 and 206–222, respectively.

55. Rosemond Tuve, *Images and Themes in Five Poems by Milton* (Cambridge, Mass.: Harvard University Press, 1962), p. 104.

56. Ibid., p. 105.

57. Ibid., p. 106.

58. Ibid.

59. Damon, p. 472.

60. S. Foster Damon, *A Blake Dictionary* (Providence, R.I.: Brown University Press, 1965), p. 390. See also the valuable discussion by John E. Grant in "Two Flowers in the Garden of Experience," in *William Blake: Essays for S. Foster Damon*, ed. Alvin H. Rosenfeld (Providence, R.I.: Brown University Press, 1969), pp. 356–357.

61. *Blake's Apocalypse*, p. 140.

62. Ibid., p. 139.

63. See George Wingfield Digby, *Symbol and Image in William Blake* (Oxford: Oxford University Press, Clarendon Press, 1957), pp. 5–53; Northrop Frye, "The Keys to the Gates," in *Some British Romantics*, ed. James V. Logan, John E. Jordon, and Northrop Frye (Columbus, Ohio: Ohio State University Press, 1966), pp. 3–40.

64. *Blake's Apocalypse*, p. 140.

65. Jean H. Hagstrum, "The Fly," in Rosenfeld, ed., *William Blake: Essays for S. Foster Damon*, pp. 369–371, 380.

66. *Blake's Apocalypse*, p. 136. My language here.

67. Damon, p. 276.

68. Jean Hagstrum can hardly be accused of not taking the implications seriously—for he regards the identification as the "burning center" of the poem and identifies it as "the fiery chariot of inspiration"—but he is nevertheless, it seems to me, thoroughly entrapped by the poem's savagely sentimental rhetoric: "The Fly," pp. 376–377.

69. Edgar Wind, *Pagan Mysteries in the Renaissance*, new and enlarged edition (New York: Barnes and Noble, 1968), p. 97. Hereafter cited in the text as Wind.

70. See Miss Raine's article cited below, note 71, and also George Mills Harper, *The Neoplatonism of William Blake* (Chapel Hill, N.C.: University of North Carolina Press, 1961).

71. Kathleen Raine, "The Little Girl Lost and Found and the Lapsed Soul," in Pinto, ed., *The Divine Vision*, pp. 17–64.

72. The *Book of Thel* plate is reproduced in Hagstrum, *William Blake*, plate 49B; the *America* plate in Erdman, *Blake*, p. 117.

73. See Northrop Frye, *Fearful Symmetry* (Princeton, N.J.: Princeton University Press, 1947) pp. 433–434, and the discussion in Grant, "Two Flowers in the Garden of Experience," pp. 355–362. Plate 28 is also discussed by David V. Erdman in "The Suppressed and Altered Passages in Blake's *Jerusalem*," *Studies in Bibliography*, 17 (1964), 18–20, and by W. D. Paden and Garland H. W. Zuther in "Blake's *Jerusalem*, Plate 28: A Further Correction," *Notes and Queries*, 12 (1965), 182–183. Grant (p. 359) has discovered in the final plate of the *Blair's Grave* series an analogue to the sidesaddle embrace of the revised version of *Jerusalem's* plate 28, discussed below in connection with the third Lyca plate.

74. *The Piper and the Bard*, pp. 142–156.

75. See Frye, *Fearful Symmetry*, p. 134; Milton O. Percival, *William Blake's Circle of Destiny* (1938; reprint ed., New York: Octagon Books, 1964), pp. 242–250.

76. See *The Piper and the Bard*, pp. 148–149.

Part II. The Descent into Night

1. See David V. Erdman, *Blake: Prophet against Empire*, 2nd ed. (Princeton, N.J.: Princeton University Press, 1969), p. 312, and, by the same author, "Blake: The Historical Approach," in *Discussions of William Blake*, ed. John E. Grant (Boston: D. C. Heath and Co., 1961), p. 19.

2. "Reflections in a Mirror," in *Northrop Frye in Modern Criticism*, ed. Murray Krieger (New York and London: Columbia University Press, 1966), pp. 135–136.

3. Geoffrey Hartman, "Ghostlier Demarcations," in Krieger, ed., *Northrop Frye in Modern Criticism*, p. 125.

4. "Blake's *Night Thoughts*: An Exploration of the Fallen World," in *William Blake: Essays for S. Foster Damon*, ed. Alvin H. Rosenfeld (Providence, R.I.: Brown University Press, 1969), pp. 131–157; "The World without Imagination: Blake's Visions of Leviathan and Behemoth," in *Energy and the Imagination* (Oxford: Oxford University Press, Clarendon Press, 1970), pp. 171–199.

5. See G. E. Bentley, Jr., ed., *Blake Records* (Oxford: Oxford University Press, Clarendon Press, 1969), pp. 271–272. It is not known whether Palmer actually communicated his feelings to Blake, but the artist's ardent temperament and the fact that he claims to have been in Blake's studio when an impression of some of the cuts was taken on Blake's press make it an irresistible inference that he must have.

6. For Paley, see note 4 above. Also see Mark Schorer, *William Blake* (1946: reprint ed., New York: Vintage Books, 1956), pp. 153–154, and Erdman, *Blake*, pp. 448–455.

7. Hartman, "Ghostlier Demarcations," pp. 126–127.

8. John Hollander, "Blake and the Metrical Contract," in *From Sensibility to Romanticism*, ed. Frederick W. Hilles and Harold Bloom (New York: Oxford University Press, 1965), pp. 293–310.

9. Ibid., p. 307.

10. G. E. Bentley, Jr., "*The Four Zoas* and the Critics," in *Vala or The Four Zoas: A Facsimile of the Manuscript* ... (Oxford: Oxford University Press, Clarendon Press, 1963), pp. 168–170.

11. Northrop Frye, "Notes for a Commentary on *Milton*," in *The Divine Vision*, ed. Vivian de Sola Pinto (London: Victor Gollancz, 1957), p. 116. Hereafter cited as Frye, "Commentary."

12. Max Plowman, *An Introduction to the Study of Blake* (1927; reprint ed., London: Victor Gollancz, 1952), p. 83. It is interesting that in a recent annotated facsimile edition, *William Blake: The Book of Thel, a Facsimile and a Critical Text* (Providence, R.I.: Brown University Press, 1971), the editor, Nancy Bogen, specifically associates the bent tree (and the title page generally) with the pastoral elegiac tradition, but then dismisses it firmly in her interpretation of the poem (p. 21).

13. *Blake's Apocalypse* (Garden City, N.Y.: Doubleday & Co., 1963), p. 62.

14. Robert F. Gleckner, *The Piper and the Bard* (Detroit: Wayne State University Press, 1959), pp. 157–174.

15. I am pleased to discover independent confirmation of this view in Eben Bass, "*Songs of Innocence and Experience*: The Thrust of Design," in *Blake's Visionary Forms Dramatic*, ed. David V. Erdman and John E. Grant (Princeton, N.J.: Princeton University Press, 1970), p. 205.

16. *Blake's Apocalypse*, p. 61.

17. G. E. Bentley, Jr., ed., *William Blake: Tiriel: Facsimile and Transcript ... and a Commentary ...* (Oxford: Oxford University Press, Clarendon Press, 1967), pp. 3–4.

18. Ibid., p. 47.

19. Ibid., p. 46.

20. *Thel* often refers to Job, as well as to other books of the Bible: see Robert F. Gleckner, "Blake's *Thel* and the Bible," *Bulletin of the New York Public Library*, 64 (1960), 573–580.

21. For Thomas Wright the emblem is "the key to the whole of Blake." The serpent is Urizen, and the children are the imagination mastering reason. *The Life of William Blake*, 2 vols. (Olney, Eng.: Thomas Wright, 1929), I, 25.

22. *Blake's Apocalypse*, p. 58.

23. *An Introduction to the Study of Blake*, p. 87.

24. Gleckner has shown that the phrase echoes I Peter 5:4: "And when the chief Shepherd shall appear, ye shall receive a crown of glory that fadeth not away." See "Blake's *Thel* and the Bible," pp. 578–579.

25. Merritt Y. Hughes, ed., *John Milton: Complete Poems and Major Prose* (New York: The Odyssey Press, 1957), p. 410.

26. Lines 26.11–27.9 (E311) have a number of interesting, if rough, analogues elsewhere in Blake: *Tiriel*, 7.14–20 (E281) and the related situation in "The Little Girl Found"; compare the "Argument" to *The Marriage of Heaven and Hell* and *The Book of Urizen*, VII.5–10 (E79–80).

27. See Frye's brilliant article, "Blake's Reading of the Book of Job," in Rosenfeld, ed., *William Blake: Essays for S. Foster Damon*, pp. 221–234.

28. Paley, *Energy and the Imagination*, pp. 261–262.

29. Jean Hagstrum, *William Blake: Poet and Painter* (Chicago and London: University of Chicago Press, 1964), p. 126.

30. Ibid.

31. In the color-print *Good and Evil Angels*, reproduced in Anthony Blunt, *The Art of William Blake* (New York and London: Columbia University Press, 1959), plate 32b.

32. The notion of a systematic iconography of left and right originates with Joseph H. Wicksteed's *Blake's Vision of the Book of Job* (London: J. M. Dent & Sons, 1910), esp. Appendix A, pp. 133–136.

33. By Wright, *The Life of William Blake*, II, 167.

34. *Energy and the Imagination*, pp. 163–164.

35. The reference has a bearing, however, on the imagery of "The Tyger": see *The Song of Los*, 3.22–24; *Milton*, 28.21–28; and Northrop Frye's note 56 in *Fearful Symmetry* (Princeton, N.J.: Princeton University Press, 1947), pp. 448–449—from all of which may be deduced the sense in which "The Tyger" is an "African" poem.

36. Erdman argues just this, *Blake*, p. 272.

37. *The Mirror and the Lamp* (New York: Oxford University Press, 1953), p. 250.

38. Ibid., pp. 250–256.

39. In an article which reached me after this book was written, George Quasha argues that the harp-smashing may reflect Blake's judgment of his own nature rather than an adverse reaction to the nature of his poem. See "Orc as a Fiery Paradigm of Poetic Torsion" in Erdman and Grant, ed., *Blake's Visionary Forms Dramatic*, pp. 283–284.

40. For the *America* version of *War* Blake put into the breach in the

city wall (for Damon the flesh, p. 339) a huge angel chained by the feet. It used to be customary to identify this figure as Urizen (Wright, *The Life of William Blake*, II, 132; Damon, p. 339), but Erdman calls him Orc (*Blake*, pp. 75, 450). The latter identification makes better iconographic sense, but in terms of the imagery of the text, as we have seen, it is impossible to make any distinction. We may as well identify the creature as the "Demon red" and be done with it. Under the heading "A Note on the Mundane Shell," Erdman illuminates the wall itself at the end of his recent essay, "*America*: New Expanses," in Erdman and Grant, ed., *Blake's Visionary Forms Dramatic*, pp. 111–112.

41. In his painting *Satan Watching the Endearments of Adam and Eve* (one *Paradise Lost* version of "Night") it is interesting that Blake suggests a visual equation: Adam with Eve equals Satan with Serpent (flying overhead), the Satan having the same face as Adam, and the position of his hand curling round the head of the serpent being an exact mirror of Adam cradling the head of Eve.

42. Peter F. Fisher, *The Valley of Vision*, ed. Northrop Frye (Toronto: University of Toronto Press, 1961), p. 228.

43. Michael J. Tolley's essay "*Europe*: 'to those ychain'd in sleep,'" in Erdman and Grant, ed., *Blake's Visionary Forms Dramatic*, pp. 115–145, reached me too late to influence these pages. He casts further light on the Miltonic references, and confirms my sense of the poem's ironies by agreeing to refuse Erdman's rather mechanical identification of Orc at the end with Christ. Tolley's reading, while unlike mine in many respects, agrees in finding *Europe* a dark poem indeed.

44. A clear indication of Blake's mature attitude toward Oothoon is M., 18.39–42 (E111), where she shines in the "Shadowy Females bosom" as a generated representative of Jerusalem.

45. *Blake's Apocalypse*, p. 109.

46. George Mills Harper makes some analogous suggestions in "Apocalyptic Vision and Pastoral Dream in Blake's *Four Zoas*," *South Atlantic Quarterly*, 64 (1965), 110–124.

47. The April letter is in E, pp. 696–697, but July must be consulted in *Blake: Complete Writings*, ed. Geoffrey Keynes (Oxford: Oxford University Press, 1966), pp. 826–829, or in some other complete edition.

48. Bentley hints at the same thing in his facsimile edition of the poem, p. 164.

49. There is a good account of the biblical imagery of the passage in *Blake's Apocalypse*, p. 329.

50. Ibid., p. 308, referring to *Paradise Lost*, I.63.

51. His edition, p. 167.

52. Damon, p. 160.

53. D. J. Sloss and J. P. R. Wallis, *The Prophetic Writings of William Blake* (Oxford: Oxford University Press, Clarendon Press, 1926).

54. H. M. Margoliouth, *William Blake's Vala: Blake's Numbered Text* (Oxford: Oxford University Press, Clarendon Press, 1956), p. xiii.

55. See Bentley's edition, pp. 157–166.

56. Ibid., pp. 168–170.

57. Margoliouth edition, p. 140; Bentley edition, p. 163.

58. Bentley edition, p. 163.

59. Ibid.

60. See Jean Hagstrum, "'The Wrath of the Lamb': A Study of William Blake's Conversions," in Hilles and Bloom, ed., *From Sensibility to Romanticism*, pp. 311–330.

61. In two extant copies of J., one of them being the Stirling copy which was the basis of the Blake Trust colored facsimile, Blake altered the order of plates in Chapter 2.

62. This connection has been noted by Denis Saurat, *Blake and Milton* (1935; reprint ed., New York: Russell & Russell, 1965), pp. 50–51, and by Frye, "Commentary," p. 131. Incidentally, here and in some of the discussion which follows, I do not mean to leave the impression that the rainbow is always a sinister, ironic, and hopeless image. This is manifestly untrue—but it *is*, like so many other key images in Blake, painfully ambivalent. For more hopeful rainbow iconography, consult Jean Hagstrum, *William Blake: Poet and Painter* (Chicago and London: University of Chicago Press, 1964), pp. 112–113, and Edward J. Rose, "'Forms Eternal Exist For-ever': The Covenant of the Harvest in Blake's Prophetic Poems," in Erdman and Grant, ed., *Blake's Visionary Forms Dramatic*, pp. 460–461.

63. S. Foster Damon suggests that Hayley may have been a suppressed homosexual. Consult "Hayley" in Damon's *A Blake Dictionary* (Providence, R.I.: Brown University Press, 1965).

64. See citations in note 75 above.

65. *Blake's Apocalypse*, p. 260.

66. For discussion see Frye, *Fearful Symmetry*, pp. 356–403; *Blake's Apocalypse*, pp. 365–433; Karl Kiralis, "The Theme and Structure of William Blake's *Jerusalem*," in Pinto, ed., *The Divine Vision*, pp. 139–162; Edward J. Rose, "The Structure of Blake's *Jerusalem*," *Bucknell Review*, 11, no. 3 (1962–63), 35–54; and Henry Lesnick, "Narrative Structure and the Antithetical Vision of *Jerusalem*," in Erdman and Grant, ed., *Blake's Visionary Forms Dramatic*, pp. 391–412. Of these the discussions by Frye and Rose seem to me the most helpful.

67. Thomas J. J. Altizer, *The New Apocalypse: The Radical Christian Vision of William Blake* (East Lansing, Mich.: Michigan State University Press, 1967).

68. Edward J. Rose remarks, "The fallen world is pulled inside out like a sleeve": "The Structure of Blake's *Jerusalem*," p. 54.

69. Frye's suggestion in *Fearful Symmetry*, pp. 433–34. But Frye's interpretation was uninformed by the bibliographical and critical work on this plate done and inspired by David Erdman. See note 73 above.

70. Damon, p. 453.

71. See Frye, *Fearful Symmetry*, p. 368; William Smith, *A Smaller Dictionary of the Bible* (London: John Murray, 1870), p. 191.

72. Paley, *Energy and the Imagination*, p. 167.

73. For a quite different view of "circumcision," see Edward J. Rose, "Circumcision Symbolism in Blake's *Jerusalem*," *Studies in Romanticism*, 8, no. 1 (Autumn 1968), 16–25.

Appendix A. A Note on the Orc Cycle

1. Morton Paley, *Energy and the Imagination* (Oxford: Oxford University Press, Clarendon Press, 1970), p. 115.

2. Ibid., p. 120.

3. See G. E. Bentley, Jr., ed., *William Blake: Tiriel, Facsimile and Transcript ... and a Commentary ...* (Oxford: Oxford University Press, Clarendon Press, 1967), pp. 50–51; and David V. Erdman, *Blake: Prophet against Empire*, 2nd ed. (Princeton, N.J.: Princeton University Press, 1969), p. 131.

Appendix B. Blake as Radical Christian

1. Peter F. Fisher, *The Valley of Vision*, ed. Northrop Frye (Toronto: University of Toronto Press, 1961), p. 7.

2. Ibid., p. 8.

Appendix C. The Four Zoas: Nights VII

1. Morton Paley, *Energy and the Imagination* (Oxford: Oxford University Press, Clarendon Press, 1970), p. 263.

INDEX

Note : All works, including Blake's, are indexed under their authors' names.